A MILITARY HISTORY
of
CHINA

A MILITARY HISTORY
OF
CHINA

edited by
David A. Graff and Robin Higham
Kansas State University

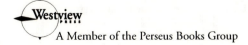

A Member of the Perseus Books Group

Copyright © 2002 by Westview Press, A Member of the Perseus Books Group

Westview Press books are available at special discounts for bulk purchases in the United States by corporations, institutions, and other organizations. For more information, please contact the Special
Markets Department at The Perseus Books Group, 11 Cambridge Center, Cambridge MA 02142, or
call (617) 252-5298.

Published in 2002 in the United States of America by Westview Press, 5500 Central Avenue, Boulder,
Colorado 80301–2877, and in the United Kingdom by Westview Press, 12 Hid's Copse Road, Cumnor
Hill, Oxford OX2 9JJ

Find us on the World Wide Web at www.westviewpress.com

A Catalog-in-Publication data record is available from the Library of Congress
ISBN 0-8133-3736-4 (HC) ISBN 0-8133-3990-1 (Pbk.)

The paper used in this publication meets the requirements of the American National Standard for
Permanence of Paper for Printed Library Materials Z39.48–1984.

10   9   8   7   6   5   4   3   2   1

CONTENTS

LIST OF MAPS

CHRONOLOGY

Neolithic Period	5500–3000 B.C.E.
Longshan Period	3000–2000 B.C.E.
Shang	1500–1045 B.C.E.
Western Zhou	1045–770 B.C.E.
Eastern Zhou	770–256 B.C.E.
Spring and Autumn	722–481 B.C.E.
Warring States	453–221 B.C.E.
Qin	221–206 B.C.E.
Western (Former) Han	202 B.C.E.–9 C.E.
Xin (Wang Mang)	9–23 C.E.
Eastern (Later) Han	25–220 C.E.
Three Kingdoms	220–263
Western Jin	265–317
Northern and Southern Dynasties	317–589
Northern Wei	386–534
Northern Zhou	557–581
Sui	581–618
Tang	618–907
Five Dynasties	907–960
Northern Song	960–1126
Southern Song	1127–1279
Yuan	1279–1368
Ming	1368–1644
Qing	1644–1912
Republic	1912–1949
People's Republic	1949–Present

EDITORS' NOTE

This book is intended to provide an accessible, one-volume introduction to Chinese military history covering both traditional and modern China. No other book currently available in English embraces as broad a range of topics and chronological periods in its examination of China's martial heritage. Since this volume is aimed primarily at a nonspecialist audience, we have tried to hold both sinological jargon and scholarly apparatus to a minimum. All dates are converted to Western forms, and where Chinese terms appear, English translations are provided.

Romanization of Chinese words and proper names generally follows the Pinyin system used in the People's Republic of China, which is somewhat simpler and less intimidating to the uninitiated than the older Wade-Giles system with its hyphens and apostrophes. Most letters are pronounced more or less as in English, with four notable exceptions. The "q" in Pinyin is pronounced like our "ch" (as in the word "chin"). The Pinyin "x" represents a "sh" sound, and "c" is really a "ts" (as in our word "its"). Finally, the "zh" combination stands for a "j" sound (as in "jack"). For a few familiar names, we have retained older, usually nonstandard forms. Chiang Kai-shek, for example, is more immediately recognizable than the Pinyin equivalent (Jiang Jieshi), and the same is true for Canton (Guangzhou). We spell the Chinese name of the Nationalist Party in Pinyin (Guomindang), but have chosen to retain its Wade-Giles-derived acronym KMT in place of the less familiar Pinyin equivalent (GMD). Personal names follow the Chinese sequence, with last name first.

We have incurred a number of debts in the process of preparing this book. Rob Williams, Carol Jones, and Steve Catalano, our editors at Westview Press, shepherded the volume through to completion. John Beck and his associates provided expert copyediting assistance. The maps were drawn by Don Graff, with the exception of the map of the Eurasian steppelands, which was created for this book by Elaine Ng. Jim Ehrman solved a number of electronic information transfer and retrieval problems for us. To these individuals and all the others who have assisted us along the way, we offer our warmest thanks.

D. G., R. H.

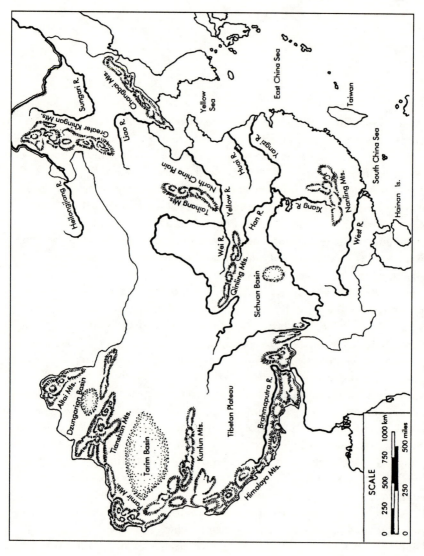

Map 1.1   Physical Map of China. Adapted by Don Graff and based upon *China: An Interpretive History*, Joseph R. Levenson and Franz Schurmann (Berkeley: University of California Press, 1969), pp. 144–145.

ONE

Introduction

Robin Higham and David A. Graff

Armed conflict has always played an important role in Chinese history. Most of China's imperial dynasties were established as a result of success in battle, and the same may be said of the Nationalist (Guomindang KMT) and Communist regimes in the twentieth century. Periods of dynastic decline were marked by great peasant rebellions, and the collapse of central authority repeatedly gave rise to prolonged, multicornered power struggles between regional warlords.

Questions of military institutions and strategy have always occupied a prominent place in Chinese political thought, and the armed confrontation between the sedentary Chinese state and the nomadic peoples of the Inner Asian steppe was one of the most fundamental themes of Chinese history prior to the twentieth century.

China's modernization efforts in the nineteenth and twentieth centuries were stimulated by repeated defeats at the hands of the Western powers (and later Japan), beginning with the Opium War of 1839–1842, and by the need to respond to the challenge of domestic rebellions such as that of the Taipings (1850–1864). Indeed, it is arguable that the pursuit of "wealth and power" has been a common denominator of all Chinese regimes from the twilight of the Qing dynasty to the People's Republic (PRC) in the post-Deng era.

In spite of this history, the existing literature has tended to neglect or downplay the role of war and the military. Works on premodern China have emphasized (and reflected) the Confucian pacifism and antimilitary bias of the scholar-official class, while the literature on the nineteenth and twentieth centuries gives pride of place to intellectual, cultural, and political developments. The English-language literature on Chinese military

1

history, ancient or modern, is extremely limited; for premodern China in particular, there is only a handful of books, several of which are now out of print. This volume is intended to fill the gap by offering a wide-ranging overview of the major themes, issues, and patterns of Chinese military history, from the first millennium B.C.E. to the present day. It is designed to provide nonspecialists and newcomers to the subject with basic orientation in fifteen key areas, and each chapter concludes with suggestions for further reading and research.

THE LAY OF THE LAND

The People's Republic of China covers roughly the same land area as the United States, and is somewhat larger than Europe (from Moscow west to the Atlantic). In contrast to the United States and Europe, however, China is not richly endowed with arable land. Most of the country's territory is mountain, desert, or arid plateau, and there is no counterpart to the vast arable expanse of the American Midwest. The largest zone of flat, fertile land, the North China Plain along the lower reaches of the Yellow River, is only a little larger than than the combined land area of Illinois and Iowa. In southern and western China, arable land (and human population) is concentrated in the much smaller river valleys and coastal lowlands. Population is especially sparse in the vast, arid western territories of Xinjiang, Tibet, and Qinghai, which account for nearly half of China's total land area. The country's highest mountains are found in the far west, in the Himalaya and Pamir ranges along the fringes of the Tibetan plateau, and the greatest rivers, the Yellow and the Yangzi, flow eastward from the Tibetan highlands to the Pacific Ocean. These western territories were little touched by Chinese settlement until very recent times. Together with the Gobi Desert in today's Mongolia, they formed an all but insurmountable barrier to the westward and northward expansion of the sedentary, agricultural lifestyle of the Han Chinese.

For most of China's history, these western and northern territories were left in the hands of peoples whose languages, cultures, and ways of life were dramatically different from those of their Han neighbors. Some, such as the Iranian and Turkish oasis dwellers of Xinjiang and the Tibetans of the Yarlung Zangbo (Brahmaputra) valley, were small-scale agriculturalists, but the dominant mode of livelihood was pastoral nomadism. The outer regions were linked to the Chinese heartland by the exchange of horses and other livestock for the products of China's farmers and artisans, including grain, silk, and metalware. Trade in luxuries extended even farther, along

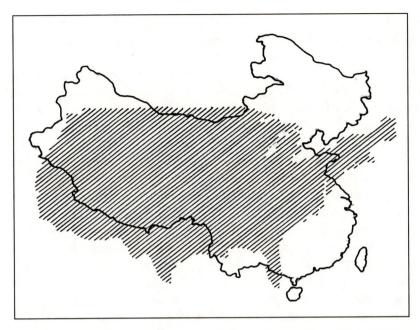

Map 1.2   Relative size of China and the 48 contiguous United States. Adapted by Don Graff based upon *Interpreting China's Grand Strategy*, Michael D. Swaine and Ashley J. Tellis (Santa Monica, CA: Rand Corporation, 2000)

the fabled Silk Road that connected China with the Middle East and the Mediterranean world. Given the vast distances, harsh landscapes, and tough customers along the way, however, there was very little direct contact between the two ends of the Eurasian landmass before Europeans found their way to China by sea in the early years of the sixteenth century.

The territory of today's China can be divided into two zones. The first, "China proper," was and is densely populated, agricultural, and inhabited mainly by the Han majority; in imperial times its people were ruled directly by the Son of Heaven. The second zone consists of Tibet, Qinghai, Xinjiang, Inner Mongolia, and the three Manchurian provinces; in earlier times this zone also included the territory that is now the independent republic of Mongolia. These lands were (and in some cases still are) very sparsely populated and inhabited by non-Han ethnic groups. At some times in Chinese history these areas paid tribute to the Middle Kingdom and were treated as vassal states; at other times, however, they were fiercely independent and threatening. The power of China in this region has fluctuated greatly over the centuries. The Former Han and Tang dynasties dominated Xinjiang, but

Song and Ming did not. Tibet was first attached to the empire by the Mongol Yuan dynasty, but recovered its independence when the Yuan gave way to a new native Chinese dynasty, the Ming. Today's PRC owes its shape largely to the Manchus, who conquered China and established the Qing dynasty in 1644. They brought their own homeland, Manchuria, into the empire, and went on to subdue Mongolia, Tibet, and Xinjiang. Of this Qing legacy only "outer" Mongolia has been lost, primarily as a result of Russian pressure in the early part of the twentieth century.

The theater in which Chinese military history was acted out included not just the territory of today's China (and Mongolia), but covered a vast, subcontinental region of East Asia. The Korean peninsula was administered as an integral part of the Han empire, and was the scene of Chinese military interventions by the Sui and Tang dynasties during the seventh century, by the Ming dynasty in the 1590s, by the Qing in the 1890s, and by the Communists in the 1950s. Northern Vietnam, including today's Hanoi, was ruled by the Qin, Han, and Tang dynasties, and Chinese armies sometimes penetrated even farther south. Han and Tang armies pushed deep into what is now the territory of the former Soviet republics of Central Asia. Mongol-led forces based in China invaded Japan, Burma, and Java in the thirteenth century, and a Qing army marched into Nepal in the 1790s. In the first half of the fifteenth century the Ming "treasure fleets," led by Zheng He and his associates, explored the Indian Ocean littoral, and in the last three decades the People's Republic has been striving to establish its military dominance in the South China Sea. In periods when China was united and strong, most military encounters took place along the periphery as the country's rulers sought to assert their suzerainty over neighboring states and peoples. During periods of division and civil war, on the other hand, the locus of most military action was the densely populated heartland of "China proper."

RESOURCES AND INFRASTRUCTURE

In ancient and imperial times, the Chinese heartland was richly endowed with the resources needed to support military endeavors. First and foremost among these resources was China's large population, recorded at more than 56 million by the Han census of 157 C.E., when the population of the Roman Empire was not more than 46 million. During the Song period China's population rose to an estimated 120 million, and between 1650 and 1850 it is believed to have tripled to 410 million.[1] These numbers made it possible for the country's rulers to maintain very large military

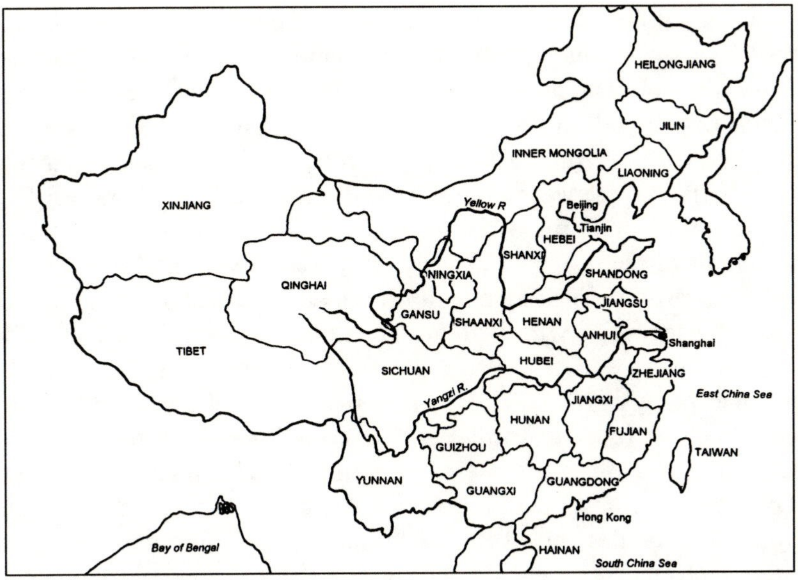

Map 1.3   China's provinces in the second half of the twentieth century. Adapted by Don Graff based upon *Interpreting China's Grand Strategy*, Michael D. Swaine and Ashley J. Tellis (Santa Monica, CA: Rand Corporation, 2000)

establishments, nearly a million men in the early ninth century and possibly as many as four million under the late Ming. The vast majority of the people, however, were farmers who provided the grain that was needed to feed the troops. When necessary they could be pressed into service as porters for the army, and as corvée laborers they built the roads and canals over which the imperial army moved and the city walls and frontier fortifications that buttressed the defense of the realm. In some periods women as well as men might be called up for labor service.

Other resources provided the materials for the instruments of war. Timber from the mountain fringes of the Sichuan basin made possible the construction of the great river flotillas that swept down the Yangzi to conquer the south in 280 and 589, and the forested hills of the Yangzi watershed and the coastal provinces of Zhejiang and Fujian provided for the huge treasure ships of Zheng He's fleet in the early Ming. Under the Northern Song dynasty, deposits of iron in Shandong, northern Jiangsu, and the Henan–Hebei border region were the basis for an arms industry that supplied China's soldiers with spearheads, arrowheads, swords, helmets, and armor for both man and horse. In the early eleventh century, foundries in these areas not far from the capital city of Kaifeng were producing 58,000 tons of iron a year, much of which went to meet the needs of the military.[2]

The Chinese heartland was wanting in regard to only one of the essential tools of premodern warfare. Its forested mountains and densely populated farmland were not well suited for the raising of horses, and this was especially true of the warmer and wetter lands south of the Yangzi River. Although the great majority of Chinese soldiers through the ages marched and fought on foot, cavalry forces were vital because they provided a powerful offensive element on the battlefield and they alone were capable of keeping up with highly mobile nomadic opponents. When imperial control extended over the grasslands of the steppe margin, state herds of as many as 700,000 head (as in the middle of the seventh century under the Tang dynasty) provided the basis for cavalry forces that extended the emperor's authority to even more distant regions. When control over the pastures was lost, however, the cavalry component dwindled and Chinese armies found themselves at a grave disadvantage against mounted opponents.

On the defensive, at least, investment in infrastructure made possible by China's vast human and material resources could compensate for a shortage of horses. Towns and cities were surrounded by massive walls built of stamped earth (*hangtu*), and the same method was used to construct the early versions of the northern frontier fortifications that became known as the Great Wall. During the Song and Ming periods, fortifications became more elaborate and walls acquired facings of stone or brick. Some of these city walls still had defensive value as late as the Civil War of 1946–1949. Since water transport was by far the most cost-effective means of moving bulky goods in premodern times, imperial governments also devoted considerable attention to augmenting and connecting China's rivers with man-made canals. The most famous of these, the Grand Canal, was first opened by the Sui dynasty at the beginning of the seventh century to connect the Lower Yangzi region with the Yellow River and the area around today's Beijing; carefully maintained by subsequent dynasties, parts of the canal remain in use today. State granaries were established at key points on the riverine transportation network, both to provide for the needs of military campaigns and to give relief to the population in the event of famine.

It was only after the Western imperialist onslaught began in the Opium War of 1839–1842 that the military resources and infrastructure characteristic of more than two thousand years of Chinese history began to see significant changes. Steam-powered vessels gave the British and other foreign interlopers easy access to China's internal waterways, which now became

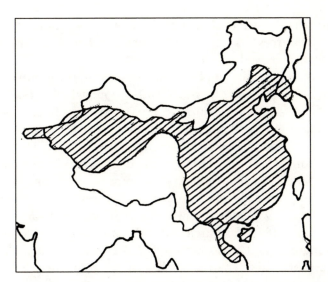

Map 1.4   A Strong dynasty: Han circa 100 B.C.E. Adapted by Don Graff based upon *Interpreting China's Grand Strategy*, Michael D. Swaine and Ashley J. Tellis (Santa Monica, CA: Rand Corporation, 2000) p. 42

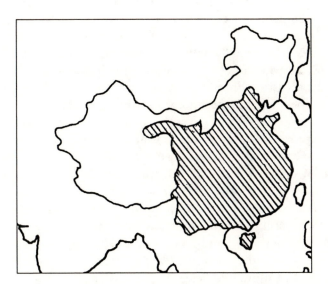

Map 1.5   A weak dynasty: Ming circa 1640 C.E. Adapted by Don Graff based upon *Interpreting China's Grand Strategy*, Michael D. Swaine and Ashley J. Tellis (Santa Monica, CA: Rand Corporation, 2000) p. 42

avenues for invasion. The climax of the Opium War came when water-borne British forces cut the Grand Canal where it meets the Yangzi at Zhenjiang, then moved upstream to attack the city of Nanjing. Foreign warships would continue to ply China's rivers until Communist field artillery denied HMS *Amethyst* passage of the Yangzi in 1949. By the last decades of the nineteenth century, China's most capable statesmen and military leaders were well aware that the empire would have to adopt key Western technologies in order to defend itself effectively. These included not only steamships and modern rifles and artillery, but also the railroad and the telegraph. The first Chinese steamships were built in the 1860s, but telegraphs and railroads—far more intrusive presences in the ancestral landscape—had to wait much longer. A short railway line built by foreigners near Shanghai in 1876 was purchased and dismantled by Qing authorities the following year, and it was not until after 1900 that China's first major trunk lines were built. The telegraph (and later telephone and wireless communications) allowed closer control and better coordination of armed forces, and the railway held out the hope that the country could be more effectively defended by forces operating on interior lines. The railway was a two-edged sword, however. Fears that foreign-financed and -controlled rail lines would permit foreign penetration of the Chinese hinterland contributed to the mood of crisis that preceded the Wuchang Uprising of 1911, which precipitated the fall of the Qing dynasty. The nation's rail network did indeed facilitate the Japanese invasion and occupation of eastern China in 1937–1945, but at the same time the invaders found their communications, logistics, lines of advance, and zones of occupation tied to the railway lines. The new technology offered unprecedented opportunities, but also imposed its own constraints on military operations.

The new prominence of steamships and railways from the late nineteenth century onward required the exploitation of new resources, most notably coal. Several areas of northern China (particularly Shanxi province) were found to hold rich reserves of coal, which remained an important fuel source even at the end of the twentieth century. As late as 1980 there were still some 10,000 steam locomotives operating in China, and diesel and electric locomotives will not likely bury the last steam engine until the second decade of the twenty-first century. Military aviation (from 1913) and motor vehicles demanded another sort of fuel. For more than two decades, China's need for oil was largely met by the great oilfield opened at Daqing in Manchuria in the early 1960s. Today, however, China no longer produces all of the petroleum needed by its rapidly growing economy, and the quest for new oil reserves is an important factor behind the assertion of sovereignty over the South China Sea. Initially dependent on waterborne transit, China turned to rail transportation in the twentieth century and is only now beginning to create a modern highway system.

In spite of these changes, Chinese military logistics in the twentieth century did not represent a surgical break with the imperial past. Mao's armies in 1949 still moved in the traditional manner, by horse and foot, and many PLA units continued to rely on horse, donkey, and even camel transport long after the establishment of the People's Republic. Even without considering China's relative poverty, labor-saving devices did not always make sound sense. As the Chinese intervention in Korea in the winter of 1950–1951 showed, packing supplies in by porters who could disappear in the daytime was more effective than hauling things in train and truck convoys easily detected by the enemy's aerial reconnaisance. And the size of China's population (1.158 billion in the 1992 census and about 1.3 billion in 2001) meant that labor was always cheap relative to capital equipment. In recent years, however, China's large population has come to be regarded more as a burden than an asset. The country is no longer self-sufficient in grain, and the imposition of birth control policies reflected the fear that economic advances and improvements in the standard of living would be eaten up by population growth.

An additional resource needs to be mentioned, one that was by no means unimportant in premodern times and has become essential in today's world of high-technology warfare: educated, literate, highly skilled, and innovative personnel. Clerical personnel were a presence in Chinese armies throughout the imperial period (as evidenced, for example, by the Han-period documents of military administration recovered from Edsengol in Inner Mongolia), and the spread of woodblock printing during the Northern Song period must have led to an increase of popular literacy. Well-known Chinese innovations of the imperial period included not only printing, but also paper, gunpowder, and the mariner's compass. After 1500 C.E., Chinese technology began to lag behind that of the West, probably due more to revolutionary developments in Europe than stagnation in China. After the middle of the nineteenth century, however, the Chinese began to master one Western technology after another, from the steam engine and the telegraph to jet aircraft, the atomic bomb, and intercontinental ballistic missiles. The gap has not been entirely closed today, but it is clear that the West's continued technological superiority is now dependent on continuing innovation.

ACTORS, INTERESTS, AND INSTITUTIONS

The idea of the proper relationship between the soldier and the farmers who made up the vast majority of the population has been reformulated many times over the course of Chinese history. During the Spring and Autumn period (722–481 B.C.E.) warfare was mainly the province of aristocratic elites, but during the Warring States (453–221 B.C.E.) and Han (202 B.C.E.–220 C.E.) periods huge armies were formed from peasant conscripts. Later periods saw the appearance of hereditary military households and "militias" of farmer-soldiers, such as the *fubing* of the Tang dynasty. From the eighth century onward, a long-service, mercenary soldiery distinct from the farming population tended to predominate, even as scholars sang the praises of the sturdy (and inexpensive) yeomanry of earlier times. Throughout the history of imperial China, an important role was played by specialized units recruited from among non-Han peoples both within and outside the borders of the empire; these included aboriginal infantry from the mountains of the south and cavalry raised from the nomadic peoples of the steppe frontier. During some periods (such as the early Tang), steppe allies and auxiliaries made a decisive contribution to the expansion of Chinese power, and at some times (most notably under the Mongol Yuan) warlike steppe peoples were themselves rulers of China.

It is testimony to the extreme diversity of military institutions in China's imperial past that the twentieth century brought little that was entirely new, at least in the way of recruitment and terms of service. The men of early Republican and warlord armies were generally long-serving regulars recruited for pay, much like the soldiery of late Tang and Song times. The Nationalist government began to introduce a European-style conscription system in the mid–1930s. During the Sino–Japanese War of 1937–1945 this tended to degenerate into brutal press-ganging, but the original conception (and the system put in place in Taiwan after 1949) bore a remarkable resemblance to the cadre–conscript system of the early Western Han, with a relatively short period of active service followed by a much longer time in the reserves. The People's Republic of China has also adopted a conscription system, though the sheer size of the population and the fact that during the Mao years military service offered one of the very few paths of upward mobility for young peasant males meant that men who were not willing volunteers were seldom called upon to serve. The ancient ideal of the farmer-soldier was revived in the militia system of Mao's China; in the mid–1970s there were reported to be 15 to 20 million people, both men and women, enrolled in the "basic" militia.

This brings us to the understudied subject of women in Chinese warfare. Women were, of course, always present as victims and as support personnel (much in evidence, for example, in the labor gangs that built airfields for U.S. bombers in the 1940s). At times, however, they were much more active participants. There is evidence that a Shang dynasty queen led military campaigns around the beginning of the twelfth century B.C.E., and nearly two thousand years later a daughter of the founder of the Tang dynasty raised forces to support her father's bid for the throne. At the other end of the social hierarchy, charismatic shamanesses emerged from time to time to lead peasant rebellions. The story of Mulan, the young woman who took her father's place in the ranks, may be fiction, but actual women have been participants in combat. The Taiping rebels in the mid-nineteenth century organized military units composed entirely of women, and women served—and fought—with the Red Army on the Long March. Approximately 135,000 women are serving in the People's Liberation Army today, though as in most other contemporary military establishments they are assigned to support rather than combat roles.

Military leaders were recruited in a variety of ways in different periods of Chinese history, and came from a wide range of backgrounds. During the Han dynasty, some of the most prominent commanders were kinsmen of imperial consorts who received appointments on the basis of their connections rather than any obvious aptitude for command. In some periods, such as the Sui and early Tang, military and civil elites were not sharply differentiated, and members of powerful aristocratic families might hold both civil and military positions in the course of an official career. A sharper distinction between civil officials and military officers had appeared by the middle of the Tang period, however, and continued to be evident under most of the later dynasties. Men from elite, landowning families tended to pursue careers in the civil bureaucracy; these required a high level of literacy and considerable book learning, since recruitment was usually by means of a very demanding series of written examinations. Military officers, on the other hand, tended to come from more humble backgrounds. They were often promoted from the ranks, and many were illiterate or semiliterate at best. The Tang, Song, Ming, and Qing dynasties did offer military examinations, but these tended to emphasize horsemanship and archery more than knowledge of military texts. Civil bureaucrats and military officers were often rivals for influence at court, and the civil officials attempted to assert their dominance over the military sphere in various ways and generally had the upper hand. Civil officials with no practical military training or experience of command at the lower levels were sometimes sent out to direct military campaigns. One such scholar-general was the Ming philosopher Wang Yangming (1472–1529); another was Zeng Guofan, the victor over the Taiping rebels in the mid-nineteenth century.

The behavior of Chinese rulers was congruent with the superiority (if not absolute supremacy) of civil over military elites. Most emperors never acted as generals or led their armies in battle, and the exceptions were mostly dynastic founders, who were often military men from humble origins who had battled their way to the throne. Civil officials usually held the view that an emperor was too valuable an asset to be risked on the battlefield (his defeat or capture might be interpreted as signalling the loss of Heaven's mandate), and that his principal function was to preside over the ritual of imperial government in the capital. Even Wudi, the "Martial Emperor" of the Han dynasty who launched repeated expeditions against the nomadic Xiongnu, never led a military campaign in person.

The training and recruitment of Chinese military leaders changed considerably in the early twentieth century. Military academies such as Baoding and Whampoa were set up in imitation of Western models, and as a consequence growing numbers of officers could boast a modicum of modern, professional training. At the same time, however, this professionalizing trend was offset to a considerable extent by the vicissitudes of Chinese politics. The breakdown of civil authority during the warlord period threw political power into the hands of military leaders, and the rise of two great revolutionary parties, the Guomindang and the Chinese Communist Party, that sought to take and hold power by means of armed force further blurred the distinction between civil and military leadership roles. The Nationalist leader Chiang Kai-shek was both generalissimo and head of state, and many Communist leaders (such as Mao Zedong and Deng Xiaoping) worked both sides of the civil–military divide. It has only been in the last two decades that maturation and routinization of the political systems in both Communist China and Taiwan have produced a distinctly civilian political leadership and confined military leaders to their professional sphere.

IDEOLOGY AND STRATEGY

In recent years there has been much interest in the qualities and characteristics that have made the Chinese approach to warfare different from that of other societies (especially the European and European-descended societies usually labelled as "the West"). Some authors, pointing to the Confucian tradition and certain passages in Sunzi's *Art of War*, have argued that China's traditional grand strategy has emphasized defense over offense and displayed a preference for nonviolent solutions to security problems. Sunzi, after all, tells us that the acme of military excellence is to subdue the enemy without fighting, while the *Mencius*, one of the core texts of the Confucian canon, maintains that the truly virtuous ruler, by means of his transforming influence, can bring his enemies to submit voluntarily without recourse to physical coercion. Others, most notably the Western military historian John Keegan, have argued that China has followed an "Oriental" style of warmaking characterized by caution, delay, the avoidance of battle, and the use of elaborate ruses and stratagems. This style of warfare is contrasted with a "Western way of war" that stresses direct, face-to-face confrontation and the rapid resolution of military conflicts by main force.[3]

Setting aside momentarily the question of whether these are accurate representations of either the Chinese or Western approaches to warfare, strategy anywhere in the premodern world had necessarily to be shaped within the bounds of a common set of material constraints. The management of campaigns had to take into account when in the spring the grass would be long enough to sustain the horses, how much surplus grain would be in the granaries, and when the rivers would flood and be impassable. In all periods up almost to the present, armies were limited to about thirty miles a day if mounted and fifteen if on foot, but even these rates of march required an excellent supply or foraging system. Horses required twenty-six pounds of forage and fifty gallons of water a day, and each soldier needed approximately three pounds of grain. East or West, an army was a veritable vacuum cleaner scouring up the resources of the surrounding countryside; its presence might easily lead peasants to hide their sustenance and flee to cover. Very large armies could only be supplied by water transport, and thus had great difficulty moving far from rivers, canals, and seacoasts.[4] This explains why campaigns were limited geographically and seasonally. In both Europe and China, transportation and supply dictated that the areas most likely to be fought over were the great river valleys and the arable plains.

The difference between premodern warfare in China and the West was probably not as great as prescriptive texts such as the Chinese military classics might lead us to believe. Despite the literary emphasis on caution and avoidance of the risks of combat, battle was no less common an occurrence in imperial China than it was in the ancient Mediterranean world or medieval Europe. The Greeks and Romans made use of stratagems just as the Chinese did, and writers who see a distinctive "Western way of war" do not take into account the reluctance of medieval Byzantine and Latin commanders to risk their armies in pitched battles. Moreover, the contents and recommendations of the principal Byzantine military treatises bear a remarkable resemblance to their medieval Chinese counterparts. There are other points of similitarity. In his recent study of Chinese strategic culture, the political scientist Alastair Iain Johnston found that the Chinese military classics (including Sunzi) show a preference for violent, aggressive solutions to security problems—provided that one has the capability to carry them out. He also found that the military activity of the Ming dynasty (1368–1644) corresponded to what might be predicted by a Western realpolitik or "structural realist" model of state behavior: In its early years, when the state was militarily powerful, Ming China engaged in far more campaigns against its neighbors than was true later on, after the regime and its armed forces had begun to weaken.[5]

A cursory examination of the military history of other major dynasties, such as the Han and Tang, would seem to reveal much the same pattern. It was during their vigorous early or middle years that these regimes launched offensive campaigns to dominate peripheral regions such as Korea, Vietnam, Xinjiang, and the Mongolian steppe. As the dynasties began to weaken and internal problems arose, however, the aggressive use of military force tended to be replaced by other strategies emphasizing diplomacy, appeasement, and the construction of static defensive installations. What Johnston calls "the Confucian–Mencian paradigm" was not entirely without influence, however. Within the ruling circles of the empire, support for aggressive military action tended to come from strong emperors, groups closely connected to the throne such as consort families and eunuchs, and aristocratic and military elites. Opposition to such strategies, on the other hand, was most likely to come from scholar-officials educated in the Confucian tradition. They blamed the Han emperor Wudi for wrecking the economy of the empire with his repeated campaigns against the nomadic Xiongnu, and opposed Tang Taizong's attempt to subdue the northern Korean kingdom of Koguryo in the middle of the seventh century. Their attitude probably derived in part from the Confucian belief that the need to use force was a sign of the failure of virtue, and in part from a desire to restrain the power of rival elites (such as military men and eunuchs).

In contrast to the antimilitary bias evident in China's heavily Confucian elite culture, some have pointed to a more favorable attitude toward things martial in Chinese popular culture. They note such things as the widespread practice of martial arts in the cities and villages and the popularity of operas, folktales, and works of fiction dealing with the exploits of martial heroes.[6] It is important to note, however, that these heroes are usually Robin Hood–type social bandits rather than regular soldiers in the service of the state. Ordinary people in many cases took extreme measures (including self-mutilation) to avoid being conscripted for military service, and soldiers were often regarded (with good reason) as being little better than brigands. In the twentieth century, the Chinese Communists largely succeeded in overcoming the negative image and making soldiers respectable by holding them to higher standards of behavior and emphasizing the unity of army and people.

THE LITERATURE

China can claim a very ancient tradition of writing about war. The thirteen chapters attributed to Sunzi, probably China's earliest surviving military treatise, are thought to date from the fifth century B.C.E., and the author of the Sunzi appears to quote from an even earlier work on the art of war that is now no longer extant. Many other military manuals were written in later centuries, and full-blown military encyclopedias appeared during the Song and Ming dynasties (some two thousand years after Sunzi's time).

When it comes to the description of actual military events as opposed to the prescriptive contents of the treatises, however, the Chinese corpus of military literature is much less impressive. The battle narratives and other descriptions of military operations that we find in the dynastic histories tend to be laconic in the extreme; such matters as weapons, tactics, detailed orders of battle, and logistics are largely neglected, while the attention of the historian is drawn to clever and unusual stratagems. A fair amount of space is devoted to the councils of war held before and after a battle, but in between them the account of the combat itself may be no more than two or three sentences. This pattern is already evident in such pioneering early histories as Sima Qian's *Historical Records* (*Shiji*) of circa 100 B.C.E. and Ban Gu's *History of the Former Han Dynasty* (*Han shu*) dating from the first century C.E.

This state of affairs can be explained by the gulf that usually existed between scholars and soldiers in imperial China. History was written by elite scholar-officials who seldom had any military experience. They had little interest in the technical details of warfare, and preferred to focus on matters of statesmanship, ethical behavior, and moral principle. Military leaders, on the other hand, were often poorly educated or even illiterate. These men and their activities were viewed with distaste by the scholar-officials, who tended to subscribe to the Confucian view that the use of violence represented a failure of statecraft and indicated that its user might lack the virtue needed for governance by moral suasion.

While neglecting the details of military operations, traditional Chinese historians nevertheless displayed considerable interest in military institutions. Beginning with Ouyang Xiu's *New Tang History* (*Xin Tang shu*), written in the eleventh century, the Chinese dynastic histories include chapters on the military that address such matters as organization, recruitment, and terms of service. Unlike combat itself, military institutions were seen as a worthy object of scholarly attention. This attitude no doubt owed something to the fact that the scholars writing the histories were also government officials, and military administration—as opposed to combat command—was always an important responsibility of the civil bureaucracy in imperial China. Beyond this, however, military institutions were considered to be a vitally important area of imperial policy and one that could be directly linked to the rise and fall of dynasties; great significance was often attached to the means of recruitment and the nature of the relationship between the soldier and civilian society as a basis for military power and dynastic stability. These attitudes have shown remarkable staying power. Even in the twentieth century, much of the finest Chinese scholarship on military history—such as Gu Jiguang's work on the Tang *fubing* militia, Luo Ergang's study of the Qing Green Standard Army, and Wang Zengyu's work on the Song military—has been devoted to military institutions.[7]

The volume of Chinese writing on military history has increased tremendously since the middle of the twentieth century, and this is especially true with regard to accounts of military operations. This may be seen both as a consequence of China's experience of almost constant warfare between 1911 and 1949 and as a product of Western influence insofar as a significant portion of this literature has come in the form of officially sponsored staff histories imitating the compilations published by the major belligerents following the two world wars. A typical example of this genre is the massive *History of the Nationalist Revolutionary Wars* (*Guomin geming zhanzheng shi*) compiled between 1970 and 1982 under the auspices of Taiwan's Armed Forces University. Similar works, such as the three-volume *Battle History of the Chinese People's Liberation Army* (*Zhongguo renmin jiefangjun zhanshi*), have been issued by the PRC.[8] The same style has also been applied to the military history of imperial times, as, for example, in the ten-volume *History of Warfare in China through the*

Ages (*Zhongguo lidai zhanzheng shi*) published in Taipei in 1967 and the twenty-volume *Comprehensive History of Chinese Military Affairs* (*Zhongguo junshi tongshi*) published in Beijing in 1998. The last several decades have also seen an outpouring of memoir literature from former soldiers on both sides of the Taiwan Strait.

In contrast, relatively little work on Chinese military history has been published in English and other Western languages. Among the most important contributions in English are William W. Whitson's *The Chinese High Command*, a monumental history of the People's Liberation Army; *Chinese Ways in Warfare*, a pioneering collection of case studies of military operations in imperial China edited by John K. Fairbank and Frank A. Kierman Jr.; and the volumes on traditional military technology prepared by Joseph Needham and Robin Yates for *Science and Civilisation in China*.[9] In general, however, the level of sophistication found in writing on Chinese military history in both Chinese and English has not matched that in other fields of military history. For the most part, the ideas of innovative Western military historians, from Hans Delbrück to John Keegan and Martin van Creveld, have yet to be applied to the study of Chinese warfare.

As already stated, the goal of this volume is less ambitious. It offers an introduction to fifteen of the major topics in Chinese military history from antiquity to the present day. Given the vast size and scope of the subject, a truly comprehensive treatment is out of the question in a single volume. Many matters of great importance—such as arms production, logistics, the role of women in warfare, the use of divination and other "magical" techniques on the battlefield in ancient and imperial times, popular attitudes toward the military, and the recruitment and training of martial elites—receive little attention in this book, and some have yet to be thoroughly explored anywhere. The field is still to a very large extent wide open, and if this volume succeeds in stimulating further research it will have more than accomplished its purpose.

NOTES

1. Tang Changru, *Wei Jin Nanbeichao Sui Tang shi san lun* [Three discourses on the history of Wei, Jin, Northern and Southern Dynasties, Sui, and Tang] (Wuhan: Wuhan daxue chubanshe, 1993), 29–30; John K. Fairbank and Merle Goldman, *China: A New History*, enl. ed. (Cambridge, MA: Belknap Press, 1998), 89; Susan Naquin and Evelyn Sakakida Rawski, *Chinese Society in the Eighteenth Century* (New Haven: Yale University Press, 1987), 24–25. For the Roman population, see Colin McEvedy and Richard Jones, *Atlas of World Population History* (New York: Facts on File, 1978), 21.

2. Robert Hartwell, "Markets, Technology, and the Structure of Enterprise in the Development of the Eleventh-Century Chinese Iron and Steel Industry," *Journal of Economic History* 26 (1966): 32–33, 36, 38.

3. John Keegan, *A History of Warfare* (New York: Alfred A. Knopf, 1993), 214, 221, 332–333, 380, 387–388; also see Victor Davis Hanson, *The Western Way of War: Infantry Battle in Classical Greece* (New York: Oxford University Press, 1990).

4. See Donald W. Engels, *Alexander the Great and the Logistics of the Macedonian Army* (Berkeley and Los Angeles: University of California Press, 1978).

5. Alastair Iain Johnston, *Cultural Realism: Strategic Culture and Grand Strategy in Chinese History* (Princeton: Princeton University Press, 1995).

6. See Morton H. Fried, "Military Status in Chinese Society," *American Journal of Sociology* 57 (1951–1952): 347–355.

7. Gu Jiguang, *Fubing zhidu kaoshi* [Examination and explanation of the *fubing* system] (Shanghai: Shanghai renmin chubanshe, 1962); Luo Ergang, *Lüying bingzhi* [A treatise on the Green Standard Army] (Chongqing: Commercial Press, 1945); Wang Zengyu, *Songchao bingzhi chutan* [Preliminary investigation of the military institutions of the Song dynasty] (Beijing: Zhonghua shuju, 1983).

8. Military History Research Department of the Academy of Military Science, *Zhongguo renmin jiefangjun zhanshi*, 3 vols. (Beijing: Junshi kexue chubanshe, 1987).

9. See Joseph Needham and Robin D. S. Yates, *Science and Civilisation in China*, vol. 5, *Chemistry and Chemical Technology*, pt. 6, *Military Technology: Missiles and Sieges* (Cambridge: Cambridge University Press, 1994). A very recent addition to the literature is Bruce A. Elleman, *Modern Chinese Warfare, 1795–1989* (London and New York: Routledge, 2001).

TWO

Continuity and Change

Edward L. Dreyer

From the perspective of military history, Chinese history divides naturally into three periods. The first of these is Ancient China, from earliest times to the end of the Spring and Autumn period (722–481 B.C.E.). Separating fact from later idealizations has long been the major challenge confronting students of this period, but certain things are clear about its military history: The major weapons system was the two-wheeled Bronze Age war chariot, and the aristocratic and "feudal" social order symbolized by the chariot remained the ideal for most Chinese intellectuals throughout the following imperial period.

The second period is Imperial China, which began militarily with the Legalist reforms in the state of Qin during the Warring States era (453–221 B.C.E.), reforms which Qin's rivals adopted with less success. After conquering all of China, the Qin ruler and his advisors invented the title *huangdi*, translated as "emperor" and used by successive imperial dynasties until 1912. Elements of continuity and change in the history of Imperial China, and more detailed periodization within it, are discussed later, but the persistence of Confucian values, the Legalist state, and the military threat from the nomadic societies of Inner Asia throughout this long span of history point to the comparability of the many dynasties included therein.

The third period is Modern China, beginning with the defeat of the Qing (Manchu) empire in the Opium War (1839–1842) and continuing down to the present. In the military as in other areas, China's efforts to respond to the West have led to drastic change, even as the continuing evolution of the major Western nations has made it difficult for other societies to catch up.

ANCIENT CHINA

Ancient China during the Shang dynasty (ca. 1500–1045 B.C.E.), the Western Zhou (ca. 1045–770 B.C.E.), and the Spring and Autumn era was a Bronze Age society whose military expression was the war chariot with two spoked wheels. Commanded by an aristocratic archer, the chariot's crew included a driver and sometimes a third person armed with a spear. While few believe the Shang were foreign conquerors, the place of the chariot in Shang culture is one aspect of the rapid diffusion of the war chariot throughout Eurasia in the middle of the second millennium B.C.E. Archaeological study of Shang sites has revealed elaborate royal burials in which chariots and bronze weapons were interred along with human and animal sacrifices. Despite these rich details, most aspects of military and social organization during the Shang remain uncertain.

The overthrow of the Shang by the Zhou introduced the worship of Heaven (*tian*) and the concept of the Mandate of Heaven (*tianming*) as the basis of political legitimacy. A feudal social order, resting militarily on a class of aristocratic chariot warriors (*shi*), is present from the beginning in authentic Western Zhou sources; it is not certain whether this was new or inherited from the Shang. During the Western Zhou the king (*wang*) ruled through his "Six Armies" of chariots, assigning territories to the feudal lords (*zhuhou*) to govern as fiefs. To emphasize his own authority, the king often transferred individual lords from fief to fief. The book *Rituals of Zhou* (*Zhouli*) and other later sources, mostly compiled in the third century B.C.E., describe in exact but unverifiable detail the offices, ceremonies, land system, and other aspects of the Western Zhou regime. These institutions had by then come to represent the moral and political ideal for the Confucian school of political philosophy. According to the *Rituals of Zhou*, each chariot was associated with five squads (*wu*) of five infantrymen to form a platoon (*liang*). Four platoons made a company (*zu*), five companies a brigade (*lü*), five brigades a division (*shi*), and five divisions an army (*jun*) of 12,500 infantry and 500 chariots, the highest level of the hierarchy. Whether or not this really existed in the Western Zhou, the model was emulated again and again, most recently in the twentieth century when it influenced the nomenclature for military units of modern Chinese armies.

The Western Zhou ends with the move of the Zhou kings to Luoyang after a military catastrophe in the west. In the following Spring and Autumn era the kings are much weaker and the feudal lords correspondingly stronger. Old proprieties still exist, but are growing weaker. The *Commen-*

tary of Zuo (*Zuozhuan*), the principal source for this period, provides much detail as it deplores these trends. It also describes, often vividly, the wars and battles among the feudal lords. The chariot continues to be the major weapon, and the activities of the chariot-mounted *shi* class receive the most attention, even if infantry are assumed to be present. Battles are preceded by rituals and moralizing speeches, and it is thought to be proper to allow the enemy to deploy fully before attacking him. During the Spring and Autumn period warfare continued to be stylized and ceremonial even as it grew more violent and decisive within these parameters, as the military hegemon (*ba*) and his "way of force" (*badao*) came to dominate Chinese society.

The destruction of the state of Jin inaugurated the Warring States era, in which great social and political change was accompanied by the end of the system of chariot warfare and the adoption of new military forms. The ritual and ceremony that had been a principle of Spring and Autumn warfare was replaced by an emphasis on deception, treachery, and stratagems whose sole moral justification was victory. This approach to warfare is codified in Sunzi's *Art of War* and the other military classics from this period, a body of work always considered morally dubious by later Confucian intellectuals.

The heightened intensity and ruthlesness of warfare in the Warring States was matched by changes in weapons and the composition of armies. Chariots disappeared and cavalry was adopted, despite the cultural challenge this posed for robe-wearing Chinese men. But most of the Warring States armies were composed mainly of infantry conscripts, equipped with iron swords, iron-tipped spears, and, most important, crossbows, whose intricate trigger mechanisms required a high level of metalworking skill. The thousands of terracotta soldier statues guarding the tomb of the first emperor, Qin Shi Huangdi, are arranged in precise formations and grouped according to type of weapon, a large percentage being crossbowmen. The conventions of Chinese historiography are such that this sort of detailed deployment information is not presented for the many battles described in the standard dynastic histories.

IMPERIAL CHINA

The military history of Imperial China before the nineteenth-century Western impact shows considerable variation from period to period, depending on changing historical circumstances and the differing social bases of successive dynasties. It also shows continuity related to the persistence of the major cultural factors that came together in the Han period. These cultural factors include Confucianism, the Legalist state, and hostility to the nomads of Inner Asia. All three of these emerged individually during the Warring States period that preceded the Qin unification, but should be viewed analytically as part of Imperial China.

Confucianism

Chinese society is sometimes called "Confucian society," and its dynasties variants of the "Confucian state." While these formulations have been challenged, they indicate something of basic importance: Formal histories and other literary works are the chief sources for Chinese history, including military history, and they are composed overwhelmingly from a viewpoint that can properly be called Confucian. For the ancient period, the Chinese classics generally believed to have the most historical content (such as the *Zuozhuan, Shujing,* and *Zhouli*) survive because of selection (sometimes aided by fabrication) by later Confucians, and the standard histories, from their beginnings in Han times to the 1739 *Ming History* (the twenty-fourth of the standard histories and the last to be compiled under dynastic rule), all were the work of historians who saw themselves explicitly as Confucians. Often the historians were major political figures as well. Whatever the contribution of Confucius himself, the Confucian canon as understood in later times seems to have been shaped during the Warring States period under the guidance of Mencius (372–289 B.C.E.). The explicit adoption of Confucianism as official ideology, and the composition by Sima Tan and Sima Qian of the *Historical Records* (*Shiji*), the first of the standard histories, were major developments in the long reign of Han Wudi (141–87 B.C.E.).

Confucian doctrine saw war as a necessary evil. Military force had to be used to resist invasion, suppress rebellion, and reunify China after periods of division. Confucian officials were not reluctant to use military power on such occasions; indeed, one recent study argues that force was the preferred option when circumstances were right.[1] The military skills of chariotry and archery were two of the six skills of a Confucian gentleman. Yet when Duke Ling of Wei asked Confucius about military tactics, Confucius denied any knowledge of the subject, and he left the next day (*Analects* 15.1). The ideal was the monarch who had received the Mandate of Heaven because of his virtue and who ruled through ritual and moral example. War was necessary because barbarians and "petty people" (*xiaoren*) among the Chinese could not be ruled through such ideal means. Understandably, the Confucian tradition had no place for the ideas of conquest, expansion, and imperial rule over subject peoples that were driving forces in, for example, Roman and Ottoman Turkish history. Emperors who seemed to enjoy war and conquest too much were usually opposed by their officials and/or condemned by history (examples include Qin Shi Huangdi, Han Wudi, Sui Yangdi, Tang Taizong, and Ming Yongle), while emperors who decisively moved from war to peace, and from military (*wu*) to civil (*wen*) values (such as Han Gaozu and Song Taizu) were correspondingly praised. Nor, as the aftermath of the early Ming naval expeditions demonstrates, was there ever any prospect of commerce-driven overseas colonial expansion, even though Ming China had both the economic development and the nautical technology to be a major player in the creation of colonial empires through seapower had Confucian values permitted such activity.

The Legalist State

Confucian values gained unchallenged dominance within Chinese education and society during the reign of Han Wudi and held this dominance for the rest of the history of Imperial China. Nonetheless, the state that Confucian-educated officials administered originated in an environment hostile to Confucianism, the expansionist Qin regime of the Warring States period. Legalist thinkers from Shang Yang (d. 338 B.C.E.) to Li Si (d. 208 B.C.E.), both of whom were Qin prime ministers, held that people should be socially regimented, bureaucratically administered, rewarded only for success in war and agriculture, punished for the slightest transgressions, and subject to the absolute will of the ruler. The goal of the Legalist thinkers and the purpose of organizing the state in this way was to permit Qin to defeat, conquer, and absorb its rivals, a process completed with the conquest of all China in 230–221 B.C.E. Qin fell soon afterward and Legalism was discredited and blamed for its fall, but the autocratic, bureaucratic, centralized empire that Qin Legalism had created remained the master institution of Chinese political life for the next two thousand years, and its restoration was always the primary goal of Chinese political actors during periods of dynastic breakdown. Officials of successive dynasties thus had the means to raise tax revenues and to mobilize the population for war or for labor service to a degree that was unusual for a preindustrial society. Military activities might have been dysfunctional for various reasons, but most dynasties were capable of formidable military efforts.

The Northern Nomads

In theory, China was the Middle Kingdom (*Zhongguo*), bordered by different kinds of "barbarians" in each of the four primary directions. In reality, the successive nomadic and seminomadic peoples living in the steppe and desert environments of Mongolia and Manchuria have been the most significant "barbarians" in Chinese military history. Three of the directional terms for "barbarians" (*yi, rong,* and *di*) and a common general term for foreigners (*hu,* also often translated as "barbarian") usually refer to Inner Asian nomadic or seminomadic peoples. The Xiongnu, Türks, Kitan, and Mongols all practiced largely nomadic ways of life, while the Xianbi and their Jurchen and Manchu successors combined nomadism with agriculture to a degree that facilitated their rule over Chinese populations. The Mongols and Manchus both conquered all of China and ruled it for long periods, and both Mongol- and Manchu-language sources show us ruling elites animated by ideals of war and conquest that often diverged from Confucian values. Similar ideals motivated the elites of the other peoples mentioned, though we know of them largely through Chinese sources. While the Xianbi, Kitan, and Jurchen did not conquer all of China, they each established durable dynasties of conquest over substantial Chinese populations.

All of these non-Chinese peoples were formidable because their male populations of military age were all warriors bred to the saddle and trained in the mounted archer mode of fighting that dominated Inner Asia. This threat emerged during the Warring States period. Chinese reactions included the building by the border states of Zhao and Yan of walls that were the precursors of the Qin wall, and the adoption of cavalry by King Wuling of Zhao in 307 B.C.E. after a culturally charged debate: Riding on horseback involved adopting elements of Inner Asian dress, including trousers. All succeeding dynasties made extensive use of cavalry. This is most obvious in the regimes founded by Inner Asian peoples, but those of Chinese origin also went to great efforts to maintain mounted forces. This included maintaining stud farms for horses in the border areas, recruiting ethnically Chinese cavalry forces whose training was modeled on that of the nomads, recruiting troops directly from the Inner Asian peoples, and establishing (with much reluctance) commercial relations in which tea and other Chinese goods were traded for horses.

Change over time during the long history of Imperial China is more subtle than the continuities. Chinese historians have usually emphasized the cyclical nature of their history, with its repeated establishment and overturning of the "Mandate of Heaven." Nevertheless, close study reveals long-term changes in many areas. In the military sphere these include the perceptions and positions of the educated elite, military officers and soldiers, personnel and institutions of non-Chinese origin, and weapons and military technology.

The Educated Elite

Over the long history of Imperial China the educated elite official class increasingly came to see itself as purely "civil," leaving military functions to be performed by others. In the Han (202 B.C.E.–220 C.E.) and the Six Dynasties (220–589), a successful official career might include provincial governorships and other positions having direct command of troops. In the Tang (618–907) this could still happen, but the civil and military positions were more sharply distinguished, and the An Lushan rebellion (from 755) was preceded by a personnel policy of placing only professional soldiers in command of troops. The An Lushan rebellion began a long period of dynastic weakness, followed by division during the Five Dynasties (907–960), and educated opinion blamed China's problems on the militarism of the standing armies and the barbarian generals prominent within them. During the Song (960–1279) strong antimilitary attitudes became dominant within the educated elite, which largely avoided political involvement during the period of Mongol rule that followed. In the Ming (1368–1644) and Qing (1644–1912), the civil and military chains of command were sharply differentiated, and even when civil officials had military responsibilities, they exercised them by giving orders to the military officers who actually led the troops. Meanwhile, the lifestyle of the educated elite emphasized separation from manual labor and other forms of physical activity, including warfare.

Military Officers and Soldiers

Over the long run of Imperial China, the military service obligation of the general population evolved from being nearly universal, as in the Qin and Han, to a burden imposed on a minority. While both the Tang *fubing* system and the Ming *weisuo* system employed the principle of soldier-farmers liable to conscription, in both dynasties this principle applied only to a minority of the population. In the Tang *fubing* membership seems to have been seen as a benefit in the early reigns of the dynasty, later evolving into a burden, while in the Ming *weisuo* membership seems to have been viewed as a burden from the beginning. In the Song the troops of the standing army were poorly paid and used for menial work, while military officer status was conferred on many officials doing low-level work disdained by true scholar-officials. Coupled with the hypertrophy of "civil" values among the educated elite, these attitudes and patterns of treatment led to the denigration of soldiers (including officers), noticeable from Song times onward and expressed in the often-quoted saying, "Good iron isn't used for nails; good men aren't used as soldiers." Occasional efforts of civil officials to revive the militia ideal of classical antiquity seldom worked as intended.

"Barbarian" Personnel and Institutions

The influence of foreign examples on dynastic military institutions expanded. One would expect this of the various non-Chinese dynasties of conquest, which arose, after all, because Inner Asian peoples and their military institutions prevailed in warfare. Yet the Sui-Tang *fubing* military system was the lineal descendant of similar institutions in the redoubtably barbarbian Western Wei of the Tuoba Xianbi, while the Ming *weisuo* system continued the essential features of the Yuan military system, itself an imposition of Mongol tribal patterns on a part of the Chinese population. This leaves the Song unique among the later dynasties of Chinese origin in that its military institutions were not directly derived from a non-Chinese model. These long-term changes culminated in the Manchu Qing dynasty, with its co-opted Chinese civilian elite, its Green Standard Army of Chinese troops, and its banner forces organized on Inner Asian models. By the time of the Opium War the Qing military was in decline, but in the two previous centuries the Qing changed China's military frame of reference permanently by incorporating Mongolia, Xinjiang, and Tibet. On the eve of the new challenge represented by Western ideas and British sea power, the Qing had solved the enduring threat of invasion by the nomadic peoples of the north.

Weapons and Military Technology

China has been an "advanced" country, in comparison to its contemporaries, through most of recorded history, losing ground only after the Industrial Revolution began in Britain. The major innovations in weaponry that influenced Western military history have their counterparts in China. Any list would include the crossbow, armor, the stirrup, fortifications, gunpowder weapons, and shipbuilding.

In the Qin and Han conscript armies, infantry and cavalry replaced chariots as the principal arm, and the infantry were armed with spears, bows, and in particular crossbows (*nu*), a weapon in whose technology the Chinese remained superior. Later descriptions of Chinese armies usually include units of archers mixed with crossbowmen, the latter presumably needing protection between rounds due to their longer reloading time. The intricate trigger latch mechanism of the crossbow was a closely guarded state secret under the Han. Battle accounts (too often, unfortunately, influenced by literary conventions) often mention the sky being darkened by clouds of arrows. Evidence for the actual conduct of battles is sketchy, but discharges of arrows (including crossbow bolts) were crucial to victory. Even though infantry bearing shields, swords, and spears existed, there is no trace of either a "phalanx" or a "legion" style of infantry fighting.

Qin Shi Huangdi's tomb army is wearing armor, and there are many later representations of armored Chinese soldiers. Most of the armor is of the scale or lamellar variety, in which overlapping metal plates of varying size are sewn onto a cloth background. Such armor is relatively light and flexible at the expense of protective strength, and in the West infantry and cavalry trained for shock tactics and reliance on edged weapons tended to move on to armor composed at least partly of large plates, of which there are a few Chinese examples.

The idea that the stirrup, by permitting the evolution of shock cavalry armed with the lance, was a primary factor in the creation of European feudalism has received a surprising degree of credence, though recent reevalution of the four-horned Roman saddle has undermined its central thesis.[2] In China the spread of the stirrup is associated with the development of the armored cavalryman, mounted on an armored (barded) horse and armed with a lance. Literary references to "armored cavalry" occur as late as the Tang, and a vivid pictorial representation of mounted warriors looking like European knights occurs in a tomb dated to 357 C.E. Nevertheless, it may be stated with confidence that the social outcomes attributed to the stirrup in Europe did not occur in China. Knightlike cavalry were part of the ruling class of north China during the Northern and Southern Dynasties period. This class, which evolved into the governing aristocracy of the Sui and Tang, was largely Xianbi in origin but also included other Inner Asian peoples and Chinese who had adopted barbarian ways. Far from devolving into feudalism, the Sui and Tang dynasties erected a powerful and enduring version of the centralized, bureaucratic empire previously built by the Qin and Han. And, stirrupped or not, the cavalry future belonged to the Inner Asian warrior whose strength was his skill with the bow rather than the lance.

China has always been a country of cities rather than castles, and city walls were not only a means of defense but also a symbol of the city's status in the hierarchy of rule. The walls were formidable defenses. While there are many recorded examples of long sieges and much literature on siege-craft, it remained the case that the best way to take a city was by treachery or surprise during a period of confusion, and a siege was more likely to be won by protracted blockade than by a successful assault. China's urban for-tifications did not evolve the low, relatively cannon-proof bastions of the *trace italienne*, as European cities did in the sixteenth century while China lived peacefully under the rule of the Ming. Afterward, the thick earthen walls of the major Chinese cities remained highly resistant to the gunpow-der weapons that were becoming more prominent in Chinese warfare.

The basic formula for gunpowder was known to the Song, weapons in-corporating gunpowder were used prominently during the Yuan, and in the Ming Yongle reign (1402–1424) a special headquarters was established in Beijing to coordinate the training of gunners. Firearms added to the de-fensive strength of the Great Wall, itself a Ming creation, and the Chinese element of the Manchu banner system seem to have been valued, in part, as artillery specialists. However, we cannot discern a "gunpowder revolu-tion" in Chinese military history. In the Ming, Qi Jiguang's successful and widely emulated military organization had gunners serving alongside bowmen, swordsmen, and spearmen in the same primary (squad-level) formations, and in the Qing Zeng Guofan's Hunan Army battalions com-bined newer and older weapons in the same way. Firearms originated in China, but in China they remained just another missile weapon. One does not see efforts to standardize manufacture, reduce the number of calibers, or create new tactics and organizations to exploit the potential of a new weapons system.

Marco Polo's descriptions of Chinese ships were part of his credibility problem in Europe, and Europeans also found it difficult to credit the early Ming naval voyages. It is now accepted that China built wooden ships as large or larger than any ever built in Europe, and, having invented the compass, navigated them beyond the sight of land to Africa and other dis-tant coasts. But these capabilities did not add up to a navy; in the latter part of the Ming and in the Qing, China's seagoing forces consisted of small ships and boats tethered to the military organizations of specific provinces.

China's long history of technological progress provides scant comfort for theories that see certain kinds of social and political change as the inevitable result of specific technologies. Neither the stirrup nor gunpowder had the dramatic consequences in China claimed for them in Europe. With respect to shipbuilding technology, Ming China's withdrawal from the sea was deliberate and dramatic, and had long-lasting consequences. It compares to Tokugawa Japan's "giving up the gun."[3] In both cases, ruling establishments feared and prevented technology-driven change.

Military Institutions

Within the context of the factors of continuity and change already discussed, we may see three broad (and partly overlapping) subperiods in the evolution of Imperial China's military institutions and practices, each of which transcends any single dynasty, and each of which came to an end due to a crisis of Chinese civilization involving the two basic military threats: domestic rebellion and foreign invasion. The first subperiod is bounded by the rise of Qin in the Warring States and the end of the last of the Six Dynasties in 589 C.E., the second by the consolidation of the Northern Wei in the fifth century and the final Mongol conquest of the Song in 1279, and the third by the Kitan conquest of part of north China in the tenth century and the fall of the imperial system as a whole in the twentieth century. We will label these subperiods Han, Tang, and Mongol–Manchu.

HAN. The two Han dynasties continued to employ the cadre-conscript army developed by the state of Qin during the Warring States, just as they continued the bureaucratic system and other Qin institutions. Similarly, the military systems of the Three Kingdoms, the ephemeral Western Jin (265–316), and the later south China regimes collectively called the Six Dynasties evolved from the Later Han state of affairs in which rival warlords controlled armies of dependent soldiers (*buqu*).

The career and reforms of Shang Yang (d. 338 B.C.E.) in Qin are described in a hostile and caricatured way in the sources, but they converted Qin permanently into the strongest of the seven warring states well over a century before the final Qin conquest of China. Shang Yang abolished hereditary status and created a new set of "titles of nobility" (*jue*) that could be conferred on any male subject, but only for success in war or agriculture. The population was organized in mutual responsibility groups and governed by officials who could not be natives of the areas they governed. These officials were rewarded (or punished) strictly for their success (or failure) in carrying out their orders. The other states contemporary with Qin undertook less comprehensive and less successful reforms, but Qin retained the leadership that Shang Yang's reforms had conferred. Qin's greatest general, Bai Qi (d. 257 B.C.E.), made it a deliberate policy to massacre the armies of the states he defeated in order to maintain Qin's comparative advantage.

While the first Han emperor made a great show of moderating the severity of Qin laws and experimented with a limited revival of feudalism, in the end the Han continued most Qin institutions, including the Qin military system. For most people conscription was the most important element of that system. Men were drafted for two years, serving as infantry, cavalry, or sailors according to their background. For a small minority this meant service in the capital, and for a larger minority service along the walled defenses of the northern frontier, whose operation in Han times is understood in unusual detail from surviving contemporary documents.[4] Most conscripts seem to have served their time within their native province (*jun*, "commandery"), whose governor (*taishou*, literally "grand defender") was also their commander in case of invasion. The founding of the Han coincided closely with the unification of the Xiongnu under Maodun, and Han Wudi's resort to war against the Xiongnu is associated with the creation of specialist cavalry forces that could fight in the Xiongnu manner, most famously by Huo Qubing (d. 117 B.C.E.). But Wudi's wars against the Xiongnu and his annexations of territory in Korea, south China, and Vietnam were made possible by the mobilization of large numbers of mostly infantry troops, and this capacity was retained under his successors.

Guangwudi (r. 25–57), the founding emperor of the Later Han, lightened the military burden by eliminating the annual summer mobilization of the reservists. The Later Han maintained military pressure on the Xiongnu, and finally broke them up for good. Except for the adventures of Ban Chao (d. 102) in the Western Regions (now Xinjiang), which were a classic example of indirect rule maintained by locally recruited troops, the Later Han was not committed to territorial expansion. Despite coups and conflicts in Luoyang, relative peace prevailed in the provinces, along with increasing concentration of landownership. When the Later Han confronted its major military crisis, the Yellow Turban rebellion (from 184), the fastest way to mobilize large armies was to recruit among the dependent clients of already powerful notables; a breakdown to warlordism followed quickly.

Cao Cao (155–220) was the most successful of these warlords, and his descendants were the rulers of Wei, the most powerful of the Three Kingdoms. His rivals founded Shu-Han (221–263, in Sichuan) and Wu (formally 229–280, at Nanjing). The Jin dynasty of Sima Yi and his descendants ended the Three Kingdoms and briefly ruled over a reunified China. After the rebellions and invasions of the early fourth century, the Jin ruled south China from Nanjing until 420, where four more Chinese dynasties followed until 589.

Many scholars believe that under these dynasties peasants were reduced to the status of serfs, and that armies also were composed of soldiers who were unfree dependents (*buqu*). While some of this theorizing is in the service of a Marxist periodization of Chinese history, it is very clear from the histories of these dynasties that a warlord pattern had developed: For whatever reason, soldiers were at the disposal of their generals, and central authority was correspondingly fragile. While expressions of disdain for soldiers can be found in the literature of the period, many eminent literary figures also exercised high military command, and the warlord founders of two dynasties (Liu-Song and Liang) had sons who compiled major literary collections (Liu Yiqing and Xiao Tong, compilers of the *Shishuo xinyu* and the *Wenxuan*, respectively). The Sui conquest of Nanjing ended this line of evolution.

TANG.   In 493 Tuoba Hong, the Northern Wei emperor posthumously titled Xiaowendi, played a trick on his Xianbi clan leaders. Pretending to lead them in an invasion of south China, he instead made them stop at the still impressive ruins of Luoyang, the capital of the Later Han and Western Jin, which he made his own capital. North China had been overrun early in the fourth century by various Inner Asian peoples who diplayed an uncharacteristic hostility to Chinese civilization. After the disorders of this period, the brief stabilization of the Northern Wei in the fifth century as the first of the important "dynasties of conquest" begins the second period of military evolution. The Northern Wei created early forms of the equal field (*juntian*) land system and the *fubing* military system that became major institutions under the Sui and Tang dynasties. Most important, the Northern Wei attempted to create a society in which the military skills of the Xianbi would be complemented by bureaucratic and literary skills of the Chinese educated elite. Later dynasties of conquest made the same attempt, and in military matters

Inner Asian influence was important even in dynasties (Sui, Tang, Ming) usually considered Chinese.

After the breakup of the Northern Wei, Yuwen Tai (505–556) and his descendants ruled the northwest first through puppet emperors of Western Wei and then as emperors of the Northern Zhou, and there both the soldier-farmer (*fubing*) military system and the mixed Chinese and Inner Asian Guanzhong aristocracy that commanded it evolved to provide military means and leaderhip for the Sui and Tang empires. The Yuwen rulers were not of Chinese origin, while the Sui founder and the father of the Tang founder were married to sisters from the Xiongnu Dugu clan. By the end of the sixth century, surnames within the Guanzhong aristocracy did not indicate purely Chinese or Inner Asian ancestry because of intermarriage, and similarly the *fubing* soldiers included elements capable of fighting on foot or on horseback. Under the *fubing* system each headquarters (*fu*) commanded about one thousand farmer-soldiers who could be mobilized for war. In peacetime they were self-sustaining on their land allotments, and were obliged to do tours of active duty in the capital. These tours were usually one month long (two months for the most distant units), and their frequency depended on the distance of each unit from the capital. The *fubing* soldiers permitted the Sui and Tang founders to conquer China, but attempts at foreign conquest were less consistently successful. Obsessive efforts to subdue the Korean kingdom of Koguryo ultimately cost the second Sui emperor his throne and his life. Tang Taizong (r. 626–649) fought both Türks and Tibetans to peace on favorable terms, but failed to overcome Koguryo. That goal was accomplished by his son Gaozong (r. 649–683), though the final winner was not Tang China but its ally, the southern Korean kingdom of Silla, which succeeded in unifying the entire peninsula under its own rule. Japan, which had supported Paekche, the third Korean kingdom, was alarmed by these developments and responded by imitating the *fubing* and other Tang institutions in the Taika reforms.

Most of the *fubing* units were located in the northwest, and the system was best suited for the annual campaigning cycle of an expanding empire. Under Empress Wu (r. 684–705) the *fubing* system declined, and under Xuanzong (r. 712–756) a standing army stationed on the northern frontier evolved in its place. This army reached a strength of half a million men and eighty thousand horses by the 740s. Its Chinese personnel included many men displaced by economic changes since the founding of the Tang, and its non-Chinese personnel included Koreans, Kitan, Türks, and Sogdians. The new standing army thus preserved the Chinese–Inner

Asian mixture characteristic of the early Tang, but the old Guanzhong aristocracy ceased to have much involvement with it and its higher ranks came to be filled from within. Having accepted the decline to uselessness of the *fubing* system, the Tang court had no central army to resist the An Lushan rebellion, and could only counter it by appealing to other frontier commanders whose social background was similar to An Lushan's and who could move swiftly from loyalty to rebellion when their autonomy was challenged. Despite impressive successes by the court, the pattern of regional warlordism continued until the fall of Tang. While the replacement of the *fubing* system with the standing army was a major discontinuity in China's military development, this discontinuity occurred in a period of peace as a result of a deliberate policy decision of the Tang government. While it led to disorder, it was not caused by defeat.

Recognizing the need for a central army as a counterweight to the troops of the regional warlords, the post–An Lushan Tang emperors created the Divine Strategy (*Shence*) Armies, whose eunuch commanders grew increasingly powerful as the Tang declined. The Privy Council or Bureau of Military Affairs (*Shumiyuan*), originally a eunuch agency, was taken over by generals during the Five Dynasties (907–960), while continuing to command the central armies (*jinjun, qinjun*) at the personal disposal of the emperors. The Five Dynasties were politically unstable, each ending in a violent overthrow, but they were militarily successful, since the territory ruled from Luoyang expanded and the troops were increasingly concentrated in the central armies.

The Song founder continued this system, making modifications in the interest of political stability. He retired his principal generals, turned the Bureau of Military Affairs into a department controlled by civil officials, and moved the capital to Kaifeng to make supply via the Grand Canal easier. The chain of command over the central army troops concentrated in the capital area was changed regularly to prevent any general from developing a dangerous personal ascendancy over a particular body of troops. Under the first three Song emperors, the army was efficient enough to reunify the south Chinese states (the Ten Kingdoms) with the empire, but was not strong enough to destroy the two states ruled by Inner Asian peoples (Tangut Xixia and Kitan Liao) that together dominated the northern frontier. The long-term trend in the Northern Song was for the central army to become larger and more expensive, while its soldiers became poorer and less capable militarily and its civilian administrators more intrusive and abusive. The relative ease with which the Jurchen Jin conquered Kaifeng and the rest of north China illustrated the decay to the

Song military system. The Hangzhou-based Southern Song depended militarily on an exiguous combination of warlord-led improvised armies and naval power (exercised along the Yangzi as well as on the ocean). The execution of Yue Fei, the most prominent of the warlords, restored political stability even as it dimmed the hope of reconquering the north. When the Mongols completed the destruction of the Southern Song in the 1270s, they ended both the much-discussed "early modern" economic developments of the Song and the continuous line of military evolution that had begun in the Northern Wei.

MONGOL–MANCHU.   While the Mongol conquest of the Song might be seen as the beginning of the third period of evolution, in fact the Mongols derived both ideas and personnel from their Kitan and Jurchen predecessors in the conquest of north China. Both of these dynasties organized their tribal populations into military units that were also social organizations, and employed the decimal system as the partial basis for this organization (in the Jin *meng'an-mouke* system, the *meng'an* is an obvious cognate for the Mongolian *mingghan*, or "thousand"). Both dynasties also assigned troops to princely appanages (*ordo*, whence the English "horde"), and made these a vital part of their military systems. In general the Kitans welcomed Mongol rule, and many Jurchens came to accept it; both nations collaborated in the further Mongol conquest of China.

After his elevation in 1206 but before his invasions of north China, Chinggis (Genghis) Khan organized his Mongolian population on a tribal military basis. Every warrior, with his family and possessions, was assigned to a particular unit and forbidden to leave it on pain of death. Both the military obligation and the specific rank within the unit were hereditary. The units were decimal: *tumen* (ten thousand), *mingghan*, *jaghun* (hundred), and *arban* (ten). The Mongols also imposed this system of decimal organization and hereditary obligation and status on their Chinese soldiers.

The succeeding Ming dynasty (1368–1644) originated in rebellion against the Mongols, but they derived their own soldier-farmer (*weisuo*) system from the Mongol model, even though they compared it explicitly to the Tang *fubing* system. Hereditary military personnel were assigned military colony lands to cultivate under the direction of hereditary military officers, and armies for active service were mobilized from this pool of theoretically ready personnel. In a process somewhat resembling the history of the Tang military, the Ming *weisuo* system also evolved into a recruiting agency for a standing army based on the northern frontier, whose military efficacy was based on the spread of firearms technology and, later, on the building of the Great Wall.

In the early seventeenth century Nurhachi and his successor organized the Manchu—formerly Jurchen—people into a military system, the Eight Banners, that had Inner Asian roots traceable to the Mongols and their predecessors, but was also influenced by Ming institutions of direct rule over Jurchen tributary people. The main theme continued to be hereditary enrollment in specific units. Before the Manchus conquered China proper, they organized some conquered Chinese and Mongols into the Chinese and Mongol Eight Banners. As with the Yuan dynasty's military forces at their height, the banner forces combined Inner Asian cavalry skills with Chinese abilities in engineering and firearms to create a military power that neither a purely Inner Asian nor a purely Chinese society could resist.

The Manchu conquest of China was aided by the defection of Ming armies, elements of which the Manchus organized into their Green Standard Army (*lüying*), the other half of the Manchu military system. The military ranks and other terminology of the Green Standard forces can mostly be traced to the standing army of the middle and late Ming. Eventually outnumbering the banner forces, the Green Standard troops played an important part in the Qing conquest of south China. Thay also provided the personnel for Qing naval forces, whose signal success was the conquest and incorporation of Taiwan in 1683. As the Qianlong reign (1736–1795) ended, the variety of military forces at the disposal of the Qing dynasty, all of which were derived by various paths from the Yuan, seemed to have answered conclusively all of the military challenges posed by the history of Imperial China. Internal order was secure. The nomadic threat had been ended by the conquest and inclusion within the Qing empire of Mongolia, Tibet, and Xinjiang. And the annexation of Taiwan had deprived seagoing pirates and smugglers of their main base off the Chinese coast.

MODERN CHINA

During the modern period that begins with her defeat in the Opium War, China has faced a Western challenge whose military component alone would have forced major changes in Chinese society. The Western impact also confronted China with a major threat from the sea. The effect of the Western challenge was the destruction of the political and social order of

Imperial China and the creation of successor regimes influenced by the West. The Qing and its successors responded in various ways, with varying degrees of success, to wars and crises since 1839. However, these years witnessed sustained military and technical developments in the world as a whole, most of it not driven by events in China, and as of the beginning of the twenty-first century one may still debate the relative weight of the "traditional" as opposed to the "modern" in China's armed forces and society.

The Opium War was decided by a British naval expedition blocking the southern end of the Grand Canal. In the Arrow War (1856–1860), sea power allowed the British to land an expedition that captured Beijing. In the Sino-French War (1884–1885), naval defeats forced the Qing to make peace despite a credible performance by their land forces. Earlier Chinese history provides several occasions on which naval considerations were important (naval defections in the fall of the Southern Song, Fang Guozhen's interdiction of the sea route to the capital in the final years of the Yuan, the disruption caused by Zheng Chenggong during the founding of the Qing), yet the rulers of China were seldom sympathetic to maritime trade or other economic aspects of sea power, and never developed a theory of sea power. In the late nineteenth century the regional leader Li Hongzhang built up the Beiyang Fleet, only to see it destroyed by the nascent Imperial Japanese Navy in the Sino–Japanese War of 1894–1895. In the twentieth century sea power (and later air power and the high-technology aspects of land warfare) could be afforded only by nations with the sort of advanced industrial economy that China has only recently begun to acquire. Despite her extensive territory, China is very vulnerable to attack by sea, as her modern economy has grown in the coastal areas around the original Treaty Ports and is dependent on ocean shipping. In the Sino–Japanese War of 1937–1945, the Japanese blockaded the entire Chinese coast and captured all of the urban centers of China's modern economy, after which China's continued belligerency had no military significance. An armed conflict with the United States in the near term would very likely highlight China's vulnerability to attack from the sea.

Efforts to modernize China's land forces contributed to the collapse of the Confucian imperial order, but in strictly military terms the armies created by these efforts were more effective at fighting each other than at defeating foreign enemies. The great success of the late-nineteenth-century reformers was the elite-mobilized "militia armies" that suppressed the Taiping and other rebellions and permitted Zuo Zongtang to bluff the Russians into a satisfactory territorial settlement in Central Asia. But defeats at the hands of the Japanese and the combined great power expedition against the Boxer "Rebellion" in 1900 persuaded the Qing rulers that it was necessary to create a truly modern army on the Western model, even if this meant abolishing the traditional education and examination systems. The new armies so created were instrumental in overthrowing the Qing in 1911–1912, and afterward fought with each other during the warlord period. The Guomindang "Party Army" (*dangjun*) led by Chiang Kai-shek imposed an imperfect unity on China in 1926–1928, but the various military groups were notoriously incapable of coordinating to resist the Japanese. The Communist People's Liberation Army (PLA) developed a peasant-based style of revolutionary war that ultimately prevailed in the 1946–1949 civil war and the subsequent conquests of Hainan and Tibet. Afterward the PLA fought fairly well in the Korean War and easily triumphed in the 1962 border dispute with India, but analysts were not impressed with its performance in the brief conflict with Vietnam in 1979.

As of the beginning of the twenty-first century, the future direction of Chinese society, including its military component, is uncertain. "Socialism with Chinese characteristics" is usually considered a fig leaf covering a growing capitalist economy, but there has been little corresponding progress toward a democratic political order since 1989. While the PLA of today is visibly burdened by the block obsolescence of its inventory of ships, aircraft, and other equipment, it is more subtly burdened by the fact that a fully modern military can be created only by a modern, open society. Current problems in the PLA, including continued regional loyalties and the unwillingness of PLA units to divest themselves of their economic enterprises, actually reflect the survival of attitudes and practices from previous Chinese history. While Chinese military leaders envy American performance in the Gulf War and Kosovo and talk about "information warfare" as a force equalizer, one supects that, as the paradigmatic modern society, the United States will continue to determine the direction of military progress, and that China's efforts to match and surpass this progress will continue to be hindered by too much baggage from her long history.

SUGGESTIONS FOR FURTHER READING

Frank A. Kierman Jr. and John K. Fairbank, eds., *Chinese Ways in Warfare* (Cambridge: Harvard University Press, 1974) is a collection of studies covering a broad span of ancient and imperial history, as is the more recent volume, Hans van de Ven, ed., *Warfare in Chinese History* (Leiden: E. J. Brill, 2000). For a general introduction to Chinese history including its military side, Denis Twitchett and John K. Fairbank, eds., *The Cambridge History of China* (Cambridge: Cambridge University Press, 1979–) now has several relevant volumes, including vol. 1, *The Ch'in and Han Empires, 221 B.C.–A.D. 220* (1986); vol. 3, *Sui and T'ang China, 589–906, Part 1* (1979); vol. 6, *Alien Regimes and Border States, 907–1368* (1994); and vol. 7, *The Ming Dynasty, 1368–1644, Part 1* (1988). Several volumes of Joseph Needham's *Science and Civilisation in China* (Cambridge: Cambridge University Press, 1954–) directly concern military history, including vol. 4, pt. 3, *Civil Engineering and Nautics* (1971); vol. 5, pt. 6, *Military Technology: Missiles and Sieges* (1994); and vol. 5, pt. 7, *Military Technology: The Gunpowder Epic* (1986). Ralph D. Sawyer translates and discusses *The Seven Military Classics of Ancient China* (Boulder, CO: Westview Press, 1993), and Alastair Iain Johnston, *Cultural Realism: Strategic Culture and Grand Strategy in Chinese History* (Princeton: Princeton University Press, 1995) extracts from them a paradigm for the strategic behavior of imperial Chinese regimes. Arthur Waldron, *The Great Wall of China: From History to Myth* (Cambridge: Cambridge University Press, 1990) deconstructs one enduring myth about Chinese military history. There is a very large secondary literature on Chinese military history and Chinese military institutions in Chinese and Japanese, but most of the work in English is derivative; an outstanding exception is Ch'i-ch'ing Hsiao, *The Military Establishment of the Yuan Dynasty* (Cambridge: Harvard University Press, 1978).

SUGGESTIONS FOR FURTHER RESEARCH

The best corrective to overconfident generalizations is more research on the many wars documented in the traditional Chinese sources. The Chinese Military History Society (on the World Wide Web at *http://www.ksu.edu/history/institute/cmhs*) includes many scholars now working on such projects.

NOTES

1. Alastair Iain Johnston, *Cultural Realism: Strategic Culture and Grand Strategy in Chinese History* (Princeton: Princeton University Press, 1995).
2. Ann Hyland, *Equus: The Horse in the Roman World* (New Haven: Yale University Press, 1990).
3. See Noel Perrin, *Giving Up the Gun: Japan's Reversion to the Sword, 1543–1879* (Boulder, CO: Shambhala, 1980).
4. See Michael Loewe, *Records of Han Administration*, 2 vols. (Cambridge: Cambridge University Press, 1967).

THREE

State Making and State Breaking

David A. Graff

In its broadest outline, Chinese history is often understood in terms of a succession of great dynasties—Han, Tang, Song, Ming, Qing—and Chinese military history can be presented as the successive conflicts between those dynasties and the "barbarian" inhabitants of the Inner Asian steppe, such as the Xiongnu, Türks, Jurchen, and Mongols. Like most simplifications, this is also a distortion. The great dynasties were separated by periods of internal chaos and civil war, and for every great dynasty there were many lesser regimes to complicate the chronological tables. Some, such as the Qin (221–206 B.C.E.) and the Sui (581–618), had a major impact on Chinese history despite their brevity. Many others, such as Northern Wei (386–534), never succeeded in establishing their control over all of the historically Chinese territory inhabited by ethnic Han populations. For long periods, China's territory was divided between two or more imperial states. The competition between the Three Kingdoms of Wei, Wu, and Shu-Han covered much of the third century C.E., and the empire was divided again when barbarian invaders overran much of north China in the early years of the fourth century. This new division between north and south lasted until the Sui reunification in 589; during this time five dynasties succeeded one another in the Yangzi valley, while a bewildering profusion of ephemeral local regimes rose and fell in north China. The decline of the Tang dynasty in the second half of the ninth century ushered in yet another age of disunity. Between 907 and 960 five dynasties ruled over the north in rapid succession, while "ten kingdoms" divided the south between them. The subsequent reunification by the Song emperors lasted only until 1127, when a Jurchen invasion initiated a new period of north–south division that ended with the conquest of Southern Song by the Mongol Yuan dynasty in 1279.

Instead of revolving around the defense of an external frontier against foreign powers, China's military history is to a very large extent a record of internal conflicts. Under the loose hegemonies exercised by the Shang and Zhou dynasties, most armed struggles seem to have occurred within the territory that later came to be known as "China proper," and were fought between groups whose descendants eventually came to regard themselves as Chinese. A well-known example is the conquest of the Shang people based in the eastern part of the North China plain by Zhou invaders coming from the Wei River valley in or around the year 1045 B.C.E. As the Zhou court weakened during the Spring and Autumn period (722–481 B.C.E.), conflict intensified between the "central states." The *Commentary of Zuo* (*Zuozhuan*), our main source for the history of this period, has far more to say about the battles between the states of Jin, Qi, Lu, Zheng, and Chu than about the threat posed by the barbaric Rong and Di peoples. By the third century B.C.E., the scores of small states mentioned in the *Commentary of Zuo* had given way to only seven powers, whose attention was focused primarily on their competition with one another rather than with the horsed nomads who were beginning to appear on the northern steppe. It was this milieu that gave birth to Sunzi's *Art of War* and the other Chinese military classics, which assume a Chinese opponent and devote virtually no attention to the special problems of dealing with mounted nomads and other exotic foes. After the unification of China under the Qin dynasty in 221 B.C.E., the empire's internecine conflicts showed recurrent patterns that continued to be seen as recently as the first half of the twentieth century. This chapter focuses on those patterns, and on the period from the creation of China's first unified empire in 221 B.C.E. to its final collapse in 1911.

The Dynastic Cycle

The Chinese long ago identified a cyclical pattern in their history, a rhythm associated with the rise and fall of dynasties. Imperial regimes emerged out of the chaos of civil war to impose order and reunify the country. They enjoyed a period of vigor (including expansion into foreign lands) but then, after the passage of several generations, fell gradually into decline. Eventually rebellions broke out that brought down the dynasty and ushered in a new period of civil war, out of which a new unifier would emerge to repeat the process. The traditional Chinese explanation for this dynastic cycle was wrapped in Confucian moralism and rooted in the ancient concept of the "Mandate of Heaven." Heaven gave its blessing to a dynastic founder on account of his superior virtue. When one of his royal heirs strayed from the proper path, Heaven indicated its displeasure through portents (such as comets, earthquakes, and other unusual phenomena); if he did not mend his ways, so the theory went, rebellions would break out and Heaven would transfer its support to a more virtuous leader and his new dynasty. In the Chinese dynastic histories, last emperors are often portrayed as monsters of depravity, moving from lurid orgies to acts of sadistic cruelty and all the while ignoring the tearful remonstrances of upright ministers. The archetype of the "bad last emperor" was the last Shang king, Di Xin, who invented the "roasting" punishment, arranged naked frolics amid forests of meat and pools of wine, and had one of his loyal ministers cut open to determine whether "the heart of a sage has seven apertures."[1]

Modern scholars have had little use for this moralistic interpretation of the dynastic cycle, preferring to emphasize socioeconomic explanations. Circumstances were always propitious for a new dynasty emerging from a period of civil war. The slate had been wiped clean, as it were, and the dynastic founder was in a position to establish new laws and institutions and to fill his administration with new men. Rival leaders had been eliminated in the fighting, and deaths from war, famine, and disease meant that the survivors would enjoy a more favorable ratio of population to land and an improved standard of living. As time passed, however, the administrative system ossified and corruption set in. Farmland was bought up by government officials and other wealthy individuals who used their political influence to make their holdings tax exempt. This increased the tax burden on the small farmers, compelling many to abandon their holdings, which in turn drove taxes even higher for those who remained. These conditions might be exacerbated by population growth resulting from several generations of peace and prosperity, and they provided fertile ground for the peasant rebellions that would eventually bring down the dynasty. At least one modern historian has argued that the very belief of traditional Chinese scholar-officials in the dynastic cycle helped to make the pattern a reality: "When Chinese statesmen thought they discerned the classic symptoms of dynastic decline, they qualified the support they gave to the ruling house and thus contributed to its ultimate collapse."[2]

Yet other scholars have taken a thoroughly skeptical view of the dynastic cycle, maintaining that the fall of individual dynasties was the result of chance events and poor policy decisions, with no underlying logic or inevitability. They may well be correct, yet it is difficult to deny that certain recurrent patterns can be discerned in the rise and fall of Chinese dynasties.

PATTERNS

The Chinese imperial state was structured to prevent the emergence of regional power centers that might successfully challenge the authority of the central government. Institutional details varied from dynasty to dynasty, but imperial statesmen were usually well aware of the danger posed by a "tail too big to be wagged." During the heyday of the Tang dynasty in the early eighth century, for example, there was no regularly established level of administration between the approximately 350 prefectures and the center. The prefectures were grouped into ten province-size "circuits," but these were provided with itinerant surveillance commissioners rather than real provincial governors. Commanders of local military units who mobilized troops without receiving permission from the capital might face the death penalty. Very similar arrangements for circuits of inspection and the control of troops had prevailed under the Han dynasty more than five hundred years earlier. Even after the emergence of the province as a regular unit of administration under the Ming and Qing dynasties, authority was quite deliberately fragmented. The Qing Green Standard and banner troops belonged to entirely separate structures, and within each province some units reported to the civil governor while others were under the authority of an independent military chain of command. Thanks to measures of this sort, Chinese dynasties were seldom threatened by powerful regional leaders emerging from their own administrative system, unless the exigencies of dealing with a major peasant rebellion had already necessitated a significant devolution of authority to provincial governors and regional military commanders.

The vast majority of the people of imperial China were farmers, and the rise and fall of the major dynasties was in most cases accompanied by agrarian unrest and rebellion. These peasant uprisings had various causes and contributing factors, including drought, floods, famine, pestilence, government exactions, and exploitation by corrupt officials and wealthy landowners.

The classic example of a revolt precipitated by natural disaster was that of the Red Eyebrows, who brought down the short-lived Xin dynasty of the usurper Wang Mang and created the conditions that made possible the restoration of the Han dynasty. Dikes along the silt-clogged Yellow River failed between 2 and 6 C.E., allowing the stream to flow southeastward into the Huai River. This resulted in the inundation of a vast swath of the North China plain and drove large numbers of people to seek refuge in the highlands of the Shandong peninsula. The regions affected by the flooding had been inhabited by some 28 million people, nearly half the population of the empire. The number of refugees far exceeded the ability of the government to provide relief, giving rise to famine. The starving people turned to roving banditry as their only hope of survival, and their small bandit groups eventually coalesced into the vast plundering horde of the Red Eyebrows.

Some six hundred years later, flooding in some of the same regions contributed to the downfall of the Sui dynasty as outlaw bands began to appear in the marshes and hill country along the lower course of the Yellow River. In the early 870s, the lands between the Yellow River and the Huai were afflicted by drought, floods, and plagues of locusts. The government was unable to relieve the resulting famine, which swelled the ranks of the bandit armies that were emerging as a major threat to Tang authority. The peasant uprisings against the Mongol Yuan dynasty that broke out in the 1350s were preceded by drought, famine, and the great Yellow River flood of 1344 that wrecked the irrigation system in the Huai valley. North China also experienced unusually harsh weather conditions for much of the two decades that preceded the fall of the Ming dynasty in 1644; terrible droughts alternated with major floods and the occasional insect infestation, leading to widespread starvation and outbreaks of epidemic disease. It was reported that starving peasants flocked to join anti-Ming rebel groups by the tens of thousands.

Peasant uprisings in imperial China were typically preceded by natural disasters, but not every flood or drought led to rebellion. Agriculture in north China was heavily dependent on moisture-laden monsoon winds from the Pacific encountering cooler air currents from the heart of Asia at the right place and time to produce the needed amount of rainfall. If the currents failed to meet, there would be drought; if they met for too long, on the other hand, the result was likely to be excessive rainfall and flooding. These were fairly frequent occurrences, with China's dynastic histories noting 1,621 floods and 1,393 droughts over the space of 2,117 years.[3] Given the ubiquity of such events, government policy must also have been an important factor determining whether adverse weather conditions would give rise to large-scale rebellion. When the imperial government was vigorous, distribution of relief grain and the prompt and effective use of military force could prevent serious outbreaks. When the effectiveness of government declined, however, relief grain was often unavailable and local officials were unable or unwilling to excuse peasants from their tax and corvée obligations. In the last years of the Ming dynasty, unpaid imperial troops helped to drive many peasants into revolt by requisitioning their crops. The most terrible episodes of flooding, moreover, can be blamed on a less effective government as much as on natural conditions, since they resulted from the failure of officially supervised water conservancy efforts on the Yellow River. Once the disaster had taken place, repair efforts could become an additonal irritant. The Yuan government's call-up of corvée labor to restore the Grand Canal and the Yellow River dikes in 1351, for example, drove many hard-pressed peasants to take refuge with rebel groups.

Government exactions and impositions could give rise to rebellions even in the absence of natural calamities. The great revolt against the Qin dynasty that began in 209 B.C.E. has traditionally been attributed to the heavy burden of labor service that the first emperor had imposed on his people, including the construction of roads, palaces, and the Great Wall. Although some modern scholars have questioned this received version, it is still undeniable that the first anti-Qin outbreaks occurred among groups of men assigned to forced labor or conscripted for military service on the frontier. Some eight hundred years later, the unreasonable demands of the state in the last years of the Sui dynasty converted what had been a controllable level of brigandage along the lower reaches of the Yellow River into a blaze of rebellion that threatened the survival of the regime. The specific cause in this instance was the obsession of the second Sui emperor with the military subjugation of the northern Korean state of Koguryo, which led him to conscript vast numbers of soldiers and porters from the farm population of areas near the Yellow River that had recently suffered from flooding. Many of these conscripts promptly deserted to swell the ranks of the bandit gangs in the hills and marshes, and the emperor's repeated failures on the Korean frontier encouraged the resisters and eventually persuaded government officials and members of the local elite in many regions of the empire to turn against him.

The popular response to natural disaster, famine, and other crises of survival took two basic forms, dubbed the "predatory" and the "protective" by modern scholars.[4] The predatory mode was adopted by peasant communities that found themselves more or less destitute, and involved the formation of bandit gangs to roam the countryside and prey on those communities that were somewhat better off. Bandit groups often began small and then coalesced to form great bandit armies, such as the Red Eyebrows of Han times or the Nian rebels of the mid-nineteenth century, that swept across vast regions. In response to the predatory threat, the better-off communities organized themselves for self-defense. Leadership was normally assumed by local elites and landowners, whose kinsmen, tenants, and retainers would form the nucleus of a protective militia force. Such forces often abandoned their home communities to take refuge in more defensible terrain, building fortified encampments in hilly or mountainous areas. This was a very common response when barbarian invaders swept over most of north China in the early years of the fourth century, and quite similar behavior was seen in the same areas in the nineteenth century and even the first half of the twentieth century. In the unsettled conditions that followed the Japanese invasion, for example, the four hundred peasant households of Laowo, Henan, took refuge in a massive, earth-walled fort in 1938. The line between protector and predator was easily crossed when survival demanded it. Protectively oriented communities that found themselves deprived of their livelihood readily turned to banditry, just as they resisted excessive state exactions by turning to rebellion. As rebel movements grew in size, they often came to include both predatory and protective elements uneasily united in opposition to the rapacious demands of the state.

Even among the predatory forces, leadership was seldom in the hands of ordinary peasants. The typical leader of a large, semipermanent bandit gang in the nineteenth or early twentieth century was what one authority has called the "village aspirant," a young man from a relatively well-to-do farm family with perhaps some literacy and ambitions of rising in the world. The ninth-century anti-Tang rebel leader Huang Chao, an unsuccessful candidate in the imperial civil service examination, fits this pattern remarkably well, as does the nineteenth-century Taiping leader Hong Xiuquan. There are also examples from various periods of leadership provided by men who had been local subofficials, military subalterns, or professional criminals such as salt smugglers. Liu Bang, one of the early rebel leaders against the Qin dynasty and the eventual founder of the Han, had been the leader of a unit of one thousand households. Two other early anti-Qin rebels were men of substance in their communities who had been placed in command of a unit of conscripts before they launched their rebellion. Among the leaders of the anti-Yuan rebels in the mid-fourteenth century were cloth merchants, salt smugglers, and Buddhist monks. Li Zicheng and Zhang Xianzhong, the two most important anti-Ming leaders in the 1630s and 1640s, were at least marginally literate and had probably seen some military service. Many of Li's followers were not peasants, but transport workers from the empire's network of post stations who had been let go by the cash-strapped Ming government.

In some periods, spiritual leaders and religious beliefs played an important role in mobilizing rebel forces. Although the anti-Qin rebels and the Red Eyebrows do not seem to have been animated by religious visions, the great Yellow Turban revolt against Han rule which erupted in 184 was led by the Daoist master Zhang Jue and his two brothers, who practiced faith healing and called for confession of sins. The religious element was less prominent in Sui and Tang, but reemerged several centuries later in Buddhist guise. The anti-Yuan rebellions in the 1350s were largely the work of White Lotus sectarians, who believed in the imminent arrival of Maitreya, the Buddha of the future. The White Lotus ideology would reappear in several unsuccessful revolts against the Qing dynasty in the eighteenth and nineteenth centuries. Regardless of whether the framework and terminology was Buddhist or Daoist, these ideologies of rebellion shared a common millenarian outlook: The world was seen to be approaching a cosmic turning point when violence would sweep away the iniquitous old order and usher in a new golden age of peace and prosperity for the followers of the rebel movement. The mutant Christian ideology of the nineteenth-century Taiping rebels may be understood as a new variation on a very old theme.

Sectarian revolts inspired by "heterodox" ideas had great difficulty attracting support from members of the social and cultural elite, who were usually committed to a more rational Confucian outlook. As was the case during the Taiping Rebellion, they often inspired fierce resistance by Confucian-educated gentry and local elites. Other sorts of peasant rebels and bandits, however, could expect to gain some support from members of the elite if they managed to hold government forces at bay for an extended period of time and occupy towns and cities. Chen Sheng, the first to rebel against the Qin dynasty, was soon joined by learned men and ritualists who resented the government's harsh treatment of Confucian scholars. When bandit armies entered the Nanyang area of southwestern Henan some two hundred years later, many of the powerful landowning families there joined forces with them to bring down the usurper Wang Mang. Elite defection was also an element in the rebellions that ended the Sui and Ming dynasties. Opportunism was an important factor, but scholars who entered the rebel camp might also be moved by the belief that Heaven had transferred its mandate from the ruling house to the rebels, who badly needed to be instructed in court ritual and Confucian norms of government. The more ambitious of the rebel leaders, for their part, welcomed the administrative talent and the aura of respectability that the scholars provided. This mutual dependence of plebeian leaders and Confucian scholars helps to explain why successful rebels in imperial China replicated the pattern of the previous regime rather than moving in a truly revolutionary direction.

Widespread and moderately successful peasant rebellions could also inspire government officials, military commanders, and other members of the elite to launch their own independent risings against a faltering dynasty. The first revolts against Qin, led by the likes of Chen Sheng, were soon followed by the efforts of royal families and noble houses displaced by the Qin conquest to restore their ancient patrimonies. The great Yellow Turban rebellion against the Eastern Han dynasty in 184 was quickly put down, but not before it had provided the court's generals and governors with the opportunity to establish themselves as regional warlords who fought one another for dominance while paying little more than lip service to the authority of the emperor. The peasant rebellions against the Sui dynasty in the second decade of the seventh century encouraged many of the regime's own officers to revolt and carve out their own states in various parts of China; one of these opportunistic officials—Li Yuan, a relative of the last Sui emperor—succeeded in occupying the capital and establishing the Tang dynasty. As sectarian risings broke out against the Mongol Yuan dynasty in the 1350s, Yuan militia commanders such as Chen Youding in Fujian showed more interest in establishing their own regional regimes than in putting down the rebels. After the rebel armies of Li Zicheng entered the Ming capital of Beijing in 1644, most of the remaining Ming generals also began to behave as autonomous warlords.

During several of China's interludes of rebellion and civil war, such as the Sui-Tang interregnum and period of the anti-Mongol uprisings, the major contenders for power eventually led forces that were patchwork quilts of bandit gangs, landlord militias, and units of government troops that had surrendered or defected. These coalitions were led by men of various stripe, but almost always suffered from tensions between their plebeian and elite elements, their predatory and protective forces. A further source of instability was the loyalty of most of the fighting men to their own immediate unit commanders, whether former bandits or militia leaders, rather than to the man at the very top of the chain of command. Given these structural weaknesses, the defection of cities and military units was a fairly frequent occurrence in the civil wars of imperial China.

As the more capable and successful rebel leaders subdued their local rivals, often absorbing the defeated troops into their own political structures, the competing factions decreased in number and grew in size. A limited number of powerful regional hegemons emerged. In 620, for example, the newly founded Tang regime of Li Yuan held the Wei River valley and adjacent territories. To the east, the plains of Henan were dominated by a renegade Sui general named Wang Shichong. The plains north of the Yellow River (modern Hebei) were the realm of a former bandit chief named Dou Jiande. Another bandit leader, Du Fuwei, held sway between the Huai River and the Yangzi. The vast territories south of the Yangzi were in the hands of Xiao Xian, a scion of the the ruling house of the defunct southern dynasty of Liang. Two lesser leaders, formerly regimental-level officers in the Sui military, controlled most of today's province of Shanxi and the Ordos region within the great bend of the Yellow River. A similar balance of regional forces existed in the early 1360s, after the initial round of uprisings against the Yuan dynasty. The Yangzi valley was divided between the three powers of Wu (based at Suzhou), Ming (based at Nanjing), and Han (based at today's Wuhan). Five weaker regimes held Sichuan, Zhejiang, Fujian, Guangdong, and Yunnan, while semiautonomous Yuan militia commanders dominated the north. The formation of such regional states was characteristic of China's periods of rebellion and civil war.

Some of the regional leaders were essentially separatists whose principal concern was to preserve their independence for as long as possible. Others harbored the ambition of overcoming their rivals to reunify "all under Heaven" and establish a new imperial regime. These ambitious, expansionist leaders signalled their intentions and sought to gather support by taking imperial titles and assuming other trappings of legitimacy, instituting proper court ritual and appointing men to high offices. They competed with one another in several ways. One was the manipulation of symbolic propaganda, which in some periods might involve the discovery of numinous stones, purple clouds, and other auspicious portents. Another was to send envoys to persuade uncommitted local leaders to submit to their authority. The most important and effective means of competition, however, involved military force. The major contenders raised large armies and sought to conquer their opponents' territories. Campaigns usually centered around the capture of walled cities, administrative centers whose control ensured domination of the surrounding countryside, and battles in the open field were often precipitated by efforts to relieve besieged cities. Victory in a major battle could produce a decisive shift in the balance of power. The great Tang victory at Hulao near Luoyang in 621 eliminated both Wang Shichong and Dou Jiande and delivered the eastern plains to Li Yuan, just as Zhu Yuanzhang's victory in the Boyang Lake campaign of 1363 led to the annexation of the Han state on the middle Yangzi and a vast increase in Ming power. Chinese civil wars often exhibited a "bandwagoning" pattern, with subordinate elements of the defeated coalition and uncommitted local leaders rushing to align themselves with the winning side after a major battle. Participants seemed to expect the restoration of imperial unity, and local leaders without imperial ambitions of their own were more interested in ending up in the good graces of the eventual winner than in defending their independence to the last ditch.

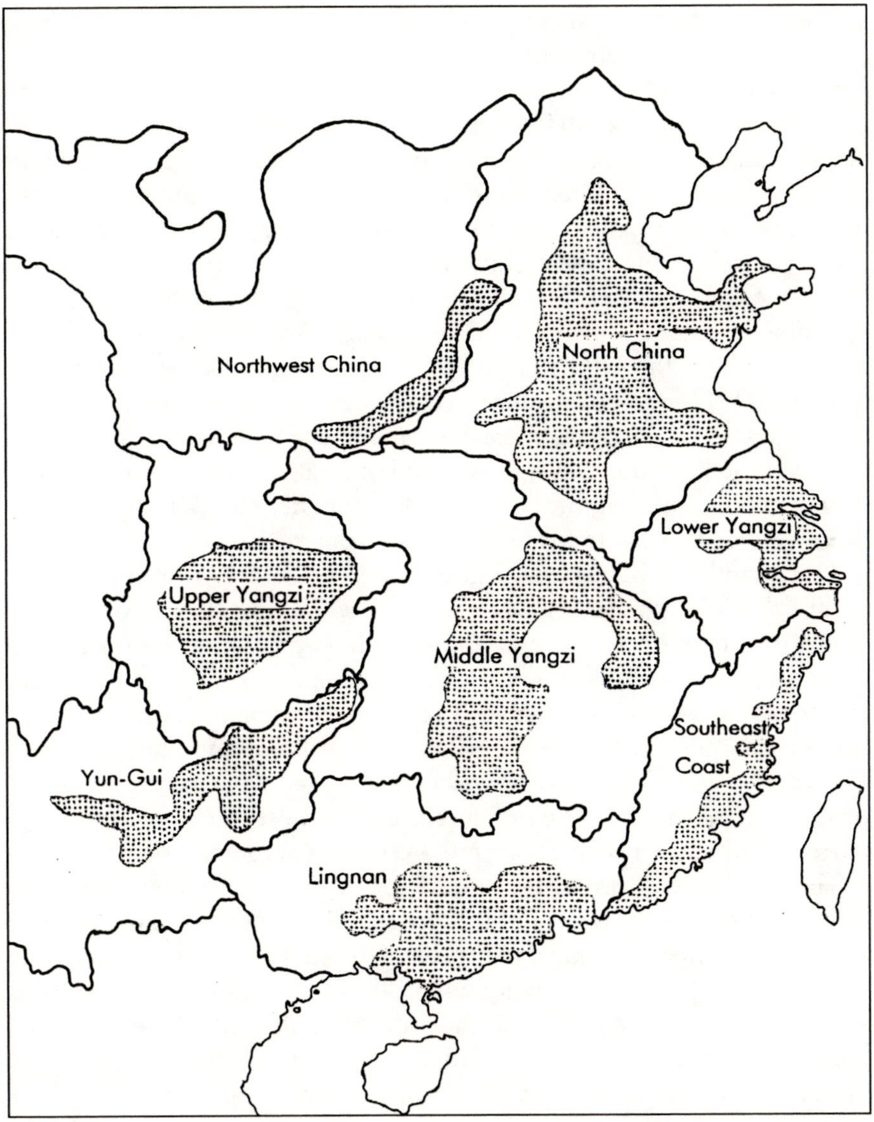

Map 3.1   China's physiographic macroregions according to G. William
Skinner. Adapted by Don Graff based upon *The City in Late Imperial
China*, G. William Skinner (ed.) (Stanford: Stanford University Press,
1977), p. 214.

The shape of China's internal conflicts was also influenced by geography. The major rivers flowing from west to east, and particularly the mighty Yangzi, facilitated "horizontal" offensive operations, while "vertical" campaigns from north to south found the rivers to be obstacles rather than highways of conquest. China's many mountain ranges divided the country into discrete, easily defensible regions in which new dynasties could be incubated and autonomous regimes could hold out for decades. One such region is the Wei River valley of northwest China, the "land within the passes," which gave rise to the Qin, Han, Sui, and Tang dynasties. Another is the territory corresponding to today's province of Shanxi, which sheltered the regime of the Shatuo Türks in the first half of the tenth century and the warlord Yan Xishan from 1911 to 1949. The greatest of all the regional bastions, however, is the mountain-ringed Sichuan basin on the upper Yangzi in the southwest. This was the last important territory to hold out against the Eastern Han founder Liu Xiu (Guangwudi) and the Ming founder Zhu Yuanzhang, and it was also one of the last to fall to the Communists in 1949.

The boundaries of regional regimes often coincided with those of the eight "physiographic macroregions" into which the anthropologist G. William Skinner divided the territory of China proper. Each of these is a drainage basin largely bounded by hills or mountains. The peripheral areas of each macroregion are rugged and sparsely inhabited, while the major population centers are found in the river valleys and bottom lands of the regional "core," where transportation is cheapest and agriculture most productive. In imperial times, Skinner noted, most of China's trade occurred within rather than between the various macroregions.[5]

The cellular structure of the empire surely influenced the pattern and outcome of China's civil wars. During a period of dynastic dissolution and chaos, competing regimes initially established themselves in different macroregions (or in important subdivisions of the same macroregion). Reunification required the consolidation of control over one's own region, followed by the invasion and subjugation of adjacent regions. If population, arable land, and other resources were more or less evenly distributed among the major contenders, expansion could be an arduous and drawn-out process. Once one of the contenders had managed to extend his control over several populous regions, however, he tended to aquire a momentum that enabled him to dispose of his remaining opponents relatively easily. Liu Xiu, for example, began his rise to power in 24 C.E. from a territorial base in the northern part of the North China plain. It took him six years to subdue his rivals on the plain and in the Shandong peninsula, but once he had, the autonomous governors of southern China fell into line with minimal resistance. Liu's last rival, Gongsun Shu in Sichuan, was not eliminated until 36, but the ultimate victory of his new Eastern Han dynasty was a foregone conclusion after 30. A similar pattern can be seen in the founding of the Ming dynasty more than a thousand years later. The balance of power in the Yangzi valley between the states of Han, Ming, and Wu was shattered by the Ming victory over Han in 1363. The annexation of the Han territories then provided the Ming leader Zhu Yuanzhang with the resources to guarantee the conquest of Wu in 1367. And with all of the Middle and Lower Yangzi macroregions in his hands, Zhu was able to overrun most of the rest of China in 1367–1368.

The civil wars that surrounded China's dynastic transitions rarely lasted more than fifteen years from the breakdown of the old imperial regime to the consolidation of its successor. (Unsuccessful rebellions, such as that of the Taipings in the nineteenth century, also tended to run their course within the same time frame.) The usual pattern saw one of the major contenders defeat his rivals one by one and add to the resources at his disposal until his ultimate victory was all but inevitable. On those relatively rare occasions when several of the weaker regional powers were able to cooperate effectively to check the expansion of their strongest competitor, however, military stalemate and political division could last for a very long time. In the last years of Eastern Han, Cao Cao succeeded in eliminating all of his rivals in north China, but his attempt to conquer the Yangzi valley and the far south was stymied when his two remaining opponents, Sun Quan and Liu Bei, joined forces to defeat him in the famous Battle of Red Cliff in 208 C.E. This battle ushered in the three-way balance of power between Cao's Wei state in the north, Liu's Shu-Han in Sichuan, and Sun's Wu state based on the lower Yangzi that dragged on until 263. The peasant rebellions against the waning Tang dynasty in the late ninth century also gave rise to a prolonged period of disunity, as the conflict between the Liang regime based on the Henan plains and the Shatuo Türk state in Shanxi (and later the incursions of the nomadic Kitan people from the northern steppe) permitted several autonomous regional regimes to cement their control over the south. Imperial unity was not restored until the second half of the tenth century, under the Song dynasty.

Even after a new imperial regime had defeated it major rivals and brought an end to the civil wars, its authority over the empire was usually far from complete. An important element contributing to the unifier's victory in the civil war was his willingness to make deals with potential opponents. Territorial governors appointed by the previous dynasty, fence-sitting local strongmen of various stripe, and the semiautonomous followers of other contenders for power were all won over with promises that they would be confirmed in office (or appointed to higher offices) and left in effective control of their own territories and armed forces. Care was usually taken to distinguish between major rivals with imperial pretensions and the lesser leaders who supported them; the former were marked for elimination, whereas the latter might be won over to one's own side by the right offer. The founders of the Tang dynasty created a large number of new units of local administration to accommodate de facto local power-holders within their state structure. They defeated the last serious armed challenge to their rule in 623, but it has been argued that several more decades passed before their government was able to extend its authority to the grassroots level and extract revenues from key areas of the North China plain.[6] Dynastic founders were willing to trade local autonomy for nominal recognition of their authority because it spared them the trouble and expense of capturing every last county town and mountain fortress; it brought the violence and chaos of the civil wars more quickly to an end, and permitted the new emperor to get on with the work of reconstruction.

In many cases, dynastic founders thought it necessary or desirable to leave very large territories in the hands of their most powerful confederates. After he destroyed his great rival Xiang Yu in 202 B.C.E., the Han founder Liu Bang left his allies and generals in control of ten hereditary kingdoms which together accounted for well over half of the territory (and population) of the empire. Much the same approach was adopted by the Manchu founders of the Qing dynasty after 1644. They welcomed Ming generals who defected with their armies, and the most important of them were rewarded with large and virtually autonomus states, or "feudatories," in the southern provinces of Fujian, Guangdong, Guangxi, and Yunnan. Such arrangements were, however, never more than interim solutions dictated by expediency. By 195 B.C.E. Liu Bang had squeezed out all but one of the original ten kings and replaced them with his own sons and brothers, and even these Liu family kings would be stripped of most of their power by the middle of the second century B.C.E. Once their realm was on a firm footing, the Manchu rulers in the seventeenth century also moved to rein in their overmighty subjects. An attempt to abolish the feudatories in 1673 provoked a major revolt that lasted until 1681, but this revolt ended in the complete defeat and elimination of the feudatories. New dynasties also worked to extend their authority at the local level, and eventually succeeded in replacing semiautonomous local strongmen with bureaucratic representatives of the center who were normally prohibited from holding office in their home areas. Local or regional autonomy was never a stable equilibrium state, but a stage in the process of reintegration leading to restoration of centralized imperial rule.

CHANGE OVER TIME

After this extended discussion of the recurrent patterns of imperial China's civil wars, it is well worth noting that no two periods of rebellion and disorder followed exactly the same pattern. Some saw heterodox religious sectarians playing a prominent role, while others did not. Some led quickly to reunification; others did not. In contrast to other periods of rebellion, the peasant risings against the Ming dynasty in the 1630s and early 1640s opened the door to the conquest of China by a non-Chinese people, the Manchus. Chinese culture was far from static over the more than two thousand years of the imperial era, and many periods had their own unique characteristics. During the "medieval" period from the fall of Eastern Han through the Tang, for example, pedigree and hereditary status counted far more than at other times, and the most viable and successful contenders for power were those who came from aristocratic families. This was in sharp contrast to the periods before and after, when humble men such as Liu Bang and Zhu Yuanzhang were able to fight their way to the imperial throne. The Ming dynasty was unique in the annals of imperial China because it conquered the north from a base in the Yangzi valley. All the other dynasties that ruled over a united China began in the north and then spread their control over the Yangzi valley and the far south. The Ming case was not a fluke, but the consequence of long-term demographic and economic shifts. For most of China's history, the most populous and economically developed parts of the country had been the North China plain and the Wei River valley. By the time of the Song dynasty, however, centuries of southward migration, land reclamation, and urbanization had finally tipped the balance in favor of the south. The next dynasty after the Ming, the Qing, came from the north, to be sure, but it was something of an anomalous case since it was established by foreign conquerors rather than domestic rebels. The first insurgent group to unify China after the imperial period, the nationalists of the Guomindang, pushed north from their original base in Guangdong during the Northern Expedition of 1926–1928 to establish nominal (if not actual) control over almost all of China proper.

It is also worth noting that many transfers of political power in imperial China were accomplished without peasant rebellions and civil wars. A number of dynasties came to power through palace coups or military revolts. This was the usual pattern for the regimes that held south China during the period of division between 317 and 589, and also for the "Five Dynasties" that dominated the north between 907 and 960. There were many anomalous cases. China's longest period of division was ushered in not by a peasant rebellion, but by a prolonged civil war among princes of the ruling Jin dynasty in the early years of the fourth century that created an opening for "barbarian" peoples, both within and beyond China's borders, to rebel against Jin authority and carve out their own kingdoms in the north. Another anamalous episode was the An Lushan rebellion, which broke out in 755 and nearly put an end to the Tang dynasty. It was launched by a Tang frontier commander who had been allowed to become too powerful, and his followers were professional soldiers rather than impoverished peasants. Although it was ultimately unsuccessful, the revolt left the Tang empire permanently divided. The fighting was brought to an end in 763 with a compromise solution that left several of the rebel generals in control of their armies and territories in return for their nominal acceptance of imperial authority. Some of these military provinces became virtually independent kingdoms, where leadership was passed from father to son and no taxes were paid to the Tang court, and even armies that had been loyal to the court during the rebellion began to emulate the ex-rebel provinces by choosing their own leaders and asserting local autonomy. This period of more than a century when autonomous provinces dominated by professional soldiers with a keen sense of economic and political self-interest paid little more than lip service to the imperial court—but made no effort to claim the throne for themselves—was unique in the annals of imperial China.

SUGGESTIONS FOR FURTHER READING

The civil wars of imperial China are one of the better studied areas of Chinese military history, and there are a number of monographs in English dealing with particular dynastic transitions. One of the most important, and perhaps the most thorough of them all, is Hans Bielenstein's study of the overthrow of Wang Mang and the establishment of the Eastern Han dynasty. This was published in four installments in the *Bulletin of the Museum of Far Eastern Antiquities* (BMFEA; Stockholm) over the space of twenty-five years, with the general title of *The Restoration of the Han Dynasty.*[7] The volumes of greatest interest to the military historian are vol. 1, *With Prolegomena on the History of the Hou Han Shu*, in BMFEA 26 (1954), and vol. 2, *The Civil War*, in BMFEA 31 (1959). The second volume includes a substantial discussion of military tactics and techniques as well as a narrative history of the conflict. The end of Eastern Han is covered in Rafe de

Crespigny, *Generals of the South: The Foundation and Early History of the Three Kingdoms State of Wu* (Canberra: Australian National University Faculty of Asian Studies, 1990), and the collapse of the Sui dynasty is treated in Woodbridge Bingham, *The Founding of the T'ang Dynasty: The Fall of Sui and Rise of T'ang* (Baltimore: Waverly Press, 1941). The principal works on the fall of the Tang dynasty and the Tang–Song interregnum are Wang Gungwu, *The Structure of Power in North China during the Five Dynasties* (Kuala Lumpur: University of Malaya Press, 1963; reprint, Stanford: Stanford University Press, 1967), and Robert M. Somers, "The End of the T'ang," in *The Cambridge History of China*, vol. 3, *Sui and T'ang China, 589–906, Part 1*, ed. Denis Twitchett (Cambridge: Cambridge University Press, 1979), 682–789. For the rebellions and civil wars that led to the establishment of the Ming dynasty, the best guide is Edward L. Dreyer, *Early Ming China: A Political History, 1355–1435* (Stanford: Stanford University Press, 1982). For the Ming–Qing transition, finally, there is the extremely thorough and detailed two-volume study, Frederic Wakeman Jr., *The Great Enterprise: The Manchu Reconstruction of Imperial Order in Seventeenth-Century China* (Berkeley and Los Angeles: University of California Press, 1985). The many excellent studies of the great nineteenth-century rebellions and the warlord period in the early twentieth century are also relevant to this subject.

SUGGESTIONS FOR FURTHER RESEARCH

Several of the works mentioned are already more than thirty years old, and all of them deal with military events within the conventional framework of political and institutional history. There is definitely room for new analyses of imperial China's internal conflicts that incorporate intellectual and religious history, social science perspectives, and the study of popular culture. It is also worth noting that even the basic outline of the civil wars and rebellions during the period of division from 317 to 589 has yet to receive serious attention from scholars writing in Western languages.

NOTES

1. Sima Qian, *Shiji* [Historical records] (Beijing: Zhonghua shuju, 1959), ch. 3, pp. 105–106, 108. Also see Arthur F. Wright, "Sui Yang-ti: Personality and Stereotype," in *The Confucian Persuasion*, ed. Arthur F. Wright (Stanford: Stanford University Press, 1960), 47–76.
2. Arthur F. Wright, "On the Uses of Generalization in the Study of Chinese History," in *Generalization in the Writing of History*, ed. Louis Gottschalk (Chicago: University of Chicago Press, 1963), 42.
3. Ray Huang, *China: A Macro History* (Armonk, NY: M. E. Sharpe, 1997), 25.
4. Elizabeth J. Perry, *Rebels and Revolutionaries in North China, 1845–1945* (Stanford: Stanford University Press, 1980), 3–4.

FOUR

The Northern Frontier

David C. Wright

For two thousand years, the primary military and diplomatic preoccupation of the Chinese empire was the northern frontier. From the Xiongnu tribes that menaced the Qin (221–206 B.C.E.) and Han (202 B.C.E.–220 C.E.) empires to the Manchus who conquered China as the last imperial dynasty, the Qing (1644–1912 C.E.), premodern China was harassed, intimidated, and partially or even fully conquered by its northern nomadic neighbors. Indeed, the history of premodern China's foreign relations is largely a history of war, or preparation for war, with the nomads. Steppe empires built by Xiongnu, Türks, Uighurs, and Mongols menaced China from a distance, while "conquest dynasties" such as the Tuoba Wei, Kitan Liao, Jurchen Jin, and Manchu Qing succeeded in imposing alien rule over portions or all of historically Chinese territory.

The *New Tang History* (*Xin Tangshu*), a work largely written and edited by the Song dynasty Confucian scholar Ouyang Xiu (1007–1072), contains specific strategic recommendations for dealing with the threats posed by the nomads:

> Our Chinese infantrymen are at their best in obstructing strategic passes, while the barbarian cavalrymen are at their best on the flatlands. Let us resolutely stand on guard [at the strategic passes] and not dash off in pursuit of them or strive to chase them off. If they come, we should block strategic passes so that they cannot enter; if they withdraw, we should close strategic passes so that they cannot return. If they charge, we should use long two-pronged lances; if they approach, we should use robust crossbows. Let us not seek victory over them.
>
> They are like unto all manner of insects, reptiles, snakes, and lizards. How could we "receive them with courtesy and deference"?[1]

Of course, this passage also reflects deep frustration and hostility. This was typical of many eleventh-century Chinese intellectuals who were greatly distressed by China's past and present humiliations at the hands of its "barbarian" neighbors to the north. Ouyang Xiu's literary career flourished at a time when portions of northern China had been conquered and ruled for several decades by the barbarian Kitans and their Liao dynasty (916–1125). He had no way of knowing it, but the situation would only worsen after his death; the Jurchens and their Jin dynasty were to conquer the northern half of China early in the twelfth century, and by the end of the thirteenth century all of China would fall to the Mongol conquerors of Khubilai Khan, grandson of Chinggis Khan.

The region inhabited by the "barbarians" was the Eurasian steppeland, an enormous belt of land that extended, with some intervening desert and forested lands, from the Carpathian Basin of Hungary in the west to Korea in the east, and from the Manchurian, Siberian, and Russian forests on the north to the Caucasus, Pamirs, and Yellow River (including a portion of the North China plain) on the south.[2] A generally arid, continental climate prevails throughout most of the steppeland region, which often experiences extremes of summer heat and winter cold. China was by no means the only civilization to be menaced by mounted archers from this region. The Middle East, and particularly Persia, was also much imperiled by them, and barbarian threats to Europe are recorded by Herodotus (ca. 485–425 B.C.E.), who described the Scythians, and Ammianus Marcellinus (ca. 330–395 C.E.), who covered the Huns known to the later Roman Empire. Nevertheless, approximately one-third of the length of the steppeland bordered on China's north, and China more than any other Eurasian civilization clashed with nomadic warriors and empires.

WHY ALL THE FIGHTING?

Historians who have considered the long and troubling history of Sino–nomadic warfare have often sought to adduce reasons for it. The traditional Chinese explanation expressed revulsion at the harsh and nonsedentary ways of nomadic tribes and implied that warlike tendencies were somehow ingrained in their natures, which seemed less than fully human. These attitudes are perhaps best typified by the great Han-dynasty historian Sima Qian (c. 145–87 B.C.E.), who in his *Historical Records* (*Shiji*) describes the Xiongnu as shiftless, primitive, shameless, and pugnacious:

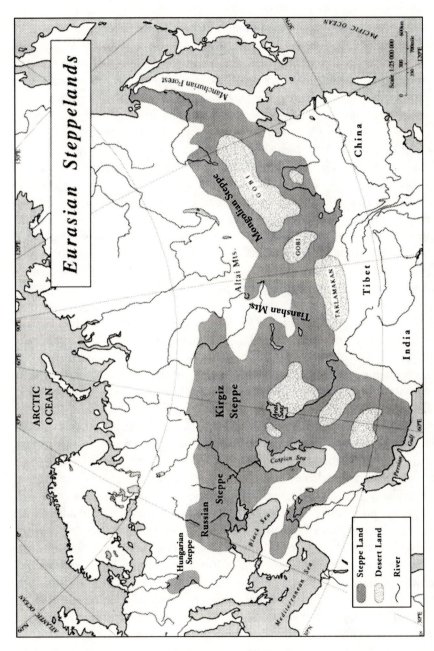

Map 4.1   Eurasian steppelands SOURCE: Provided by David Wright. Drawn by Elaine Ng.

As early as the time of Emperors Yao and Shun and before, we hear of these people, known as Mountain Barbarians, Xianyun, or Hunzhu, living in the region of the northern barbarians and wandering from place to place pasturing their animals. The animals they raise consist mainly of horses, cows, and sheep. . . . They move about in search of water and pasture and have no walled cities or fixed dwellings, nor do they engage in any kind of agriculture. Their lands, however, are divided into regions under the control of various leaders. They have no writing, and even promises and agreements are only verbal. The little boys start out by learning to ride sheep and shoot birds and rats with a bow and arrow, and when they get a little older they shoot foxes and hares, which are used for food. Thus all the young men are able to use a bow and act as armed cavalry in time of war. It is their custom to herd their flocks in times of peace and make their living by hunting, but in periods of crisis they take up arms and go off on plundering and marauding expeditions. This seems to be their inborn nature. For long-range weapons they use bows and arrows, and swords and spears at close range. If the battle is going well for them they will advance, but if not, they will retreat, for they do not consider it a disgrace to run away. Their only concern is self-advantage, and they know nothing of propriety or righteousness.[3]

There is really nothing uniquely Chinese about Sima Qian's description of the Xiongnu and their lifestyle; as A. M. Khazanov has pointed out, Ammianus Marcellinus describes the Huns in much the same terms.[4]

Sima Qian does not directly comment on the significant tactical and operational advantages the nomads enjoyed over the Chinese. The nomads' military superiority was primarily the result of their mobility and their superb horsemanship and marksmanship. Equestrian skills, which nomads learned at a very early age, were of course important for herding their animals from one pasturage to another. But they were also useful for hunting, something nomads also engaged in to supplement their diets and hone their military skills. The nomads' ability to shoot arrows accurately while riding their horses at full gallop gave them an enormous tactical advantage over the huge armies of infantrymen that Chinese generals often fielded against them. In addition, of course, the figure of a galloping nomadic cavalryman offered a difficult target for Chinese archers to hit. The nomads' mobility was often their greatest defensive as well as offensive asset. Because they had no cities or villages to defend, they often allowed Chinese armies to pursue them out into the steppes, there to be weakened by logistical difficulties and their own inability to live off the grasslands.

Sima Qian, perhaps because he was so overawed by the military acumen of the nomads, also failed to note that China's population always vastly outnumbered that of the steppes. In ecological terms, the "barbarians" he so deplored were pastoral nomads. They were pastoral because they domesticated and husbanded animals (mainly sheep), and nomadic because they were highly mobile, riding on horseback or on simple carts from one naturally occurring stretch of grassland to another in the steppes north and west of China's borders, living in collapsible and portable tentlike shelters made of wooden latticework frames covered with felt. Pastoral nomads chose not to corral their animals and feed them cultivated hay the way their agricultural neighbors in China did, and they valued the mobile life of the nomad over the stationary life of the farmer. Their mobility demanded a simple and efficient economy, and as a result nomads were seldom as wealthy or technologically innovative as their sedentary neighbors.

They were also never as populous. An ecology based on pastoral nomadism might sustain more people per surface unit of land than an exclusively hunting and gathering one does, but neither way of life can come close to matching the demographic sustaining power of agriculture. But militarily, pastoral nomadic societies made up for their small populations and technological backwardness with superior mobility and tactical skills. Nomadic cavalrymen were often quite literally able to run circles around large groups of Chinese foot soldiers, shoot arrows into their midst, and then quickly withdraw out of the range of Chinese archers. Nomadic cavalrymen greatly outmanned by Chinese foot soldiers could and often did achieve smashing victories against them.

The Chinese attempted to develop countermeasures against such tactics. Sustained campaigns into nomadic territory in what is now Mongolia did occasionally weaken nomadic power, as did the Han Emperor Wudi's massive excursion into the Xiongnu homeland in 119 B.C.E. But such campaigns were rare because they imposed huge financial and logistical burdens on the Chinese state. Other responses to the nomadic threat were more tactical in nature. One type of long weapon was used to trip or injure the hoofs of the nomads' horses, but this of course was useful only when the nomads attacked Chinese infantrymen at close range. Another obvious countermeasure for the Chinese was to learn to be cavalrymen themselves. Mounted Chinese warriors did sometimes prove effective against nomadic warriors, but this was the exception rather than the rule. For most Chinese, horsemanship was an acquired skill, not second nature as with their opponents. In short, Chinese cavalrymen by themselves could rarely hope to match the skill of the mounted nomadic warrior on the battlefield. In addition, Chinese horses were seldom as good as the horses bred out on the steppes, possibly because the nomads took measures to keep their best stock from falling into Chinese hands.

Modern historians have suggested other theories to explain the prolonged pattern of Sino–nomadic warfare. Some have suggested that the basic ecological incompatibility of agricultural and nomadic peoples inevitably produced periodic misunderstanding, friction, and open warfare. Others maintain that famine or drought in the steppe regions might have led nomadic peoples to attack sedentary civilizations for food. This theory, while appealing upon first glance, must be regarded at most as an insightful piece of speculation because it can neither be proven nor disproven; there is simply not enough meteorological information in historical sources. More recent attempts to explain Sino–nomadic warfare are by Mongolian historian Sechin Jagchid, Russian anthropologist A. M. Khazanov, and American anthropologist Thomas J. Barfield. In his book on the subject, Jagchid briefly describes the ecology of pastoral nomadism and then argues that the Chinese were almost always the ones at fault for outbreaks of Sino–nomadic hostility and warfare, because the nomads needed three basic commodities that their simple pastoral economies could not produce: grains, textiles, and metals. When the Chinese were willing to permit mechanisms such as intermarriage of royal families, tribute missions, and border markets to facilitate the transfer of these goods to the nomads, peace prevailed. But when the Chinese, for whatever reason, closed down these mechanisms, nomads were ultimately driven through sheer economic necessity into raiding China. Thus, in Jagchid's view, the nomads were essentially peaceable and were far from the warlike people characterized in almost all imperial Chinese historical materials. Jagchid's argument is essentially economic and has been called the "trade-or-raid" thesis.[5]

Thomas J. Barfield's perspective is quite different. While he agrees with Jagchid on the material dependency of pastoral nomads on the Chinese, he sees the nature of this dependency in different terms. What the nomads needed from the Chinese, he argues in his important survey of Sino–nomadic interaction, was not subsistence commodities but luxury items, which nomadic empires used to strengthen their weakest link: that between local chieftains and regional rulers. Barfield's is, then, essentially a political argument.[6]

A. M. Khazanov's perspective on this question also emphasizes the material dependency of nomadic societies on civilized societies. But Khazanov points out that conquest, when and where it was possible, was the most profitable way for pastoral nomads to secure the items they needed from civilized societies: "Wherever nomads have the corresponding opportunities their raids and pillaging become a permanent fixture."[7] Thus, the nomads may have been more rational than some traditional historians have thought. Raiding was in fact probably the easiest way for the nomads to get what they needed from China, but they were astute enough to know that they very often could not get away with this for very long.

The Great Wall of China

One very common misconception about the northern Chinese frontier that must be dispelled right from the start concerns the Great Wall of China. The standard textbook account claims that it was either constructed or connected from earlier wall segments during the Qin dynasty in order to keep the "Huns" and other "barbarians" at bay; over the centuries thereafter the Wall was supposedly alternately shored up or allowed to fall into states of disrepair, but its site was always known. The best-preserved sections of the Great Wall today, near Badaling (not far from Beijing), are the results of Ming dynasty repairs. Historian Arthur Waldron, however, questions this and argues that the Great Wall of China as we know it today is not an ancient structure, but was built for the first time during the Ming dynasty.[8]

Even a brief perusal of a good Chinese historical atlas will show that the Wall did not usually define precisely the geographical extents of Chinese and nomadic polities. Moreover, ecological boundaries between sedentary and pastoral nomadic societies were sometimes fluid and seldom were neatly demarcated by anything as dramatic and final as a fixed wall. Thus, theories about the Great Wall of China that see it as a definitive ecological, linguistic, and cultural demarcation or emphasize the inherent permanence of China's "walled frontier" should probably now be revised or discarded altogether.[9]

But Waldron has not completely proven his case. There remains, for instance, the matter of an eleventh-century poetic reference to the Wall (or a wall) by Su Song, a Song dynasty literatus who twice travelled to the Kitan Liao state in the eleventh century in diplomatic missions. In a poem he wrote in 1077 upon crossing Gubei Pass, a well-known point along the modern Great Wall, Su Song noted that he was once again crossing over "the ten-thousand *li* wall of the Qin monarch."[10] It is of course possible that this is a literary trope, but its focused geographical and chronological specificity by a scholar-official who twice travelled by Gubei on diplomatic business seems at least to indicate that Su Song knew that some sort of Qin wall was once here. That the Ming also chose to run its Great Wall through Gubei suggests that both dynasties understood its strategic importance.

HAN AND XIONGNU

The Xiongnu, sometimes identified with the Huns known to the late Roman Empire, were the first great steppe empire to threaten the security of an organized and unified Chinese state. The Xiongnu and the Han dynasty, in fact, rose to power at roughly the same time. During the very early years of the Han dynasty, the founding emperor, Gaozu (Liu Bang), was defeated in a major battle with the Xiongnu and narrowly avoided capture. The Han both feared and respected the Xiongnu after this, and for the next few decades the so-called intermarriage (*heqin*) system was the basic framework for diplomatic relations between the two powers. The original peace agreement, which was expanded over the years, contained the following provisions:

1. A Chinese princess given in marriage to the leader of the Xiongnu.
2. Fixed annual payments of food, silk, and wine to the Xiongnu.
3. Equal or "brotherly" status between the two powers.
4. A fixed border between the two powers.[11]

The intermarriage system endured as the basic vehicle for Han–Xiongnu relations until the Han emperor Wudi (r. 141–87 B.C.E.) cancelled it and initiated hostilities with the Xiongnu in 133 B.C.E. Wudi seems to have concluded that the provisions of the intermarriage system were demeaning to China and that the Chinese had endured insults and humiliation at the hands of the Xiongnu long enough. As part of his overall program of territorial expansion, Wudi decided to face down the Xiongnu militarily and outmaneuver them diplomatically. Han Wudi's strategy was fourfold:

1. To push the Chinese frontier back to the old Qin boundaries.
2. To ally with the Yuezhi and Wusun, old adversaries of the Xiongnu.
3. To expand into the Tarim Basin and occupy a long segment of the Silk Road there, thus "cutting off the right arm" of the Xiongnu by depriving them of their revenues from the oasis city-states there involved with overland trade.
4. To launch destructive punitive expeditions into Xiongnu territory.[12]

In 119 B.C.E., Han armies drove deep into Xiongnu territory and destroyed an important headquarters of the *shanyu*, or leader of the Xiongnu. Three decades later the two powers had more or less exhausted themselves and stalemated each other into an uneasy period of détente.

By Wudi's death in 87 B.C.E., however, it was becoming clear that the real losers in the decades-long confrontation were the Xiongnu. Their defeats at the hands of relatively minor nomadic adversaries in the 70s and 60s B.C.E. indicated their internal weakness, and a Xiongnu civil war also did much to further weaken their power and prestige. By 54 B.C.E. the majority of the Xiongnu agreed to surrender to the Han.

During his lifetime, Han Wudi had long insisted that the Xiongnu accept a new framework, the so-called tribute system, for relations between the two powers. The elements of the new system were much more symbolically favorable to the Han than the old intermarriage system elements had been, so the Xiongnu had long feared and resisted the tributary system in the belief that it would entail actual subjugation to the Han. They repeatedly demanded the restoration of the intermarriage system, but the Han would not assent to this. The tributary system contained three major elements:

1. Far from receiving a royal princess from the Han in marriage, the Xiongnu would now send a hostage from their royal family to reside at the Han capital.
2. The Xiongnu *shanyu*, or an envoy personally representing him, would come periodically to China to pay homage.
3. The Xiongnu would send tribute to China in return for imperial gifts from China.[13]

After 54 B.C.E. and the surrender of the majority of the Xiongnu to the Han, the Xiongnu quickly discovered that this "tributary system" was, in reality, a sham that did not involve actual submission to Han power. The Chinese demanded mere ritual and material submission to the Han emperor, and in return for this they bestowed imperial gifts out of all proportion to the value of the tribute. Thus, tribute missions turned out to be enormously profitable to the Xiongnu, and soon they were requesting permission to conduct them more and more frequently. The tributary system was in fact an institution that the Xiongnu could manipulate for their own material benefit, as they had the former intermarriage system. Chinese intellectuals eventually caught on to the Xiongnu attitude, which they interpreted as "insincerity."[14]

By 43 B.C.E. the Xiongnu had resolved their differences and reunified themselves, and they continued to manipulate the tributary system to their own advantage. They now saw it more or less as the same old intermarriage system, but in a new ritualized package that seemed to make the

Chinese feel better. The tribute system provided peace until 8 C.E. and the usurpation of the Han throne by Wang Mang, who like Han Wudi before him changed relations with the Xiongnu and tried to subjugate them. The Xiongnu balked at this and went to war with Wang Mang's new regime, which at any rate was overthrown in 23 by Han restorationists. Then the Xiongnu themselves disintegrated into civil war by the late 40s, resulting in a north–south split among the Xiongnu: the Southern Xiongnu submitted to Han authority, while the Northern Xiongnu remained independent and defiant. In 89 the Southern Xiongnu and the restored Han dynasty attacked the Northern Xiongnu and greatly defeated them. Most of the remaining Northern Xiongnu then submitted to the Han, but a small, defiant minority followed a leader to the north and west, far away from Han China. A controversial theory dating to the eighteenth century attempts to equate these Xiongnu with the Huns who entered the Carpathian Basin in Hungary in 375 and eventually, under the leadership of Attila, threatened Rome in 452.[15]

CHINA'S FIRST CONQUEST DYNASTIES

In Chinese history the period from the collapse of Han in 220 until the complete reunification of China under the Sui dynasty in 589 is known as the Six Dynasties, a period during which pastoral nomadic peoples took advantage of China's division and internal weakness and conquered the northern portion of the country, while a series of weak native Chinese dynasties ruled in the south with their capital at Jiankang (modern Nanjing). One such dynasty, the Eastern Jin, harbored ambitions against the barbarian occupiers of northern China and seemed for a time to be making good on its vow to reunify China under its rule. In 383 the Eastern Jin turned back a barbarian invasion at the Battle of the Fei River in Anhui, and by 417 the dynasty had reconquered a portion of the Silk Road. By 420, however, the Eastern Jin fell due to internal strife, and barbarian rule over the north was assured for another 168 years while a series of short-lived native Chinese dynasties ruled over southern China. Southern and northern China had more or less fought one another to a standstill that lasted from 420 until the Sui reunification of China in 589. From the fourth through the sixth centuries, several barbarian peoples conquered portions of northern China and ruled over it with semibarbarian, semi-Chinese regimes that were dubbed "conquest dynasties" by early twentieth-century Japanese historians of China. These differed from the classic steppe empire model established by the Xiongnu in that they actually occupied and governed Chinese territory; while the Xiongnu often fought with the early Han and intimidated it into establishing the intermarriage system, the early Xiongnu seldom if ever seriously thought of actually occupying and administering Chinese territory. The conquest dynasties, on the other hand, were familiar enough with Chinese ways that they learned the rudiments of governing an agricultural society and collecting taxes.

Barfield has pointed out that throughout Chinese history, most of the conquest dynasties (with the very significant exception of the Mongolian Yuan of the thirteenth and fourteenth centuries) seem to have been "Manchurian" in origin, or from the area the Chinese now call the Northeast. This is probably because the natural environment of the region accommodates all ecologies, including agriculture, pastoral nomadism, and hunting and gathering. Manchuria was thus a sort of training ground or experimental laboratory for barbarian peoples who harbored ambitions of conquering portions or all of China. Several more conquest dynasties followed in Chinese history: the Kitan Liao (916–1125), the Jurchen Jin (1126–1234), and the pre-Yuan Mongols (1234–1279) ruled over significant portions of northern China, while the last two conquest dynasties, the Mongol Yuan (1279–1368) and the Manchu Qing (1644–1912), succeeded in conquering all of China and ruling as alien emperors. Thus, in the last 1,003 years of imperial Chinese history, alien regimes conquered and ruled over some or all of Chinese territory for 730 years, or more than 70 percent of the time. Serious historians of China cannot, therefore, ignore or skim over times when non-Chinese peoples ruled China.

Conquest dynasties have been called "dualistic" because they applied "barbarian" laws and administrative techniques to the non-Chinese peoples and Chinese methods to the Chinese. Conquest dynasties might thus be thought of as multicultural, or at least multiethnic. The first significant conquest dynasty was the Tuoba Wei, which ruled a portion of northern China from 386 to 439 and over all of northern China from 439 to 535.

Tang China and the Türks and Uighurs

The Türks, or Tujue as they are known in Chinese histories, had their homeland in the Altai Mountains and were originally subjects of the Rouran. But during the mid-sixth century they overthrew their Rouran masters and themselves became rulers of the steppe, with a far-flung empire from Manchuria in the east to the Caspian Sea in the west. Civil war had broken out among them by 581, however. This seriously weakened their empire and divided them into Eastern and Western segments. The

Eastern Türks themselves also fell into civil war, and one of the rival khans submitted to the Sui in 584. Eventually the Eastern Türks helped Tang forces capture Chang'an from the Sui in 617, the year before the Tang dynasty was founded.

The founding emperors of the Tang dynasty (618–907) were ethnically part Türk. The first Tang emperor, Li Yuan (Tang Gaozu, r. 618–626), was a cautious man vis-à-vis the Türks, but his son, the young Li Shimin (Tang Taizong, r. 626–649), was more confrontational. He proved his mettle on two separate occasions during the 620s. In 624, while still a prince and during the Türks' menacing of the Chang'an region, Li Shimin rode out with a hundred men to challenge rival Türk khans to personal combat. When they refused, he spread misinformation among them that destabilized their polity. In 626, right after Li Shimin had deposed his father and assumed the Tang throne, the Türks threatened Chang'an again, probably wishing to probe the new emperor's strength and resolve. Much to the distress of his advisers, Li Shimin galloped out of the gates of Chang'an and rode to the Wei River with only six men. He berated the Türk khan across the river for his aggression. When an attendant remonstrated with him for despising the enemy in this manner, Li Shimin responded that he wanted to disabuse the Türks of their notion of internal Tang weakness. Bad weather, internal divisions, and major Tang campaigns against them eventually led to the submission of the Eastern Türks to the Tang in 630, and with this the first Türk empire came to an end. Li Shimin reigned as emperor over the Chinese and Heavenly Khaghan over the Türks, and several thousand prominent Türk families moved to Chang'an and became Tang government officials.

Türk submission to Tang China began to unravel after Li Shimin's death in 649. His successor, Gaozong, generally favored the indigenous Chinese elite at the expense of the Türk officials. Discontent among the Türks arose with a new generation that lacked its parents' and grandparents' memories of the great Taizong. Rebellion against the Tang broke out in 679, and in 680 many Türks abandoned their defense posts at the Tang frontier and fled back to their homeland in Mongolia. The Türk empire was soon reborn, and its leaders immediately began attacking China again, not to invade and hold Chinese territory, but to intimidate China into making economic concessions.

In fact, the Bilgä khaghan, one of the major leaders of the second Türk empire who reigned from 716 to 734, urged his people to avoid the mistakes of their predecessors under the first empire by staying away from China; better for them to exploit China from a distance than to approach it too closely and risk being drawn into the Chinese morass. He literally carved in stone his admonitions to the Türks of his generation:

> Deceiving by means of (their) sweet words and soft materials, the Chinese are said to cause the remote peoples to come close in this manner. After such a people have settled close to them, (the Chinese) are said to plan their ill will there. (The Chinese) do not let the real wise men and real brave men make progress. If a man commits an error, (the Chinese) do not give shelter to anybody (from his immediate family) to the families of his clan and tribe. Having been taken in by their sweet words and soft materials, you Turkish people, were killed in great numbers. O Turkish people, you will die! If you intend to settle at the Choghay mountains and on the Tögültün plain in the south, O Turkish people, you will die! . . . If you stay in the land of Ötükän, and send caravans from there, you will have no trouble. If you stay at the Ötükän mountains, you will live forever dominating the tribes![16]

The second Türk empire endured until 744, when internal succession disputes weakened it and the Uighurs, who were former subjects to the Türks, came to power and established their own steppe empire, the wealthiest and most sophisticated that East Asia had yet seen. The Uighurs built a capital city and central storehouse of sorts called Karabalgasun, in modern Mongolia. They were a more stable polity than the Türks because their linear or vertical succession system made transitions to power much less ambiguous and controversial. The Uighurs developed a writing system for their language and seem to have learned even better than the Türks how to exploit and intimidate China from a distance. They secured annual payments of silk from the Tang and got the best of the silk–horse trade that developed between themselves and the Chinese. They also intermarried with the Tang imperial family, and during the middle of the eighth century the Uighurs helped the Tang quell the great An Lushan uprising. Uighur horsemen sometimes rode haughtily through the streets of Chang'an, but the Tang Chinese endured this because they knew they owed their dynasty's survival to them. Ultimately, however, the riches extracted from China and stored at Karabalgasun proved too big and irresistible a target for other steppe peoples. In 840 the Kirgiz, a warlike tribe living along the Yenisei River, swept down into Karabalgasun and destroyed it. The Uighur empire could not endure the loss of its capital and collapsed soon thereafter. The Kirgiz, for their part, retreated to their Yenisei homeland and were not heard from again in Chinese history. Other northern frontier peoples closer to home would soon emerge to threaten China's northern borders and even conquer large sections of northern China.

SONG CHINA AND THE KITAN LIAO AND JURCHEN JIN

A proto-Mongolian people known as the Kitan came to power in Mongolia, Manchuria, and northern China in 907, the same year as the fall of the Tang. (China did not achieve lasting national unification until 960 and the founding of the Song dynasty.) The Kitan regime eventually became known as the Liao and ruled over Manchuria, southern Mongolia, and parts of northern China (including modern Beijing) as a classic conquest dynasty until 1125, when it was destroyed by the Jurchens, who ruled over an even greater portion of northern China as the Jin dynasty (1126–1234), a conquest dynasty par excellence.

A portion of northern Chinese territory that came to be known as the Sixteen Prefectures of Yen and Yun had been lost to the Kitans in 936, and the founding Song emperor refused to consider China completely reunified until this territory was recovered. As it turned out, however, the Song never did govern this territory, although two attempts were made in the late tenth century to recover it militarily. In 976 the Song attacked the Liao but was beaten back with heavy losses; during the campaigns even the founding Song emperor himself was injured by two arrows. His brother and successor tried again in 986 to recover the territories and met with some initial success, but was ultimately forced to withdraw after Liao generals managed to cut his supply lines. The accession in 997 of Zhenzong, the timid and naive third Song emperor (r. 997–1022), emboldened the Kitan to make their own incursions into Song territory. Low-level clashes between the two states broke out between 1001 and 1003, but the real conflict began in the summer of 1004, when Kitan cavalry launched several reconnaissance raids deep into Song territory. By the fall the Kitans' hostile intentions were obvious even to Zhenzong, and he reluctantly began making preparations for a major military confrontation with the Liao. He accepted advice from his two imperial counsellors to rally the Song troops and overawe the Kitan by personally leading an expeditionary force from Kaifeng (the Northern Song capital, just south of the Yellow River) to Shanyuan, the first major town on the north side of the river.

Meanwhile, the Kitans were advancing steadily southward into Song territory, and by late 1004 they seemed poised to overwhelm Shanyuan, cross over the Yellow River, and advance to Kaifeng. Zhenzong wavered in his resolve and momentarily considered withdrawing to Jiangsu or Sichuan, but ultimately his bravest and most competent imperial counsellor, Kou Zhun, persuaded him to proceed with the expedition to Shanyuan in January 1005, which according to Song sources had the desired effect of rallying and encouraging the troops. Meanwhile, Song armies had managed to outflank the main Liao offensive and had made their way northward, thus threatening to cut off the Liao armies deep in Song territory. Both sides recognized that they had fought each other to a standstill, and peace negotiations began in November, although sporadic fighting continued. Peace was concluded at Shanyuan on January 19, 1005. The Song essentially bought off the Kitan; if they would stop menacing Song territory, the Song would drop its territorial claims to the Sixteen Prefectures and would agree to annual payments to the Liao of 100,000 ounces of silver and 200,000 bolts of silk.

The Treaty of Shanyuan began over a century of peace between Song and Liao and made the eleventh century one of the most peaceful, prosperous, and innovative (both technologically and intellectually) in Chinese history. Minor skirmishes and disagreements over border delineations broke out in the 1040s and again in the 1070s, but for the most part the peace held. The treaty also led to the exceptional development of "equal diplomacy" between Song and Liao, with a body of Chinese diplomatic language and ritual that regarded the Liao not as an inferior or tributary state, but as a full-fledged equal. After the fall of the Liao to Jurchen forces in the 1120s and the withdrawal of the Song capital from Kaifeng to Hangzhou, annual payments and equal diplomatic treatment on the Shanyuan model were transferred to the Jurchens and their Jin dynasty, although for a brief time from the 1140s to the 1160s the Southern Song was forced to accept the humiliating self-designation of "vassal" (*chen*) vis-à-vis the Jin.

THE MONGOL CONQUEST OF CHINA

The rise of the Mongols and their world empire was an important geopolitical and military development in thirteenth-century Eurasian history. In 1206 a conqueror named Temüchin united by force the tribes of Mongolia and was proclaimed Chinggis (Genghis) Khan, or supreme khan of nomadic peoples north of China. In 1209 Chinggis Khan attacked the minor border state of Xi Xia and secured its nominal submission. His campaigns against the Jin began in 1211 and continued intermittently throughout his life. At his death in 1227 Chinggis Khan had not fully subjugated the Jin; that task was left to his son and successor, Ögödei Khan (r. 1229–1241), who accomplished it in 1234.

The final conquest of the Jin left the Mongols the rulers of the steppe and of northern China. During the rest of his reign Ögödei Khan concentrated on campaigns against Russia and eastern Europe. His nephew and ultimate successor, Möngke Khan (r.1251–1259), expanded the Mongol world empire in different directions with campaigns against the Middle East, Korea, and China. Mongolian armies under the command of Möngke's younger brother Hülegü set out for the Middle East, where during the 1250s they conquered Persia, sacked and butchered Baghdad, overthrew the Abbasid Caliphate, and encountered European Crusaders in the Holy Land. The Mongol campaign against Korea began in 1252, and by 1258 their general Jaliyar had conquered the peninsula.

Meanwhile, in 1256 Möngke and his younger brother Khubilai launched a campaign against a much greater prize than either Korea or the Middle East: Southern Song China. Popular stereotypes about the weakness and effeteness of the Southern Song's military notwithstanding, the conquest of Southern Song China was the most difficult military task the Mongols undertook. The Southern Song fought bravely against the Mongols and was finally conquered in 1279, nearly three decades after the Mongols began their attack.

The campaign was complicated by several factors, chief among them the terrain. Much of northern China is flat and relatively dry, and Mongol cavalry usually made short shrift of any resistance offered them there by Chinese infantrymen. In southern China, however, a wet climate and mountainous terrain frequently made progress on horseback tough going, as did the ubiquitous irrigation ditches, waterways, and muddy rice paddies. The heat and humidity of central and southern China were also distressing to the Mongols, who on at least one occasion suspended a campaign until autumn brought more tolerable temperatures. And then there was always the Yangzi River that bisected central and southern China. Any conquest of all China would necessarily mean that the Mongols and their allies would need to deal with the Yangzi. This, in turn, meant that they would need a large navy. The Mongols knew nothing about building or using a navy. In this campaign they were aided and advised by scores of Chinese defectors who had concluded that the political future of China was with the Mongols rather than the moribund Southern Song government.

Möngke's strategy was to attack down the Yangzi River from Sichuan in the west with a naval force that he hoped would destroy the economic foundations of Southern Song China. Möngke envisioned a grand multipronged attack that would defeat the Southern Song: He would come down the Yangzi with his naval force, while Khubilai moved down through

Hubei and other generals advanced along China's east coast. In planning and strategy it all looked quite good, but in 1259 the entire offensive was called off because of Möngke's death in Sichuan. The Mongols now had to convene a grand tribal council or *khuriltai* to select a new khan.

After much nasty politicking and bickering, Khubilai was enthroned in 1260 as the new khan. When his overtures to the Southern Song were rebuffed, he resumed the China campaigns, which were to be a central preoccupation of his for the first nineteen years of his reign. The Southern Song proved to be a very tough nut to crack, and there are even scattered indications that the Chinese defenders of the dynasty used some gunpowder weaponry against the Mongol invaders. The Mongol naval attack on the fortified city of Xiangyang on the Han River (a northern tributary of the Yangzi) was waged for five years before the city surrendered in 1273. Chinese, Jurchen, Korean, and even Persian engineers and strategists helped out during this key siege and built a great catapult and mangonel to hurl huge stones at Xiangyang's walls.

After the surrender of Xiangyang, Khubilai chose the Mongol general Bayan to continue the China campaign. Bayan's armies swelled with Chinese defectors such as Lü Wenhuan, the gallant defender of Xiangyang, who were convinced that the Mongols would be the new rulers of China. Bayan's sheer numbers, the high morale of the Chinese defectors who threw in their lot with him, and the tactical advantage afforded by his superior artillery made him invincible. Bayan occupied towns along the Yangzi that surrendered to him and utterly devastated those such as Changzhou that repeatedly resisted his overtures. In January 1276 the Southern Song capital at Hangzhou finally surrendered to the Mongols and submitted the dynasty's official seal to Bayan. A few die-hard Song loyalists fled farther south and set up a scion of the Song royal family as a claimant. On March 19, 1279, however, these pretensions came to an end when the last Song emperor, a child, perished in the arms of a Song loyalist who jumped with him into the sea off southern Guangdong province. From this time until his death in 1294, Khubilai reigned as Grand Khan of the Mongol world empire and as emperor over China.

YUAN CHINA

The Mongols started out as a steppe empire but ended up a conquest dynasty. This political transformation from intimidation to administration was remarkable and seems to have been begun by Möngke and finished by Khubilai, two grandsons of Chinggis Khan who had grown up with some familiarity with the Chinese world and probably some knowledge of the early Tang emperors' dual positions as khans of the nomads and emperors to the Chinese.

Khubilai and subsequent Yuan emperors did not please everyone among the Mongolian elite. Mongol accommodationists approved of Khubilai's adoption of Chinese-style administrative techniques for China. Steppe traditionalists, on the other hand, were suspicious of this and deplored Khubilai's seeming fascination with the Chinese world. They seem to have resented Khubilai's removal of the capital of the Mongol world empire from Karakorum in Mongolia to Beijing in China. Thus, as with emperors of native Chinese dynasties, Khubilai had to worry about threats and challenges from the northern frontier. At the very beginning of his reign, Khubilai was challenged by a hardline steppe partisan named Ariq-böke and fought a four-year civil war before finally defeating him. Another steppe dissident and rival named Qaidu was a continual challenge to Khubilai.

Yuan administration in China after Khubilai's death was very unstable and unpredictable because it was determined by the orientations or worldviews of the much lesser emperors who succeeded him. Yuan governance after Khubilai was a comedy of jarring errors and lurching inconsistencies as accommodationist and traditionalist emperors sought to reverse the policies and approaches of their predecessors. By the 1350s Yuan rule over China was so disorganized and decentralized that a native Chinese insurgent named Zhu Yuanzhang was able to overthrow the dynasty in 1368. Zhu became founding emperor of the Ming dynasty and spent much of the rest of his life recentralizing imperial power and concentrating it in his own hands. Ming administrative centralization and political "despotism" was probably more of a reaction against Mongol government than a continuation or result of it.

MING AND MONGOLS

The Ming was the only major native Chinese dynasty that did not have a powerful unified nomadic steppe empire on its northern border. This may well have been, as Barfield argues, because the Ming largely refused to accommodate the Mongols commercially, thus depriving them of the material prerequisites of nomadic empire.[17] After all, Ming China had thrown off the Mongol yoke with the greatest of difficulty and was quite fearful of contributing to its own reconquest. But this very fear of Mongol revanchism also led to seemingly incessant nomadic raiding on China's northern frontiers. Definitive peace between

Ming China and the Mongols was not reached until 1571, near the end of the dynasty.

The first Ming emperor (Taizu; r. 1368–1398) and his son (Chengzu, or the Yongle emperor; r. 1402–1424) personally led campaigns deep into Mongolia, probably not for conquest but to keep the Mongols divided and off balance. After about 1400, the Mongols were increasingly divided into two competing groups: the Western Mongols or Oirats in the Altai Mountains and the Eastern Mongols in central and southern Mongolia. Construction of the Great Wall began during the Yongle emperor's reign, and thereafter there seem to have been few if any Ming excursions north of it. As early as 1389 three Mongolian groupings known as the Three Commanderies submitted to the Ming and served in the Ming armies in order to escape recriminations by other Mongols. These Mongol tribes and also several Jurchen groups who submitted to the Ming around 1400 were allowed to offer tribute to China twice a year, which as usual proved handsomely profitable for them.

By the mid-fifteenth century, however, these tribute relations were largely disrupted as Esen-tayiši came to power and attempted to establish a steppe empire unifying all Mongols under his rule. Esen was an Oirat and not a member of the Chinggisid lineage, so he could not lay claim to the title of khan, but only to *tayiši*, more or less "grand master." For his legitimacy he maintained a Chinggisid khan as a puppet and claimed to be acting on his behalf. In 1449 Esen launched a huge attack on Ming China in three columns and managed to march nearly all of the way to Beijing. A chief eunuch at court, perhaps thinking of the Shanyuan precedent, convinced the Zhengtong emperor (r. 1435–49) to go out and meet the Mongols in battle. This turned out to be a disastrous strategic miscalculation, however, because Esen surrounded the imperial encampment at Tumu and eventually captured the emperor. Thinking that he now had a valuable bargaining chip for pressuring the Ming into concluding a tributary alliance with him, he pressed his attack on Beijing but failed to take the city. And the Ming, as it turned out, responded to the capture of the Zhengtong emperor simply by enthroning another, Jingtai (a monarch whose posthumous title, Daizong, means something like "substitute emperor"), who reigned from 1449 to 1457, when the old emperor finally reclaimed his throne, this time as the Tianshun emperor. Seemingly deprived of the value of his imperial captive but apparently still fearful of recriminations lest any harm befall him, Esen gave the hapless emperor back to the Ming in 1450. Esen was eventually assassinated in 1454 or 1455 by jealous and disgruntled Mongols who were disappointed with the failure of his China campaign and resentful of his outright assumption in 1453 of the title of khan. With his death the frequency of tribute missions diminished, and by 1500 they had fallen off altogether.

By the mid-sixteenth century, the main raids on Ming northern frontiers were led by the Altan-khan (1507–1582) of the Tümed Mongols from his base at Guihua. Unlike Esen-tayiši, the Altan-khan was a member of the Chinggisid lineage and could thus legitimately be called "khan." The purpose of his raiding was to compel the Ming to reinstitute the tribute system that had previously applied to the Three Commanderies. The Altan-khan's raids grew larger until, in 1550, Mongol cavalrymen once again were at the very walls of Beijing. This frightened the Ming court into establishing border markets and allowing the Altan-khan to present tribute, but mutual suspicions and antagonisms soon led to the curtailment of the missions and the border markets, and fighting broke out anew.

Definitive peace between Ming China and the Altan-khan was not established until 1570, largely due to the intelligent policy recommendations of Wang Chonggu, a border official who understood the reasons for the raids. Wang convinced the Ming court to reopen border markets and establish tribute relations with the Altan-khan in 1571, after which the Mongol raids dropped off sharply (although they did not cease altogether) and peace with the Mongols largely prevailed. From 1571 to the end of the dynasty there was little further threat from the Mongol quarter to the security of the Ming empire. By the early seventeenth century the Ming's foreign policy and defense preoccupations were primarily with another frontier people: the Jurchens, a Manchurian people of mixed ecology who would eventually become known as the Manchus and conquer all of China by the end of the seventeenth century.

For most of its history, imperial China was either threatened or conquered, partially or fully, by its northern nomadic neighbors. It seems that major native Chinese dynasties were invariably either threatened by steppe polities at various stages of organization or else overrun by conquest dynasties. Imperial China's failure to solve its barbarian problem definitively before the advent of the Manchu Qing dynasty was a function neither of Chinese administrative incompetence nor of barbarian pugnacity, but of the incompatibility and fixed proximity between very different societies, ecologies, and worldviews. Many statements in historical records strongly suggest that the Chinese and the nomads had clear ideas of their differences and were committed to preserving them against whatever threats the other side posed. A tidy apothegm from Carlyle, "All battle is well said to be misunderstanding," is placed at the front of Sechin

Jagchid's work on Sino–nomadic relations, a book dedicated "to the myriads of people who, because of misunderstanding, suffered and died along nomadic sedentarist frontiers."[18] But it may be that the Chinese and the nomads clashed so fiercely and for so long not because they misunderstood each other, but because they understood themselves and each other only too well. For them, battle and conquest are perhaps best said to have been understanding after all.

Suggestions for Further Reading

The best single-volume survey of Sino–nomadic relations is Thomas J. Barfield, *The Perilous Frontier: Nomadic Empires and China, 221 BC to AD 1757* (Oxford: Basil Blackwell, 1989). Barfield's book is based on previously translated primary sources, and some of his theories and perspectives are controversial. But the book is still a good survey for beginning and advanced students alike. Sechin Jagchid and Van Jay Symons, *Peace, War, and Trade Along the Great Wall: Nomadic–Chinese Interaction through Two Millennia* (Bloomington: Indiana University Press, 1989) is also based on primary materials but seems more difficult to read because it is topically rather than chronologically organized. Anatoli M. Khazanov, *Nomads and the Outside World* (Cambridge: Cambridge University Press, 1984) is a fine anthropological treatment of the historical interactions between pastoral nomads and civilized societies, including China. Owen Lattimore, *Inner Asian Frontiers of China* (New York: American Geographical Society, 1951) and *Studies in Frontier History: Collected Papers, 1929–1958* (London: Oxford University Press, 1962) remain important reading, although some of Lattimore's conclusions now seem somewhat inadequate.

The single most important book on Han–Xiongnu relations is still Ying-shih Yü, *Trade and Expansion in Han China: A Study in the Structure of Sino–Barbarian Economic Relations* (Berkeley and Los Angeles: University of California Press, 1967). Tang–Türk relations are covered in detail in Pan Yihong, *Son of Heaven and Heavenly Qaghan: Sui-Tang China and Its Neighbors* (Bellingham: Western Washington University, 1997). Aspects of Tang–Türkic relations are also covered in Christopher I. Beckwith, *The Tibetan Empire in Central Asia: A History of the Struggle for Great Power among Tibetans, Turks, Arabs, and Chinese during the Early Middle Ages* (Princeton: Princeton University Press, 1987). Liu Mau-ts'ai, *Die chinesischen Nachrichten zur Geschichte der Ost-Türken (T'u-küe)*, 2 vols. (Wiesbaden: Otto Harrassowitz, 1958) is also an important work. Colin Mackerras, *The Uighur Empire According to the T'ang Dynastic Histories: A Study in Sino–Uighur Relations, 744–840* (Columbia: University of South Carolina Press, 1972) is a documentary study of Tang–Uighur relations, but unfortunately it contains some errors of translation.

The most extensive treatment of the Treaty of Shanyuan in a Western language is still Christian Schwarz-Schilling, *Der Friede von Shan-yüan (1005 n. Chr.): Ein*

Beitrag zur Geschichte der chineschen Diplomatie (Wiesbaden: Otto Harrassowitz, 1959). On Song diplomacy and foreign relations in general, see Morris Rossabi, ed., *China among Equals: The Middle Kingdom and Its Neighbors, 10th–14th Centuries* (Berkeley and Los Angeles: University of California Press, 1983). On various aspects of Song–Liao diplomacy, see Jingshen Tao, *Two Sons of Heaven: Studies in Sung–Liao Relations* (Tucson: University of Arizona Press, 1988).

David Morgan, *The Mongols* (Oxford: Basil Blackwell, 1986) is a solid and readable general survey of the Mongol world empire. Paul Ratchnevsky, *Genghis Khan: His Life and Legacy* (Oxford: Basil Blackwell, 1991); Thomas Allsen, *Mongol Imperialism: The Policies of the Grand Qan Möngke in China, Russia, and the Islamic Lands, 1251–1259* (Berkeley and Los Angeles: University of California Press, 1987); and Morris Rossabi, *Khubilai Khan: His Life and Times* (Berkeley and Los Angeles: University of California Press, 1988) are all biographies of individual Mongol khans. Chinggis Khan's attacks on the Jurchen Jin are treated in detail in Henry Desmond Martin, *The Rise of Chingis Khan and His Conquest of North China* (Baltimore: Johns Hopkins University Press, 1950).

The field of Ming–Mongol relations is largely dominated by Henry Serruys, whose major book-length studies include "Sino–Mongol Relations during the Ming II: The Tribute System and Diplomatic Missions (1400–1600)," *Mélanges Chinois et Bouddhiques* 14 (1969); "Sino–Mongol Relations during the Ming III, Trade Relations: The Horse Fairs (1499–1600)," *Mélanges Chinois et Bouddhiques* 18 (1975); and "The Mongols in China during the Hung-wu Period (1366–1398)," *Mélanges Chinois et Bouddhiques* 11 (1956–59). Dmitrii D. Pokotilov, *History of the Eastern Mongols during the Ming Dynasty from 1368 to 1634* (Philadelphia: Porcupine Press, 1976) is also a useful survey. Arthur Waldron, *The Great Wall of China: From History to Myth* (Cambridge: Cambridge University Press, 1990) contains much coverage of Ming–Mongol relations. The nonpareil account of the capture of the Ming emperor Zhengtong in 1449 is Frederick W. Mote, "The T'u-mu Incident of 1449," in *Chinese Ways in Warfare*, ed. Frank A. Kierman Jr. and John K. Fairbank (Cambridge: Harvard University Press, 1974), 243–272.

SUGGESTIONS FOR FURTHER RESEARCH

There is still no authoritative and up-to-date survey of Sino–nomadic relations that draws on both primary sources and modern scholarship. The history of China's first conquest dynasties during the Six Dynasties period is so complicated that it would probably make writing (and reading) a book-length monograph on the subject quite difficult. Three biographies of important Mongol khans are now available, but one still needs to be written on Ögödei. Morris Rossabi's biography of Khubilai covers aspects of Khubilai's campaigns against Southern Song China, but a full-length study in English of the entire scope of the conquest would be useful.

NOTES

1. Ouyang Xiu, *Xin Tangshu* [New Tang history] (Beijing: Zhonghua shuju, 1975), ch. 215A, p. 6025.

2. A concise geographical description of Central Eurasia and the steppelands can be found in the chapter by David C. Montgomery in Denis Sinor, *Inner Asia: A Syllabus* (Bloomington: Indiana University, 1969), 7–17.

3. Sima Qian, *Records of the Grand Historian*, vol. 2, trans. Burton Watson (Hong Kong and New York: Columbia University Press, 1993), 129.

4. Anatoli M. Khazanov, *Nomads and the Outside World* (Cambridge: Cambridge University Press, 1984), 8.

5. Sechin Jagchid and Van Jay Symons, *Peace, War, and Trade Along the Great Wall: Nomadic–Chinese Interaction through Two Millennia* (Bloomington: Indiana University Press, 1989).

6. Thomas J. Barfield, *The Perilous Frontier: Nomadic Empires and China, 221 BC to AD 1757* (Oxford: Basil Blackwell, 1989).

7. Khazanov, *Nomads and the Outside World*, 222.

8. Arthur Waldron, *The Great Wall of China: From History to Myth* (Cambridge: Cambridge University Press, 1990).

9. See, for example, Owen Lattimore, *Inner Asian Frontiers of China* (New York: American Geographical Society, 1951), 21–25, and *Studies in Frontier History: Collected Papers, 1929–1958* (London: Oxford University Press, 1962), 73–84. By no means do I mean here to denigrate the whole of Lattimore's scholarship or to downplay his important role in establishing and popularizing Sino–nomadic relations as a field of historical inquiry.

10. David C. Wright, "Wealth and War in Sino–Nomadic Relations," *Tsing Hua Journal of Chinese Studies* 25 (1995), 138. The passage reads "Qin wang wanli cheng" and is from Su Song, *Su Weigong wenji*, vol. 1 (Beijing: Zhonghua shuju, 1988), ch. 13, p. 169.

11. Ying-shih Yü, *Trade and Expansion in Han China: A Study in the Structure of Sino–Barbarian Economic Relations* (Berkeley and Los Angeles: University of California Press, 1967), 43–44.

12. Barfield, *The Perilous Frontier*, 54.

13. Yü, *Trade and Expansion*, 43.

14. Barfield, *The Perilous Frontier*, 60, 63.

15. For a brief outline of the debates surrounding this theory, see David C. Wright, "The Hsiung-nu–Hun Equation Revisited," *Eurasian Studies Yearbook* 69 (1997): 77–112.

16. Talat Tekin, *A Grammar of Orkhon Turkic* (Bloomington: Indiana University Press, 1968), 261–262.

17. Barfield, *The Perilous Frontier*, 230–231.

18. Jagchid and Symons, *Peace, War, and Trade Along the Great Wall*, v.

FIVE

Water Forces
and Naval Operations

Peter Lorge

Naval warfare and operations were crucial to the creation and unification of the Chinese empire for over two thousand years, yet this fact has usually been overlooked in the military history of China. China has generally been seen as a continental power that failed to develop an effective navy. This orientation is frequently contrasted with Europe's seafaring, outward-looking attitude, which drove it to explore, exploit, and dominate the rest of the world. Defenders of Chinese culture often bring up the six voyages of the Muslim eunuch-admiral Zheng He to the Indian Ocean between 1405 and 1433, or even Khubilai Khan's attempted invasions of Japan in 1274 and 1281, to argue that China was not exclusively inwardly focused. Yet these adventures were exceptions that neither demonstrate the general importance of naval operations in China nor explain the specific roles that navies usually played in warfare.

China is divided by several large rivers running roughly east–west that had to be crossed by any would-be conqueror attempting to assemble a unified Chinese empire. It is thus not surprising to find that every history of the creation of a major Chinese dynasty is laced with accounts of naval operations and warfare. Without a strong navy, no unification of China was possible. While the Mongols were off conquering much of Eurasia, the Southern Song navy blocked their southward progress for nearly half a century. But a conqueror's naval needs were not limited to river crossing. Rivers were also the most efficient means of transporting men and supplies for campaigns. Hence, control of the rivers was a prerequisite for conquest and control of the empire, but the sea was of limited military importance.

That is not to say that the sea was completely unimportant. A fair amount of sea trade was transacted at various times in Chinese ports, which greatly profited the imperial treasury through customs duties. But the government's interest in profits from seaborne trade did not mirror a similar interest in spreading its influence through a fleet of warships. This was not due to an inward focus by Chinese statesmen so much as to practical considerations of costs and benefits. An oceangoing navy was expensive and served no apparent function, since China was seldom menaced from the sea. Ironically, it was the Mongols, a nomadic steppe people, who made the most use of the Chinese and Korean navies in their campaigns of conquest. The offensive and defensive naval needs of Chinese emperors were usually limited to the rivers and canals of their own territory, not the sea coast. There were some exceptions to this, such as the Tang invasions of Korea by sea in the seventh century, but the government was content, for the most part, to leave the ocean to the merchants and let the merchants take care of themselves.

Naval operations encompasses a much broader range of activities than ship-to-ship combat. As mentioned, control of waterways was crucial to army logistics. Spanning a river with a pontoon bridge is as much a naval operation as an engineering one, and frequently involved the navy in defending the bridge once constructed. In many cases, the success or failure of a naval operation to take control of a waterway or protect a bridge determined the outcome of the land campaign. Large armies could be effectively tied to rivers by their logistical dependency, and the strategy of many campaigns was dictated by the floods and droughts that could ruin an army's riverine supply lines. Operations were not limited to the natural river system; the earliest canals in China were immediately exploited for their military potential.

It is almost impossible to separate the technological, logistical, and purely military aspects of naval operations, and no attempt will be made to do so here. Chinese navies were quick to take advantage of any effective innovation in weaponry or sailing. Fire weapons and true cannon appeared on Chinese ships soon after they appeared on land, and seaworthiness improved dramatically over the centuries. But what is more important to remember in the history of this vast continental power is that it was how ships were used—their vital role in empire building—that is most remarkable. Far from being ignored, naval operations were involved in creating Chinese empires from the very beginning to the very end.

The first recorded use of ships in a military operation occurred circa 1045 B.C.E., when King Wu of Zhou ferried 300 chariots, 3,000 men of his personal guard, and 45,000 infantrymen across the Yellow River at Mengjin in forty-seven ships to attack the Shang capital.[1] These were not specialized warships, but vessels commandeered for the operation. Even so, the importance of this operation is clear: A naval contingent of some kind was necessary to span a geographic feature that would otherwise have protected a strategic goal. King Wu's use of ships for military purposes was probably not the first instance of this sort of operation in China. By the first millennium B.C.E. Chinese (to use a somewhat anachronistic term) had been transporting themselves on the water for thousands of years. An oar for a small boat was unearthed in 1978 at a Neolithic site at Hemudu (on the coast of Zhejiang) and dated to 5000 B.C.E. But the pattern set by King Wu was to be repeated throughout Chinese history as dynasty succeeded dynasty and states warred with each other.

Over the succeeding centuries, ships became more specialized. The ships that ferried King Wu's army across the Yellow River were gradually replaced with transport vessels and warships purpose-built for their tasks. Warships were first constructed in the states of Wu, Yue, and Chu in southern China during the Spring and Autumn period (722–481 B.C.E.), as well as in the state of Qi in the northeast. The first recorded naval engagement took place in 549 B.C.E., although no details are available beyond the fact that Chu launched an unsuccessful naval expedition against Wu. It was reported that King Kang of Chu, who launched the attack, was the first Chu ruler to carry out naval expeditions, beginning in 559 B.C.E. when he first took the throne. Some transport vessels at that time could carry fifty men with three months' supply of food and make the thousand-plus-mile trip from Sichuan in the west down the Yangzi River to Chu in less than ten days, covering more than a hundred miles a day.[2]

The development of ships in general, and warships in particular, was aided by advances in woodworking that were themselves a by-product of improved iron tools. Yet the means of naval warfare were still limited to galleys carrying troops of men armed with bows and hand-to-hand weapons. There were several kinds of warships available to the state of Wu: Large Wings, Medium Wings, Small Wings, Tower Ships, and Bridge Boats. Large Wings (the name perhaps coming from the motion of the oars) were 3.5 meters wide and 23 meters long, bearing a crew of ninety-one men (of whom fifty were rowers). These two-decked vessels were supplied with four long hooks, four spears, four axes, thirty-two crossbows, and 3,200 arrows. The high number of oarsmen indicates that speed was particularly important. Medium Wings were 3.1 meters wide and 22 meters long, Small Wings were 2.8 meters wide and 20.7 meters long. All of these vessels had ramming beaks. Tower Ships were used for assaulting the walls of fortifications adjacent to rivers or other bodies of water. They were used in the same way as siege towers on land, to enable the attackers to shoot down at a wall's defenders. Bridge Boats were fast galleys that served the same function as light infantry and cavalry, and they may well have also had ramming beaks.[3]

These ships were first explained by Wu Yuan, also known as Wu Zixu, who came to serve the king of Wu after the king of Chu killed his father and elder brother. In 506 B.C.E. Wu was ordered to construct a canal running from Suzhou through to Lake Tai and then on to the Yangzi River. Shortly after this more than 100-kilometer canal was completed, the king of Wu used the canal to launch a successful attack on Chu. The utility of canal building for military operations was clear, so the next king of Wu ordered another canal dug, this time connecting to the Huai River in the north. Upon its completion in 484 B.C.E., a successful attack was launched against the state of Qi using the 185-kilometer canal. This new canal now allowed the Wu army to travel all the way to the Central Plains of northern China by ship, transiting from the Huai River to the Si River and then on to the Ji River. These canals were constructed in order to allow the north–south transfer of troops for military campaigns. By connecting the major east–west rivers, these man-made water routes spanned the natural geographic divisions that separated many of the individual states of early China.

The state of Wu was also an innovator in launching China's first recorded use of oceangoing ships in a campaign, resulting in the first naval battle at sea in 485 B.C.E. Yet Wu's advances in naval warfare were also to prove its undoing. The rival state of Yue carefully trained its own navy, and in a series of naval engagements combined with land operations destroyed the state of Wu in 475.

Naval warfare was now a regular part of Chinese warfare, and it continued to develop as a result of its increasing frequency. By the early part of the Han dynasty (202 B.C.E.–220 C.E.), Chinese ships had added several layers of superstructure and moved from clinker-built to carvel-built construction. In addition, anchors, rudders, sweeps, and sails had all come into common use. The Han navy, the first independently established navy in Chinese history, was actually called the "Tower Ship Navy," an indication of the central place of the tower ship. This incarnation of the earlier tower ship would continue in use through the thirteenth century, its multiple levels of superstructure serving to protect and provide firing platforms for a substantial complement of soldiers or marines. A variety of smaller ships supplemented the tower ships.

When the Han dynasty was first founded the navy was not powerful enough to suppress the independent kingdoms in the southeast that had broken away from the collapsing Qin dynasty (221–206 B.C.E.). The southeast was and has remained the center of China's maritime culture. Not only does it include an extensive coastline, but inland the area is laced with a vast network of rivers and streams. Three southeastern kingdoms escaped the initial Han consolidation: Dongou, Nanyue, and Minyue. In 138 B.C.E. Minyue attacked Dongou, and the king of Dongou sought Han help. The Minyue navy withdrew without engaging the Han navy, but Dongou was promptly incorporated into the Han empire.

In the fall of 112 B.C.E., having settled the northern border seven years before, the Han emperor sent a larger naval force of 100,000 men to attack Nanyue. The kingdom fell the following year. When the Han navy originally set out to attack Nanyue, Minyue was asked to send a naval force to aid the effort. Although Minyue agreed to the request, the force it sent halted well short of Nanyue, claiming that unfavorable winds prevented it from advancing. Having destroyed Nanyue, the Han commander proposed attacking Minyue on the way home. The Han emperor rejected this idea, and ordered his navy to return to base to refit and await further orders. The Minyue ruler in turn went into open rebellion, and a combined land and naval campaign destroyed the kingdom in 110 B.C.E.

Even before the last shreds of Han sovereignty disintegrated in 220 C.E., the empire had already effectively split into three kingdoms: Wei in the north, Wu in the southeast, and Shu in Sichuan. The balance between them was maintained by geography and naval power. Shu was protected by a ring of mountains, but, despite its position upstream on the Yangzi, could not strike out at Wu because it was unable to develop an effective navy. Wu, on the other hand, had an extremely powerful navy that allowed it to fend off the well-developed land forces of Wei. Yet because its own land forces were considerably weaker than Wei's, Wu was limited in its ability to project power northward.

In the spring of 208 Wei began to build a navy that would allow it to project power southward. This buildup, and the campaign that followed, led to perhaps the most famous battle in all of Chinese history: the Battle of Red Cliff. In mid-year, more than 100,000 infantry and cavalry boarded ship to begin Wei's drive to unify the empire. The Wei force was successful in its drive down the Han River and into the Yangzi. Once on the Yangzi, however, the navies of Shu and Wu united to defeat Wei's large but not particularly skillful fleet. Wei's fleet, now swelled to a force of some 150,000 men (here we should note the proclivity of Chinese sources for giving the number of men rather than the number of ships), anchored beneath Red Cliff chained stem to stern in a continuous wall. The combined

Wu–Shu fleet opened its attack on this static formation by launching ten fire ships into the Wei lines. In the ensuing battle, Wei's fleet was entirely destroyed, thus temporarily putting an end to its unification attempts.

Naval operations played an important role in the centuries that followed, as the back-and-forth warfare of the third through sixth centuries kept the political divisions of China in flux. In 581 the Sui dynasty started to bring this period to a close and constructed a large empire like that of the Han. Late in 588 the Sui emperor sent a vast force across the Yangzi to extinguish the southern kingdom of Chen. The construction of more than one thousand Yellow Dragon ships, in addition to a wide variety of other vessels, had begun in 584. Some 100,000 Chen soldiers waited on the south bank of the Yangzi. This was more in the nature of a vast amphibious landing than a naval battle. Five hundred thousand Sui troops invaded Chen along eight routes, seven of them crossing the Yangzi and one approaching from the sea. Despite some spirited resistance by the Chen army on the upper reaches of the river, the kingdom fell early in 589.

The Sui dynasty itself proved short-lived. It was succeeded by the Tang dynasty (618–907). The Tang emperors made extensive use of naval forces in their campaigns against the Korean kingdoms of Koguryo and Paekche in the middle decades of the seventh century. In 663, the Tang navy defeated a Japanese fleet in a great battle fought on the southwestern coast of the Korean peninsula. Although it does not appear that Tang was a period of dramatic innovation in naval technology or practice, this was nevertheless a time of cultural and commercial developments that laid much of the groundwork for naval advances under the Song dynasty. Many of the innovations first attested during the Song (960–1279) may have been of earlier design. It was during the Song, for example, that the use of the compass for navigating is first mentioned (at the very end of the eleventh or the beginning of the twelfth century). There were several other Song improvements in maritime technology. Ships were considerably strengthened by the addition of crossbeams bracing their ribs. Rudders that could be raised or lowered allowed ships to operate in a broader range of water depths, and the teeth of anchors were arranged circularly instead of in one direction, making them more reliable.

The most significant naval development during the Song was the widespread use of a Tang invention: the man-powered paddle-wheel boat. By the early twelfth century paddle-wheeled warships were being manufactured by the dozen. Not only were the numbers of these vessels increasing, their size and the number of paddle wheels was also growing. Ships were built with as many as thirty-two wheels, and some could carry a thousand soldiers. Oceangoing vessels also began to proliferate. Tang developments in this area were built upon to create still larger and more seaworthy vessels armed with a variety of early gunpowder weapons.

Naval warfare in the Song was both more extensive and more sophisticated than in Tang times. It also provides a good example of the way that a navy was vital to continental conquest. In 974 the Song undertook to conquer the Southern Tang, a kingdom based on the Yangzi River. Although conceived in territorial terms, the entire campaign turned on the ability of the Song navy first to span the Yangzi with a pontoon bridge and then to protect that link from repeated attacks by the powerful Southern Tang navy. Every attack on the pontoon bridge jeopardized the army's success on land. The Southern Tang ruler only surrendered after the last of his navy was destroyed or captured, despite the fact that the Song navy had surrounded his capital for some ten months. With the conquest of the Southern Tang, the Song navy faded in importance for nearly a century and a half.

In 1127 the Jurchen Jin from Manchuria captured the Song capital, Kaifeng, on the Central Plains. Song sovereignty seemed on the verge of collapse, with both the emperor and the retired emperor captured. The immediate reach of the Jin army, however, was limited to the land north of the Huai River. A new Song emperor established himself in southern China and began to reconstruct a semblance of a government. Under these circumstances the Song navy became vital to the survival of the state. The contrast between the Jin and the later Mongols is instructive. Jin superiority on land was more than offset by naval weakness, and Jin's failure to develop an effective navy prevented it from conquering the Song. The Mongols, on the other hand, realized that a strong navy was a necessary prerequisite to conquering the south.

The Jin responded to the appearance of the new Song emperor by crossing the Yangzi River and chasing him south. He was forced to take ship and wait at sea for the crisis to pass. The Jin army was unable to maintain itself in southern China and retreated north. When it reached the Yangzi, however, it found its way blocked by Han Shizhong's 8,000-man navy. Jin reinforcements waited on the north bank, while the Jin army on the south bank found itself threatened by the gathering Song forces. The Song navy, with its large oceangoing warships, wreaked havoc on the small Jin vessels. The 100,000-man Jin army was entirely stymied until a Chinese collaborator pointed out that all of the Song navy's advantages and the Jin navy's disadvantages would be reversed when there was no wind. So, on a windless day, the smaller Jin ships rowed out and shot fire arrows into the becalmed Song navy, destroying most of it. The Jin troops were finally able to recross the Yangzi. This narrow escape probably contributed to keeping the Jin on the north side of the river for another thirty years. Han Shizhong's men had held up the Jin army for forty-eight days.

The next major Jin invasion came in 1161. This 600,000-man invasion force was divided into four major routes, one of which was an attack from the sea. The Jin naval force, however, fell victim to a Song fleet under Li Bao. Li's fleet of 3,000 men and 120 ships regularly attacked the Jin territory by sea, and so was quite familiar with the sailing routes. He attacked the Jin's 600 ships and 100,000 troops at their base. Li's force confidently engaged the much larger Jin fleet, knowing that their opponents were poor sailors and unaccustomed to fighting at sea. The Song navy's fire arrows made short work of the Jin fleet, annihilating the entire Jin force in this single engagement.

While Li Bao was disposing of the Jin seaborne force, the main army under the Jin emperor came up against another Song fleet, this time on the Yangzi River. The original Song commander of the border defenses elected to fall back from the Huai River and defend the Yangzi line instead. He was promptly sacked, but before his replacement could assume command of the Yangzi River forces, matters came to a head. The Jin army outnumbered the Song army by nearly ten to one, yet it had failed to make proper provision for crossing the river. Its ships were constructed with the wood from dismantled houses. Command of the Song navy fell to Yu Yunwen, a civil official with no military experience. Yu proved himself a master of naval warfare, however, repeatedly inflicting devastating defeats upon the Jin. It was simply impossible for the Jin army to cross the Yangzi at that point, so the Jin emperor shifted his army downstream hoping to find another way across. Yu anticipated this and, while his navy was then limited by lower water levels, its continued presence on the river dissuaded the Jin emperor from further attempts to cross. Yu and the Song navy had rendered superior Jin army numbers moot. The invasion had foundered on its lack of an effective navy.

The Mongols did not repeat the Jin's mistakes. They completely overran the last of the Jin state by 1234 and, despite earlier cooperative efforts with the Song, found themselves contemplating the same sorts of invasions that the Jin had attempted in the twelfth century. For the moment, the Huai and Yangzi river defenses were not seriously assaulted as Mongol armies occupied themselves with the rest of Eurasia. It was only when Khubilai became khan in 1260 that the continued existence of the Song in southern China came to the fore. Khubilai had originally shifted his power base into China in order to exploit Chinese resources in his struggle for supremacy with the other Mongol princes. Now firmly rooted in China and secure in his rule, he saw that vast riches could be extracted from the wealthy south. It was also clear that a navy would be required for any serious action against the Song, Mongol efforts in Sichuan having already been repulsed through a coordinated defensive system of forts and fortified cities.

The Mongol navy owed its creation to Khubilai. As was explicitly pointed out in his court, "If there were no Yangzi then that country [the Song] would also not exist."[4] Construction of five thousand warships and training of 70,000 troops in naval warfare began in 1270. Three years later a further two thousand ships and more than 50,000 troops were added to the growing Mongol navy. The navy continued to grow into an overwhelming force. Several thousand Mongol ships took part in the 1273 campaign against the Song. Once the Song lost control of the Yangzi River, its fate was decided. The final tattered remains of the dynasty, including an infant emperor, were destroyed in a climactic sea battle off the island of Yaishan (near today's Hong Kong) in 1279.

In the course of destroying the Song, Khubilai turned his navy to other military adventures. He attempted to invade Japan twice, in 1274 and again in 1281. The Mongol navy also attacked Vietnam in 1282 and 1287. These campaigns represented the high point of Mongol naval power. Subsequent Mongol expansion on land and sea lost the explosiveness that characterized their efforts during the thirteenth century, and Mongol control of China was fairly short-lived. By the mid-fourteenth century the Mongol regime had begun to implode, and rebellions sprang up all over China.

The leader who would emerge to found a new dynasty, the Ming (1368–1644), started his career in southern China. Zhu Yuanzhang became the only ruler ever to unify China and establish a stable regime by moving from south to north. Not surprising, naval operations were vital to the growth of his power. By 1360 the Ming was situated on the middle reaches of the Yangzi River, sandwiched between the forces of Han upstream and Wu downstream. Han was the much greater threat, due to both its greater size (its subject population in 1359 was 14 million, as compared to the Ming's 8 million) and aggressiveness. Wu, by contrast, was only slightly larger than the Ming, and much less aggressive.

War between these southern rivals centered around the capture of walled cities. These cities were the economic and political keys to the surrounding territory, and frequently commanded the transportation and communication routes. Combined with the extensive use of ships for transporting men, horses, and provisions, the importance of attacking walled cities led to vessels with extremely tall stern structures purpose-built to overtop walls along waterways. As we have seen from our earlier discussions, this was not a new innovation, but rather the revival of an old idea. These large vessels, combining both transport and siege functions, maneuvered poorly, but were still effective in naval combat because of their size. In spite of the extensive use of fire weapons, including cannon, naval combat was still frequently decided by hand-to-hand combat.

A turning point in Ming fortunes came during the 1363 Boyang Lake campaign against Han. Although a Ming ambush three years earlier near Nanjing had virtually destroyed the Han navy and greatly strengthened that of the Ming, internal rebellions removed Ming pressure long enough for the Han to rebuild their navy. Early in 1363 Wu momentarily distracted the Ming downstream, giving Han a good opportunity to attack the city of Nanchang, on the Gan River off Boyang Lake. Nanchang was vital to the control of Jiangxi province, and lay much closer to the Han center of power than to that of the Ming.

Particularly large ships were constructed for Han's attack on Nanchang, with tall stern castles and iron-plated archers' towers. This was an all-out effort by the Han ruler Chen Youliang, for which he had gathered some 300,000 men and vast quantities of supplies. Ideally, the enormous size of the Han vessels would allow them to quickly carry the main cities and towns as they proceeded downstream, avoiding protracted sieges. However, the fleet was hung up on the siege of Nanchang.

The Han fleet arrived on June 5 and, despite some initial success in breaching the city's outer wall, remained stuck there until August 28, when an approaching Ming fleet some 100,000 men strong drove them off. The ensuing fleet action on Boyang Lake was an uninspired slugging match, led by the rival rulers. If Chen destroyed the Ming fleet, then Nanchang would fall. Zhu, on the other hand, had only to raise the siege to succeed in his objective. Yet the Ming fleet was outnumbered by the Han fleet, and its ships were smaller. Its only advantage lay in its position across the line of retreat of the Han fleet, whose deeper draft vessels were now restricted by lower water levels. From August 30 to September 2 the two fleets fought a series of bloody engagements that weakened and demoralized both sides. Still, Zhu Yuanzhang was succeeding in his objective of raising the siege, and Chen Youliang had failed to win anything like a decisive victory despite his superior strength. Ironically, it was the different drafts of the main ships in the shallow lake that had contributed to the indecisiveness of the fighting. The Han ships were frequently unable to approach the Ming ships in shallow water, so although the Ming fleet was weaker in all respects, it retained the initiative.

The Ming fleet withdrew on the night of September 2, threading its way through the straits leading from the lake to the Yangzi River. It then took a position upstream from the mouth of the straits, again blocking the Han fleet's line of retreat. Despite several important defections to the Ming cause, the Han fleet was still considerably stronger. By the time the battle was joined on October 3, however, the Han fleet was in a do-or-die situation. It had simply run out of food. Combat quickly broke down into clumps of opposing vessels drifting downstream locked in hand-to-hand combat. The results of that day's fighting would have been similarly inconclusive except for two major incidents: Chen You-liang's death from a stray arrow, and the capture of his son, the designated successor to the Han throne. The remains of the leaderless fleet surrendered the following day.

In retrospect, this inelegant and bloody naval campaign was a turning point in the development of Ming power. Zhu Yuanzhang was able to expand into Han territory over the next two years and increase his power to the point where he could overrun Wu in 1367. The following year Zhu declared the founding of a new dynasty, and launched campaigns into north China and along the southern coast. Naval forces played a key role in conquering the southern provinces of Guangdong and Fujian, and they also played a significant role in supplying the northern campaigns. With the remnants of Mongol power driven back to the steppes, though not destroyed, Zhu turned his attention in 1371 to conquering the Xia regime in Sichuan. A two-pronged attack began in early summer and was over by September. The Ming fleet virtually shot its way into Sichuan, using cannon to destroy the booms deployed to block its progress up the Yangzi River.

Despite continuing increases in the number and size of vessels during Zhu Yuanzhang's reign, the navy was shifted to a defensive role as part of a generally defensive foreign policy. The Ming court's attitude toward foreign trade would vary not only from emperor to emperor, but also over the course of individual reigns. At the same time, however, overseas trade continued to grow without regard for the government's desires. By the mid-sixteenth century the issue of overseas trade came to a head when some court officials connected it to the endemic problem of piracy along the southeastern coast. While there was undoubtedly some truth to the belief that trade and piracy were related, many prominent local families along the coast were engaged in the lucrative overseas trade. Locally, then, central government efforts to suppress piracy by suppressing trading were extremely unpopular, and ultimately backfired. Legitimate merchants who had been interested in helping the government capture real pirates found their livelihood criminalized. They were thus forced to become pirates themselves.

Zhu Wan was originally sent to suppress piracy along the Fujian and Zhejiang coast in 1547. He was forced to recruit his own staff because local officials refused to cooperate with him in his intention to prohibit trade. Whatever the effect of his efforts on piracy, Zhu was fairly successful in suppressing trade. He repeatedly attacked merchant fleets and executed many of those he captured. Unfortunately for him, his actions earned him the enmity of officials from those provinces. Zhu was impeached in 1549, and committed suicide early the next year to avoid disgrace.

Although Zhu Wan was gone and his fleet dispersed, the Ming court did not change its policy on overseas trade. Faced with an even stricter ban, merchant fleets under the leadership of Wang Zhi began coordinated raids against the southeast coast in 1552. These raids came on the heels of famine and drought, further exacerbating already difficult conditions in the region. By 1554, these raids had been so successful, and the government response so ineffective, that the pirates established fortified bases on the mainland from which to raid further inland. Chinese pirates were joined by Japanese warriors, causing all of them to be labeled *wokou* (Japanese bandits). Much of the countryside was left to be pillaged, while government armies stayed in the walled cities after repeated defeats in the field in 1553 and 1554. During all of this, it seems that Wang Zhi and many of his fellow Chinese merchants were still looking for a way to return to the peaceful pursuit of trade. The emperor had decided upon extermination of the bandits, however, closing off the possibility of allowing men like Wang to surrender and serve the government by destroying the other pirates. Wang eventually did surrender and was executed because his captor could not deliver the pardon he had promised. Even so, the underhanded dealing of the government had eliminated some of the major pirates, and improved imperial forces began to take their toll. This was largely a victory of land forces, though, rather than a massive naval effort. The worst depredations were over by the 1560s.

The fear of pirate raids surfaced again in 1592, after the Japanese invasion of Korea. Naval operations were to play a crucial role in both this invasion and a second one in 1597. The Japanese army had to bring most of its supplies and all of its men to Korea by sea. Its logistics were further complicated by Korean partisans, who actively denied the Japanese control of the countryside. Confronted by the formidable Ming armies in the field, and with their communications attacked at sea, the Japanese forces received the order to retreat even before their warlord Hideyoshi died (in Japan) in 1598. Without control over the sea lanes, the Japanese invasion force was always in danger of being cut off from retreat. Korean admiral Yi Sun-sin's "turtle boats," iron-plated galleys armed with cannon, wreaked havoc on the Japanese navy (although Admiral Yi is not much credited in the Chinese sources). The Koreans were saved by their navy, and that of the Ming.

The Ming navy would also preserve the last shreds of the Ming cause when the dynasty fell to the Manchus in the seventeenth century. In the 1640s, the dynasty was caught between internal rebellion and the rising Manchu Qing regime north of the Great Wall. These twin threats prevented an adequate response to either, and Beijing fell in 1644, first to the rebel leader Li Zicheng and then to the Manchus. A new Ming emperor was enthroned in Nanjing, the first capital from which Zhu Yuanzhang had ruled the empire, following the suicide of the sitting emperor when Li Zicheng's army entered Beijing. While the Manchu forces were overrunning north China, the new Ming court was attempting to achieve some semblance of normality amidst bitter factionalism. By June of the following year the Qing army had captured Nanjing as well as the new emperor. Ming loyalist forces still held out in southern China, however, relying upon naval strength that they hoped the Qing could not counter. Yet at the same time the men in control of those forces, principally Zheng Zhilong, were reluctant to do more than defend the south. Fragments of Ming rule survived for some years, with one court spending much of its time on Zhoushan Island off the coast of Zhejiang.

Qing efforts to eradicate these Ming remnants concentrated on destroying the various resistance forces on the mainland while building up a navy capable of taking Zhoushan Island. In addition, they made every effort to suppress trade with the island. The Qing fleet overwhelmed the Ming navy in October of 1651, then battered Zhoushan City into submission with cannon fire. Regent Lu, representing one of the last threads of Ming rule, fled by sea to seek the protection of Zheng Chenggong, the son of Zheng Zhilong. Zheng Chenggong (also known as Koxinga) had taken command of the Zheng family navy after his father surrendered to the Qing. The younger Zheng had been born in Japan of a Japanese mother, and represented exactly the sort of trader-pirate that had plagued the Chinese coast in the 1550s.

The Qing had great difficulty overcoming Zheng because of his over-whelming naval strength and his bases in areas nearly inaccessible by land. By 1655, after two years of fruitless attempts by the Qing court to induce him to surrender on favorable terms, Zheng actually began to ex-pand northward. A Qing fleet was destroyed trying to capture Jinmen Is-land off the Fujian coast in 1656, inducing the Manchus to turn to less direct methods. Their previous prohibition on coastal trading was ex-tended to encompass more of the coastline, while amnesties were offered to pirates who surrendered and served the Qing. This brought the Qing valuable sailors and ships, but Zheng's northern expansion was ulti-mately hobbled much more by his limited ability to sustain a land attack and his lack of familiarity with the waters of the Yangzi River and the north. After a crushing defeat on land outside Nanjing in 1659, he re-treated to defend his territory from the expected Qing counteroffensive. Zheng recognized that he needed a more secure base farther from the mainland. In 1661, he shifted his base to Taiwan, driving out the Dutch. He died the following year. His son held out for another two decades, but there was a limit to what purely naval force could do.

The Qing would have little use for a navy for quite some time after Ad-miral Shi Lang finally subjugated Taiwan in 1683. It was not until it was confronted by another group of trader-raiders, this time Europeans, in the nineteenth century that the Qing court had to once again take up the serious matter of naval affairs. As with all previous dynasties, the Qing had been forced to develop some naval capability during its conquest of the Chinese empire. And just like many of its predecessors, it later found itself desperately trying to erect a naval line of defense against attacks on its sovereignty.

Suggestions for Further Reading

Very little had been written on Chinese water forces and naval warfare prior to the middle of the nineteenth century. The technology of shipbuilding and navi-gation is addressed in Joseph Needham, *Science and Civilisation in China*, vol. 4, pt. 3, *Civil Engineering and Nautics* (Cambridge: Cambridge University Press, 1971). Needham devotes some attention to the tactics of ship-to-ship combat, as does Rafe de Crespigny, *Generals of the South: The Foundation and Early History of the Three Kingdoms State of Wu* (Canberra: Australian National University Fac-ulty of Asian Studies, 1990). De Crespigny also offers a detailed account of the Battle of Red Cliff. Other examples of naval battles and coastal operations can be found in Frank A. Kierman Jr. and John K. Fairbank, eds., *Chinese Ways in War-fare* (Cambridge: Harvard University Press, 1974); the contributions of Edward

L. Dreyer (dealing with the Boyang Lake campaign of 1363) and Charles O. Hucker (dealing with the Ming antipiracy campaign on the Zhejiang coast in the 1550s) are especially valuable. The rise and fall of Chinese maritime power from the Song dynasty through the Ming is treated in three important articles by Jungpang Lo: "The Emergence of China as a Sea Power during the Late Sung and Early Yuan Periods," *Far Eastern Quarterly* 14 (1955): 489–503; "The Decline of the Early Ming Navy," *Oriens Extremus* 5 (1958): 149–169; and "Maritime Commerce and Its Relation to the Sung Navy," *Journal of the Economic and Social History of the Orient* 12 (1969): 57–101. The most accessible treatment of the Ming admiral Zheng He's voyages to the Indian Ocean is Louise Levathes, *When China Ruled the Seas: The Treasure Fleet of the Dragon Throne, 1405–1433* (Oxford: Oxford University Press, 1994). Bruce Swanson, *Eighth Voyage of the Dragon: A History of China's Quest for Seapower* (Annapolis: Naval Institute Press, 1982) is primarily concerned with naval modernization since the late nineteenth century, but devotes approximately seventy pages to the Ming voyages and the water forces of the Qing dynasty. Zhang Tieniu and Gao Xiaoxing have written an overview of China's premodern naval history, *Zhongguo gudai haijun shi* [History of the Ancient Chinese Navy] (Beijing: Bayi chubanshe, 1993). There is no comparable survey in English.

SUGGESTIONS FOR FURTHER RESEARCH

The small amount of existing work on premodern Chinese naval history frequently suffers from a perceived need to compare the Chinese navy with European developments, or to fit Chinese navies and naval exploits into European historical models. Very little progress will ever be made in understanding Chinese naval history if it continues to be directed toward explaining why China did not embark upon a sustained and vigorous program of ship-borne world exploration leading up to a system of global trade and power projection.

There are five areas of research on premodern Chinese naval history that can profitably be explored: naval battles, logistics, administration, technology, and strategic thought. The almost entirely undeveloped state of the field has left all five areas equally unexplored. At the most basic level, Chinese naval history must begin by creating a corpus of detailed battle studies of individual encounters and larger campaigns. This history would necessarily discuss naval warfare both as part of related land campaigns and separately, in its own right. Just as naval warfare needs to be discussed in connection with larger campaigns and in its own right, so too would any research on logistics need to stress both how the need to supply armies and navies led to certain battles or directed campaign strategy, and how logistic capability itself developed and was used. Naval logistics may well have formed the strategic backbone of many campaigns. One of the most peculiar oversights in Chinese naval history is the almost complete lack of discussion of the administration of the imperial navies. Chinese historical source material is usually particularly strong in the areas of government administration and bureaucracy, and it seems likely that this avenue of research could be easily and profitably pursued. The late Joseph Needham lamented the primitive state of knowledge of Chinese naval technology, and his comment deserves seconding. Finally, research must begin to explore the extent of Chinese thinking on naval operations. This is a topic so unexplored that it cannot even be said for certain if there is anything extant that would constitute premodern naval strategy. It is highly unlikely, however, that this topic entirely escaped comment in the vast archives of Chinese history.

NOTES

1. Zhang Tieniu and Gao Xiaoxing, *Zhongguo gudai haijun shi* [History of the ancient Chinese navy] (Beijing: Bayi chubanshe, 1993), 5.
2. Sima Qian, *Shiji* [Historical records] (Beijing: Zhonghua shuju, 1959), ch. 70, p. 2290.
3. Zhang and Gao, *Zhongguo gudai haijun shi*, 8–10.
4. Liu Minzhong, *Ping Song lu*, quoted in Zhang and Gao, *Zhongguo gudai haijun shi*, 113.

SIX

Military Writings

Ralph D. Sawyer

Without doubt, China has the longest continuous tradition of military literature of any culture, dating from about 500 B.C.E. right through the present, with only a brief hiatus during the early twentieth century when various Western doctrines temporarily predominated.

Military thought, understood as the conscious study of battlefield events and the forces that shape them, may have had rudimentary precursors in the Neolithic (5500–3000 B.C.E.) when battles were fought with stone and wood, but certainly began to evolve in the Longshan period (3000–2000 B.C.E.) with the development of fortification technology and the incipient stage of bronze weapons. Warring States and later historical writings perceive well-planned campaigns in the rise of the Xia, Shang, and Zhou dynasties, while such traditional chronicles as the *Commentary of Zuo (Zuozhuan)*, *Discourses of the States (Guoyu)*, *Intrigues of the Warring States (Zhanguoce)*, *Historical Records (Shiji)*, and *Bamboo Annals (Zhushu jinian)* attribute complex tactics and coordinated strategy to the clashes of the Spring and Autumn period (722–481 B.C.E.). Although the sophisticated dialogues appearing in these works are late reconstructions, in aggregate they preserve sufficient vestiges of tactical thought to indicate Spring and Autumn military leaders had already formulated a number of combat principles. However, without further archaeological or textual discoveries, it remains unknowable whether a truly systematic body of thought had evolved prior to Sunzi.

Some twenty of the generally acknowledged four to five hundred military writings currently extant—mere remnants of the many that perished over the centuries through neglect, suppression, and war—merit introduction. However, China's military history is not to be found in these theoretical works which, in fact, have an unknown relationship with actual combat, but instead in its many historical writings, especially the annals and biographies found in the expansive *Twenty-Five Dynastic Histories*. In aggregate, the numerous court discussions and memorials also preserve extensive source materials for the study of military thought and ideas. In addition, Warring States and slightly later philosophical and political writings, including the *Book of Lord Shang* (*Shangjunshu*), *Guanzi, Xunzi,* and *Huainanzi,* often contain succinct chapters on military affairs. Siege practices are visible mainly in the *Mozi*, scattered *Lüshi chunqiu* chapters provide important insights on theory and values, and several paragraphs on the nature and appropriateness of warfare in the *Mencius* long furnished a basis for moralizing whenever court discussions were held about the feasibility of mounting aggressive campaigns against external, "barbarian" peoples. Finally, a whole host of early writings, such as the *Wu-Yue chunqiu, Yanzi chunqiu,* and even the *Rituals of Zhou* (*Zhouli*) preserve essential accounts, narratives, and martial discussions; the pivotal *Daodejing* contains focal military chapters and espouses a philosophical perspective that fundamentally influenced traditional military concepts; and a number of forgeries and fabrications, such as the *Guiguzi* and the *Xinshu* attributed to Zhuge Liang, also affected military theory.

Although evidence exists that tactical ideas were committed to writing before 500 B.C.E., Sunzi's *Art of War* (*Sunzi bingfa*)—often viewed as virtually synonymous with Chinese military thought—marks the known beginning. The turbulent Warring States period (453–221 B.C.E.) saw the composition of numerous political and other books, among which six important martial texts survive: *Simafa, Wuzi, Sun Bin bingfa, Taigong liutao, Weiliaozi,* and *Huangshigong sanlue*. Whatever other military works may have been penned in the centuries before Li Quan's Tang-dynasty *Taibai yinjing*, such as those by Cao Cao and Zhuge Liang, have largely vanished except for remnants and late reconstructions. Finally, Wang Zhen's intriguing early ninth-century meditation on ending warfare (*Daodejing lunbing yaoyi*) and the incisive *Tang Taizong Li Weigong wendui,* attributed to the great Tang general Li Jing, conclude the formative period of Chinese military thought. Thereafter, with the exception of the manuals written by the Ming general Qi Jiguang, even the most insightful works tend to be primarily compilations and overview.

The Song philosophical impulse to analytical classification is equally evident in such military writings as the *One Hundred Unorthodox Strategies (Baizhan qilue)* and the *Hundred Terms from Military Tactics* (*Bingfa baiyan*). (The former selects the hundred most important tactical principles found in the classic military writings and illustrates them with appropriate historical battles; the latter offers often ethereal topical discussions.) Imperial concern over the lack of classical military knowledge in the Song dynasty resulted in the famous compendium of miltiary science known as the *Essentials of the Military Classics* (*Wujing zongyao*), and subsequently, in 1080, in the *Wujing qishu* or *Seven Military Classics*, a collection of seven preexisting martial books settled upon after some dispute: *Sunzi bingfa, Simafa, Wuzi, Weiliaozi, Taigong liutao, Huangshigong sanlue,* and *Tang Taizong Li Weigong wendui.* The various extant commentaries, apart from Cao Cao's on Sunzi, were stripped out. Designated as the core texts for the newly founded military academy and required content for military examinations, these seven naturally became disproportionately influential. A few other significant writings appeared in the empire's concluding centuries, including the *Caolu jinglue, He boshi luelun, Huqianjing, Beizheng lu, Dengtan bijiu,* and the encyclopedic *Wubeizhi,* but their content was mostly accretional, their knowledge and practices minimally evolutionary.

SUNZI BINGFA

Despite the *Art of War*'s cryptic nature and short length, as the commonly acknowledged progenitor of China's military writings it constituted a repository of critical ideas and first principles that had to be thoroughly pondered, and inescapably influenced military and nonmilitary thought alike for over two millennia. The source of innumerable sayings and concepts that have entered the Chinese language to shape basic thought processes and expectations, it continues to be actively studied in many contexts and remains the foundation of classically oriented attempts to construct a modern operational doctrine "with Chinese characteristics." However, apart from having been condemned by the literati over the centuries for its "vicious orientation" and inhumanity, it is also a text much beset by controversy. The identity and even existence of its author, Sunzi or Sun Wu, are much debated, as is his role in transforming Wu into a powerful state capable of conquering mighty Chu and nearby Yue near the end of the sixth century B.C.E. Second, Sunzi's relationship with the *Art of War* is also questioned, with some views identifying him as the sole author and others denying any connection whatsoever. Third, the book's date is also vehemently disputed. Traditionalists who attribute it to Sunzi himself (as suggested by his *Shiji* biography) understand it as an insightful meditative distillation of late Spring and Autumn military experience that must have been composed at the end of the sixth century B.C.E. and slightly modified thereafter by his disciples or other editors, accounting for the few obvious anachronisms. Others consider it a late-fifth-century product that reflects the expanding scope of warfare, or even attribute it to the early fourth century and perceive a strongly accretional nature. While showing slight variations and much about the text's evolution, the bamboo-slip editions recovered by archaeologists in recent years have not substantially contributed to resolving these debates.

The brief, enigmatic *Art of War* often seems to take the form of notes, perhaps because of the inherent constraints imposed by using bamboo slips as the recording medium. Although each of its thirteen chapters is marked by a distinct thematic emphasis, the views, concepts, and principles remain consistent throughout. Nevertheless, the last two chapters on incendiary warfare and spies (for which the book was excoriated in both China and the West) may have been appended by later hands. Even though much of the book actually consists of concrete pronouncements applicable to operational situations and explications of specific tactical principles, at least half presents a core vision of national strategy, warfare objectives, and conceptual material that became fundamental to Chinese military thought. Briefly summarized, because warfare is dangerous and expensive, Sunzi advocated achieving victory without fighting wherever possible. However, when unavoidable, and only if based on thorough intelligence, military actions should be taken to achieve predetermined objectives expeditiously. This should be accomplished by manipulating and destabilizing the enemy, thereby creating circumstances in which overwhelming strategic power can effect a decisive victory through the utilization of unorthodox methods and exploitation of environmental advantages.

Because military campaigns entail the fate of the people and warfare is therefore deemed the greatest affair of government, martial study and preparation cannot be neglected. Moreover, the state must be united and fully in harmony with the ruler's intent for success to be achieved. However, unlike the later military classics, the *Art of War* is little concerned with the people's welfare, being focused instead on developing the overwhelming strategic power that, when applied in concrete situations, can be imagized as a torrent roaring down a mountain from a burst dam, carrying everything before it. However, mere might alone is inadequate; it is the creation of strategic advantage that forges victory. This is achieved through maneuvering one's own army while simultaneously manipulating the enemy through lures, deceit, forced marches, subversion, and other means that will weaken them and make them susceptible to a concentrated, unexpected attack. The enemy's spirit should equally be targeted, because the dispirited are easily defeated.

Implementing these measures requires thorough knowledge of the enemy, generally obtained through scouts and spies. Thereafter, councils can calculate the feasibility of achieving state objectives through warfare, determine the requisite operational strategy, and plot concrete tactical efforts. Hostile forces should never be engaged if the victory is not certain, but once committed, actions should be decisive yet taken with an eye to preserving the enemy as well as oneself. Foolish and wasteful assaults, such as upon fortified positions (generally misunderstood as applying simply to cities), should be eschewed in favor of making the enemy vulnerable, spreading his defenses, and attacking his vacuities and gaps. The commander should be formless and unfathomable, utilize secrecy and deception to fullest advantage, vary his tactics, and employ the unorthodox (*qi*) and orthodox (*zheng*). The commander should also be cognizant of the topography and consciously take advantage of the various configurations of terrain, especially the "fatal terrain" that can be employed to elicit the utmost effort from one's troops.

THE *WUZI*

The *Wuzi*, the second of the ancient military classics, has traditionally been attributed to Wu Qi, the great general who enjoyed inordinate battlefield success against Qin in the first century of the Warring States period before perishing in Chu while serving as a high official (because he instituted severe governmental reforms inimical to entrenched aristocratic interests). Even if the book's core originated with Wu Qi, it has suffered both extensive losses and serious accretions (including references to cavalry forces), and may not have attained final form until the early Han. Nevertheless, in conjunction with the *Art of War* it has always been considered one of the twin foundations of Chinese military science even by nonmilitary officials and therefore essential to martial contemplation.

Wu Qi believed that governments must implement benevolent policies; otherwise, they will be unable to nurture the military forces crucial to the state's survival. Harmony must be fostered if the people are to sustain martial efforts, but organization and training make victory possible. Commanders must be properly qualified, the troops selected, rewards and punishments properly established, and constraint and measure imposed in all aspects. Thereafter, tactical opportunities must either be discovered through active probing or created. Enemy commanders must be manipulated and all flaws in the character of their troops exploited. Numerous tactical measures are also discussed, providing many insights into the era's military practices. However, although the book's focus is more concrete than the *Art of War*, the *Wuzi*, throughout its few extant chapters, still stresses the larger issues that significantly affect the state.

THE *SIMAFA*

Traditionally associated with the legendary Sima Rangju, a fabled commander of the turn of the fifth century B.C.E., the *Minister of War's Methods* was probably compiled in the fourth or early third century B.C.E. from various materials, including some recounting relatively idealized early Zhou practices that may date from the Western Zhou period. Whether the extant five chapters comprise mere remnants from the 155 reportedly included in early Han dynasty versions cannot be verified, but what remains, although limited in scope, is cogent and consistent. Moreover, the *Simafa* has traditionally been accorded great respect, certain concepts and key sentences frequently being quoted in court discussions and later military manuals. Particularly important is the dictum, "Even though a state may be vast, those who love warfare will inevitably perish. Even though calm may prevail under Heaven, those who forget warfare will certainly be endangered."

In emphasizing fundamental issues of government and organization rather than operational principles and tactics, the *Simafa*'s thrust differs fundamentally from the other classic military writings. Although many of the tactical resolutions it proposes for varying situations are common to other late Warring States works such as the *Taigong liutao*, the *Simafa* is defined by its ruminations on the nature of warfare and the surprising conclusion that war is necessary because only through killing can power be created and order brought to the world. However, violence is only appropriate in limited circumstances, when justified by virtue and righteousness. (Since the people's welfare is paramount, rescuing them from suffering and repression stands chief among them.) Effective training must precede any military campaign; when in the field, constraint and measure should be imposed. The examples of antiquity should be studied for crucial lessons, including different approaches to conflict.

Two aspects command attention: the clear distinction that must be made between the civil and the martial (or civic and warrior realms), and the nature and role of *qi* (spirit or the will to fight). The *Simafa* points out that they are intertwined because the spirit and attitude appropriate to a warrior, focused on action and death, are disjunctive with those found in court, where sedate movement and deferential discussion prevail. Thus, the attitudes of the latter cannot be imposed on the former; otherwise, the army will be doomed because practicing inappropriate ritualized forms of behavior (the *li*) quickly subverts and erodes warrior values. Moreover, since *qi* ensures victory, the army's *qi* must be studied and manipulated, exploited when required but constrained when less urgent. Rewards and punishments provide the means, oaths and harangues the final impetus for achieving this.

SUN BIN BINGFA

Reputedly a lineal descendant of the great Sunzi, Sun Bin's historicity is attested by a highly dramatic biography in the *Shiji* and numerous references in late Warring States writings. A brilliant strategist who was maimed through the machinations of his enemies, he still managed to direct Qi's forces in vanquishing Wei twice in the mid-fourth century B.C.E. at the famous battles of Guiling and then Maling, where crossbows were employed en masse for the first time. His book was well known into the Han, but somehow disappeared thereafter until it was rediscovered in a Han dynasty tomb in 1972 and laboriously reconstructed from hundreds of fragmented bamboo strips. Unfortunately, the resulting work consists of two distinct parts: fifteen chapters in expanded dialogue format with Sun Bin explicitly identified as the speaker, followed by fifteen integrated, purely expository essays on particular topics (presumably by later hands). The book was probably compiled by Sun Bin's disciples within decades of his death. Although numerous textual and interpretive problems plague the enigmatic passages, both halves of this book preserve extremely valuable material for studying middle Warring States thought.

Sun Bin's Art of War (or *Military Methods*, to distinguish it in English from *Sunzi bingfa*) may be said to generally take Sunzi's assertions on the nature and importance of warfare, as well as many of of his other concepts, as fundamental preliminary to focusing on concrete issues, especially tactical and operational questions. Even though the subject matter ranges widely, *Military Methods* emphasizes manipulating the enemy and then ruthlessly exploiting the resulting weakness. Following thorough evaluation and planning, Sunzi's crucial techniques of being deceptive, luring the enemy onto difficult terrain, destabilizing their formations, and thwarting their plans are to be employed. Furthermore, while stressing swiftness, Sun Bin advocates dividing both one's own and the enemy's forces, the former to facilitate maneuver, the latter to create gaps and vacuities. Flaws and weaknesses in enemy commanders should be targeted and enemy troops emotionally coerced. Contrary to Sunzi's blanket admonition, cities may be attacked when dictated by potential profits and the likelihood of an easy conquest.

Even when not specifically discussed, Sunzi's concept of strategic power (*shi*) underlines most of Sun Bin's methods and pronouncements. Since the various configurations of terrain previously identified by Sunzi facilitate the creation of temporary strategic advantage, the topography must be constantly surveyed. The unorthodox provides the general method for engaging a dissimilar enemy, deploying into selected formations the concrete means for wresting victory in varying circumstances. Formations, terrain characteristics, and recurring tactical situations are discussed in some detail throughout the book. Only an astute, experienced commander of exemplary character can actualize these advantages, only well trained and organized troops can implement them. Finally, the soldiers' fervor must be controlled through a remarkable series of stages that constitute a true martial psychology so that their spirit reaches its zenith just when entering battle.

THE *WEILIAOZI*

Some historians believe the *Weiliaozi* originated in Wei Liao's conversations with King Hui of Liang, others attribute its beginnings to his discussions with the first Qin emperor while the latter was still young. Since the text was clearly composed somewhere between the late fourth and the middle third centuries B.C.E. and tomb text versions show it existed before the Han—contrary to claims of Tang dynasty fabrication—it is clearly a middle to late Warring States book. Moreover, because its two halves dramatically differ in focus and orientation, it must have been cobbled together from two distinct sources rather than being an integral work from a single author that then underwent the usual modifications and accretions.

The first half is a strongly theoretical work that integrates benevolent policies with strict discipline and draconian law enforcement. In seeking to unite civil government with martial spirit, it stresses conceptual and organizational issues to the almost complete exclusion of tactics. Because material welfare is the foundation of the state's survival and the means to military procurement, a vibrant agricultural and commercial economy must be fostered. Furthermore, a strong, contented populace will furnish the loyal, enthusiastic military forces necessary, particularly when they are properly controlled through strict disciplinary measures. The *Weiliaozi* continues the *Simafa*'s insights into *qi* and its manipulation, emphasizing the need to nurture the warrior spirit while depriving the enemy of their will.

The *Weiliaozi* also attaches great importance to organization and unity in both civil and military administrations. Its entire second half, which may preserve actual Qin regulations, advocates imposing strong measures to control the troops and always punishing battlefield failures and camp infractions severely, frequently with death. This will forge a stalwart, responsive army capable of maneuvering and executing unorthodox tactics and of readily exploiting emerging weaknesses. This sort of force will not just overwhelm the enemy, but also overawe them with its unity, spirit, commitment, and death-defying dedication. Much in the spirit of Sunzi, the *Weiliaozi*'s well-known opening paragraphs debunk the era's beliefs in auspicious days and portents, stressing that man alone is responsible for battlefield success or failure.

TAIGONG LIUTAO

The longest of the *Seven Military Classics*, the *Six Secret Teachings* (from the character *tao*, which has the basic meaning of "bowcase" and thus suggests a container that could conceal things) is a comprehensive work that ranges widely over all aspects of grand strategy, military conceptualization, tactics, organization, and theoretical fundamentals. Traditionally attributed to the sagacious Taigong (also known as Lü Shang), who served as an advisor and military commander to the Zhou kings when they vanquished Shang, it is clearly a heterogeneous work compiled in the Warring States period either shortly after Sun Bin's *Military Methods* or at the start of the third century B.C.E. Apart from preserving innumerable concrete tactics for particular situations and unique descriptions of military equipment, several chapters advocate total warfare, including the use of subversive methods to corrupt and undermine the enemy, causing it to be much condemned by later Confucians. Its sixty chapters are grouped into six *tao*—the Civil, Martial, Dragon, Tiger, Leopard, and Canine—each of which generally pursues a single theme. For example, the Civil primarily focuses upon government, general strategy, administrative matters, and state building.

The basic vision is common to most of the military writings: Establish benevolent yet strict government that espouses virtue, emphasizes the people's welfare, and nurtures the state's prosperity. The ruler, who should be constrained and impartial, must manifest an image of righteousness in order to inculcate the proper values and build a competent, devoted bureaucracy. Thereafter, should the state need to engage in warfare against a pernicious enemy, every means should be employed—but without treating the common people as the enemy. Victory can only be secured with qualified generals who impose severe discipline through a strictly organized military hierarchy. Training is paramount, for then the army will be able to exploit advantages of terrain, weaknesses in the enemy, and flaws in commanders.

The final three *tao*, some thirty chapters, focus on the actual practice of warfare, not only discussing equipment, logistics, and the nature of the army's component forces (chariots, infantry, and cavalry), but also explicating dozens of tactical situations (such as mountain and marsh warfare) rarely seen in other works. Swiftness and deception are always essential, certainty and aggressiveness requisite. Chaos in the enemy's ranks must be fostered and then exploited; environmental factors, such as steep hills and rainy conditions, must be turned to advantage; traps and ambushes should be established; the initiative should be seized; and the enemy should be continuously evaluated and probed, constantly manipulated and exhausted both physically and psychologically. Suitable operational forces must be chosen from among the infantry, chariots, and cavalry, and difficult terrain thereby overcome.

HUANGSHIGONG SANLUE

Despite its storied association with Zhang Liang, one of the chief strategists in the rise of the Han dynasty, the *Three Strategies of the Duke of Yellow Rock* was probably composed late in the Former Han dynasty by integrating highly disparate Warring States material within a new, heavily Daoist perspective known as *Huang-lao*. The last of the classic military writings, the book is organized into three sections, entitled Superior Strategy, Middle Strategy, and Inferior Strategy, presumably reflecting the theory that civilization had inexorably declined since legendary antiquity, thereby requiring stronger, more aggressive measures for each increasingly disordered stage. However, a closer examination reveals that the strategies should be appropriately employed in accord with differing circumstances rather than simply in a particular era of turmoil.

Four threads of thought pervade this somewhat ethereal but intriguing work: Confucian concepts of virtue and benevolent government; the activist measures of Legalism intended to strengthen the state and re-store civic order; Daoist values of harmony, noncontentiousness, yield-ing, and esteeming life; and the intrusive realism of military combat, mandating strict command and control measures. Warfare, which should only be conducted to mitigate suffering and extirpate evil rather than to profit the state, depends upon the people's willing allegiance and participation. The soldiers must be strongly motivated rather than merely willing to defend the state. Rewards and punishments provide the means of coercion, swiftness in execution the method for precluding dis-order and disaffection. The general must be an exemplary figure: loved yet awesome, capable yet receptive, unquestioned in authority and free of doubt. Finally, in accord with the Dao, military actions require restraint yet decisiveness. Because simple strength, bluntness, and directness are not always advisable, appropriate techniques from among the hard and soft, weak and strong, should be selected, even admixed, to achieve the predetermined objectives.

TANG TAIZONG LI WEIGONG WENDUI

The *Questions and Replies between Tang Taizong and Duke Li of Wei* pur-portedly records an actual dialogue between the Tang dynasty's second emperor and his most prominent general, Li Jing, also honored as Duke Li of Wei. However, doubts that such sophisticated dialogues could be genuine, particularly as some of the language and concepts apparently date to the Song, have prompted numerous questions about its authentic-ity. Most likely the book was compiled by an experienced strategist in the late Tang or early Northern Song period, possibly from notes or a core work containing the views of these two dynamic historical figures. It briefly enjoyed great credence when included in the *Seven Military Clas-sics*, but subsequently encountered much condemnation.

Irrespective of its provenance and its greater stress on conceptions and reasoning rather than tactics, the book's three lengthy chapters con-tain important material on Tang and possibly Song military theory and practices. The discussants tackle several key issues from earlier military writings, evaluate historical battles, and unravel Li Jing's intentions in mounting victorious battlefield actions in the dynasty's early days. (Li Jing was not only instrumental in helping consolidate the dynasty's power, but from 618 on also expanded the Tang domain in pacification campaigns in the south and later against the Türks. Continuing as Tang Taizong's confidant after the latter usurped power in 626, he remained prominent until his own death in 649.) The dialogues explicate the nature and employment of the orthodox and unorthodox; previous military writings; organization and training; selecting and using men appropriately; the vacuous and substantial; the employment of battlefield formations; methods for conquering and using barbarians; command and control; the cavalry's functions; rewards and punishments; being deceptive and manifesting changes; strength and weakness, including how to manipulate the army's *qi*; appointing generals; the basis and means for waging warfare; and warfare's necessity and appropriateness. Although many of their conclusions merely expound principles and ideas first conceptualized by Sunzi, the dialogues show a wide appreciation of the entire body of classic military writings.

TAIBAI YINJING (TAIBAI YINFU)

Nothing is known about this book's author, Li Quan, except that he apparently held provincial-level military posts and was probably active for at least twenty years (roughly from 745 to 765). Thus, he must have experienced the devastating warfare that engulfed China during An Lushan's rebellion (755–763) and witnessed the subsequent erosion of Tang power. He was an astute yet thorough student of military affairs and the classic martial texts, but only the *Taibai yinjing* and his commentary on Sunzi's *Art of War* (in the *Shijiazhu* edition) survive intact. However, the *Tongdian* and other later texts adopt many chapters in their entirety, and numerous short paragraphs from his lost works are also preserved in such compilations as the *Taiping yulan*.

According to the author's prefatory remarks, dated 759, the title refers to the planet Venus (*Taibai*), which governs military affairs, and the moon (*Yin*), which is associated with attacking and slaying. The book was conceived as a subtle work discussing the ethereal and unorthodox aspects of military art rather than simplistic open-field tactics. A lengthy hundred chapters in all, its ten categorical sections of varying length constitute a veritable repository of Tang military theory and practice. Although opening with a contemplation of Heaven and Earth, it immediately emphasizes the role and necessity of human effort, without which any advantage of environment will be squandered. Still, more than any previous work, the *Taibai yinjing* is pervaded by the concepts of *yin* and *yang* and thus emphasizes the formless and the hidden, though not because Li Quan was enamored of mystical doctrine. Rather, he employs a unique vocabulary to advance a new means of conceptualizing warfare, one that emphasizes being unfathomable so as to effect unexpected victory with minimal effort and expense, in consonance with Sunzi's thought.

Although tactics are surprisingly absent, the book is similar to the *Taigong liutao* in comprehensiveness, with many chapters focusing upon important concepts and poignant sayings from the classic military writings, especially the *Art of War, Wuzi,* and *Liutao.* However, the defining theme throughout the disparate chapters is the need for flexibility, for employing unorthodox methods to wrest spatial and temporal advantages that will allow strategic power (*shi*) to overwhelm the enemy. The foundation for victorious military campaigns is a sound, virtuous national leadership that harmonizes the people and unites them in the state's enterprises. In conjunction with this, an efficient military organization with superlative command and control techniques, proven methods for motivating men, and thorough knowledge of all aspects of military science must be nurtured. Accordingly, there are extensive discussions of formations and deployments, planning, preparation (including logistics and camp measures), weapons and equipment (such as for fording rivers, and for incendiary and aquatic warfare), medical and veterinary issues, rewards and punishments, the commander's qualifications, military organization, and creating elite forces.

Even though some of them have a pastiche character, the chapters are internally consistent and reasonably well integrated. However, there is a major disjuncture between the first part of the book, comprising roughly 60 percent of the material, and the final four sections, which subsume chapters on sacrifices to such legendary martial figures as Chi You, numerous methods for prognostication, calendrical indications for auspicious days, and even techniques for physiognomizing men and horses. Insofar as the classic military writings prior to the *Taibai yinjing* largely embraced Sunzi's stress on human agency, this marks an astonishing shift. Whether these contents were amassed by Li Quan himself or simply cobbled on by later hands because of the ethereal orientation pervading the earlier chapters is unknown, but they certainly initiated a trend toward including vast amounts of such speculative material in subsequent works. Although so overwhelmingly detailed as to suggest that these methods could never have been contemplated, much less consulted, in real military contexts, these chapters provide a remarkable source for studying the principles underlying divinatory systems. Their very extensiveness also indicates that prognostication played a much greater role than previously imagined, perhaps explaining its vehement condemnation in the *Weiliaozi.*

ENCYCLOPEDIAS

The Tang dynasty also produced the first encyclopedia to include a significant military section, the famous *Comprehensive Canons* (*Tongdian*) largely compiled in the last decades of the eighth century by Du You, a scholar also known for his commentary on the *Art of War*. (Much military knowledge and thought is preserved in the various commentaries appended to the classic martial writings by such scholars and military men as Shi Zhimei, whose voluminous late-twelfth-century jottings on the *Seven Military Classics*, the first comprehensive commentary to the entire corpus, became known as "lectures.") The *Tongdian* consists of nine major sections focusing on government affairs, including one devoted to military matters that basically selects, parses up, and distributes important passages from the classic martial and historical writings under various military topics, all insightfully interspersed with Du's narrative. Thereafter, the well-known *Taiping yulan* and its companion *Taiping guangji*, both compiled under imperial sponsorship by Li Fang and others late in the tenth century, encompass selected military materials under such broad topics as "chariots" and "boats," thereby fortuitously preserving otherwise lost passages as well as illuminating textual variants and errors. Finally, the still extant portions of the enormous *Yongle Encyclopedia* (*Yongle dadian*), compiled in the first decade of the fifteenth century, contain several volumes of military writings, as does the massive *Gujin tushu jicheng* ("imperially approved synthesis of books and illustrations past and present") compiled in the early eighteenth century.

Although several other lesser-known encyclopedias also preserve materials of interest, two other compendia are devoted exclusively to military issues and affairs, the *Essentials of the Military Classics* (*Wujing zongyao*) and the *Wubeizhi*. The former was undertaken by imperial directive in 1040 when Emperor Renzong was persuaded his military officials lacked an understanding of China's classical military writings. Essentially a cut-and-paste job, it arranges passages from the classics (without identifying their origins, as was common) in every imaginable topical category. It also includes several chapters on divination and prognostication, and appends two important anonymous works of the Song period, the *Xingjun xuzhi* and the *Baizhan qifa*. A so-called continuation of the work known as the *Xu wujing zongyao* and written in the late Ming dynasty focuses largely on formations and deployments.

China's second military encyclopedia, the *Wubeizhi*, is roughly three times the size of the *Wujing zongyao*. Compiled single-handedly by Mao

Yuanyi in the second decade of the seventeenth century, it essentially drew upon all the writings extant at the end of the Ming. The material is arrayed in five comprehensive sections that focus on military writings; the evaluation of historical battles; deployments, training, control, and weapons use; operational matters for field campaigns; and finally prognostication, a section that also includes substantial chapters on riverine and open-water warfare as well as border peoples and affairs. Many early books and obscure materials, such as the *Taibai yinjing*, are preserved complete, accounting for the encyclopedia's great length.

JIXIAO XINSHU AND LIANBING SHIJI

The last great Chinese military writer was Qi Jiguang (1528–1588), who composed these two lengthy but exemplary military manuals devoted to training and the practical aspects of warfare in the Ming dynasty. Although born into a hereditary military family established six generations earlier by Qi Xiang, a noted general who had helped establish the Ming dynasty, he cultivated both civil and martial skills before entering active military service in Beijing when only seventeen. Quickly rising in rank and responsibility, he first served for several years as a northern defense commander, during which time his strict discipline and troop organization wrested important victories and deterred Mongol aggression. In addition, he passed the local military exam, thereby earning a minor place in palace discussions, and wrote his first appraisal of the contemporary military situation, complete with recommendations for repulsing the enemy.

While only twenty-four, he was posted to Zhejiang and entrusted with defeating the so-called Japanese pirates who had been entrenched for some two centuries in the coastal area (thanks to the collusion of local officals and powerful families) and preyed upon local shipping, towns, and merchants. In several battles in which he participated—including one in which he personally shot the enemy commander to turn the tide—the marauders were severely defeated. Over the years, as he became responsible for increasingly greater areas, the pirates were invariably vanquished and expelled further from the coast. After pacifying the region, he was appointed area commander for northern Hebei at the age of forty and assumed responsibility for defending the area along the Great Wall. Here he showed his ingenuity in constructing numerous watchtowers and perfecting his training methods, successfully deterring enemy aggression for a decade and a half. Ironically, the resulting lack of armed clashes, dramatically in contrast to his aggressive record in the south, led to accusations of laxity and dereliction that eventually led to his retirement and death just before his sixtieth birthday.

Qi Jiguang's fame rests less upon his impressive field achievements at a time when the Ming military was increasingly weak and hollow than upon the two books he penned to instruct soldiers in their craft. Although many of the chapters are devoted to describing essential field practices, military organization, and the proper employment of weapons (often illustrated for the first time) and always emphasize the substantial over the formal and flowery, the underlying views may be traced back to Sunzi and Wuzi. Qi believed that soldiers should be physically qualified, well trained, and tightly organized under a strict system of discipline wherein the individual squads would employ mixed weapons to engage in the critical task of slaying the enemy. (Cannon were also to be integrated into the army as a whole rather than deployed with individual units.) All forces should be capable of both offensive and defensive warfare, able to create opportunities and exploit them, identify configurations of terrain and utilize them. The people constitute the foundation, because without a stable, engaged populace, armies will lack the fervor for battle. In addition, their courage must be fostered and respect for their role sustained. Their material welfare must be sufficient and their weapons superior; only then will the army be able to bring overwhelming power to bear, just as Sunzi advocated. The component forces of chariots, cavalry, and infantry all have their appropriate roles, and are therefore mixed in the ideal combat battalion. Moreover, no doubt because of his long service in the coastal areas, Qi's books, in contrast with previous works, include considerable material on naval forces and their training. Much of the text and most of the illustrations (although often poorly redrawn, as with the spear tips dropped off, turning them into staffs) were incorporated in the *Wubeizhi*, and his books were much studied in the late Ming and Qing dynasties.

SUGGESTIONS FOR FURTHER READING

For an overview on dates and authorship, see Robin D. S. Yates, "New Light on Ancient Chinese Military Texts: Notes on Their Nature and Evolution, and the Development of Military Specialization in Warring States China," *T'oung Pao* 74 (1988): 549–603, as well as the individual introductions and notes to the translations in Ralph D. Sawyer, *Seven Military Classics of Ancient China* (Boulder, CO: Westview Press, 1993) and *Sun Pin Military Methods* (Boulder, CO: Westview Press, 1995).

Among the numerous Chinese military texts, only those found in the *Seven Military Classics* and a few others have been translated into English. Sunzi's *Art of*

War has seen many versions over the past two centuries, but the most useful are those of Samuel B. Griffith (Oxford: Oxford University Press, 1963), Ralph D. Sawyer (Boulder, CO: Westview Press, 1994), and Roger Ames (New York: Ballantine, 1993), with the first two emphasizing military history. With the exception of the *Wuzi* (included as an appendix in Griffith's *Art of War*), the only readily available English translations for the other *Seven Military Classics* are Sawyer's. *Sun Bin bingfa* may be found in two translations: D. C. Lau and Roger Ames, *Sun Pin: Art of Warfare* (New York: Ballantine, 1996), and Sawyer, *Sun Pin Military Methods*. Other translations of Chinese military writings include *One Hundred Unorthodox Strategies: Battle and Tactics of Chinese Warfare* [*Baizhan qilue*] (Boulder, CO: Westview Press, 1996) and Wang Zhen, *The Tao of Peace* [*Daodejing lunbing yaoyi*] (Boston: Shambhala, 1999), both translated by Ralph D. Sawyer; Harro von Senger, *The Book of Stratagems*, trans. Myron B. Gubitz (New York: Viking, 1991); several comic book editions of the classics; and various English-language versions of Sunzi published in the People's Republic of China that, irrespective of the writer's insights, tend to be useless for scholarly purposes.

Although vernacular (modern) Chinese versions of the various military classics, especially Sunzi's *Art of War*, proliferate, apart from the series published by the People's Liberation Army Press (Jiefangjun chubanshe) in Beijing over the last two decades—and, to a lesser extent, that published by the Commercial Press (Shangwu yinshuguan) in Taiwan—few are of any scholarly value, often eliding difficult passages or dropping them altogether. Even the PLA editions suffer in inexplicably converting all the characters of the ancient texts into simplified modern forms. Conversely, many of the ancient texts are being republished in readily accessible formats by both PRC and Taiwan presses, including the PLA's fifty-volume *Collection of Chinese Military Books* (*Zhongguo bingshu jicheng*). A number of modern Japanese scholarly editions also append useful commentaries as well as contemporary translations. Unfortunately, with the exception of Sunzi's *Art of War* and Sun Bin's *Military Methods,* most of the so-called tomb texts—lost texts recovered from ancient tombs over the past three decades—still await transcription, modern annotation, and publication.

SUGGESTIONS FOR FURTHER RESEARCH

Notwithstanding the existence of these historical texts, the fundamental questions regarding the nature and function of military thought in traditional China remain unanswered. Although military officials were often commissioned from among the pool of experienced generals or, from the Song dynasty on, successful examination candidates, normally they were civil officials constrained by a distinctly different mindset and temporarily entrusted with military responsibilities. Moreover, particularly in the earlier periods, many commanders were directly appointed from the ruler's own clan or were relatives of his consorts. However, individual schools or family traditions of military thought clearly existed, and

SEVEN

The Qing Empire

Paul Lococo Jr.

In the year 1600 the land known to us as Manchuria was nominally a part of the Ming realm. However, Ming control was tenuous, and in fact most of the land was divided into numerous small, semiautonomous territories ruled or administered by traditional clan and tribal chieftains. Nurhachi, a chieftain of the Aisin-Gioro clan, soon came to exert real authority over the land of Manchuria and then turned his energies to China. Over the next two hundred years the Manchus conquered China and established an empire in Asia the size and power of which had not been seen since the Mongol empire of the thirteenth century.

Though diplomacy, politics, and economic manipulations played their role, this empire was acquired and maintained primarily through military means. Throughout this two-hundred-year period, Manchu leaders (civil as well as military) demonstrated an ability to be flexible and adaptable with regard to military matters, in the process transforming a traditional "steppe nomadic" military force into one more professional and designed to expand and secure the Qing realm.

THE MANCHU CONQUEST OF CHINA

The Organization of the Eight Banners

The name "Manchu" was not applied to the peoples of the northeastern region of China until 1635. Before this time they were more commonly referred to as Jurchens, descendants of those who had created the Jin dynasty in northern China in the twelfth century. The Ming dynasty (1368–1644) court took special care to see that the peoples of this region were divided, and tribal chieftains were formally enrolled as part of the

Ming military system with responsibility to maintain order in the region. This system of divided, semiautonomous competing tribes worked reasonably well until the late sixteenth century, when the Ming became progressively weaker and its hold on the region less secure.

Taking advantage of the new situation, the Manchu tribes became united under a dynamic chieftain by the name of Nurhachi (1559–1626). Chinese historical sources record that Nurhachi, after suffering a harsh early life, utilized conquest, marriage alliances, trickery, and bribery to create a powerful rival to Ming China. As the tribes and peoples of Manchuria came under his control, Nurhachi created what he called the "Eight Banners," administrative divisions into which all Manchu families were placed. These were named for the different colored flags, or banners, that marked each one. Although the banners resembled new tribal divisions, they soon became the primary source for the Manchu military organization, with each banner required to raise, support, and train a certain number of troops. Henceforth, the term "Eight Banners" refers mainly to the military arm of the Manchus.

Banners were primarily administrative organizations. For actual battle, subunits of the banners, called *niru* and each composed of roughly 200 to 300 men, were gathered together under a commander chosen by the ruler. A banner commander, then, did not lead "his" banner in combat, making it difficult to launch military opposition to Nurhachi and his successors. Originally, *niru* commanders gained their position through inheritance, but by the early eighteenth century all were appointed bureaucratically.

By the early 1600s Nurhachi, with his army of disciplined warriors toughened through constant training and raiding, was able to unite all the peoples of the area into one polity. The banners that he had created formed the basis for his power, and for that of his descendants. He had created an efficient military system for carrying out his campaigns of unification and plunder, and later the campaigns of conquest.

Creation of the Chinese Banners

The Eight Banners of Nurhachi proved capable of forcibly unifying most of Manchuria. But if the Manchus intended to do more than raid China, their numbers were much too small. Beginning in the late 1620s Nurhachi's successors incorporated allied and conquered Mongol tribes into the Eight Banner system, eventually forming eight Mongol banners. Yet the most significant modification to the banner system was the formation of eight banners of Chinese, or "Han-Martial," as some call them.[1]

As time went on, raids on the regions of southern Manchuria settled by Han Chinese became more successful, and the Manchus began capturing whole Ming garrison units. Many of these garrisons were acquired as a result of military defeat, but others joined voluntarily, convinced by Manchu blandishments about restoring a "pure" China in contrast to the increasingly corrupt Ming. While the first Chinese additions to the Manchu military force were merely sprinkled into existing banners as replacements, eventually the sheer numbers of Chinese soldiers caused Manchu leaders to form them into the "Old Han Army" (*Jiu Han jun*). This force was especially useful in providing much of the infantry support the Manchus had lacked.

In 1631 a separate Chinese artillery corps was formed, artillery being one area in which the Manchus were seriously deficient. Most of the major defeats suffered by the Manchus to this time had come from Ming cannon fire. Indeed, Nurhachi died through wounds suffered as a result of Ming artillery. Already in 1637 the Qing Manchu armies had so many Chinese troops under their command that they were divided into two separate wings, and two years later the Chinese troops were organized into four banners, eventually forming eight Chinese banners in 1642.

Throughout the 1630s and 1640s, as the banner soldiers gained more combat experience, they also became more professional and bureaucratized. Banner forces were taken on numerous raids into China, as well as more organized expeditions to pacify Inner Mongolia and conquer Korea. In one important move, the Manchu rulers began to appoint a nonbanner Chinese to each banner to oversee daily administrative affairs. These civil officials reported directly to the court. In addition, changes were introduced into the booty system, rationalizing that as well and taking it one step further to a salary system. All booty was distributed by the emperor and his agents, with 30 percent retained by him for imperial affairs. Eventually, after the conquest of China, all bannermen received a set salary rather than a share of booty. These administrative and institutional changes both improved the fighting ability of the banners and centralized power more fully in the hands of the emperor and his advisors.

Overview of the Conquest of China

In 1636 Nurhachi's successor, Hong Taiji, proclaimed the establishment of the Qing dynasty, meaning "pure." With the now clearly stated aim of rulership of China, the Manchus became one more threat the Ming had to consider as it reached its final days.

The actual fall of the Ming dynasty was effected by rebel armies that had plagued the Ming since at least the 1620s. Manchu Qing armies took advantage of the situation to ally with one of the last intact Ming armies and destroy the rebel forces. While banner armies were essential to the conquest, in fact most of the fighting, especially in southern China (where the land was not quite suitable for the mainly cavalry forces of the banners), was done by allied or surrendered Ming units. Much of the south was given to the commanders of these Chinese armies as "feudatories" of the Qing. While owing nominal allegiance to the Qing court, these southern generals ruled their territories quite autonomously.

The most disciplined and effective forces in the years of the conquest were without doubt the Qing banner forces. The Manchus did not refrain from ruthlessness when they deemed it necessary, as happened in the taking of the wealthy and strategically important city of Yangzhou in southern China. The city mightily resisted the Manchu attack, decimating the attacking bannermen with withering cannon fire. Yangzhou did not fall until May 1645, and as punishment for its resistance the city was brutally sacked for ten days. Tens of thousands were slaughtered and raped, and news of this was spread as a warning to others in China who had thought to resist the Qing. However, cities, towns, and territories that accepted Qing rule were generally spared and usually had their taxes significantly reduced as well, since the Manchus strove mightily to present themselves as a Chinese dynasty restoring peace and order. This was an attitude maintained almost without interruption throughout the Qing dynasty, and it worked to gain the acceptance of the Chinese populace and educated gentry class. Basically, the Manchus ruled in as traditionally Chinese a manner as possible, resorting to brutal suppression only when the dynasty's legitimacy was resisted or its control of China appeared threatened.

The last Ming pretender to the throne was captured in 1662 by a Chinese general allied with the Manchus and immediately executed. In that same year the last armed remnants of Ming resistance fled to the island of Taiwan, where they hoped to organize a later military campaign to recover the mainland. A naval expedition led by admiral Shi Lang, a surrendered Ming loyalist who had served under the Taiwan regime, recovered Taiwan for the Qing in 1683. With this came the acquisition of the last of the Ming official seals, and the end of any serious anti-Qing resistance.

Three Feudatories Rebellion

The most serious threat faced by the Qing after their initial conquest of China came not from Ming loyalists, but from the surrendered Ming generals who had been given feudatories in return for their assistance. By far the most powerful of these generals was Wu Sangui, whose defection to the Manchus in 1644 was key to their successful destruction of the anti-Ming rebels. In 1673 Wu persuaded two of the other autonomous generals to join him in a revolt against the Qing that has been called the Three Feudatories Revolt. Massive human and material resources were required before this revolt was suppressed, but as a result the Qing court gained much tighter control of China.

In return for his early assistance to the Qing conquest Wu Sangui had been given the title of "prince" and nearly complete control over several southern provinces. Other provinces had similarly been given to two other former Ming generals, though Wu was even allowed to maintain his own private army. This army numbered over 100,000, and its maintenance was dependent on subsidies from the court in Beijing. Indeed, by the early 1670s these subsidies totalled nearly half the imperial budget. This situation not only drained the Qing court's finances, but was also a potential threat. When the emperor Kangxi decided in 1673 to end the subsidies and place the southern provinces under direct imperial administrative control, Wu revolted.

The Qing court had not been completely unprepared for revolt, and for years immediately prior to its outbreak had been quietly transferring surplus funds to the capital in preparation for this sort of emergency. Yet however prepared it felt, when Wu first raised his standard of revolt the Qing court became very nervous and began pulling its troops in to the center. The Kangxi emperor, though only nineteen years old, took firm command and provided central direction.

Throughout 1673 and 1674 Wu's forces met with an almost unending string of successes, both in defeating Qing armies and in convincing other Chinese generals to join the revolt. Especially in their southern bases, Wu's armies were experienced and benefited from their knowledge of the terrain. While the Manchu troops were scattered throughout the empire, Wu had his troops mostly concentrated. The feudatory armies in these early years were led by many competent and experienced officers. Moreover, Wu and his supporters stressed their identity as Chinese opposing the "barbarian" Manchus.

Success possibly came too fast, for in early 1675 Wu, instead of pressing his attack, worked to consolidate his newly acquired territories. Once in control of the important grain-producing province of Hunan, he even offered to allow the Qing to keep control of Manchuria and Korea if they would leave China immediately. There are also some indications that Wu was willing to allow the Qing to keep much of the north, reprising the north–south division of China of Jin–Song times.

These early successes were due almost as much to Qing failures as to rebel advantages. Banner commanders did not perform well at all. They appeared shaken by the defeats of the early months and were often gripped with indecision. Several Manchu military commanders advocated retreat to Manchuria, but even this began to seem untenable. Qing disorder and defeat led a string of Chinese generals to defect, and even some Mongol tribes rose against the Manchus, at one point threatening the original Qing capital at Mukden in Manchuria (today's Shenyang).

Survival of the Qing came about through new strategy, a focus on imperial advantages, and rebel forces that collapsed under the weight of success. A major reason for the poor performance of the banner commanders was that most of the brightest had been serving primarily in civil positions over the previous years, leaving the military under less experienced and competent commanders. Kangxi, following the counsel of his court military advisors, ruthlessly dismissed commanders and promoted those who gained combat merit.

The Qing court also drastically reduced its reliance on the Eight Banners, instead trusting huge new Chinese armies (reportedly numbering over 900,000 at their peak), usually under Manchu or Chinese banner commanders. Defections continued to threaten Qing positions at times, but a surprisingly large number of these Chinese armies remained loyal to the Qing. Meritorious and loyal Chinese commanders could expect rapid promotion, many to a level equal to the top Manchu military commanders. In fact, the main political and military story of the Three Feudatories Revolt is how few of the elite Chinese actually joined the rebellion. Qing efforts at projecting an image of Confucian rectitude, providing law and order, and generally ruling China as would be expected by Chinese had proved successful. And Wu Sangui was not a plausible leader of the Ming-restorationist cause. After all, his defection to the Qing nearly thirty years earlier had been fatal to the Ming dynasty.

At the same time, the Qing command utilized the advantages it possessed in logistics and transportation networks. Few of the breadbasket provinces under imperial control were ever under serious threat, while wealthy areas under Wu's command were in a state of almost constant fighting and disorder. Rebel armies were only nominally unified, unlike the imperial armies, and defections went both ways. The Qing court showed leniency to generals who returned to the imperial fold. Wu Sangui had to tax mercilessly to be able to minimally fund his revolt, and he often could not afford to pay his troops or equip them with such things as artillery and handguns. By contrast, the Qing commanders took great pains to ensure that their troops were not only fed, but equipped with the best weapons they could get.

The revolt was essentially over by early 1680, though several more major campaigns were needed to gain full control over the remaining rebellious provinces. As territories were recovered, the court placed civil officials in charge, and not until the second half of the nineteenth century would military commanders again be given much autonomous authority.

Organization of the Qing Military in the Eighteenth Century

Once the Three Feudatories Revolt had been crushed and Taiwan brought into the Qing realm, reforms were effected in the Qing military system. These reforms to the structure and organization of the Qing military established its essential form for almost two hundred years. The military system established by the Qing came closest to resolving the age-old Chinese concern—how to maintain an effective military force, yet insure that it could not threaten the ruling dynasty. The Qing military was successful in carrying out the imperial will, engaging in many large-scale military expeditions that added huge lands to the Qing empire. And yet, as important as the military was to the security of the empire, not until the twentieth century was the dynasty to be threatened again with military mutiny or revolt.

Bureaucratization

The Qing court learned much from its near disaster with the Three Feudatories Revolt. A trained, professional, disciplined military force was essential to the dynasty's survival. It was only after the near debacle of the Three Feudatories Revolt that the Qing military became fully transformed from its origins as a traditional steppe-nomadic type of fighting force to one much more professional, and that administration of all the various military branches of the Qing was brought under central control.

Qing military forces were divided into two major branches. First, the Eight Banners resumed their role as the main strike force of the dynasty, and a central banner office was maintained at the imperial palace. To ensure their military effectiveness, the civil functions of the Qing Eight Banners were drastically reduced. Second was what was called the Green Standard Army. Originally composed of surrendered Ming armies, this was the main force that had defeated Wu Sangui's rebels. After the rebellion, this army too was completely bureaucratized and administered by the Board of War.

At the top of the whole military apparatus, and very much in control, was the emperor. By the early eighteenth century the emperor was advised on military matters by a new office called the Grand Council. Much like a general staff, the Grand Council advised the emperor on military affairs and planned, organized, and oversaw campaigns. However, commanders of garrisons and major expeditions answered directly to the emperor, not the Grand Council. This body was advisory only, although at times individual Grand Councilors were assigned to lead expeditions.

Reorganization of the Eight Banners

The poor performance of the Eight Banners during the early years of the Three Feudatories Revolt led to major changes in the institution. The Qing leadership determined that too many bannermen had been used in civil functions, taking many of the most effective soldiers away from military duties. As Manchu control of China became more secure during the course of the Three Feudatories Revolt, banner officers were returned to their units and training and discipline emphasized. From this time it was rare that middle- or lower-ranking banner officers were used in civil functions. Some banner generals were placed in top civil positions throughout the rest of the dynasty, but often the banner designation of these officials was more social than functional. In other words, these were Manchu "generals" who only served civil functions, never leading troops in direct combat.

Militarily, by the early eighteenth century there had developed a core of competent, veteran Manchu (and some Chinese) high-ranking officers who were called on to lead military expeditions or serve as subordinate commanders or staff to the leaders of expeditions. There was constant replenishment of this key leadership group throughout the eighteenth century, with most beginning their careers as small unit leaders and rising through the ranks as they distinguished themselves in combat. Most of those who reached the very top military ranks were related to the imperial family through blood or marriage.

Membership in the banner military force was hereditary, although all officer positions were filled through appointment by the emperor. It was quite common for a banner soldier who distinguished himself in combat to be promoted to the officer ranks. There were even a few cases of these commoners rising to some of the senior banner positions.

The garrison system of the Eight Banners reflected their dual role as defenders of the dynasty's position and the main military arm of the imperial court. Over half of the banner force was placed in garrisons near the capital or in Manchuria, the Qing homeland. The rest of the banner force was posted in garrisons located in or near key cities throughout the rest of China, and at strategic points along key waterways, such as the Yangzi River and Grand Canal. To reinforce the elite nature of the bannermen and to keep them from becoming too tied to local areas, garrisons were kept in segregated walled compounds and rotated with the capital garrisons from time to time. Also, only banner officers could take their families along with them to provincial garrisons. Even in the mid-eighteenth century, however, this regulation was often ignored.

Over time the banners underwent significant internal changes as well. As the number of bannermen swelled due to population increase, many Chinese and Mongol banner units were reclassified as civilians or placed in the Green Standard Army. So while in 1700 a majority of bannermen were Chinese, by 1800 the large majority were Manchu. Also, the banners reflected the changing nature of warfare. Originally an almost all-cavalry force, by the mid–1700s the large majority of bannermen were infantrymen equipped with firearms. Most banner cavalry units were maintained in Manchuria or the capital region. Also, the Mongol banners by this time were almost solely cavalry units.

Green Standard Army

During the later years of the campaigns to defeat the Three Feudatories, the Qing court came to rely increasingly on Chinese units, called the Green Standard Army. This military force, which numbered over 600,000 during most of the eighteenth century, had by 1700 come to serve primarily as a constabulary force, designed to maintain local law and order and quell small-scale disturbances, but also contributing the bulk of forces dispatched in major campaigns. The Green Standard Army was extremely fragmented, with literally thousands of large and small outposts throughout the empire, many with as few as twelve men. During peacetime it was rare for one officer to command more than 5,000 men.

The Board of War, based in the Imperial City and directly under the control of the emperor, administered the Green Standard Army. The board did not have operational control over the soldiers of the Green Standard Army, even those few posted to the capital region, but it dealt with issues such as recruitment, pay and provisions, promotion, and rewards and punishment.

Operational control of the Green Standard Army was on the surface very complicated. There was no general-in-chief based at the capital, and in fact no officer higher than the provincial commander-in-chief (*tidu*). Provincial garrison units involved in operations outside their province came under the control of the emperor and any officials he had designated, rather than the provincial commander-in-chief. However, even within a province the provincial commander-in-chief, nominally responsible for all Green Standard troops in the province, had direct control of no more than 5,000 men. Provincial governors had their own contingents of about 5,000 men, and several other garrisons were commanded by officers who answered directly to the governor-general (an official above the governor who normally oversaw two or more provinces). Most of the rest of the provincial Green Standard force answered to one of several brigade generals scattered throughout the province. These brigade generals usually had both administrative and operational control over their men, but only within strictly defined territories. The provincial *tidu* had command authority over most of the brigade generals, except those commanding garrisons located at strategic spots, such as along the Grand Canal or next to major port cities (such as Shanghai or Guangzhou). The *tidu* also had the right to engage in direct communications with the emperor and the Grand Council.

Strictly speaking, the Green Standard Army was not a hereditary force, although the dynasty directed its recruiting efforts primarily at sons and other relatives of serving soldiers. Enlistment was considered a lifetime occupation, but it was generally very simple to be reclassified as a civilian. During emergencies (usually in regions engaged in ongoing combat operations) conscription might be resorted to, but the Qing preferred to utilize local militia forces to augment its regulars. Militiamen—and sometimes whole militia units—who had distinguished themselves in combat were often incorporated into the regular Green Standard Army.

Green Standard officer ranks were filled in three main ways: (1) from the Eight Banners (officers who, although serving in the Green Standard Army, received pay and evaluations through the banner office), (2) through promotion from the ranks after a soldier had distinguished himself in battle (though this was much more common within the banners than in the Green Standard Army), and (3) by means of the military examination system. The military examinations had much less prestige than the civil service examinations, and were considered much less rigorous.

Examinees were evaluated on their knowledge of the traditional Chinese military classics (especially Sunzi's *Art of War*), as well as tests of physical strength and endurance: horseback riding, archery, and lifting heavy rocks. Surprisingly, there was no test of handgun marksmanship, despite the fact that the Green Standard Army relied heavily on firearms by 1700. The obsolete nature of the military examination did not come under serious criticism until well into the nineteenth century, after defeats at the hands of the European powers.

There was also a small Green Standard Army naval component, but this was never large and was designed mainly to suppress pirates. There were numerous patrol craft armed with small cannons, and combatants were all regular Green Standard soldiers. This force was fairly effective in keeping the peace along the main waterways, but very poor at coastal security. Faced with large pirate gangs, the court often preferred to incorporate the pirates into the Qing navy rather than fight them. The pitiful state of the Qing navy can be attributed to the fact that from the conquest of Taiwan in 1683 until the mid-nineteenth century, China was not faced with any serious threats from the sea.

Except for some of the elite Manchu cavalry forces, who relied primarily on mounted archery, almost all of the bannermen and Green Standard Army soldiers were armed with matchlocks. Each major garrison produced its own weapons, although there were also some large production facilities in the capital. The matchlock remained essentially unchanged for nearly two hundred years, but until serious confrontation with Western powers in the nineteenth century it was still at least equal, and often superior, to the weapons possessed by the Qing's adversaries.

CAMPAIGNS OF THE QING IN THE EIGHTEENTH CENTURY

The dispersed nature of the Qing military provided a useful local constabulary force and, coupled with the meticulous control of military leadership, made it difficult for any commander to rebel against the dynasty. The Qing military system was effective at preserving the dynasty's position of power, providing for local security and allowing for several large-scale, complex military campaigns during the eighteenth century. The major expeditions of the dynasty for the most part took place far from the center of Qing power and resources, necessitating a patient buildup of men and materiel. The preparations for these major expeditions were governed by very clear regulations that were based on experience from the Kangxi reign period.

The system of military fragmentation and control was originally designed to prevent the possibility of Qing military forces being utilized against the dynasty. Thus, the decision to engage in a major military operation had to come from the emperor himself. Once a determination had been made to launch an expedition, the emperor appointed a special imperial commissioner as commander, with broad powers over both the administration and the conduct of the campaign. Almost all of those appointed as imperial commissioner were Manchus or Chinese bannermen. There were occasions when a Green Standard officer who had previously distinguished himself in combat leadership was appointed imperial commissioner. The most famous of these was Yue Zhongqi (a descendant of the great Song general Yue Fei), who led a major expedition into western Sichuan in the 1740s. Once an imperial commissioner had been appointed, usually in a personal ceremony before the emperor, the Grand Council then sent detailed orders to the appropriate military and civil officials to prepare troops, horses, supplies, and fodder. All of this was carried out only after the emperor had personally signed off on all the orders.

The eighteenth-century emperors, especially Qianlong (r. 1735–1796), were fortunate in having at hand several high-level military officials who had had extensive prior experience in military command. During peacetime these generals rarely had command over more than a few thousand troops. They served instead as high civil officials, their appointments considered as part of their reward for leading victorious military expeditions. Civil offices brought material rewards as well as prestige, since holding the position of governor of a province could make one quite wealthy through the bribery and graft that was a normal part of civil government in the Qing.

The emperor, Grand Council, and imperial commissioner organized the campaigns, creating a staff for the imperial commissioner to manage logistics, intelligence, and actual operations in the field. Great care was taken in assigning men to this staff, as well as to subordinate positions. Normally, veteran officers were chosen, and they usually brought along many soldiers who had fought with them on previous campaigns.

Through experience and regulation the Qing military were able to manage numerous expeditions that required the organization and transport of enormous quantities of supplies. The wealth of China in this era meant that the demands of these military operations had only a minor impact on the economy of the empire. Not until the very last years of the eighteenth century (during efforts to suppress the White Lotus Rebellion) did total military expenses (both for garrison forces and to finance major campaigns) take up more than about 25 percent of the imperial budget. This shift in resources had more to do with corruption than with any new financial demands from the military. The impact of military financing on China's economy and the Qing budget compares quite favorably, in fact, with eighteenth-century European states. The ability to effectively mobilize the available resources gave the Qing almost insurmountable advantages over their opponents. None of the enemies confronted by the Qing could come close to possessing the resources necessary to challenge Chinese dominance.

China in the eighteenth century was almost certainly more secure in its borders for a longer period than it had been at any previous time in its history. It was a very peaceful and prosperous land, a center of world trade exporting vast quantities of both agricultural and industrial (primarily handicraft) goods. A major reason for this security was the dynasty's constant attention to containing any military disturbances along its extensive frontiers. The Qing court was aware that failure to quell disruptions on its borders could lead to major military threats. Qing leaders understood, in particular, the importance of maintaining the security of their Inner Asian frontiers; after all, the Manchus were themselves from this region. Hence, complete domination of the Mongols was a major goal of early Qing rulers. In addition, several military campaigns were launched to subjugate Tibet and the western regions of Sichuan, and to force Burma, Nepal, and Vietnam to accept or resume tributary relationships with China.

Subduing the Zunghar Mongols

The lands called Zungharia are located in western Mongolia and part of present-day Xinjiang. The Zunghars, a tribe of Mongols, first took advantage of the Ming dynasty's chaos, and later the Qing dynasty's preoccupation with Wu Sangui's rebellion. Zunghar leaders expanded and consolidated the territory under their control. By the late seventeenth century the Zunghars had constructed a capital city and the beginnings of a bureaucratically administered state system. And they continued to be very expansionary, threatening not only the Qing realm but neighboring Mongol tribes and Tibet as well.

The Manchu Qing conflict with the Zunghars for domination of the region was the beginning of what became a series of campaigns over several decades. It originated during the reign of the Kangxi emperor and culminated with the final subjugation of the Zunghars during the reign of the Qianlong emperor in 1759. Thus was much of Inner Asia brought under control, finally ending the many-centuries-long conflict between China and its northern neighbors.

During the first armed struggles in the late seventeenth century, the Manchus met with, at best, stalemate. They relied on cannon to decimate the Zunghar cavalry, but the Zunghar leader sheltered his forces behind camels armored with thick layers of felt, which seems to have limited the damage to his men. Finally, in 1696 Kangxi personally led a Qing force that was aided by disaffected Mongols and, at Jao Modo, scored what was thought to be a decisive defeat of the Zunghars.

After this victory, the Manchus did not occupy the recently acquired lands of Mongolia but used allied Mongol tribes to patrol the border. Over the next few decades the Zunghars resumed their threats to Qing interests, attacking Tibet and several Qing outposts near their territory. The dynasty could not rest easy until the Zunghars had been fully pacified. Not only was there fear of a major Mongol empire on their borders (an empire that might include Tibet as well as the Mongol lands), but also concern that the Zunghars might form some sort of alliance with Russia, which was then sniffing around the area.

A major Qing offensive force was destroyed in 1730 during the emperor Yongzheng's reign (1723–1735), and this alarmed the court even more as the Zunghars streamed into the Qing's northern territories. In response, the Yongzheng court withdrew from the region and bolstered its garrisons along the border. Essentially conceding Zunghar dominance of the northern regions, the Qing action was reminiscent of Ming defensive strategy in the fifteenth and sixteenth centuries. The Qing court also allowed extensive trade relations, which often were a face-saving means of presenting tribute to the Zunghar khan.

Mongol internal conflicts in the 1740s reduced the threat to the Qing empire. Then, in the mid–1750s, the Qianlong court took advantage of the confused situation to the north to launch another series of major military campaigns. With a force predominantly composed of bannermen and Mongols, Qing commanders met success quickly and too easily. In fact, the Zunghars had withdrawn and regrouped many of their fighters, and swiftly retook many of the lands recently lost to the Qing. Several more expeditions were needed before the Zunghars were completely defeated.

The early phases of the war were fought on the Qing side by Manchu bannermen utilizing traditional mounted archery, supported by Chinese banner artillery. When the cavalry was able to hold the Mongols long enough for the artillery to arrive, the results were devastating. With their mobility neutralized, the Zunghars suffered terrible casualties. In the later phases of the war, the Qing organized enormous expeditions in which banner cavalry and artillery were supported by tens of thousands of Green Standard infantry. At one point the Qing general Zhaohui and his vanguard fell into an ambush. Expert generalship and a disciplined force that did not collapse under pressure allowed the Qing army to hold on until reinforcements arrived.

The Zunghars found that they could score only small victories over isolated units, and increasing numbers of their subordinate tribes were defecting to the Qing. The Zunghars had created a typical Inner Asian "empire," which was in reality more like a confederation. Unity depended on the ability of the khan to reward his followers, through either spoils acquired in military action or tribute. As the Qing took increasing control over the Zunghars' resource base and defeated the main Zunghar armies, many tribes found it easy to leave the khan and accept Qing tributary status.

After a smallpox epidemic wiped out almost half the Zunghar population, Manchu success was assured. By 1759 Qing armies succeeded in destroying the last Zunghar resistance. As punishment for their spirited opposition, Qianlong ordered the remaining Zunghar population exterminated.

Wars along the Other Frontiers

Ending China's many-centuries-long competition with the Mongols was probably the most striking achievement of Qing arms, but Chinese armies were also engaged in many other military endeavors during the seventeenth and eighteenth centuries. Two of these campaigns in particular illustrate the ability of the Manchu dynasty to mobilize vast numbers of men, often combat veterans, supply them through a complex logistical system that tapped the wealth of the whole empire, and engage in major combat in a variety of often hostile terrains. The campaigns in Jinchuan (western Sichuan) required Qing armies to fight in mountainous lands, while the campaigns in Burma were fought in mostly jungle territory.

THE BURMA WAR (1764–1770).   Burma had had a checkered relationship with China ever since the Mongol conquests in the thirteenth century. From Ming times the Burmese had maintained a tributary relationship with China, though they were not as close, either politically or culturally, as Korea or Vietnam. The Burmese usually sought to keep at least a peaceful relationship in order to facilitate trade, which was a very important indicator of Burmese internal stability. When new Chinese emperors ascended the throne, the Burmese would usually send a tributary envoy.

In the 1760s, however, a more aggressive Burmese king began to encroach on Qing border regions, prompting the Qianlong emperor to order the dispatch of troops. The early years of the war saw a common pattern. Large Qing armies met with an early string of successes, forcing the Burmese to retreat, then became bogged down in the Burmese jungles. The regrouped and resupplied Burmese armies then pushed the Qing forces back. Qing military depredations—including the slaughter of the men and distribution of the women as spoils of war—created a great deal of animosity toward the imperial forces among both the Burmese and native peoples.

The later years of the war saw a different pattern: Ever larger Qing armies penetrated deep into Burmese territory only to succumb to disease. Severely weakened, the imperial armies withdrew, to be harassed by the Burmese. From 1778 until the end of the war Qing armies consisted of much better commanders leading disciplined troops, including over 40,000 bannermen from Manchuria. Most of the regional chieftains eventually returned to the Qing and supplied fighters and logistical support to Qing forces. By 1770 the Burmese were exhausted and the kingdom was on the verge of collapse into civil war. Interestingly, they had purchased several thousand flintlock muskets from the French, but these were not enough to compensate for Chinese numbers. When the Burmese offered to return to their earlier tributary status, Qianlong agreed. The small regional chieftains of southern Yunnan, however, lost most of their autonomy and were much more closely integrated into the Qing administrative structure.

THE JINCHUAN WARS (1747–1749, 1770–1776).   Throughout the early decades of the Qing dynasty the western regions of the province of Sichuan were, like southern Yunnan, autonomous lands of native non-Chinese peoples ruled by hereditary chieftains. The Qing court did not attempt to rule this mountainous and mostly sparsely populated land directly, instead posting a few small military garrisons to ensure that the local chieftains did not unite to oppose Qing sovereignty. Conflict, however, was seemingly endemic to the region and the chieftains were often involved in armed struggles with each other. The Qing government did not get involved unless the fighting threatened to expand, and then it served as a sort of "honest broker," which usually resulted in tying the chieftains even more securely to the Qing.

In early 1747 one of the local chieftains began forcibly incorporating his neighbors and openly challenged the Qing for control of the region. The first Qing efforts to recover the land met with embarrassing defeat. The mountainous region reduced the advantage of numbers possessed by the Chinese armies, and the defenders built hundreds of small and large stone towers and fortresses. Taking these towers was very costly and time consuming, but bypassing them left Qing supply lines and rear-area troops vulnerable to assault.

Concerned that defeat would inflame all the non-Chinese peoples of the western frontiers, the emperor Qianlong determined to mount a major expedition. Over 200,000 troops armed with vast quantities of firearms, artillery, and supplies invaded the region in mid–1748. Seeing their position slowly but surely crumbling, the local chieftains sued for peace. Rather than continue the very costly process of subjugation, Qianlong agreed to a negotiated peace.

The Second Jinchuan War was sparked by moves toward unification of the region by one of the major chieftains. He claimed to be no threat to the Qing, saying that he was merely responding to a personal insult. Qing garrisons were attacked, so the chieftain said, only because they got in the way. He justified himself to the Qianlong emperor by stressing that "previously, I had never thought to act incorrectly in the lands of your imperial majesty. But I need revenge to settle my spirit."[2]

Qing expeditionary armies ran into immediate problems similar to those faced in the first war: too few troops and too little artillery to tackle the myriad stone towers and fortresses of their opponents. And the Jinchuan defenders had learned how to utilize logs and packed earth to resist the cannon fire that had proved so effective before. Qing armies became bogged down, suffering enormous casualties.

Until late 1774 any successes the imperial forces had were at great cost. Thousands were needed to take each stone tower, while Qing supply lines were constantly threatened. In mid–1773 a major Qing army was cut off and ambushed. Out of an initial force of 16,000, fewer than 500 managed to get back to Qing lines. At this point the Jinchuan leaders offered to negotiate, but Qianlong demanded surrender.

The final campaigns saw the mobilization of over 200,000 men, including 10,000 bannermen from Manchuria. Most of the soldiers were used to protect communication lines. Also, newer, much-larger cannons were constructed on the spot under the supervision of European Jesuit cannon makers. Jinchuan supply lines were constantly harassed by small units of highly mobile bannermen, and Jinchuan forces were prevented from uniting more than a few thousand men at any one place. As the towers, stockades, and forts were methodically taken and destroyed, increasing numbers of Jinchuan commanders surrendered or defected to the Qing. In early 1776 the chief leader of the Jinchuan forces was captured, paraded through the streets of Beijing, and later executed

CONCLUSIONS

From their beginnings in the early seventeenth century as a fairly good example of a traditional Inner Asian military force emphasizing mounted archery, the armies of the Manchus were transformed into a much more professional force designed to serve the interests of a centrally administered empire. This transformation was deliberate and often based on hard-learned experience. By the early eighteenth century the Qing dynasty had at hand a large, well-equipped, experienced military force that maintained internal security and engaged in several large-scale expeditions to expand the frontiers of the Qing realm. It was not until the very nature of the threats changed in the nineteenth century that the security of the Qing empire was seriously threatened.

SUGGESTIONS FOR FURTHER READING

A good start on the subject that examines in general terms the traditional relations between China and its Inner Asian neighbors is Thomas J. Barfield, *The Perilous Frontier: Nomadic Empires and China, 221 BC to AD 1757* (Oxford: Basil Blackwell, 1989). Although it covers much of the late Qing as well, Pamela Kyle Crossley, *Orphan Warriors: Three Manchu Generations and the End of the Qing World* (Princeton: Princeton University Press, 1990) provides a wealth of information focusing on the Manchu bannermen and their relations with the larger Han Chinese population. The most complete discussion of the formation of the early Manchu military and the Manchu conquest of China is in Frederic Wakeman Jr., *The Great Enterprise: The Manchu Reconstruction of Imperial Order in Seventeenth-Century China*, 2 vols. (Berkeley and Los Angeles: University of California Press, 1985). For the early Qing's management of military affairs, especially the Three Feudatories Rebellion and early armed contests with the Mongols, look at Lawrence D. Kessler, *K'ang-hsi and the Consolidation of Ch'ing Rule, 1661–1684* (Chicago: University of Chicago Press, 1976). While examining Qing–Mongol–Russian relations primarily from a Russian viewpoint, Fred W. Bergholz, *The Partition of the Steppe: The Struggle of the Russians, Manchus, and the Zunghar Mongols for Empire in Central Asia, 1619–1758: A Study in Power Politics* (New York: Peter Lang, 1993) still provides a good deal of detail on the military competition with and for Mongolia. Finally, for an excellent, very detailed study of an eighteenth-century rebellion and especially the military efforts to suppress it, see Susan Naquin, *Shantung Rebellion: The Wang Lun Uprising of 1774* (New Haven: Yale University Press, 1981).

SUGGESTIONS FOR FURTHER RESEARCH

There are many areas of early and mid-Qing military history that need to be more fully explored, especially since the opening of the various Qing archives in China has made literally millions of documents available for research. Campaign histories in English are almost completely lacking, surprising since all major (and some minor) military expeditions were written up in detailed accounts by the Qing Grand Council. Descriptions of military life, in both war and peace, are also wanting, especially with regard to the rank and file. And there is much more to be done examining specific garrisons and their actions in war and peace.

NOTES

1. See Pamela Kyle Crossley, *Orphan Warriors: Three Manchu Generations and the End of the Qing World* (Princeton: Princeton University Press, 1990).
2. Zhuang Jifa, *Qing Gaozong shiquan wugong yanjiu* [The Ten Great Campaigns of Qing Gaozong] (Taipei: National Palace Museum, 1982), 132.

EIGHT

The Taiping Rebellion: A Military Assessment of Revolution and Counterrevolution

Maochun Yu

Rarely in the course of human history do we see a mighty empire decline so precipitously and helplessly as the Qing dynasty (1644–1912) of China. This dramatic decline manifested itself most poignantly in the mid-nineteenth century through a number of devastating popular uprisings all over the country, severely shaking the foundation of Manchu rule over this vast nation. In the southwest, the ethnic Miao rebelled in Guizhou province, and the Hui Muslims took up arms against the government in Yunnan from 1855 to 1873, establishing a small but violently defiant peasant government at Dali. In the north and northwest, Muslims in Shanxi, Gansu, Ningxia, and Qinghai also rose up to rebel against the dynasty in 1862. The rebellion spread to Xinjiang, where it was not put down until 1877. The fire of destruction sprang up not just in the border regions, but also in the heartland of China. In Shandong, Henan, and Anhui provinces, the Nian uprising (1851–1868) presented a powerful blow to the confidence and structure of the government. Of all these tremendous popular rebellions, however, none matches the scale, intensity, and level of destruction of the Taiping Rebellion (1850–1864).

Even when placed in global perspective, China's Taiping Rebellion, which resulted in the death of at least 25 million people, is the most destructive civil war in history. When compared with the other bloody civil war that was unfolding almost at the same time in the United States, where a little over 600,000 lives were lost, the Taiping Rebellion is staggeringly immense in its devastation. This chapter attempts to elucidate only the main strands of the military side of the Taiping Rebellion.

THE COURSE OF THE WAR

To call the Taiping Rebellion a war is to render justice to what really transpired in China during those years. "Rebellion" often implies a sense of transiency, ephemeral significance, and failure. Yet the Taiping rebellion lasted fifteen years. It involved troop movements of tens of thousands at an unprecedented frequency and the massive mobilization of land and naval forces on an unprecedented scale. It was fought in eighteen of China's provinces. Undoubtedly, the Taiping Rebellion was the largest peasant war in China's long history.

The rebellion was led by a small group of visionary peasant rebels, the chief of whom was a man named Hong Xiuquan. Hong belonged to the Hakka minority of south China, a people who had migrated from north China centuries before. Although ethnically Han Chinese, the Hakkas spoke a dialect distinct from those of the native southerners. Often meeting with hostility and discrimination, they maintained a strong sense of identity and tended to dwell in their own separate communities. Hong followed the traditional career path in his youth by diligently preparing for the imperial examinations. Four times he traveled from his home village in Guangdong province to the southern metropolis of Canton (Guangzhou) to take the exam, and four times he failed. Amid enormous anguish and frustration, Hong encountered Protestant missionaries in Guangzhou; their proselytizing literature would provide him with a powerful Christian vision as the ideological basis of the Taiping Rebellion. With his hopes of pursuing a position as a scholar-official dashed, Hong started to organize rebellious forces in neighboring Guangxi province, where years of arduous preaching and secret recruiting among the Hakka communities resulted in a major eruption in 1850, the year that marked the beginning of the momentous Taiping Rebellion.

The armed revolt against the Qing government began on Hong Xiuquan's thirty-seventh birthday, January 11, 1850. At a gigantic birthday feast in Jintian village, Guangxi, Hong virtually declared war against the Qing dynasty in front of tens of thousands of his followers. Immediately Hong and his Taiping rebels started to seize nearby county governments, mobilizing new recruits along the way, and rapidly became a nightmare for the ruling regime.

Key to the swift success of the Taiping armed rebellion was the command structure at its highest level. On top of the military echelon was of course Hong Xiuquan himself, who was called the "Heavenly King" (*tian wang*). Second in command was the "Eastern King," Yang Xiuqing, a former coal miner and the most brilliant military commander of the Taiping forces. Following Hong and Yang were four other "kings," with equal command power. The stunning cohesiveness of this supreme command is without a doubt the most important factor contributing to the impressive military victories of the Taipings in the early stages of their revolt. As time went by, the tragic erosion of this cohesiveness and the internecine power struggle among the six supreme commanders laid the foundation for the ultimate demise of the Taiping uprising.

The fundamental difference between the Taiping rebels and most other peasant uprisings in Chinese history lies in the unique vision of their leaders. The Taipings were by and large inspired by prototypical Christian ideas, dedicated to eradicating "demons" and "Confucianists." Theirs was an ecumenical vision with a long-range strategy that aimed to create a brand-new "world order" for "the new times." It was just such a vision that propelled the rebels to launch a widespread, large-scale assault on the government forces over a vast region of China. They were seldom concerned only with local campaigns. To them, every military campaign served the cosmic purpose of creating a new world order. Within a couple of years, the Taipings moved triumphantly from the back country of Guangxi province to central China, taking Quanzhou, Daozhou, Yuezhou, Hanyang, Hankou, and Wuchang. By the end of 1852, the Taipings had developed an army of over 200,000 troops. In April 1852, the Taiping high command met in Daozhou to map out a grand strategy. It was decided that instead of going straight to Beijing, the Taipings would aim to capture Nanjing toward the mouth of the Yangzi River.

The response from counterinsurgency forces on the government side was miserably ineffectual. To begin with, the Qing troops were not prepared to deal with rebellions of this size and ferocity. Yet the strategic miscalculation on the part of the court that the Taipings were local by nature and therefore best left to be dealt with by local magistrates created a magnificent opportunity for the rebels to charge forward without being seriously impeded. At the beginning of 1853, the forces of the Qing were heavily deployed in the provinces of Henan and Zhili in north-central China, a clear indication that the government had no clue about the Taipings' strategy of striking east first. In early February 1853, Hong Xiuquan led an army of over 100,000 eastward down the Yangzi River, assisted by an armada of over 10,000 water craft of different sizes. The rebels cut through feeble opposition at various cities along the way. A month later, they arrived at the outskirts of the city of Nanjing. Days of intense fighting finally broke the defenses, and the rebels established Nanjing as the capital of a new political regime with Hong Xiuquan at its head.

Shaken by the stunning defeats of its forces, the court in Beijing settled on a strategy to sandwich the new Nanjing regime. The plan called for the setting up of two massive army groups, the Southern Front and the Northern Front, that would presumably squeeze Nanjing in the middle. To counter this formidable challenge, the Taiping rebels responded by launching two major campaigns simultaneously to relieve the pressure. The first was the Northern Expedition, which aimed to capture the imperial capital of Beijing. The second was the Western Expedition to wipe out the enemy forces in the central provinces and divert the troops besieging Nanjing. The Northern Expedition got under way soon after the rebels settled down in Nanjing. In May 1853, Lin Fengxiang, Li Kaifang, and Jie Wenyuan of the Taiping cause led more than 20,000 elite soldiers northward, only to be stopped by the mighty Yellow River in Henan province where all the boats along the river had been destroyed by the local magistrates. Undeterred, the rebels moved westward along the south bank of the river in search of a ferry route, which they succeeded in locating several hundred miles further west. After crossing to the north bank, the Taiping rebels penetrated into the Beijing area, capturing Baoding and reaching the outskirts of the capital. There a critical mistake was made. Instead of directly storming into Beijing, a move which could have succeeded, the rebels roamed outside and moved toward the nearby metropolis of Tianjin, thus allowing the government forces to regroup after their initial panic and to organize effective counterattacks. The imperial forces broke the dikes of the Grand Canal to flood the rebel positions. Shortages of provisions, severe weather, and tactical blunders finally rendered the two-year-old Northern Expedition a total disaster, with virtually all the Taiping soldiers and commanders committed to the campaign killed by the government forces.

The Western Expedition fared slightly better. The rebels moved swiftly to capture such strategic choke points as Anqing, Pengze, Hukou, and Jiujiang. While fighting in Hunan, the Taiping encountered their nemesis in Zeng Guofan, whose Hunan Army would be the ultimate victor over the Taipings in 1864. But during the Western Expedition the Taipings beat Zeng Guofan hands down, propelling him to make two suicide attempts in the face of the agony and humiliation of defeat. Unfortunately for the rebels, they were abruptly called back to reinforce the besieged city of Nanjing at the very point that their offensive was succeeding. This effectively ended the Western Expedition in March 1856.

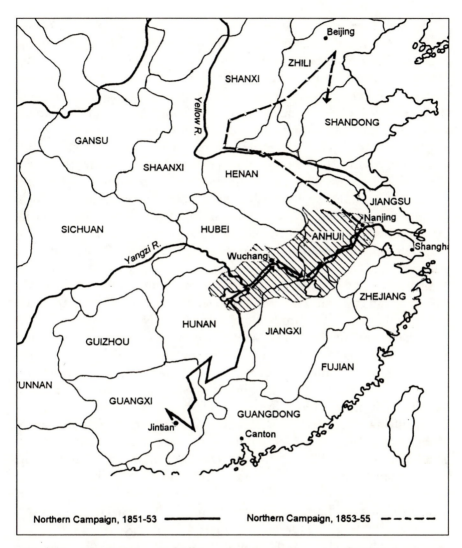

Map 8.1   The Taiping Rebellion, showing main area of Taiping control in 1854. Adapted by Don Graff based upon *The Taiping Rebellion: History and Documents,* vol. 1: *History,* Franz Michael (Seattle: University of Washington Press, 1966), map 15.

The year 1856 marks a watershed in the military development of the Taiping Rebellion. A major implosion took place within the Taiping regime. Hong Xiuquan, the Heavenly King of the Taiping Tianguo (Heavenly Kingdom of the Grand Harmony), was believed to be the real younger brother of Jesus Christ. That grand stature gave him enormous power over his followers. But he was not the only prophet in the Taiping camp. Back in 1850, when Hong was temporarily absent from the Taiping base in Guangxi, the Taiping followers began to lose faith in the cause, and trouble started to brew. In a desperate effort to save the situation, Yang Xiuqing, Hong's second-in-command, announced to the world that he could speak on behalf of "God the Father" (*tian fu*). Yang's stunning announcement secured the unity of the Taiping followers in Hong's temporary absence, but it also created a practical problem. Hong Xiuquan himself was only the younger brother of Jesus Christ, but Yang had made people believe that he himself could now enunciate the will of the father of Jesus Christ. Thus, Yang's words would in theory be more powerful and command more respect than than those of Hong. Yet since Hong's presence as the brother of Jesus was daily and constant, while Yang could only receive "edicts" and instructions from God during temporary trances, Hong acquiesced in the arrangement. The bizarre result was that Yang announced frequently that he was receiving instructions from God so as to restrain Hong and punish him for not having given Yang himself more prestige in the Taiping hierarchy. Hong had to publicly confess his "crimes." This, of course, became terribly humiliating to Hong, and in 1856 he carried out a bloody coup. Wei Changhui, one of Hong's five kings and Yang Xiuqing's rival, received the order from Hong to carry out the murderous coup in which Yang, his entire family, and several thousands of his security forces were mercilessly liquidated. Wei's hideous killings of the Taiping comrades naturally evoked disgust among the rank and file. Facing pressure from below, Hong Xiuquan eventually pointed the finger at Wei and had him executed. By the end of the year, of the half dozen veteran Taiping leaders, only Hong and an ambitiously independent king named Shi Dakai remained alive. But the implosion had so disturbed Shi that in 1857 he led tens of thousands of the Taiping troops to flee Hong and Nanjing, moving westward to the mountainous area of Sichuan. There he was captured and executed by government forces in June 1863.

Facing increasingly alarming signs of military crisis, Hong Xiuquan decided to promote a new military high command. Another half dozen or so of the young commanders, most in their twenties and thirties, were elevated to the highest military posts. Among them were Chen Yucheng, Li Xiucheng, Li Shixian, and Meng De'en. These young commanders proved to be among the most brilliant military strategists and tacticians in modern Chinese history. Starting in 1856, they led huge peasant armies to break the siege of Nanjing, the Heavenly Capital of the Taiping regime. By 1858 the two major Qing army groups designed to sandwich Nanjing, the Northern Front and the Southern Front, had met serious challenges. Led by the twenty-three-year-old prodigy Chen Yucheng, the Taiping soldiers effectively demolished the Northern Front by the end of 1858, thus greatly relieving the pressure on Nanjing. In May 1859, the Southern Front was also destroyed by Taiping troops after a superb game of deception and joint operations.

Yet the days of the Taiping were numbered, despite the many impressive military victories they had scored against government forces by the end of 1859. What the Taipings had thus far fought against were mainly the imperial armies of the Eight Banners and the Green Standards, which were notorious for their incompetence and corruption. After the Northern Front and the Southern Front were beaten by the Taipings, the Qing court was forced to place the fate of the empire into the hands of newly formed militia armies led by examination degree-holders and local elites (gentry). The most important of these forces was the Hunan Army led by the scholar-general Zeng Guofan. Zeng was appointed military governor of the Jiangsu and Jiangxi area in the wake of the demolition of the Southern Front in 1859. The Taipings were no match for Zeng, who combined brilliant military strategy with unique methods of training and leadership. Due to increasing friction between the Taipings and the Western powers in the coastal areas, Zeng was able to enlist the help of foreigners in Shanghai and other treaty ports to harass the rebels. The first important victory came to Zeng when he outmaneuvered the Taipings and captured the key city of Anqing in September 1861, which left the vast upstream flank of Nanjing extremely vulnerable to attack. In February 1862, Zeng Guofan launched his final campaign against Nanjing. It lasted over two years, with many bloody battles and troop movements on an epic scale. As the noose tightened around Nanjing, Hong Xiuquan died suddenly of illness on June 1, 1864, leaving his sixteen-year-old son as the new head of the Taiping regime. Fifty days later, on July 19, 1864, Zeng Guofan's artillery barrage finally destroyed a major section of the city wall. The government forces flooded into the city and, amid scenes of slaughter, all of the major Taiping leaders were captured and executed. The fifteen-year ordeal of the Qing dynasty was finally over.

THE MILITARY DIMENSION OF THE TAIPING MOVEMENT

The Taiping Rebellion was simultaneously a military movement and a social revolution. As a military movement, the Taipings closely tied their religious fanaticism to troop organization and command. This religious ferment greatly enhanced the cohesiveness and unity of the Taiping troops and created a strong sense of purpose while fighting the "demons" represented by the Qing court and its armed forces. It is the single most important factor behind the great Taiping victories in the early years of the war. As the Taipings began to settle in the lower Yangzi River area, however, life became more comfortable. The religious ardor was gradually replaced by lax discipline and a taste for secular pleasures, which contributed greatly to the ultimate demise of the cause.

Yet thoughout the war the Taipings posed a formidable military threat to the court. In fact, the rebels consistently routed the government forces. Even as late as 1862, the Taiping generals were able to defeat enemy forces twice the size of their own armies. Looking closely at the strategies and forces of the Taipings, we discover a system unique in the history of Chinese peasant rebellions.

First of all, the Taipings placed civic virtue and puritanical discipline at the top of their military indoctrination. The "Taiping Rules and Regulations" (*Taiping tiao gui*), the military training manual of the movement, specifically stipulated that all Taiping soldiers were expected to "obey the heavenly regulations" and "cultivate good morals"; they were not to smoke tobacco or drink wine.[1] The same manual assigned men and women to separate military units and strictly prohibited sexual relations. Looting was not permitted, which made the Taipings popular in territories beyond their original home base in Guangxi. Strict regulations required harsh punishments for violators; the most common punishment was beheading.

What did this extreme, puritanical austerity mean for the military effectiveness of the Taipings? Of all the important ramifications, nothing stands out so much as the extreme flexibility and agility of the Taipings' troop movements. As a Taiping company commander explained to a French officer at the time, "The days of distress followed the days of opulence and we found it all quite natural. It was just that which made us superior to the imperial troops. When they camp, they need big installations. They have to have fortifications, tents, and so on. We went straight on. If there were houses we stayed there, if not, we slept under the stars."[2]

The second unique feature of the Taiping military organization was its utilization of women soldiers in combat units. Since all men and women were regarded as brothers and sisters under God, no one was supposed to face discrimination because of their sex. A woman under the Taiping regime thus had the same privilege or obligation to serve in the army that a man did, as well as the same right to own her own land. To Hong Xiuquan and his associates, the employment of women combat soldiers also provided a powerful ideological weapon against what they regarded as the chief spiritual evil: Confucianism. In the orthodox Confucian order, women were expected to stay indoors and were not supposed to engage in outside social activities, let alone serve in the military. In fact, the prevailing practice of footbinding essentially rendered women useless in any type of military service because they were unable to run. The use of women in Taiping combat units was in direct defiance of the Confucian order, and it was possible because the women of the Hakka minority did not practice footbinding. In the key battles at Guilin and Changsha, Taiping women soldiers performed with valor and were highly praised.

A third unique feature of the Taiping military was that its main organizational principle was the soldier-peasant model. All citizens in the regime were required to serve as soldiers. And conversely, all layers of society were structured according to the military command hierarchy. Although soldiers were paid slightly better than farmers, the ethos and tempo of a farmer's life became the same as for a soldier. Farmers as well as soldiers were subjected to a rigid military command structure. In the Taiping system, "A corporal commands four men. A sergeant commands five corporals. . . . A colonel commands five captains. . . . A corps general commands five colonels; altogether he commands 13,125 men."[3]

The Taiping army was also remarkable for its innovative tactics. Among the most famous was the excellent use of tunnelling and demolition. This was primarily due to the personal experience of Yang Xiuqing, the Taipings' second-in-command before 1856, who had been a coal miner before the uprising and knew the power of explosives underground. The Taipings produced the best demolition experts in nineteenth-century China. In addition, the Taipings were among the first in modern China to utilize mass war propaganda in (quite literally) demonizing their enemies. These hysterical and xenophobic efforts at consciousness-raising against the Manchu rulers were for the most part quite effective.

Despite all these advantages enjoyed by the Taiping military, the peasant rebellion was eventually quelled. Ironically, the Taipings were defeated not by the regular army of the imperial court but for the most part by an exceptionally intelligent scholar-stateman who saw all the flaws of the emperor's troops and who instead envisioned and commanded a much more effective "gentry" army that eventually defeated the once-invincible Taiping troops.

ZENG GUOFAN'S VIEW OF THE QING MILITARY

Facing a momentous peasant rebellion inspired by prototypical Christian ideals, the ruling Qing dynasty would have collapsed in the mid-nineteenth century had it not been for the military genius of a prominent Confucian scholar, Zeng Guofan (1811–1872). Zeng and his military thought occupy a unique place in Chinese military history. It is true that there have been many military strategists and theorists throughout the annals of Chinese statecraft, and Zeng Guofan himself may not have been the most brilliant or original, but he was exceptional in the sense that he was one of the very few who were both theorists and practitioners of military doctrines. Few influential strategists have had the opportunity of creating, training, and commanding a huge and powerful army based upon self-taught or self-synthesized principles of war.

Zeng Guofan began his career as an outstanding military strategist not because he knew what to do, but rather because he painfully realized what not to do: Whatever the imperial army represented, he must tenaciously avoid. At a time of grave crisis for the dynasty that he supported, the regular armies of the Qing court had proved stunningly inept and ineffectual. Zeng's analysis of the Qing imperial army is classically poignant. In his view, the then current military system had the following five failings:

Hereditary Bureaucratic Military Force

The strategic core of the Qing dynasty's military consisted of two basic forces, the Manchu banners and the Chinese Green Standard Army. The troops served for life or even on a hereditary basis, with no channel for bringing in new blood from outside. As a result, these once-powerful fighting forces had deteriorated into a decadent cohort of unfit soldiers and officers by the time of the Taiping Rebellion. As a Western observer of Zeng's time noted, "The men were as heterogeneous as their clothes. Old and young, strong and decrepit, half-blind or whole deaf, none seemed too miserable objects for service."[4]

Failure to Come to the Support of Comrades in Trouble

This piqued Zeng's strongest sentiment against the imperial army. "When I daily ponder over our current military forces," Zeng wrote, "the most shameful and hateful of all aspects is what is expressed by the four characters *bai bu xiang jiu* [the defeated cannot expect rescue]."[5] The reason for this fateful shortcoming, Zeng argued, was the way the court assembled military units in time of war. Fearful of entrenched, personally bonding loyalty between a superior commander and his soldiers, the Qing court constantly broke up solid troop units and regrouped the men into new ones. Thus, the newly formed units were made up of strangers who felt no obligation to help one another. When a battle occurred, units under the same commander failed to cooperate: "One unit of soldiers is defeated, bleeding like a river, yet the other unit nearby, watchfully smiling, stays put, with no intention of offering help and rescue."[6]

Jealousy

This went far beyond the normal realm of interservice and interunit rivalry. Instead, it had become a deadly disease of the Qing army. In Zeng's analysis, low military pay and insufficient training were responsible for this problem.

Lack of Discipline and No Concern for "the People"

One historian has noted that "the people of north China feared the Imperial troops more than they feared the rebels."[7] The danger of indiscipline lay not just in the ineffectiveness of the troops, but in the alienation of the people from the government, preparing the way for the dynasty's demise.

Lack of Civilian Control

The banners and the Green Standard Army consisted of professional military men who had grown arrogant and shortsighted. During a crisis such as the Taiping Rebellion, they had proved themselves worthless. Yet it was difficult to impose civilian guidance to counteract the ignorance and incompetence of the imperial army.

Zeng's Military Innovations and the Defeat of the Taipings

The profound defects of the Qing military provided Zeng with a clear sense of direction and purpose when recruiting and commanding an army of his own. Zeng's genius is largely due to his ability to see the true picture (which required a fair amount of courage in the Chinese scheme of authoritarian imperial bureaucracy), and to act upon this picture to incorporate his own remedies into a brand-new fighting force created for the specific purpose of overcoming the court's most formidable enemies. The remedies Zeng worked out in the 1850s and 1860s were nothing short of revolutionary. Indeed, they made Zeng the father of the modern Chinese military system. The specific reforms were as follows:

First, Zeng Guofan completely overhauled the concept of "braves" (*yong*), and made these troops into a first-rate force. There had been three layers in the Qing military system: "soldiers" (*bing*), "braves" (*yong*), and "militiamen" (*ding*). The soldiers were professional, full-time military men such as the banner and Green Standard troops. They were fully supported by the court, with stable financial backing and regular military structures. They were designed to be the strategic core of the Qing army. The braves were recruited by the court, mostly during times of prolonged rebellion or civil disturbance on a grand scale, as part-time servicemen fully financed by the government. But the braves were much less privileged than the regular troops and their stipends varied a great deal. The militiamen were even less formally organized. They were local by nature. Recruited and trained by local luminaries and gentry heavyweights, militiamen acted as a local security force for the neighborhood or village. Their military usefulness during a time like the Taiping Rebellion was inconsequential, but they could help maintain the Confucian moral order and keep local toughs under control.

When the Taipings marched north through his home province of Hunan in 1852, Zeng was at home fulfilling the filial duty of mourning his mother's death. Burdened with the task of protecting his birthplace from the rebels' ravages, Zeng concluded that the regular soldiers were good for nothing and the militiamen undependable. He opted instead for the braves. It was this choice of *yong* recruits that enabled Zeng Guofan to create the greatest army of late imperial China: the Hunan Army.

The Hunan Army was an army of recruits. By strengthening this element, Zeng aimed to break with the hereditary character of the Qing standing army. Zeng recruited peasants from the mountain areas of Hunan. His recruiting standards became famous. Recruits were to be "skillful, young and strong; the simple, plain and peasant-like are the best.

Never recruit those who are slick, who are urban Philistines, and who are officious and pretentious."[8] All these bad qualities, in Zeng's view, were prevalent among the regulars.

Second, Zeng Guofan steadfastly stressed the importance of civilian command over the military. This reflects the ideal of "excellence in both literary and martial skills" (*wen wu shuang quan*). Zeng himself is revered as the quintessential scholar-general: a physically unimpressive scholar applying his brilliant intellect to the command of an awesome and ferocious fighting force. Zeng used many fellow literati as his top generals and officers of senior grade. In his Hunan Army, over half of the officers had previously been literary candidates for the imperial examinations; the top 10 percent of the army's officer corps were literati who had already passed an examination. In fact, only at the bottom of the officer ranks did the military candidates outnumber the literary candidates.[9] All the prominent leaders of the Hunan Army and other forces created later on the same pattern were without exception members of the literati class. The Hunan Army was in fact an army of peasants led by literati, as if the U.S. Army were being run by Ph.D.s in the humanities.

Third, and perhaps the most significant element in Zeng's military thought and practice, was the cultivation of moral character in all military personnel. This was strictly along the lines of Confucian virtues and mores. For the general, benevolence toward both his soldiers and the people was crucial. He had to be upright, generous, diligent, and caring, both a righteous ruler and a gentleman of good personal attributes. Among the various strands of Confucian virtues, the most important to Zeng was the value of family. A superior officer was expected to act like a father to his soldiers. Zeng often communicated with his officers in such a fashion. The establishment of a strong relationship between a benevolent superior officer and his subordinates was deemed essential in accomplishing military goals. This hierarchical structure of human relationships rooted in Confucian ethics poses a sharp contrast with the ultraegalitarian rigidity of the Taiping military order.

Instead of being motivated by an abstract ideology like that of the Taipings, a soldier in the Hunan Army was taught to fight not necessarily for the court, nor for his province, nor even for Zeng Guofan, but for his family, his parents, his brothers and sisters. To strengthen the connection between a soldier on the move and his family back home, superior officers were given the power to send a significant portion of a soldier's stipend directly to his family. Misconduct and disgraceful behavior such as desertion or cowardice in battle was interpreted as bringing shame on the family and the clan.[10] The cultivation of a morally sound fighting man was the essence of Zeng's military reform.

Fourth, a sweeping reform of military finance was indispensable to Zeng's efforts. Ever fearful of concentrating too much power in the hands of a military commander, the Qing court had devised a system of checks and balances in military finance. The banners and the Green Standard Army were all paid for by the court, but there were independent stipend commissioners to decide the scale and distribution of soldiers' pay, so that commanding officers had little to do with the financial well-being of their subordinates. The Hunan Army was partly funded with government money at the outset, but gradually developed complete financial independence through such means as imposing taxes (*lijin*) on goods in transit. With this change, a general could decide the pay of his own subordinates. And Zeng chose to pay his troops extremely well. At a time when a farm hand earned five taels of silver per year, an infantry soldier of the lowest grade in the Hunan Army was paid fifty-one taels of silver each year. A battalion commander made more than ten times what an infantry soldier did.[11] Even though moral indoctrination played the greatest role in Zeng Guofan's system, such high financial reward greatly enhanced the morale of the troops. But most important, high pay also had a strong moral utility: A well-paid soldier was less likely to loot, gamble, or commit other crimes or unethical deeds.

Following the salient tradition of classical Chinese military doctrine, Zeng Guofan placed supreme importance on the quality and power of commanding generals. Zeng had a reputation for selecting the best people for such posts. Perhaps the most unique aspect of the Hunan Army was the unparalleled control a commander had over his subordinates. It started with recruitment. Zeng Guofan recruited his protégés as army commanders, these army commanders then went on to recruit their own protégés or friends to be division commanders, who also recruited their own people. Commanders at each level had absolute authority over the level immediately below them, but the authority of higher commanding officers could not jump over intervening levels. This reform is of great significance because for the first time in several hundred years, a system of "state-owned" military was beginning to give way to a "general-owned" military. Indeed, Zeng and his many protégés could easily have made themselves independent warlords had they so desired.

Since the Taipings were mostly interested in a war of movement, Zeng's strategic approach tended to favor positional warfare. The key concepts that Zeng emphasized were calmness (*wen*) and being the "host" (*zhu*). Calmness meant the time-honored strategic quality of being cautious, planning well, and being rooted in one place. "In a battle," Zeng ruminated, "one should be calm and steady, which is the first thing one should be; only then should one seek for changes."[12] The strategy of calmness was closely linked to the concept of the host, because Zeng believed that to fight in someone else's territory as a "guest" (*ke*) has many disadvantages that can easily lead to defeat. To grasp the position of the host requires utilizing to the fullest extent the local support of people from your village, county, or province. It also involves creating situations on the battlefield to which the enemy is forced to respond. The host is always the side that determines the terms of the fight. Zeng's *wen* and *zhu* methods would become a prominent feature in twentieth-century Chinese counterinsurgency campaigns, including the Nationalists' efforts to wipe out the Communist forces in the Jiangxi Soviet.

Zeng Guofan had a specific military mission: to defeat the Taiping Rebellion and save the Qing dynasty. In this he succeeded with extraordinary gallantry and efficiency. While the well-trained, well-organized Taipings carried out their social and military campaigns with puritanical rigidity, ideological fanaticism, and utopian collectivism, Zeng trained and commanded his armies with a strong emphasis on family ties, individual responsibility, flexible yet responsible discipline, enhanced military pay, respect for intellectuals serving the army, and a strong bond between officers and soldiers. In the final analysis, Zeng Guofan won and the Taipings lost precisely because the Taipings did not understand the power of human relations as Zeng did. A deep appreciation of the Chinese way of human relations is the core of Confucianism. In this sense, the defeat of the Taipings may be viewed not just as the rout of utopian radicalism, but also as the triumph of Chinese tradition.

Suggestions for Further Reading

The Taiping Rebellion has attracted a great deal of scholarly attention. The single most comprehensive study of the conflict, dealing with both the Taipings and their opponents, is Yu-wen Jen, *The Taiping Revolutionary Movement* (New Haven: Yale University Press, 1973). Another important work is Franz Michael in collaboration with Chung-li Chang, *The Taiping Rebellion: History and Documents* (Seattle: University of Washington Press, 1966–1971); this was published in three volumes, the first providing an historical overview and the other two offering translations of Taiping documents with notes and commentary. There are also a number of specialized studies covering particular aspects of the Taiping movement, including Vincent Y. C. Shih, *The Taiping Ideology: Its Sources, Interpretations, and Influences*

(Seattle: University of Washington Press, 1967), and S. Y. Teng, *The Taiping Rebellion and the Western Powers: A Comprehensive Survey* (Oxford: Clarendon Press, 1971). The foreign contribution to the suppression of the Taipings is highlighted in Richard J. Smith, *Mercenaries and Mandarins: The Ever-Victorious Army in Nineteenth Century China* (Millwood, NY: KTO Press, 1978), while Jonathan D. Spence, *God's Chinese Son: The Taiping Heavenly Kingdom of Hong Xiuquan* (New York: W. W. Norton, 1996) focuses on the Taiping leadership circle and the mind of Hong Xiuquan himself.

The preeminent treatment of the "gentry" armies opposing the Taipings is Philip A. Kuhn, *Rebellion and Its Enemies in Late Imperial China: Militarization and Social Structure, 1796–1864* (Cambridge: Harvard University Press, 1970); another useful study is Stanley Spector, *Li Hung-chang and the Huai Army: A Study of Nineteenth Century Regionalism* (Seattle: University of Washington Press, 1964). Mary Clabaugh Wright, *The Last Stand of Chinese Conservatism: The T'ung-Chih Restoration, 1862–1874* (Stanford: Stanford University Press, 1957) considers reform, foreign relations, and the suppression of the mid-century rebellions from the standpoint of the Qing court in Beijing. For more information on the other rebellions that overlapped with that of the Taipings, see S. Y. Teng, *The Nien Army and Their Guerrilla Warfare, 1851–1868* (The Hague: Mouton, 1961); Wen-djang Chu, *The Moslem Rebellion in Northwest China, 1862–1878: A Study of Government Minority Policy* (The Hague: Mouton, 1966); and Elizabeth Perry, *Rebels and Revolutionaries in North China, 1845–1945* (Stanford: Stanford University Press, 1984).

SUGGESTIONS FOR FURTHER RESEARCH

The monographic literature on the mid-century rebellions and their suppression, extensive as it is, still has several notable gaps. The Miao revolt in Guizhou and the Muslim rising in Yunnan, for example, have been largely neglected. The time is also ripe for a reassessment of Zeng Guofan and the other scholar-generals who defeated the Taiping. The most recent book-length, English-language biographies of Zeng and his important associate Zuo Zongtang were published in 1927 and 1937, respectively.[13]

NOTES

1. "Taiping Rules and Regulations," in *The Taiping Rebellion*, vol. 2, *Documents and Comments*, ed. Franz Michael (Seattle: University of Washington Press, 1971), 139.
2. Quoted in S. P. Mackenzie, *Revolutionary Armies in the Modern Era: A Revisionist Approach* (London: Routledge, 1997), 82.
3. "The Taiping Military Organization," in *The Taiping Rebellion*, vol. 2, 133.
4. Mary Clabaugh Wright, *The Last Stand of Chinese Conservatism: The T'ung-Chih Restoration, 1862–1874* (Stanford: Stanford University Press, 1957), 197.

5. Letter from Zeng Guofan to Jiang Minqiao, in *Zeng Wen Zhenggong quanji—shouzha* [Complete Works of Zeng Guofan—Letters], vol. 2 (Hunan: ChuanZhong, 1934).

6. Letter from Zeng to Li Shaoquan, in *Zeng Wen Zhenggong quanji—shouzha*, vol. 2.

7. Wright, *Last Stand of Chinese Conservatism*, 203.

8. Zeng Guofan, "Zhao mu zhi gui" [Rules of recruitment], in *Zeng Wen Zhenggong quanji—za zhu* [Complete Works of Zeng Guofan—Miscellaneous Writings], vol. 2 (Hunan: ChuanZhong, 1934).

9. Wright, *Last Stand of Chinese Conservatism*, 200.

10. Gao Rui, ed., *Zhongguo junshi shilue* [A brief military history of China], vol. 3 (Beijing: Military Science Press, 1992), 39.

11. Wang Dingan, *Xiang jun zhi* [Annals of the Hunan Army] (Changsha: Yuelu shushe, 1983), 339.

12. Letter from Zeng to his family (dated fourth day of lunar first month, 1858), in *Zeng Wen Zhenggong jiashu* [Zeng Guofan's letters home], vol. 5 (Hong Kong: Hongwen shuju, 1953).

13. William James Hail, *Tseng Kuo-fan and the Taiping Rebellion, with a Short Sketch of His Later Career* (New Haven: Yale University Press, 1927); W. L. Bales, *Tso Tsungt'ang, Soldier and Statesman of Old China* (Shanghai: Kelly and Walsh, 1937). A few more specialized volumes have published in recent years; one example is Lanny B. Fields, *Tso Tsung-t'ang and the Muslims: Statecraft in Northwest China, 1868–1880* (Kingston, Ontario: The Limestone Press, 1978).

NINE

Beyond the Marble Boat: The Transformation of the Chinese Military, 1850–1911

Richard S. Horowitz

In the northwestern suburbs of Beijing locals and tourists throng the Imperial Summer Palace, now a public park. At the center of the park is a picturesque artificial lake, and by the northern shore stands a pavilion carved out of stone (said to be marble) in the shape of a boat. The gaudy palace and the marble boat were both creations of the Empress Dowager Cixi, built in the 1880s and 1890s. As every Chinese schoolchild learns, building the palace was an expensive undertaking, accomplished by diverting funds needed to purchase warships. In the end, the story goes, the Empress Dowager got her palace and a marble boat on which to enjoy a spring picnic, but shortly thereafter China was humiliated in a war with Japan. The mable boat became not just a pleasant place to view the lake, but the emblem of a modern Chinese navy that never was, and of the failure of the late Qing leadership to respond to the foreign threat.

This was a threat that should have been evident even in the rarefied world of the Qing court, far removed from everyday life, for the new palace replaced an older and larger one just a few miles away. The earlier Yuanming Palace (called the Old Summer Palace by foreigners) was burned and looted by British and French troops in 1860 at the end of the Arrow War. Now it is also a public park, but all that is left is a picturesque ruin, carefully maintained as a public remembrance of China's humiliation by foreign imperialism. To Chinese, the two palaces are powerful symbols of China's military failures in the nineteenth and early twentieth centuries.

There is substance behind the symbolism, for China's military experience from 1850 to 1911 is, indeed, replete with failure. Qing China badly lost the Arrow War (1856–1860) and the Sino-Japanese War (1894–1895).

During the Boxer Uprising in 1900 an allied foreign army again swept away Chinese resistance as it marched to Beijing. The military was so weak that from 1897 onward Qing diplomats could not resist foreign demands for economic concessions and military bases, and in 1904 the Chinese could only watch as the Russo–Japanese War was fought primarily on Chinese soil.

But it would be a mistake to limit our understanding of the period to the powerful symbolism of the marble boat. For there were successes as well: In the 1860s and 1870s massive domestic rebellions were suppressed, and from 1861 to 1895 Qing diplomats were able to limit concessions to foreigners, demarcate boundaries, and assert the Qing dynasty's claims to sovereignty in frontier areas. In fact, throughout this period Qing officials sought to reform their armed forces by introducing Western weapons and military methods. While they did not ultimately succeed in producing a military force able to resist foreign aggression, they did transform military organization and training, dramatically increase the coercive capacity of the Qing state, and transform the relationship of the military with state and society.

This chapter will present a very brief overview of some of the major themes in China's military transformation during this period. The efforts to transform the Qing military can be divided into two periods: the self-strengthening movement from 1861 to 1894, and the creation of the New Armies from 1895 to 1911. In each period there are three important interpretive issues: the reception of foreign technology and ideas by Chinese civil and military officials, changes in the organization of the Chinese military, and the evolving relationship of the military and the Qing state over half a century.

THE SELF-STRENGTHENING EFFORT

In 1861, responding to embarrassing defeat in the Arrow War (also known as the Second Opium War) and to continuing internal rebellion, leading officials of the Qing dynasty began to call for "self-strengthening." They initiated a range of efforts to repair the weaknesses of the Qing state, often involving the use of foreign technology and foreign methods. Military measures were at the center of this effort. Over the course of three decades troops began to use Western-style infantry firearms and artillery, and at times Western patterns of military training. New naval forces were created using armored, steam-powered ships. To provide weapons for these forces, new arsenals and shipyards were created, establishing the foundation of a modern armaments industry. The self-strengthening movement, as historians later dubbed it, was led by a rather small group of officials. Provincial leaders such as Zeng Guofan and his former subordinates Li Hongzhang and Zuo Zongtang, all of whom rose to prominence fighting the Taiping Rebellion, oversaw many of the most important projects and typically receive most of the credit. In Beijing, a new bureau of foreign affairs known as the Zongli Yamen, led by the imperial Prince Gong and masterminded by Wenxiang, a prominent Manchu grand councilor, sought to coordinate and finance many of these efforts through the 1860s and 1870s.

The self-strengthening effort began as a response to the multiple military problems faced by the Qing dynasty. Rapid population growth, systemic problems in Qing local government, currency instability, and in many cases ethnic conflict produced vast internal rebellions. The most significant were the quasi-Christian Taiping Rebellion (1850–1864) in the Yangzi valley, the Nian Rebellion (1851–1868) on the North China Plain, the Muslim Panthay Rebellion (1855–1873) in Yunnan and Guizhou, and the massive Northwestern Muslim Rebellions (1862–1877), which began in Shaanxi and Gansu provinces and later engulfed the vast territory of Xinjiang in the far northwest. There were external threats as well. Along the northern reaches of the empire, Russia was extending its control in the direction of the Pacific Ocean and seeking territorial and trade concessions. And, of course, "the West"—the British, French, Americans, and later Germans—wanted trade, railway, and mining concessions and a semicolonial realm of treaty ports, missionaries, and extraterritorial justice. The Opium War (1839–1842) and the Arrow War demonstrated that the British and French were willing to use arms in pursuit of these goals.

In confronting these threats the Qing leadership depended on an elaborate military system that had evolved since the Qing conquest. The regular military organization had two major sections, the Eight Banners and the Green Standard Army. The Eight Banners was a system of hereditary military and social organization for ethnic Manchus, Mongols, and Han Chinese whose families had long-standing loyalties to the Qing throne. Garrisons of bannermen were placed in strategic positions across the country. But while the banners were presumptively military forces, and their members provided with stipends, by the mid-nineteenth century they were primarily social organizations and their military effectiveness was limited. The Green Standard Army was ethnically Chinese but also predominantly hereditary in its organization. With the Green Standard troops spread across the country in tiny garrison units serving in constabulary as well as military roles, they were not easily concentrated into large mass armies, and when concentrated often did not perform as expected. By the mid-nineteenth century, two temporary modes of military organization existed for dealing with emergencies. "Braves" (*yong*), perhaps more adequately translated as "recruits," were soldiers hired for a particular military task, paid from emergency funds, and in normal conditions disbanded once the crisis was over. Militia (*tuanlian*) were military organizations created by local elites and trained to come together to protect their locality when it was threatened.

But by the end of the 1850s the multiple challenges to Qing sovereign authority had pressed the empire's military capacities to their limits and beyond. The regular military forces proved pitifully incompetent in the face of both internal and external military threats. Against the domesic rebels, as the banner and Green Standard armies failed to perform as expected, Qing leaders increasingly turned to large, ramified armies of recruits, which gradually formed several new permanent (or semipermanent) forces, notably the Hunan Army created by Zeng Guofan and the Anhui Army created by Zeng's protégé Li Hongzhang. These new armies gradually began to gain the upper hand against the Taipings. Qing forces had even more difficulty against the British and French. Only one engagement in the Opium and Arrow wars, the 1859 ambush of British and French flotillas at Dagu in north China, could be regarded as a Qing victory. It resulted in a still more humiliating foreign invasion of north China that forced the emperor to flee Beijing. These military travails against both domestic and foreign opponents led officials such as Wenxiang, Zeng Guofan, and Li Hongzhang to implement the first efforts to adopt Western patterns of military technology and organization.

Army reforms began with several important experiments. In the early 1860s special brigades of Chinese soldiers equipped with European weapons and led by foreign officers were incorporated into the armies of Li Hongzhang and Zuo Zongtang as they fought the Taipings. The Ever-Victorious Army (led by the colorful British soldier Charles "Chinese" Gordon) and the Ever-Triumphant Army (led by French officers) played a significant although not decisive role in the final defeat of the Taipings. More generally, units of both the Anhui and Hunan Armies began to use imported Western-style rifles in the 1860s, and some efforts were made to incorporate Western drill. There were also attempts to revive the banner and Green Standard armies. In Beijing, in the aftermath of the disastrous performance of the metropolitan banners in the Arrow War, Prince Gong and Wenxiang organized a special unit called the Firearms Division. Of-

ten called the Peking Field Force, this unit was composed of selected bannermen equipped with Russian rifles and French cannon and drilled by
British officers. Green Standard forces in the north were reorganized,
equipped with rifles, given a modicum of Western drill, and dubbed "re-
trained forces." Similarly, in the 1870s new naval units equipped with
both foreign and domestically produced steamships began to appear, and
by the 1880s these formed separate northern and southern fleets.

The modern Chinese military–industrial complex also began to develop in the mid–1860s. While our knowledge of pre–1860 arms production in Qing China is quite limited, it appears to have been a mixture of
government-run foundries for casting cannon and artisanal gunmakers
producing matchlock muskets and other small arms. Zeng Guofan realized by the early 1860s that to produce superior Western-style rifles and
artillery, more sophisticated Western manufacturing methods would have
to be imported. He began by creating an arsenal in Suzhou during the
Taiping war. This was soon moved to Shanghai and vastly expanded to
form the Jiangnan Arsenal under the aegis of Li Hongzhang when Zeng
was moved north to fight the Nian rebels. The Jiangnan Arsenal was designed to manufacture rifles, artillery, and ammunition, and even had
limited shipbuilding capacities. In 1866 Zuo Zongtang proposed the creation of an even more ambitious facility, the Fuzhou Navy Yard, intended
to provide modern warships to protect China's shores. While Zuo was
transferred shortly thereafter to the northwest to lead the Qing forces
against Muslim rebels, under the leadership of the very capable official
Shen Baozhen the Fuzhou shipyard, using French technical assistance, became the most sophisticated military manufacturing facility in China.
Another major arsenal was created in Tianjin, initially with Zongli Yamen
support, and under Li Hongzhang during the 1870s and 1880s it became a
major supplier of ammunition. Some smaller ammunition production facilities were begun as well. In the early 1870s Zuo Zongtang began to establish an arsenal at Lanzhou to support his northwestern campaign.
Smaller arsenals were created in the mid–1870s in Sichuan and Shandong.
Taken on their own terms, the new military–industrial facilities were a
dramatic improvement on the existing Chinese systems of weapons production. But Qing officials were also gravely aware that the weapons produced were not equivalent to contemporary Western production, and
Chinese-produced ammunition was often unreliable.

By the mid–1870s the initial stage of self-strengthening had come to an
end. Increasingly, financial restraints limited the creation of large new facilities. And while the Taiwan crisis in 1874 (when a Japanese military

expedition landed on the coast of Taiwan, ostensibly to punish aborigines who had murdered and otherwise mistreated both Japanese and Ryukyuan sailors) renewed concerns about the need to further improve the military, large new commitments of funds were not forthcoming. Furthermore, as many of the early supporters of self-strengthening, such as Zeng Guofan, Wenxiang, and Shen Baozhen, passed away, and Zuo Zongtang was preoccupied with his northwestern campaign against the Muslim rebels, the burden of reform increasingly fell on the shoulders of Li Hongzhang, now the governor-general of Zhili province. From 1870 on, Li's Anhui Army defended the approaches to Beijing, and in his role as superintendant of the northern ports Li also controlled the Northern Fleet. By the 1880s these were the best forces in China. The Anhui Army was equipped with modern rifles and artillery, often purchased from German or other European suppliers, and Anhui Army officers were aided by foreign (usually German) advisors. Li also sought to combine private and government investment to create strategic industries, including mines, telegraphs, and a steamship company (that could transport Qing troops in times of war). From the mid–1880s Zhang Zhidong, a younger official who had once been critical of the self-strengthening effort, began to create new facilities following a similar pattern, including a new arsenal and an iron and steel facility in the Wuhan area. These "official oversight and merchant management" (*guandu shangban*) facilities had mixed results. In the case of the China Merchants Steam Navigation Company, initial success under merchant management was later compromised as officials skimmed off profits for other uses, deterring further private investment.

The early self-strengthening period brought significant achievements. The use of Western weapons gave the Qing forces major advantages over domestic opponents. By the early 1870s the rebellions in China proper had been defeated, and by 1878 Qing armies had reasserted control of even the outlying frontiers of Xinjiang. In the meantime, the improved military situation had led to a stabilization of the international situation of the Qing state. During the 1874 Taiwan crisis, Shen Baozhen's quick mobilization of military resources put pressure on the Japanese to seek a diplomatic solution, and Qing authority in Taiwan was firmly reasserted (and as Edwin Leung has shown, contrary to the textbook explanation, the settlement did not sacrifice Qing claims in the Ryukyus).[1] In 1881 Zeng Jize's brilliant diplomacy, backed by Zuo Zongtang's military mobilization along the northwestern border, led to the Russian withdrawal from the strategically important Ili valley in Xinjiang, which Russian troops had occupied for a decade. In 1884–1885 the war with France, primarily over French demands in northern Vietnam, saw some serious defeats for Qing forces, particularly at sea. But in Taiwan, Qing troops under Liu Mingquan performed reasonably well, preventing the French from capturing the town of Danshui, and along the Vietnam–China border, after initial French advances, Qing troops defeated the French at Lang Son and were advancing toward Hanoi when the armistice was signed. The war was settled without the Qing making any new concessions or paying substantial indemnities. While hardly a victory, the contrast to the Opium and Arrow Wars was striking.

In 1894–1895 all of this unravelled. In a lightning campaign, the armies of Meiji Japan crushed Li Hongzhang's best forces in Korea and then proceeded into China. The Japanese navy smashed the northern Chinese fleet at the Battle of the Yellow Sea, and Li Hongzhang's army lost a series of battles in Korea and north China. The settlement was humiliating. China ceded Taiwan to Japan, allowed the Japanese a free hand in Korea, and agreed to pay a massive indemnity, effectively covering Japan's costs for the war. Only the self-interested intervention of Germany, France, and Russia prevented the cession of the strategically important tip of the Liaodong Peninsula and the naval base at Port Arthur. But this came at the cost of a still larger indemnity.

SELF-STRENGTHENING AND QING PERCEPTIONS OF FOREIGN METHODS

Ever since the Sino–Japanese War ended in defeat for Qing China in 1895, historians and others have focused on the slow pace at which Qing officials seemed to awaken to the need to adopt the latest Western military methods. The war made comparison with Japan both obvious and invidious. In Japan, the leaders of the new Meiji government had made the creation of a modern military their highest priority. A new conscript army was created; organized along the lines of the latest and best European models, it was led by a professionally trained and technically proficient officer corps. By the turn of the century, the Japanese army and navy were among the most efficient military organizations in the world. By contrast, the Qing leadership seemed to stand still; indeed, many argue that fierce ethnocentrism and an intense allegiance to conservative Confucian values stymied China's efforts to move into the modern world. While there is some truth to this picture, it is exaggerated. Qing officials from the early 1860s onward were enthusiastic about the superior capabilities of Western weaponry. They were, however, far less receptive to Western training and

Western institutional models; these only slowly came to be accepted, and were only effectively endorsed in the aftermath of the Sino–Japanese War and the Boxer Uprising. To understand the nature of the Qing response to Western miltiary ideas, methods, and patterns of organization, these issues must be considered in their intellectual and institutional context.

From very early on, Qing officials who actually faced Western military opponents were impressed with the efficacy of their weapons and the mobility of their ships. The famous imperial commissioner Lin Zexu, whose efforts to end the opium trade sparked the Opium War, quickly recognized the technological superiority of the British navy, particularly its maneuverable ships and powerful cannon. He created a translation bureau to try to learn as much as possible about his opponents, and one of his advisors, the prominent political theorist and military historian Wei Yuan, organized this material into the famous *Gazetteer of the Maritime Regions* (*Haiguo tuzhi*). Wei argued that arsenals and shipyards that could produce the superior European-style arms had to be established in order to develop an effective system of maritime defense. While the warnings of Lin and Wei fell on deaf ears, the Arrow War had a more dramatic impact. In Beijing, Wenxiang was unsparing in his criticism of Qing troops who had failed to defend north China: They were, he believed, poorly trained, poorly armed, and poorly led. Wenxiang tried to revive the units defending Beijing by introducing Western weapons and drill. Similarly, provincial officials such as Zeng Guofan, Li Hongzhang, and Zuo Zongtang who were fighting the Taipings became convinced that superior Western weapons were a crucial ingredient in suppressing the rebellion. In 1874–1875, a national debate over defense policy showed that senior officials across Qing China supported the adoption of Western weaponry nearly unanimously, although there were significant disagreements over what this should entail.

Curiously, however, Qing officials were far more reluctant to endorse Western training and organizational patterns. The Firearms Division was trained by British drill masters through the 1860s, but once its sponsor Wenxiang fell ill, training fell off and the unit gradually deteriorated. Likewise, Li Hongzhang's effort to incorporate Western drill into the repertoire of the Anhui Army by creating a special training center at Fenghuangshan quickly faded. In the 1870s, among the senior officers of the Anhui Army, only Zhou Shengquan (1833–1885) showed an interest not only in Western weapons (in which he was something of an expert) but also in Western training methods.[2] While foreign observers saw European-style military organization, uniforms, and culture as of central importance, to their shock and annoyance most Qing officials did not.

There were both ideological and institutional reasons for the selective response to Western military methods before 1895. At the level of perceptions, to Qing officials the modern West was not a seamless whole: Diplomats, merchants, missionaries, and adventurers who came to China had their own motives, and their products and ideas needed to be considered in that light. The modern West could not or should not simply be imitated. At the same time, the Chinese political milieu shaped the way that Western ideas and technology were received and utilized. Orthodox Neo-Confucian political theory (which had undergone a revival in the 1840s and 1850s) emphasized that leaders needed proper ethical orientations rather than specific technical skills. Therefore, efforts by self-strengthening advocates to provide official positions for specialists in Western technology were subject to intense opposition by conservatives. Specialists in foreign methods were regarded as small-minded technicians and therefore morally suspect. To conservatives, the self-strengtheners' emphasis on technology was misplaced; a moral renaissance among officials was what was needed. As one conservative critic declared in 1871, "Ever since the [foreign trouble] began in Guangdong, we have been on an unfortunate slope, and we must hope to get loyal, righteous, and heroic men, who can act for the country in managing its difficulties."[3] Good men, not gadgets, would restore the dynasty to power. Even reformers, moreover, worried about the motives of foreign advisors. During the 1860s the Zongli Yamen and Li Hongzhang, the most prominent advocates of Western technology at the time, questioned whether foreigners would be willing to sell their key technologies to China, and even more whether foreign officers serving in the Chinese military would be willing to take orders from their Chinese superiors. Early returns were not good. An attempt to purchase a flotilla of river gunboats failed in 1863 when the British commander refused to be subordinated to Zeng Guofan, and in the final days of the Taiping campaign Gordon very nearly resigned in a huff over Zeng's management of the operation. Similarly, in the late 1870s the U.S. government reneged on earlier commitments to allow Chinese boys who had been educated in the United States to study at West Point and Annapolis. Taken together, these concerns created a quandary. On the one hand, foreigners could not be trusted in positions of authority. One the other hand, Chinese who had moved outside of the traditional education system to develop Western technical expertise were seen as morally suspect.

Qing efforts at Westernizing military reforms were also limited by institutional problems. In the financial realm, the Qing government simply did not adequately support military reform efforts. During the 1850s and 1860s new revenues flowed in from taxes on commerce, especially the internal transit tax known as the *lijin* and the maritime customs system administered by Sir Robert Hart and staffed with foreigners (but which reported to the Zongli Yamen). Foreign loans guaranteed with customs revenues were also used extensively to fund military campaigns. Gradually the new tax revenues were committed to various civil and military projects, and the discretionary funds that had made the reforms of the 1860s possible disappeared. Foreign loans were generally only used for emergencies, and further financial reforms were not pursued. Consequently, after 1875 financial constraints limited reform.[4]

The structure of Qing political institutions also impeded reform, for administrative authority over both civil and military affairs was spread out among numerous provincial and metropolitan officials. This system was intended to avoid dangerous concentrations of power and maximize the choices available to the emperor, but it made the management of policies extending across provincial jurisdictions quite difficult. Only decisive involvement by the throne (i.e., the emperor or the regents ruling in his name) could produce effective policies on the national level. And yet from 1861 until 1898 the throne simply did not act to establish strong and consistent defense policies. While reforms went ahead, support was half-hearted and self-strengthening advocates were subjected to ferocious criticism from conservative officials. This opposition eroded the enthusiasm of the reformers and almost certainly deterred others from joining their ranks.

Finally, in many respects the nature of foreign imperial involvement served as a deterrent to broader economic development, particularly in areas such as railways that could be seen as strategically important. The institution of extraterritoriality, by which foreigners were not subject to the jurisdiction of Qing law courts, severely limited the willingness of Qing officials to allow foreign investment. The earliest Western residents in China's interior, Christian missionaries, were felt to be abusing extraterritoriality to protect their converts and subvert the authority of local government. Foreigners with extraterritoriality, Qing officials felt, could not be controlled. The 1876 Wusong Railroad incident, in which a railway illegally constructed by British merchants from Shanghai to Wusong was purchased and removed by the Qing government, is often taken as an example of resistance to modernization. But to Qing officials the railway constituted a serious infringement on Qing sovereignty, and allowing it to continue would simply sanction lawlessness. In this situation, the dangers of foreign investment were perceived as far outweighing its economic and military benefits. Before 1895 new projects proceeded only when the government was convinced of strategic benefits and was willing to invest its own resources and/or attract private Chinese investors.

In summary, during the self-strengthening era the majority of Qing officials quickly recognized the superiority of Western weaponry, although they were more doubtful about methods of organization and training. Reforms were slowed not only by ideological resistance, but also, and more important, by institutional problems: Financial shortfalls, poor coordination among officials, and a lack of consistent support from the top combined to limit military improvements. Western pressure for reform and foreign investment was often counterproductive, making Qing officials justifiably suspicious of the purposes of foreign investors and diplomats. In the aftermath of the humiliation by Japan, however, the Westernization of the Qing military was dramatically accelerated. Doubts about the efficacy of Western models of organization were silenced, and after 1900 the throne came down in firm support of reform.

THE CREATION OF THE NEW ARMIES AND THE ROAD TO REVOLUTION

The crushing defeat in the Sino–Japanese War initiated radical changes in military policy. In the aftermath of the war, with its best armed forces destroyed and its prestige in tatters, the Qing government found itself in a position of profound weakness. Long unwilling to give railway and mining concessions to foreign companies, the Qing government now found it could do little to resist foreign demands. From 1897 to 1899 a dramatic scramble for concessions saw the empire carved into putative spheres of economic influence for foreign powers. Within these spheres foreigners demanded and received rail and mining concessions, naval bases, and other benefits. In this context increasingly ambitious efforts were made to restore China's military strength, this time by building new armies from scratch.

The first of the new armies were sponsored by two officials, Yuan Shikai in north China and Zhang Zhidong in Hubei. In 1895 Zhang had established a new "Self-Strengthening Army" consisting of thirteen battalions of carefully selected men who were organized along European patterns and trained by a team of thirty-five German officers and noncommissioned officers. This force included cavalry, infantry, artillery, and engineering units, and also had medical and support personnel. Zhang also created a new military academy in Nanjing in 1896 to provide trained officers for his new army. When he was transferred back to his former position of governor-general of Hunan and Hubei, Zhang created another military academy in Wuchang and began to reform the troops in these two provinces. Meanwhile, at the behest of the increasingly influential Manchu grand councilor Ronglu, in 1895 Yuan Shikai, a former protégé of Li Hongzhang, began to establish a new army to prop up the weakened defenses of north China. This "newly created army" was to total some 7,000 men, trained by German instructors.

Defeat also spurred larger changes in the political sphere. The short-lived Hundred Days Reforms in 1898, sponsored by the Guangxu emperor, proposed radical reforms in government and education aimed at putting China on a more positive path along Meiji lines. It was, however, politically naive. A coup supported by Yuan Shikai, among others, forced the emperor into involuntary retirement and restored his great aunt, the Empress Dowager Cixi, to the regency she had held from 1861 to 1873 and then from 1874 until 1889, and the emperor was imprisoned at the Summer Palace. Cixi reversed most of the political and educational reforms, but military reforms initiated before 1898 continued. In 1900 a more severe disruption followed, the Boxer Uprising. Originating in drought-stricken areas in north China, the Society of Boxers United in Righteousness was a popular organization that practiced martial arts and other spiritual practices. Its members targeted and victimized Christian converts and to a lesser extent foreign missionaries, believing them to be the cause of their economic and social hardships. Encouraged by a number of antiforeign officials, the Boxers grew rapidly, slaughtering numerous Christians as they spread across north China. Eventually, with support from the Empress Dowager, Boxers marched on Beijing, and together with imperial troops surrounded the foreign legations. Eight countries proceeded to send a joint expeditionary force that, facing only limited resistance from regular Qing troops, marched to Beijing, relieved the legations, and forced another embarrassing treaty on the Qing government.

The military reforms were only strengthened by the disaster. Prominent provincial officials such as Zhang Zhidong, Liu Kunyi, and Yuan Shikai had refused to support the Boxers and stood aside as the foreign invasion proceeded. In early 1901, after the treaty was settled, the Empress Dowager began to initiate thoroughgoing reforms in government, education, and the military, known as the New Policy reforms. The military aspects of these reforms specifically built on the earlier efforts of Zhang Zhidong and Yuan Shikai. Yuan's army was rapidly expanded to form the Beiyang (or "northern") Army, which soon established itself as the preeminent military force in China. Provincial governments were ordered to establish armies along Western lines and to set up military academies to produce professionally trained officers. Separate standing armies, reserves, and gendarmerie divisions were to be created. The traditional military examination system was suspended and discussion of either dissolving or reforming the traditional Green Standard and banner armies began; in the end these were often redesignated as reserve units. Response to the New Army reforms varied from province to province. Progress was greatest where strong, reform-minded governors-general were in place, as, for example, in Zhili under Yuan Shikai and Hunan and Hubei under Zhang Zhidong. Elsewhere the process was less dramatic: Existing units were reorganized and officers trained in nascent military academies. Foreign (often Japanese) advisors were hired to train Chinese officers, and occasionally to drill Chinese troops.

In 1904 the government established a long-term plan to reorganize the New Army into thirty-six divisions totaling some 450,000 men under the oversight of the Army Reorganization Bureau. This was to be the "New Army," and it was initially expected to be completed by 1922, although this was later advanced to 1912. The goals of the reforms were to standardize the hodgepodge of organizations, pay scales, and equipment then extant, and to begin to establish firmer central control. By 1906 there were ten New Army divisions: Five were part of Yuan Shikai's Beiyang Army in north China, and the sixth was made up of Zhang Zhidong's troops in Hubei; the remaining divisions and some independent brigades were spread across the rest of China, and generally both undermanned and undertrained. Large numbers of older types of army organizations, including Green Standard and banner troops and remnants of the Hunan and Anhui Armies, continued to exist as reserve and gendarmerie forces. Progress was substantial, yet slower than authorities hoped.

While the New Policy reforms did make dramatic progress on many fronts, the Qing government was facing a crisis of legitimacy. Abroad, dissident intellectuals like Liang Qichao (a supporter of the Hundred Days Reforms) were calling for constitutional reform, while revolutionaries like Sun Yat-sen and Zou Rong spiced their calls for revolution with racist anti-Manchu rhetoric. Within the government there were tensions as well. The failure of the leading provincial officials to support the Empress Dowager's pro-Boxer policy, however correct in hindsight, suggested that the throne could not always count on the obedience of its officials, and conversely officials could legitimately see the interests of China in conflict with the demands of the highest authorities.[5] The accumulation of power by Manchu officials in Beijing exacerbated ethnic tensions. Manchu suspicions of leading Chinese officials were demonstrated by the transfer of both Zhang Zhidong and Yuan Shikai to Beijing in 1907, and the enforced retirement of Yuan two years later. Meanwhile, the central government's reluctance to cede political power to local elites and form a more democratic government bred growing resistance.

In 1911 and 1912 revolution finally felled the Qing dynasty, and the New Armies were a central part of it. The rebellion was sparked when it was discovered that soldiers in the Wuchang garrison were associated with revolutionary groups. The panicked soldiers rebelled, forcing a reluctant brigade commander, Li Yuanhong, to join the rebellion. With astonishing speed the insurrection spread among local elites and new military men. The government, facing the crisis, discovered that its New Armies were not as loyal as it had imagined; suppressing the rapidly growing rebellion was hard going. Yuan Shikai was recalled, and by early 1912 he decided that with the Beiyang Army's support for the Qing regime lukewarm at best, his most promising alternative was to negotiate the abdication of the Qing emperor. Using his unparalled influence as the creator of the Beiyang Army, he also established himself as president of the new regime.

EVOLVING MILITARY ORGANIZATION

The New Armies were the final phase in a three-stage transformation of military organization. Before 1850 Qing military institutions meshed hereditary recruitment and bureaucratic organization. During the self-strengthening era Western weapons were imported, but the military structure continued to follow either existing Qing insitutional systems or to take on new, indigenous models of organization. After 1895, new armies began to accept the Western military model whole, including organization, training, and even military culture.

For all of their success, in many respects the recruit armies of Zeng Guofan and Li Hongzhang seem like a backward step from earlier Qing military institutions. The banner and Green Standard armies, notwithstanding their hereditary mode of recruitment and antiquated weaponry, were professional and bureaucratic. During the self-strengthening era, the recruit armies of Zeng Guofan, Li Hongzhang, and Zuo Zongtang were organized along radically different principles. They were led by amateurs, men with no formal military training and often members of the literati elite, forced by circumstance to fight. Where personnel in the Eight Banners and the Green Standard forces were seen as largely interchangeable, key elements of the recruit armies were based on local and personal ties, important modes of organization in Chinese society. Zeng Guofan, drawing on the writings of the Ming-dynasty military thinker Qi Jiguang, recruited his army in his native province of Hunan and created a pyramidal structure of human relationships: He recruited commanders from among friends, relatives, and associates, and they in turn recruited their own subordinates. At the level of the battalion (*ying*, a unit of around 500 men), personal ties between commanders and recruits were so important in enforcing unity and discipline that when a commander died or retired, the battalion usually was not placed under a new commander—rather, it was disbanded and a new battalion was recruited. This was a striking contrast to the Green Standard armies, in which efforts were made to limit such local and personal connections.

To make these armies function effectively, senior officials also began to establish increasingly elaborate and specialized staff offices (*mufu*), recruiting specialized personnel to manage various functions. While the staff offices were originally associated with the official's civilian responsibilities, they quickly began to provide crucial staff and logistical support for the recruited armies. Near the end of the Taiping conflict, Zeng Guofan's military headquarters was said to have "at least two hundred officials. . . . Besides his secretaries, who numbered no less than a hundred, there were expectant officials, learned scholars, lawyers, mathematicians, astronomers and machinists."[6] Other commanders created similar staff organizations.

While the recruited armies were initially very successful, over time their training and discipline tended to break down. The emphasis on personal rather than bureaucratic organization undoubtedly had something to do with this. Where the banner and Green Standard forces had quite carefully defined training regimens, albeit using outdated weaponry such as matchlock muskets and bows and arrows, in the new recruit armies the commanders individually had to take responsibility for implementing training. With the influx of new rifles and the increased cost of training with live ammunition, many commanders did not provide sufficient opportunities for live target practice.

Leadership was also a problem. The military background of commanders was often limited to experience from the Taiping, Nian, and Muslim rebellions, with little formal military training. The problems among junior officers were even worse: Foreigners often noted the reluctance of junior officers to participate in training, and stated that they were unwilling to lead troops in battle.[7] Li Hongzhang agreed with the substance of these criticisms. In 1885 he created a new military academy to train officers for his Anhui Army (and made similar efforts to professionalize the Northern Navy). But these efforts to improve the professionalism of the Anhui Army were insufficient, and the superior discipline, mobility, and training of the Japanese armies proved decisive in 1894–1895.

In terms of organization, the Sino–Japanese War was a turning point in the history of the Qing military. The destruction of the Anhui Army's best units by Japanese forces had a double effect: It eliminated the existing Anhui Army as an effective fighting force, and it clearly demonstrated the limitations of the recruited armies. The new-model armies of the post–1895 period, exemplified by Yuan Shikai's Beiyang Army and Zhang Zhidong's Self-Strengthening Army, were deliberately built on Western lines. The heavy emphasis on personal ties was replaced with bureaucratic organization, academy education, and an emphasis on discipline, training, and overall efficiency. In theory, merit was to guide recruitment and promotion. Indeed, a central aspect of the New Army reforms was education to form a disciplined and technically proficient officer corps through the creation of military academies, such as Yuan Shikai's at Baoding. Solid performance in the ranks could also provide a way up the ladder: In the Beiyang Army at least, literate recruits were able quickly to advance to become noncommissioned officers and eventually commissioned officers.

Significantly, the culture of uniformity that by this time was a central part of European military life was also imported. Before 1895, Chinese soldiers generally did not wear uniforms. This, along with the lack of close order drill, gave them what to foreigners was a distinctly unmilitary look ("clothed in a sort of Falstaff uniform," remarked the British diplomat Rutherford Alcock).[8] The New Armies impressed foreign observers for their replication of European military culture. The Maritime Customs inspector-general Sir Robert Hart, a veteran of over half a century in China, declared after viewing the Beiyang Army maneuvers in October 1905 that the new troops were

> an immense improvement on anything before seen in China—stout men, well paid and well dressed, strict discipline willingly obeyed, arms in good condition, and officers who are really soldiers and not merely be-button'd mandarins with fans in their hands instead of swords. Even *Yuan* [Shikai], the Viceroy, and Tieh Liang, the military chief of the War Bureau, got out of their Chinese robes and put on gold-laced trousers and jackets, etc., for the occasion! *Militarism* has taken hold and root.[9]

The Chinese had embraced Western models of military organization both in form and in substance. Nevertheless, even the New Armies were lacking important elements of contemporary European military organization. In particular, the lack of centralized organization and a general staff system suggests that even these new armies had a long way to go to match their potential European and Japanese adversaries.

THE MILITARY AND THE STATE

China's military transformation is important on one final analytical level: Military transformation dramatically influenced the development of the late Qing state. We can see this in three areas: First, there were shifts in the relationship of the central government in Beijing and the provincial leaders. Second, as local elites became more involved in organizing local militia and other military activities, they became deeply involved in the political realm. Finally, the New Armies were crucial to the overthrow of the Qing regime.

The issue of central–provincial relations is a complicated one. The writings of Luo Ergang in China in the 1930s and Franz Michael in subsequent years in the United States articulated what is known as the "regionalism thesis": In the effort to suppress the Taiping and other mid-century rebellions, officials like Zeng Guofan and Li Hongzhang became, in effect, regional satraps, with essentially "personal" armies and autonomous sources of revenue from the *lijin* commercial transit tax. The Qing state, it was argued, was never able truly to reassert central control, and so the rise of these provincial leaders was a direct antecedent to the complete collapse of central control during the 1910s and 1920s.[10] While initially plausible (and still widely reproduced in textbooks), the regionalism thesis has been under constant and devastating attack for years. Kwang-ching Liu demonstrated that Li Hongzhang remained highly dependent on the central government for funds and remained a loyal central government agent, and that his more or less permanent position as Zhili governor-general was an exception. Other scholars have shown that the customs revenues remained under firm central control. While a few governors-general undoubtedly became exceptionally powerful as a result of the suppression of the rebellion, it did not represent a fundamental structural shift in the Qing state.[11]

The real shift in central-provincial relations began during the Boxer Uprising. When the central government began to support the Boxers' antiforeign activities and the siege of the foreign legations, prominent provincial officials saw this as at best futile and at worst suicidal. While in many cases they simply ignored central government edicts and waited for the storm to pass, in the crucial Yangzi valley the prominent governors-general Zhang Zhidong and Liu Kunyi, responding to intense pressure from local elites, signed the Yangzi Compact, an agreement with the British that no military action would be undertaken in the Yangzi valley—and an open rejection of an imperial edict. In the aftermath of the disaster, as the Empress Dowager Cixi initiated the New Policy reforms, the disobedience was conveniently forgotten, but the unwillingness of even loyal senior officials and local elites to listen to Beijing indicated a real break from the traditions of Qing government. The building of new armies was primarily a provincial activity, and only slowly did the central state try to take control of the process. This centralization effort had not achieved much success by the end of the first decade. Efforts to assert control by shifting Zhang Zhidong and Yuan Shikai from their positions of power, and to nationalize the railways that local elites had vigorously sought to purchase from foreign control, provided fuel for open rebellion. From 1908 onward, as reformers became disillusioned with the central government, this lack of effective control would become a fatal problem.

A second level on which military change shaped the Qing state was in the formation of local militias in the mid-nineteenth century. Philip Kuhn argued that militarization of local elites during the rebellion led them into increasingly powerful political roles and toward growing efforts to influence state activities.[12] The activism of local elites in everything ranging from paramilitary and police functions to tax collection and philanthropy was one of the most important developments in the post-Taiping period, eventually leading to local assemblies and other openly political activities. While local elites had always played significant roles in local politics, the scope and organization of these developments reached new levels, and at least in some areas, such as tax collection, there was a growing reliance on coercion in implementing these roles.

In the final decades of the dynasty, these two trends—local activism and increasing provincial power—came together. The New Policy reforms eliminated the traditional Confucian-based examination system, which had long attracted ambitious young men to pursue government service and inculcated in them politically safe ethical orientations toward service and loyalty. Now, with no alternative method of becoming involved in the government, many of these young men began to enter the New Armies and were far more literate and far more inclined than earlier Chinese soldiers to be politically active. By 1911 there were significant numbers of men in the New Armies who were increasingly committed to the revolutionary cause.

CONCLUSION

The traditional narrative embodied in the symbolism of the marble boat—of a militarily weak China conspicuously abused by Western and later Japanese imperialism and unwilling to respond effectively to the challenge—has tremendous resonance to Chinese nationalists and a degree of historical validity. But closer examination shows a more complex and interesting picture. While Qing reform efforts in the 1860s and 1870s did not create modern, Western-style armed forces, they did have a major impact on the military efficacy of China's armed forces. The suppression of rebellion and the stabilization of China's international position are clear indications of this. While Qing China through the 1870s and 1880s was hardly in a strong military position, the fact remains that Japanese threats in 1874–1875, a near war with Russia over Ili in 1880, and open fighting with France in 1884–1885 did not produce radical changes in China's position vis-à-vis the foreign powers. It was only with the crushing defeat at the hands of Japan that the scales shifted, and a dramatic effort to replicate European military patterns followed. While again this did not lead to a national military revival as its sponsors hoped, it did create a professional European-style military, dramatically more effective than the forces that had been humiliated just a few years before.

The historical significance of these efforts at military transformation is very much interwoven into the broader history of Chinese state and society in the late nineteenth and early twentieth centuries. The military transformation had direct impact on state structures: The recruit armies made provincial rather than central authorities the main locus of military reforms, and after 1900 central government authority was clearly in decline. The militarization of local elites during the great rebellions gradually led to their growing politicization, and ultimately to their significant role in overthrowing the dynasty. In the end, ironically enough, the new Western-model armies intended to save the dynasty from foreign aggression undermined it from within and bequeathed to the new Chinese republic a substantially modernized and deeply politicized military.

SUGGESTIONS FOR FURTHER READING

The starting point for those interested in late Qing military issues remains John K. Fairbank, ed., *The Cambridge History of China*, vols. 10 and 11 (Cambridge: Cambridge University Press, 1978–1980). Particularly important are the articles by Kwang-ching Liu on the "Ch'ing Restoration" and Ting-yee Kuo on "Self-

Strengthening" in vol. 10, and by Kwang-ching Liu and Richard J. Smith on "The Military Challenge" in vol. 11, with valuable material in many other chapters. The bibliographical essays at the back of each volume provide an excellent starting point for research in published primary and secondary sources.

On the Chinese military system in the 1850s, see Richard J. Smith, "Chinese Military Institutions in the Mid-Nineteenth Century, 1850–1860," *Journal of Asian History* 8 (1974): 122–161. On the self-strengthening period, there is a considerable body of work. Mary Clabaugh Wright, *The Last Stand of Chinese Conservatism: The T'ung-Chih Restoration, 1862–1874* (Stanford: Stanford University Press, 1957) is an invaluable survey. While Wright's argument that Confucianism was incompatible with modernity has been widely criticized, her empirical research is extraordinary and interpretations of specific issues remain cogent. On the recruit (*yongying*) armies, the works of the Taiwanese scholar Wang Ermin are essential. Particularly important is his analysis "Qingdai yongying zhidu" [The Brave Battalion system of the Qing Period], which is available in a collection of Wang's essays titled *Qingshi junshi shilunji* [Essays on military affairs in the Late Qing] (Taipei: Lianjing chubanshe, 1980). Wang's *Huai jun zhi* [Treatise on the Anhui Army] (Taipei: Academia Sinica, 1967) is the definitive work on the most important military force in the period leading up to 1895. Also useful is Stanley Spector, *Li Hung-chang and the Huai Army: A Study of Nineteenth Century Regionalism* (Seattle: University of Washington Press, 1964). On local militia, see Philip A. Kuhn, *Rebellion and Its Enemies in Late Imperial China: Militarization and Social Structure, 1796–1864* (Cambridge: Harvard University Press, 1970). On the efforts to create a modern navy, see John L. Rawlinson, *China's Struggle for Naval Development, 1839–1895* (Cambridge: Harvard University Press, 1967). The early history of China's modern arms industry is the subject of two excellent works, Thomas L. Kennedy, *The Arms of Kiangnan: Modernization in the Chinese Ordnance Industry, 1860–1895* (Boulder, CO: Westview Press, 1978) and David Pong, *Shen Pao-chen and China's Modernization in the Nineteenth Century* (Cambridge: Cambridge University Press, 1994), which deals with the creation of the Fuzhou Navy Yard. A useful collection of more recent scholarship related to Li Hongzhang's multifaceted role is Samuel C. Chu and Kwang-ching Liu, *Li Hung-chang and China's Early Modernization* (Armonk, NY: M. E. Sharpe, 1994).

On the creation of the New Armies after 1895, there is somewhat less material. Yoshihiro Hatano, "The New Armies," in Mary Clabaugh Wright, ed., *China in Revolution: The First Phase, 1900–1913* (New Haven: Yale University Press, 1968), is the best short account. Ralph L. Powell, *The Rise of Chinese Military Power, 1895–1912* (Princeton: Princeton University Press, 1955), while dated in its treatment of the period before the Sino–Japanese War, remains a useful general narrative on military developments after 1895. Stephen R. MacKinnon, *Power and Politics in Late Imperial China: Yuan Shi-kai in Beijing and Tianjin, 1901–1908* (Berkeley and Los Angeles: University of California Press, 1980) analyzes the role of Yuan Shikai and the formation of his Beiyang Army. Ernest P. Young, "Yuan

Shih-k'ai's Rise to the Presidency," in Wright, *China in Revolution*, considers the role of the New Armies and particularly Yuan Shikai in the overthrow of the Qing dynasty. The most complete treatment of the military's part in the fall of the Qing is Edmund S. K. Fung, *The Military Dimension of the Chinese Revolution* (Vancouver: University of British Columbia Press, 1980).

There is a startling shortage of accounts of military campaigns in English that take advantage of Chinese sources. A recent exception is Allen Fung, "Testing the Self-Strengthening: The Chinese Army in the Sino–Japanese War of 1894–5," *Modern Asian Studies* 30 (1996): 1007–1031, which offers an important corrective to textbook accounts based primarily on the reports of observers on the Japanese side.

SUGGESTIONS FOR FURTHER RESEARCH

There are vast gaps in the scholarship on this period and enormous opportunities for new research for those willing and able to use Chinese and Japanese sources. There is a considerable body of published primary source material in Chinese that has only minimally been exploited, and the First National Archives in Beijing, open to foreign scholars, is a treasure trove of new material. Detailed battle accounts of the Sino–Japanese War and the Sino–French War are badly needed, and Chinese documents can offer important new insights. While we have a fairly good idea of the larger structures of military organization, our knowledge of the actualities of life in the military, including training regimens, logistics, and other aspects of the infrastructure of war is still very limited. Research on the culture and social life of the military is also badly needed.

NOTES

1. Edwin Leung, "The Quasi-War in East Asia: Japan's Expedition to Taiwan and the Ryukyu Controversy," *Modern Asian Studies* 17 (1983): 257–281.

2. Kwang-ching Liu and Richard J. Smith, "The Military Challenge: The Northwest and the Coast," in *The Cambridge History of China*, vol. 11, *Late Ch'ing, 1800–1911, Part 2*, ed. John K. Fairbank and Kwang-ching Liu (Cambridge: Cambridge University Press, 1980), 244–245.

3. Memorial by Xu Tong in the documentary collection *Chouban yiwu shimo* [The management of barbarian affairs from first to last] (Rpt. Taipei, 1970), *tongzhi chao* 91, pp. 9b–10.

4. Richard S. Horowitz, "Central Power and State-Making: The Zongli Yamen and Self-Strengthening, 1860–1880" (Ph.D. diss., Harvard University, 1998), ch. 4.

5. Chen Shiwei, "Change and Continuity: The Political Mobilization of Shanghai Elites in 1900," *Papers on Chinese History* 3 (1994): 110–112.

6. Yung Wing, *My Life in China and America* (New York: Henry Holt, 1909), 148.

7. Rutherford Alcock, "Comments on William Gill, 'The Chinese Army,'" *Journal of the Royal United Service Institution* 24 (1881): 376.

8. Ibid.

9. John K. Fairbank, Katherine Frost Bruner, and Elizabeth MacLeod Matheson, *The I.G. in Peking: Letters of Robert Hart, Chinese Maritime Customs, 1868–1907,* vol. 2 (Cambridge, MA: Belknap Press, 1975), 1484.

10. For a clear articulation of the argument, see Franz Michael, "Introduction: Regionalism in Nineteenth Century China," in Stanley Spector, *Li Hung-chang and the Huai Army* (Seattle: University of Washington Press, 1964).

11. Among others, see Kwang-ching Liu, "The Limits of Regional Power in the Late Qing Period: A Reappraisal," *Tsing Hua Journal of Chinese Studies* (new series) 10 (1974): 207–223.

12. Philip A. Kuhn, *Rebellion and Its Enemies in Late Imperial China: Militarization and Social Structure, 1796–1864* (Cambridge: Harvard University Press, 1970), 211–225.

TEN

Warlordism in
Early Republican China

Edward A. McCord

The emergence of warlordism, a condition under which military commanders exercise autonomous political power by virtue of their personal control of military force, made the early Republican period (1912–1927) a dark chapter in Chinese history. Warlordism arose as the consequence of a militarization of politics that accompanied the fall of China's last imperial dynasty. Unlike military interventions in many countries, military rule did not appear suddenly in China as the result of a military coup. Rather, warlordism emerged over a period of time as the application of military force in political struggles over the creation and control of the postimperial government drew military commanders into politics and ultimately allowed them to parlay military power into political domination. The subsequent competition among these military commanders, or "warlords," to strengthen their own political positions led to additional military conflicts and civil wars, with devastating effects on Chinese society. In less than a decade after the 1911 Revolution, warlordism had become a defining feature of the Chinese "Republic."

The combination of personal military and political power seen in Republican-period warlordism was by no means a new phenomenon in Chinese history. Periods between dynasties had often been marked by political fragmentation among competing military leaders (the powerful military governors who arose during the collapse of the Tang dynasty being a notable example). A more immediate historical precedent occurred in the mid-nineteenth century when regional army commanders, such as Zeng Guofan and Li Hongzhang, organized and led personally-oriented armies to defeat the Taiping and other major rebellions. Rewarded with important civil positions as provincial governors or governors-general, these men wielded a considerable degree of political power, tempered only by their continued loyalty to the Qing dynasty.

The resemblance of these regional army commanders to later warlords has led some historians to trace twentieth-century warlordism to these nineteenth-century forces. However, the direct links connecting these armies and their commanders to Republican-period warlords are tenuous at best. The regional armies were first significantly reduced following the restoration of peace and then largely superseded at the turn of the century by modern-style "New Armies." Unlike the regional armies, which drew their strength from a chain of personal loyalties, these new forces were organized on a relatively nonpersonal or bureaucratic basis. More warlord armies actually originated from these modern-style forces than from the remnants of regional armies that survived to the end of the dynasty. Likewise, late Qing provincial governors, who supposedly inherited the personal military powers of regional army commanders, did not survive the fall of the dynasty to become warlords. Thus, while the personalization of military power seen in nineteenth-century regional armies, and the combination of military and civil authority under late Qing provincial governors, may have provided some inspiration for Republican-period military commanders, there was no direct line of succession from late-Qing regional army commanders to Republican warlords.

While the personalist orientation of military power under the warlords cannot be traced to late Qing military organization, the military fragmentation characteristic of warlordism was influenced by the organizational diversity of the late Qing military. China did not have a unified national army on the eve of the 1911 Revolution, but rather a hodgepodge of old and new-style forces, which were often organized on a provincial or local basis. This military fragmentation resulted in part from the dynasty's inability to harness sufficient central resources to create a truly unified national army. At the same time, this organizational diversity reflected a long-standing dynastic strategy that guarded against military usurpation by preventing the accumulation of too much military power in the hands of any one commander. The advantages of this organizational diversity were lost, though, with the fall of the dynasty. In its fragmented state, the Chinese army was in no position to act as a unifying national force in the face of political instability. On the contrary, military intervention, when it occurred, would reflect the military's own fragmented organization, and thus enhance rather than inhibit political disunity.

The rise of warlordism differed from previous periods of military fragmentation in Chinese history because it did not simply reflect a military struggle to establish a new dynasty, but political and military conflict over how to create a new, nondynastic state. The crucial part played by military men and military power in the 1911 Revolution itself had laid the groundwork for a more expansive political role by the military. Historians seeking to understand the overthrow of China's two-thousand-year-old imperial tradition in 1911 have often focused their attention on issues such as modernizing reform movements, the development of Chinese nationalist thought, and the activities of revolutionary societies. The result has often been to forget that the outcome of the 1911 Revolution, in the last analysis, was determined by military force.

The 1911 Revolution began with an uprising by the Hubei provincial New Army at Wuchang on October 10, 1911. One by one, a majority of provinces eventually followed Hubei's lead to declare their independence of the Qing dynasty and their support for the establishment of a Republic. In each case, New Army units played a leading role, either in provincial revolutionary uprisings or in providing military support for revolutionary declarations by civilian elites. The revolutionary predilection of New Army units was largely the result of the enlistment of large numbers of educated youths into these forces, inspired to no small extent by the increased status of military service in a time of rising nationalism. The susceptibility of these patriotic youths to revolutionary appeals quickly turned many New Army units into subversive threats to the dynasty they were supposed to defend. The 1911 Revolution cannot, of course, be entirely understood in military terms. The Revolution would not have occurred without a broader disaffection of the Chinese elite, of which military men were only one portion. Nonetheless, the revolutionary cause also could not have succeeded without this crucial military support.

Although setting an important precedent for military forays into politics and legitimating the use of military force for political ends, the army's role in the 1911 Revolution did not immediately result in full-blown warlordism. For example, initial revolutionary uprisings were largely carried out by activists in the rank and file of New Army units, not by military commanders, and often involved the ouster of senior officers who remained loyal to the dynasty. Thus, the personal control of military commanders over their troops, one hallmark of warlordism, was not yet evident in these military actions. A more important contribution of the revolution to the eventual emergence of warlordism was the institutionalization of military participation in government. In the aftermath of revolutionary uprisings, military men were included in the elite coalitions that organized new administrations in most rebellious provinces.

Recognizing the military demands of the revolutionary struggle, "military governors" were placed at the head of most of these provincial governments. The establishment of such positions did not necessarily mean the establishment of military rule. The participation of prominent gentry leaders in these governments helped to provide considerable continuity in civil administration. Over half of the provincial military governors who held office in the first months of the revolution were not even military men. Nonetheless, the creation of such posts would provide later military commanders with a foundation for the extension of their control over civil administration.

The military victory of the 1911 Revolution was never a foregone conclusion. The province-by-province progression of the revolution left many revolutionary forces temporarily isolated and vulnerable to military action by forces loyal to the dynasty. The Yangzi valley quickly became the focal point of a revolutionary civil war, with hard-fought battles over strategic cities such as Wuhan and Nanjing. While provincial New Armies dominated revolutionary uprisings, the Qing dynasty pinned its own hopes for the suppression of the revolt on the continued loyalty of the largest of the New Armies, the six-division Beiyang Army. To this end, the court recalled Yuan Shikai from his retirement to lead the dynasty's defense, counting on his influence as the army's founder to keep it loyal to the dynasty. Instead, Yuan played both sides of the fence. Hoping to bring the revolutionary war to a quick conclusion, the provisional president of the Republican forces, the revolutionary leader Sun Yat-sen, agreed to yield the presidency to Yuan Shikai in exchange for his betrayal of the Qing dynasty. When Yuan accepted these terms, the military balance of power shifted decisively in favor of the revolution. Using the threat of Beiyang Army defections, Yuan pressured the child emperor to abdicate and assumed the presidency of the new Chinese Republic.

The success of the 1911 Revolution in achieving the overthrow of the last imperial dynasty was unfortunately not accompanied by a consensus on the structure and distribution of political power in the new Republican regime. While Yuan Shikai advocated a centralized, bureaucratic government under a strong presidency, many revolutionary activists, emerging political parties, and elite-based provincial regimes favored increased local self-government, federalism, and a strong parliamentary system. All these arguments were framed in terms of creating greater national strength, but just as clearly reflected the personal political interests of their advocates. Having observed the political importance of military power in the revolution, neither Yuan nor his opponents were reluctant to use military force to resolve these issues. Accumulated grievances against what many saw as Yuan Shikai's dictatorial tendencies (including complicity in the assassination of his main parliamentary opponent and the negotiation of foreign loans to strengthen his military forces without parliamentary consent) finally came to a head in 1913 when Yuan arbitrarily dismissed several politically troublesome governors in former revolutionary provinces. Fearing Yuan's actions were aimed at the elimination of all political opposition, Sun Yat-sen reemerged to call for an anti-Yuan "Second Revolution."

Military force was decisive in the revolutionary attempt of 1913 as it had been in 1911. Only seven provinces responded to Sun Yat-sen's call, and most of these provinces had drastically reduced their military forces following the 1911 Revolution. Yuan had meanwhile expanded the Beiyang Army as the main "national" army (not coincidentally insuring the loyalty of its officers), and quickly defeated the forces arrayed against him. Yuan's actions in the wake of his victory confirmed Sun's worst fears. Yuan promulgated a new constitution that concentrated power in the presidency, dissolved the National Assembly and replaced it with a more subservient body, banned Sun's political party, removed independent provincial governors within reach of his armies, and abolished all local and provincial representative assemblies. Although his power over the entire country was never complete, Yuan did his best to transform the new Republic into a centralized dictatorship.

Due to the importance of military power in his own political rise and the fact that many of the military leaders to emerge as warlords originally served under him in the Beiyang Army, Yuan Shikai is sometimes referred to as the "father of warlordism." Nonetheless, having gained the presidency, Yuan was not prepared to see a devolution of political power into the hands of local military commanders. Whenever possible, he sought to keep military governorships out of the hands of the strongest commanders and to reestablish the precedence of civil governors over these military posts. Nonetheless, to the extent that Yuan continued to rely on military force to uphold his political authority, he ultimately undermined the strong central and civil state that was his goal. Yuan's failure became obvious in late 1915 when he sought to consolidate his authority even further by declaring himself emperor.

While many had been willing to accept Yuan's dictatorship as the price for peace and order, he overstepped the bounds of political tolerance with his monarchical ambitions. Revolutionary activists such as Sun Yat-sen, as well as more moderate politicians, appealed to military commanders in southwestern provinces that had not been occupied by Beiyang Army forces (Yunnan, Guizhou, Guangxi, and Guangdong) to rise against Yuan. The Yunnan Army was the first to respond. Renaming itself the National Protection Army in December 1915, the Yunnan Army initiated the National Protection or Anti-Monarchical War with a call for the overthrow of the new emperor. Expeditionary forces from Yunnan soon gained support from military forces in surrounding provinces until the entire southwest was in open revolt. Although Yuan sent Beiyang Army forces to crush the revolt, many of Yuan's own commanders were themselves uncomfortable with his imperial ambitions and were reluctant to press the war with vigor. As opposition to Yuan grew, some of his commanders began to consider their own military intervention against him. Only Yuan's death in June 1916 ended the need for further struggle.

The Anti-Monarchical War was a turning point in the emergence of warlordism. Military governors in National Protection provinces, most notably Tang Jiyao in Yunnan and Lu Rongting in Guangxi, took advantage of the conflict to throw off remaining central constraints and assume direct control over provincial administrations. In the north, a number of military commanders manipulated Yuan's need for their support to acquire broader administrative powers. Two prominent examples were Wang Zhanyuan, commander of the Beiyang 2nd Division in Hubei, and Zhang Zuolin, commander of the largest garrison force in Fengtian province, both of whom had been denied top administrative posts by Yuan. With the outbreak of the war, these men forced Yuan's agreement to their appointments as military governors and their control over civil administrations. By this means, these commanders gained direct access to official financial resources to support, and thus exert greater personal control over, the military forces at their command. For such men, then, the Anti-Monarchical War marked their transition to warlordism.

The emergence of warlordism was not, however, a uniform process. In some areas, no single military commander possessed sufficient power to gain a dominant political position. In a number of provinces, a degree of civilian authority remained or was restored at the end of the Anti-Monarchical War. Yuan Shikai's death even provided some hope that a reconstituted central government could regain control over increasingly autonomous provinces and begin to recover the political powers assumed by military men. Unfortunately, the main result of Yuan's death was to reopen, rather than resolve, the basic constitutional issues that had troubled the Republic since its inception. The ensuing political struggles only

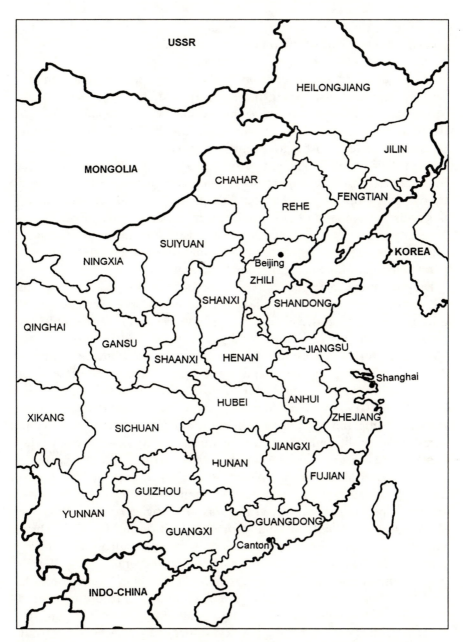

Map 10.1   China during the Warlord Period, 1916–1928. Adapted by Don Graff based upon "Provinces of China, 1916–1928," in *Warlord Politics in China,* Hsi-sheng Ch'i (Stanford: Stanford University Press, 1976).

served to confirm the political importance of the military and to complete the hold of warlordism on Chinese society.

Hopes for restored national unity at the end of the Anti-Monarchical War were based on a number of political compromises balancing the various interests that had emerged during the war. The vice president, Li Yuanhong, who now succeeded to the presidency, had revolutionary credentials (as military governor of Hubei during the 1911 Revolution) but an ambiguous relationship to revolutionary activists (having opposed the Second Revolution). Thus he was seen as a potentially neutral political figure. The continuing importance of the Beiyang Army was recognized by giving two top Beiyang Army leaders, Duan Qirui and Feng Guozhang, positions as premier and vice president, respectively. As a concession to Yuan's opponents, the National Assembly dissolved after the Second Revolution was restored, as was the provisional constitution Yuan had supplanted with his more authoritarian document.

Despite this balancing of political interests, there was still no consensus within the new government on basic constitutional issues, such as the relative powers of executive and legislative branches or the relationship between national, provincial, and local governments. Bitter political struggles soon broke out between the president, the premier, the National Assembly, and the provinces over a wide range of issues. In the absence of an appropriate political framework to resolve these issues, those who had access to military power were not reluctant to use it to achieve their political ends. Initial military pressure on political issues was largely limited to threatening public announcements by military commanders. Such pressure became more organized when the Beiyang Army and other northern military governors formed a "military governors' association" to support Duan Qirui's struggles against both Li Yuanhong and the National Assembly. Open military intervention was not long in coming. When Li Yuanhong tried to remove Duan from his position in May 1917, Duan rallied his military supporters to declare their independence of Li's government. Li then accepted the offer of another general, Zhang Xun, to mediate this conflict. As the first step in this "mediation," Zhang forced Li to dissolve the National Assembly. Then, with his own troops ensconced in Beijing, Zhang betrayed Li by declaring the restoration of the Qing dynasty. As Li fled the capital, the political future of China was again firmly in military hands.

Zhang Xun's restoration attempt provided Duan with an opportunity to lead his own military supporters to Beijing to "save" the Republic, and in the process create a new government dominated by the Beiyang Army.

Easily defeating Zhang's forces, Duan announced that the imperial restoration had destroyed the constitutional foundation of Li's government. While Duan kept his own position as premier, his Beiyang Army compatriot, Vice President Feng Guozhang, assumed the presidency in Li's place. A new constitution and a new National Assembly were then created to support their government.

Having established Beiyang Army dominance over the Beijing government, Duan and Feng turned their attention to the restoration of central authority over the rest of the country. Their main targets were southern provinces that had remained largely autonomous since the Anti-Monarchical War. Riding on their military success in Beijing, Duan and Feng agreed to use military force to achieve this political unification. In the summer of 1917, Beiyang Army troops began to move into Hunan and Sichuan provinces in the first step of a pincer movement to bring recalcitrant southern provinces to heel.

The southern provinces that had participated in the National Protection Movement against Yuan refused to accept the legitimacy of the unilateral Beiyang Army reconstitution of the Beijing government. Seeking to build on this opposition, Sun Yat-sen called for the organization of a "Constitutional Protection" movement to restore the early Republican constitution and recall the original National Assembly. Supported by the main military leaders of the south, Lu Rongting of Guangxi and Tang Jiyao of Yunnan, Sun organized an alternate government in Canton (Guangzhou). The legitimacy of this government was enhanced when both the Chinese navy and a substantial portion of the old National Assembly joined Sun in Canton. Not unexpectedly, then, when Hunan and Sichuan armies rose up against the northern invasion of their provinces, they received the political support of the Canton government and military support from other southern provinces. The result was the outbreak of yet another civil war, the Constitutional Protection or North–South War.

As in previous military conflicts of the early Republic, the dependence on individual military commanders to carry out the political objectives of the North–South War provided an opportunity for these commanders to increase their own political influence. The appearance of competing Beijing and Canton political authorities vying for the support of these commanders only served to enhance their political leverage. The end result was that while the North–South War was supposedly fought over constitutional issues, the actual course of the war was determined by the interests of the military commanders who fought it.

The ability of individual military commanders to influence political outcomes was most evident in actions taken by Wu Peifu, commander of the Beiyang vanguard in Hunan. Wu had originally been a strong supporter of military unification. Assigned to the Hunan front in early 1918, Wu's forces were largely responsible for victories that brought most of Hunan under Beiyang control. However, when Duan Qirui slighted his contribution by awarding the post of Hunan military governor to another commander, Wu negotiated a cease-fire with his southern enemies and effectively brought the northern advance, and the war itself, to a halt. Wu's action, though particularly striking in its effect, was by no means exceptional. From the other side of the conflict, Lu Rongting made it clear that he would abandon his opposition to the Beijing government if his own hegemony over Guangdong and Guangxi was guaranteed.

The independent actions taken by Wu, Lu and other commanders in the North–South War made this conflict another turning point in the development of warlordism. The constitutional issues that had framed earlier conflicts faded into the background as this and subsequent wars increasingly reflected little more than the competing interests of military commanders and military factions. In their public announcements, military commanders continued to frame their actions in terms of higher patriotic principles. Some were no doubt even sincere in their commitment to these principles. Nonetheless, military men had become political actors on the basis of their military power, and to survive as political actors this military power had to be maintained. The warlord era therefore came to be defined by the increasing number and scale of civil wars and military conflicts fought by warlords and warlord factions for political and military resources.

The appearance of competing military factions was in itself another significant feature of the North–South War. While every military commander was a potential warlord, the actual political autonomy of individual commanders could be limited by numerous constraints, including the size of their armies, access to financial and military resources, and the comparative power of other military commanders with whom they interacted. Commanders therefore usually found their interests best served by factional associations that increased their own power through collaboration with other commanders. Warlord factions were usually headed by a military leader who had attained a significant political position that gave him access to resources (tax revenues, weapons, and administrative positions) that could be used to reward his followers. While familial, school, and organizational ties were emphasized to enhance factional unity, the success of a factional leader was measured by his ability to provide these rewards. Ironically, this success could also have a detrimental effect on factional unity as access to resources increased the autonomous political interests of individual faction members. In this regard, the Beiyang Army under Yuan Shikai was a prototype for subsequent warlord factions in both their strengths and weaknesses. While Yuan initially used the Beiyang Army to establish his will over much of China, the commanders who benefited most from his success also contributed to his downfall by their unwillingness to risk their own interests by providing full support for Yuan's monarchical enterprise.

Fissures that were already apparent within northern and southern forces prior to the North–South War initially provided the foundation for the appearance of two dominant factions on each side. The Beiyang Army and its affiliates split into two main factions named after the home provinces and main bases of their top leaders: the Anhui clique led by Duan Qirui and the Zhili clique led first by Feng Guozhang. Two leading military factions also arose in the south: the Yunnan clique under Tang Jiyao and the Guangxi clique of Lu Rongting. The appearance of these dominant factions would, however, eventually be followed by additional factional divisions. The emergence of military factions also marked a shift in the direction of subsequent military conflicts, which would no longer pit the north against the south but would reflect narrower regional struggles among these factions. The overall pattern of these struggles differed somewhat in the north and in the south. In the north, large military coalitions formed and collapsed over the course of major wars fought for control of the Beijing government. In the south, military conflicts reflected the rise of provincial-based factions to challenge the dominance of the Yunnan and Guangxi cliques.

The factional breakup of the Beiyang Army into Anhui and Zhili cliques began with a division of interests over the strategy and the spoils of the North–South War. Duan Qirui had been the main advocate of military unification and used the war to strengthen the positions of his closest associates. While Feng Guozhang initially supported the war, he soon found greater political benefits, in his rivalry with Duan, in supporting a negotiated settlement of north–south differences. Feng found support from Beiyang Army commanders in central China who feared the expansion of the conflict into their domains, and from commanders such as Wu Peifu who resented Duan's lack of recognition of their efforts. When Feng died in 1919, shortly after the end of his term of office as president, Wu Peifu's immediate superior, Cao Kun, assumed leadership of the Zhili clique.

The rivalry between the Anhui and Zhili cliques eventually led to war. The prelude to this conflict was the withdrawal of Wu Peifu and other Zhili-affiliated commanders from Hunan in early 1920. In an advance agreement with his supposed southern enemies, Wu also allowed the Hunan Army to follow on the heels of his retreat and drive Duan's supporters from Hunan. Despite this loss, Duan's Anhui clique was still the strongest power in the north, controlling a broad swath of provinces across northern China and down the eastern coast. Apart from Cao's home base in south Zhili, Zhili clique commanders only controlled the Yangzi valley provinces of Hubei, Jiangxi, and Jiangsu. This disparity was reduced, though, when Cao formed an alliance with Zhang Zuolin, the emerging leader of a non-Beiyang military faction based in Manchuria, usually referred to as the Fengtian clique. In exchange for Zhang's support, Duan had originally supported the extension of Zhang's power from Fengtian to the other two Manchurian provinces of Jilin and Heilongjiang. Nonetheless, when Duan began to support the buildup of another force on the Mongolian border, which Zhang saw as his sphere of influence, Zhang shifted his support to Cao. In the summer of 1920, Cao and Zhang attacked and crushed Duan's forces between them in the Zhili–Anhui War.

The Zhili–Anhui War resulted in a major redistribution of power in north China. Duan Qirui was forced to resign, while the Fengtian and Zhili cliques joined to organize a new government in Beijing. Zhang's armies meanwhile moved up to Beijing and took control over northern provinces along the Manchurian and Mongolian borders. Most of the rest of north and central China came under Zhili control. The Anhui clique was left only with a small foothold in Zhejiang and Fujian provinces. The Zhili–Fengtian alliance did not last long. Conflicts soon arose between the two cliques over the policies and resources of the Beijing government. The result was yet another major war, the First Zhili–Fengtian War in the spring of 1922. This war pushed Zhang Zuolin's forces back into Manchuria and gave the Zhili clique total control over the Beijing government.

As internal conflicts in north China had eliminated any hope of a reconquest of the south, successive Beijing governments had sought to negotiate some resolution of their differences. Feng Guozhang's successor as president, the Beiyang Army elder statesman Xu Shichang, supported a north–south peace conference in 1919. However, this conference broke down over the refusal of military commanders on both sides to compromise over contested territory. Another attempt to entice the south back into Beijing's fold came after the First Zhili–Fengtian War, when Li Yuanhong was recalled to the presidency and the early-Republican National

Assembly restored in an obvious concession to long-standing southern "constitutional protection" demands. This effort was derailed, however, by Cao Kun's growing ambition. In the summer of 1923 Cao forced Li to resign and bribed the National Assembly to elect him president. These actions destroyed Cao's reputation as a national leader and shattered hope in many quarters for national reunification under the Zhili clique.

The downfall of the Zhili clique was not long in coming. When Zhili forces attacked the Anhui clique remnant in Zhejiang and Fujian in September 1924, Zhang Zuolin, fearing his own increasing isolation, declared war against the Zhili clique in the Second Zhili–Fengtian War. The record number of nearly 300,000 troops mobilized for this conflict reflected the increasing scale and intensity of warfare in this period. The Zhili clique began the war with a clear advantage. Its hopes for a decisive victory were smashed, however, when Feng Yuxiang, the "Christian general" whose well-disciplined army was a key factor in Zhili strength, switched sides. Seizing Beijing and forcing Cao Kun's resignation, Feng collaborated with Zhang Zuolin in a successful two-front attack that defeated the main Zhili army under Wu Peifu on the Manchurian front.

The Second Zhili–Fengtian War left the north more politically confused than at any time since Yuan Shikai's death. The Fengtian clique expanded beyond Manchuria, taking control of Beijing away from Feng Yuxiang and extending its power south along the eastern coast. Feng Yuxiang emerged as a new faction leader with control over several provinces to the north and west of Beijing. Zhili clique commanders still controlled a swath of provinces from Henan to Fujian. However, the relationship between these factions remained unsettled, and alliances were broken as quickly as they were made. Thus, while Zhili commanders resisted the advance of Fengtian armies toward the Yangzi River, Wu Peifu allied with Zhang Zuolin in an attack on Feng Yuxiang. Meanwhile, little pretense of regular constitutional government remained. The Beijing government continued to operate under a series of ad hoc chief executives, but no new president was elected. Finally, in 1927 Zhang Zuolin took direct control over the Beijing government with the title of "grand marshal."

Warlord struggles in the south led to an even greater degree of political disintegration. In the period between the 1911 Revolution and the North–South War, both the Yunnan and Guangxi armies had expanded beyond their own borders and allied with other provincial forces to form two multiprovince military factions. The Yunnan clique under Tang Jiyao sent troops into southern Sichuan and exerted influence over Guizhou and west Hunan. The Guangxi clique under Lu Rongting extended its control over Guangdong and allied with provincial forces in south Hunan. Northern threats in the National Protection and North–South Wars had encouraged the collaboration of these two factions and their local allies against a common enemy. With the removal of these threats, however, this common interest faded. The result was not just conflict between the Yunnan and Guangxi cliques, but increased resentment by other provincial armies over the occupation of their provinces by Yunnan and Guangxi troops. Over the course of 1920, the power of these two cliques was drastically reduced as the Yunnan and Guangxi armies were forced back within their own provincial borders. Internal struggles within these armies following this debacle eventually forced both Tang and Lu from power. The decline of these two factions did not, however, lead to greater peace in the south, but intensified struggles by military factions within each province for the control of provincial and local governments.

In contrast to the north, where multiprovince factions continued to fight for control of Beijing with at least the stated goal of restoring central authority, some southern warlords championed the idea of federalism as a defense against renewed northern invasions or threats from their immediate neighbors. Leading civilian politicians also supported this idea, hoping that the principle of provincial self-government would end interprovincial military conflicts, eliminate the need for military rule, and ultimately provide a federalist framework for renewed national unity. In the end, though, provincial self-government and federalism simply became slogans used by provincial warlords to justify their own power and did little to stop either inter- or intraprovincial military conflicts.

A wild card in warlord struggles of the south was Sun Yat-sen's effort to establish an alternate national government at Canton and initiate his own military campaign for national unification. While a variety of warlords gave lip service to Sun's cause, they did so mainly because an affiliation with Sun helped legitimate their own regimes. They were less willing to support Sun's military objectives or to allow Sun to interfere in their own affairs. Thus, after coming into conflict with Lu Rongting, Sun was forced to resign from his position as head of the Canton government in 1918. In 1921, Sun was invited to create a new government in Canton following the expulsion of the Guangxi army from Guangdong. In little over a year, though, Sun was again forced to leave his position in a conflict with the dominant Guangdong warlord. Only on his third attempt in 1923 would Sun finally establish a solid base in Guangdong by developing his own party army to keep his warlord enemies at bay. Although Sun, who died in 1925, would not see the results, his vision of an antiwarlord Northern Expedition was finally realized in 1926. The success of this campaign, under the leadership of Chiang Kai-shek, resulted in the nominal reunification under a new Nationalist Party (Guomindang) central government established in Nanjing in 1927. This event has conventionally been taken to mark the end of China's warlord era.

This brief survey only touches the surface of the convoluted politics and incessant warfare of the warlord period. While factional alliances provided a broad framework for many conflicts, some warlords remained independent or were only loosely allied to these factions. Numerous minor conflicts involved nothing more than the competing interests of individual commanders. Territorial bases of warlord power were also in a constant state of flux. The size of warlord bases varied from multiprovince alliances, to single-province enclaves, to subprovince garrison commands. A few warlords were able to maintain stable control over one area for fairly long periods of time, with Yan Xishan's rule over Shanxi province from 1911 to 1949 setting the record. Other regions experienced alternating patterns of territorial consolidation and fragmentation under a succession of competing warlords. In most cases, war remained the primary catalyst for these territorial and political changes.

The conditions of warlordism had a devastating effect on the lives of the Chinese people, as well as on broader nationalist aspirations. As military commanders competed to increase their own military "capital," the number of men under arms rose from under half a million at the end of the Qing dynasty to over two million in the 1920s. The dedication of this expanded military establishment to domestic struggle, however, weakened rather than strengthened its effectiveness for national defense. The political and military fragmentation represented by warlordism likewise limited China's ability to take a united stand against foreign threats. Meanwhile, with warlords in control of civil administrations, state finances were increasingly committed to military ends. The people were burdened with new taxes and loans raised by warlord rulers to support their growing armies, while funding for education and other public services was drastically reduced. Populations in war zones suffered more directly from the requisitions and abuses of passing armies as well as from battles that disrupted agriculture and commerce and destroyed their homes.

While warlordism grew from military struggles that had attempted to resolve the political problems of the early Chinese Republic, within a decade of the 1911 Revolution the devastating effects of warlord misrule and the destructiveness of warlord wars made warlordism itself China's most pressing political problem. Meanwhile, the political issues that had framed early Republican politics were also changed by the emergence of warlordism. Thus, opportunistic warlord manipulation of the Beijing government and hypocritical support for local "self-government" discredited both constitutionalism and federalism as political alternatives. At the same time, the emergence of antiwarlordism as a nationalist goal stimulated new political movements, and provided a context for both the revitalization of Sun Yat-sen's Nationalist Party and the founding of the Chinese Communist Party.

Despite the "victory" of the Nationalist Party's Northern Expedition, and the "reunification" of China under a new Nationalist government in Nanjing in 1927, it would be some time before the shadow of warlordism over China would be lifted. First, all warlords were not simply eliminated by the Northern Expedition. Many were absorbed into the Nationalist party army and, in exchange for their allegiance to the new government, allowed to retain a considerable degree of political autonomy in their garrison areas. These residual warlords would remain a thorn in the side of the Nationalist government and would not be completely eliminated until after the Communist victory in 1949. Although the warlords did eventually disappear, the legacy of warlordism was more lasting. To achieve success in a military era, both the Nationalist and the Communist parties ultimately had to find ways to accommodate military power within their political structures. The importance of the military as a foundation for political power was perhaps most obvious in Chiang Kai-shek's government, both on the mainland and in Taiwan. However, Mao Zedong also drew a lesson from the warlord era that "political power grows out of the barrel of a gun." Although Mao insisted that the party should control the gun, the People's Liberation Army has nonetheless remained a political force in the Chinese Communist Party up to the present. Finally, warlordism also left an enduring scar on the political consciousness of the Chinese people. The ability of the Communist Party to appeal to popular apprehensions about threats to national unity or the danger of political disorder are rooted, at least in part, in memories of the civil wars and political instability of the warlord era.

SUGGESTIONS FOR FURTHER READING

The two most important studies of Yuan Shikai and the Beiyang Army for the late Qing and early Republican periods respectively are Stephen R. MacKinnon, *Power and Politics in Late Imperial China: Yuan Shi-kai in Beijing and Tianjin, 1901–1908* (Berkeley and Los Angeles: University of California Press, 1980) and

Ernest P. Young, *The Presidency of Yuan Shih-k'ai: Liberalism and Dictatorship in Early Republican China* (Ann Arbor: University of Michigan Press, 1977). Both works challenge the conventional portrayal of Yuan as the "father of Chinese warlordism" with more complicated pictures of Yuan's role in this transitional period. An important study of the role of the military in the 1911 Revolution, with a particular emphasis on the revolutionary subversion of the New Armies, is Edmund S. K. Fung, *The Military Dimension of the Chinese Revolution* (Vancouver: University of British Columbia Press, 1980). The only major work to focus specifically on the issue of the origins of Chinese warlordism, examined through case studies of Hunan and Hubei provinces, is Edward A. McCord, *The Power of the Gun: The Emergence of Modern Chinese Warlordism* (Berkeley and Los Angeles: University of California Press, 1993).

A significant number of books have been published that describe individual warlords or warlord cliques. Two classic biographical studies are Donald Gillin, *Warlord: Yen Hsi-shan in Shansi Province, 1911–1949* (Princeton: Princeton University Press, 1967) and James E. Sheridan, *Chinese Warlord: The Career of Feng Yu-hsiang* (Stanford: Stanford University Press, 1966). Two additional studies of major warlord figures (Wu Peifu and Zhang Zuolin) that also delve more deeply into the relationship between warlords and imperialist powers in China are Odoric Y. K. Wou, *Militarism in Modern China: The Career of Wu P'ei-fu* (Dawson: Australian National University Press, 1978) and Gavan McCormack, *Chang Tso-lin in Northeast China, 1911–1928: China, Japan and the Manchurian Idea* (Stanford: Stanford University Press, 1977). Two excellent studies of specific warlord factions are Donald S. Sutton, *Provincial Militarism and the Chinese Republic: The Yunnan Army, 1905–25* (Ann Arbor: University of Michigan Press, 1980) and Diana Lary, *Region and Nation: The Kwangsi Clique in Chinese Politics, 1925–1937* (Cambridge: Cambridge University Press, 1974). Robert A. Kapp examines one of the more extreme examples of military fragmentation within one province in *Szechwan and the Chinese Republic: Provincial Militarism and Central Power, 1911–1938* (New Haven: Yale University Press, 1973). The best of the very few works to examine warlord politics in a more comprehensive fashion is Hsi-sheng Ch'i, *Warlord Politics in China, 1916–1928* (Stanford: Stanford University Press, 1976), which applies systems theory analysis to the relations of warlord factions. The broader factional politics that characterized warlord struggles for the control of the Beijing government are also examined in detail in Andrew Nathan, *Peking Politics, 1918–1923: Factionalism and the Failure of Constitutionalism* (Berkeley and Los Angeles: University of California Press, 1976).

A few authors have contributed more topical studies of warlordism. One example is Diana Lary's excellent study, *Warlord Soldiers: Chinese Common Soldiers, 1911–1937* (Cambridge: Cambridge University Press, 1985). One aspect of the complicated issue of how warlords armed their forces is examined in Anthony B. Chan, *Arming the Chinese: The Western Armaments Trade in Warlord China, 1920–1928* (Vancouver: University of British Columbia Press, 1982). Finally,

Arthur Waldron, *From War to Nationalism: China's Turning Point, 1924–1925* (Cambridge: Cambridge University Press, 1995) is the only book to examine a specific war and its broader impact on Chinese society.

SUGGESTIONS FOR FURTHER RESEARCH

With the focus of much past scholarship on the careers of individual warlords, the histories of military cliques, and warlord politics (largely defined in terms of relations among the warlords themselves), many issues relating warlordism to broader developments in Chinese society have barely been explored. For example, much work remains to be done on the specific economic impact of warlordism, not only on the lives of the Chinese people but on the shape of the Chinese economy. A better understanding of the development of modern Chinese political thought and institutions could result from more careful study of subjects such as the psychological effect of persistent warfare on Chinese society, the role of warlordism as both a stimulant for and an obstacle to revolutionary movements, and the impact of military rule on government administration. Finally, with the exception of the few topical studies noted, many of the classic subjects of traditional military history have been largely unexplored. Further study, for example, of developments in military organization, strategy, and logistics in relation to the actual conduct of war under warlordism is needed to round out an understanding of this period of China's history.

ELEVEN

The National Army from Whampoa to 1949

Chang Jui-te

Following the founding of the Republic in 1911, the Guomindang adopted two approaches in its efforts to gain power. On the one hand, the KMT attempted to work within the parliamentary system to gain control of the National Assembly through electoral victories. On the other hand, the party recognized the limits imposed on the legislature by the very real power of the warlords, and accordingly adopted a policy of allying with certain less objectionable warlords in order to overthrow others. Both approaches failed, however, and even the warlord Chen Jiongming, whose career had flourished under Sun Yat-sen's patronage, eventually fell out with the KMT and launched a rebellion in 1922 that almost put an end to Sun's career. At that point, Sun belatedly realized that if his revolution was going to have any chance at success, he would have to look for military support from somewhere other than his inconstant warlord allies. To that end, he decided to establish his own military force and immediately started to look abroad for potential sources of material support.

For many years, Sun Yat-sen had taken the democratic political systems of the United States and Western Europe as the model for China's development. For their part, the great powers had always considered China to be a backward country, prone to disorder, and therefore in need of a military strongman to ensure the political stability so conducive to their commercial interests. The revolutionary movement led by Sun not only contributed to this disorder, but his advocacy of nationalism and the abrogation of the unequal treaties constituted a direct threat to the interests of the great powers. For these reasons, the powers not only did not support Sun, they viewed him as an enemy and accordingly boycotted all his activities. Chen Jiongming's revolt and the hostility of the great powers persuaded Sun to reexamine the possibility of cooperating with the Soviet Union, itself still somewhat of an international pariah. Sun felt that the Soviet planned economy closely resembled his own vision for China's development. He was also very interested in the secrets behind the Soviet success in establishing an effective party machine and a powerful party army. In particular, he was impressed by the fact that the Red Army had managed to resist a strong Allied intervention despite its inferiority in all types of military equipment. Sun made contact with the Soviets and was rewarded for his efforts by a promise of aid. It should be noted that up to this point in Sun's career as a revolutionary, no country or organization had ever been willing to provide large-scale financial support, let alone assist him in establishing a revolutionary military force. The eventual Soviet offer of support was therefore hard to resist, even more so in light of the munitions embargo that had been imposed on China by the great powers since 1919.

In January 1923 the Soviet Union dispatched Adolf Joffe to Shanghai to hold talks with Sun on questions pertaining to future Sino–Soviet cooperation. At that time, Sun formally requested the dispatch of a Soviet military advisory group, and plans were made for the establishment of a party military academy. In August of that year, Sun sent his associate Chiang Kai-shek (who had received a professional military education in China and Japan) to Moscow with instructions to conduct preliminary research on the Soviet military system, including political training in the Red Army. In October 1923, in keeping with the Soviet demand for cooperation with the nascent Chinese Communist Party (CCP), the KMT carried out a series of party reforms that culminated in the inclusion of a number of CCP members under the auspices of the first "United Front." These reforms paved the way for the founding of the Whampoa military academy the following year, a move that would prove to have a decisive impact on subsequent political developments within China.

Sun's decision to develop the KMT's own military force led directly to the founding of the Chinese Nationalist Party Army Officer Academy in 1924. The choice of site was determined by Sun's own limited power base, which at that time barely extended beyond Canton (Guangzhou). The academy was located on Huangbu Island near Canton (with the name Whampoa derived from the Cantonese pronunciation). Chiang Kai-shek acted as commandant, and the school's military curriculum was set up under the guidance of the Soviet advisory group, utilizing the latest military theories and techniques, albeit with a distinct Soviet flavor. Unfortunately, the exigencies of the revolution severely limited the time available for training, so the emphasis naturally had to be on the practical knowledge and skills required on the battlefield. Like all other Chinese military schools, Whampoa was influenced by Japanese models. There was, however, one way in which Whampoa differed from the other schools: From the very beginning political instruction played a major part in the training. All told, there were more than twenty topics covered in the political curriculum, including Sun Yat-sen's own ideology of the "Three Principles of the People" (*San Min Zhuyi*), the anatomy of imperialism, Soviet studies, comparative political systems, revolutionary history, and the study of student, peasant, and labor movements. Further reflecting the Soviet experience, the Whampoa school also established a political bureau and arranged for a system of party representatives (in this case from the KMT) who were modeled after the commissars of the Red Army. They supervised day-to-day administration, participated in management decisions, directed party activities, and personally took charge of political training in their units. In general, they were responsible for ensuring that all military training and combat missions were completed, and to that end, all orders issued by military commanders had to obtain the endorsement of the party representative before implementation.

As commander of the Whampoa forces, Chiang Kai-shek often boasted that his troops were the first in China to have a party commissar system. Despite his later break with the Communists, Chiang was always a supporter of an effective commissar system and political training for his troops. In his drive to turn the KMT force into a Chinese version of the Soviet Red Army, Chiang stressed the use of Sun's Three Principles of the People as the basis for political indoctrination. This commissar system was preserved even after the success of the Northern Expedition, the split with the CCP, and the reunification of the country, with special party bureaus being retained in all formations above the divisional level. Unfortunately, over time the system lost its effectiveness as more and more party representatives were appointed from above as opposed to being elected from members within a given military unit. That, coupled with the fact that the appointees were often full-time party workers with other more pressing responsibilities, ensured that the system gradually lost its coherence and eventually came to exist in name only.

In the first eventful years of its existence, the Whampoa-based military arm of the Guomindang underwent numerous changes. In late 1924, only a few months after the school had opened, the first training regiment was activated. School instructors led this regiment, and the very first graduates acted as platoon commanders. The bulk of the ordinary soldiers were selected from the hodgepodge of other units loyal to Sun Yat-sen in the greater Canton area. As more cadets graduated, Sun added a second training regiment and officially christened the academy force the Guomindang Party Army. Sun himself acted as generalissimo, and appointed Whampoa commandant Chiang Kai-shek as his military secretary. In April 1925 Chiang was appointed commander of the constantly expanding Party Army, and in August of that same year, the Military Affairs Committee of the KMT announced the organization of a National Revolutionary Army, with the two Whampoa training regiments joining to form its first division. From this point on, all units under the jurisdiction of the Nationalist regime were collectively known as the National Revolutionary Army.

The first Whampoa graduates gave an excellent account of themselves during the Eastern (1925) and Northern (1926–1928) Expeditions. Although Sun's warlord allies did much of the fighting, the students and staff played an important role in both campaigns, and to a certain extent their determination and daring compensated for the tactical inexperience of some of their commanders. Although they were often at odds with Chiang Kai-shek and his staff over both strategic and tactical issues and considered the much-celebrated attack on Huizhou (during the Eastern Expedition) to be an unnecessary waste of lives, even the hardened Soviet advisors were impressed by the performance of the Whampoa units. They displayed a level of esprit de corps and combat tenacity that had largely been absent from the internecine squabbles of the warlords, and their enemies generally gave way before the firebrands from Whampoa. Indeed, many of the students and staff went on to play important roles in modern Chinese history. By the end of the 1940s, many of those who had once held positions on the school staff were serving as commanders-in-chief, provincial governors, or heads of central government ministries. Many Whampoa graduates, particularly those from the first four classes, went on to hold command positions at the division and corps level. These former students and staff were often seen as an elite group within the military, and were generally referred to as the Whampoa clique.

With the success of the Northern Expedition and the reunification of most of the nation, the military academy followed the KMT government to the new capital at Nanjing, and in March 1928 the new school was officially renamed the Central Military Academy. In the aftermath of unification, faced as they were with a bewildering array of disparate local and regional forces, the new government had to deal with the difficult task of standardizing both military education and military organization throughout the country. The Central Military Academy played a crucial role in this process, becoming in effect the breeding ground for the officers-cum-agents of centralization that were posted to every unit across the country. Chiang Kai-shek's task was made somewhat easier through the assistance of a quasi-official German military advisory group that came to China in the early 1930s, and the quality of the officers who graduated during this period was considered quite high.

Unfortunately, the small numbers of advisors and the demands of the ongoing anti-Communist campaigns made it difficult to expand the school quickly enough to meet the demand for junior officers. Between 1928 and 1937, the Central Military Academy only graduated 10,731 officers, a number that fell far short of even the peacetime requirements of an army as large as China's. With the outbreak of the Anti-Japanese War in 1937, the high number of casualties and the rapid expansion of the army essentially prevented Academy graduates from exerting any decisive influence on the quality of Chiang's troops. In the furious fighting that followed the outbreak of the war with Japan, the attrition rate for lower-level officers was extremely high. For example, during the fighting in and around Shanghai in late 1937, which saw Chiang Kai-shek commit his crack German-trained divisions to a battle of attrition with the Japanese, almost 10,000 lower-level officers were lost in a single three-month period. With no way to replace losses on that scale, a vacuum quickly developed. The demand for new officers grew quickly, and lowering the threshold entry requirements turned out to be the easiest way to bring in more candidates.

Prewar regulations had stipulated that only high school graduates could sit for the Academy's entrance exams. Starting in 1937, however, those standards were lowered to include junior high graduates, and it was not unheard of for some who had not even attained that level of schooling to gain admission. Prior to the war against Japan, the pay and benefits of officers had improved to the point where they were considered quite good, and as a result there were large numbers of applicants for the limited positions in the Central Military Academy and the school could afford to be selective. For example, when the school started looking for students for the twelfth class in 1935, the acceptance rate was only 7 percent. Due to the large increase in the number of students needed after the outbreak of the war with Japan, the acceptance rate rose dramatically. According to the records for the Number Six Branch School of the Military Academy, the acceptance rate in 1940 was as high as 87 percent. Not only were more candidates being accepted, both the curriculum and the training period were reduced. During the war, the time cadets spent at the

Central Military Academy and its various branch schools, including the period spent on basic training, was at most two years and seven months, with some courses lasting less than nine months. The constant pressure to produce more officers in less time was exacerbated by wartime shortages of funds and equipment, and the lack of a rigid quality-control system inevitably led to a decline in the quality of the graduates, thus undoing much of what had been accomplished in the prewar period.

Most of the original commanders of the National Revolutionary Army were graduates of the Baoding Military Academy founded by Duan Qirui in 1912. By the time of the outbreak of the war with Japan, the place of these Baoding graduates had been taken over by the new Whampoa officers. This trend was clearest among those officers who actually exercised direct control over troops, such as corps and divisional commanders. Most of those wartime general-level officers had graduated from the earliest Whampoa classes, receiving only an abbreviated course of training (six months to one year), and therefore their basic military education was limited. The Army War College was the main organization responsible for providing further in-depth tactical, strategic, and administrative training for commanders, but the number of graduates was far too small to have any significant impact. By the end of the war with Japan, there were only 2,100 War College graduates throughout the army, and most commanders had not been to the school. In the armies of most advanced nations, officer academy graduates were able to further their military education through a carefully planned rotation system among different positions, units, and specialized schools. This ensured that those officers who rose to high rank were well versed in their own trade and familiar with the workings of other branches. Officers in the National Army rarely had that opportunity, and this was reflected in their generally low level of professional knowledge.

Following the founding of the National Revolutionary Army, the steady succession of campaigns and the high number of casualties among the Whampoa officers—who tended to lead from the front in the early days—resulted in excessively rapid promotions and a corresponding decrease in opportunities to gain necessary experience at every level. These factors conspired to prevent Chiang Kai-shek from improving the quality of his commanders, and it is not surprising that at a conference in 1938 Chiang himself pointed out that in terms of military knowledge and skills his commanders were inferior to officers in Western armies, and were not even comparable to their counterparts in the Japanese Imperial Army. He even went so far as to say, "We who are commanders-in-chief are only comparable to their regimental commanders, and our corps and division commanders are only fit to act as their battalion or company commanders."[1]

The poor quality of Chiang's commanders was compounded by the lack of a sound general staff system. Although the quality of staff officers had improved by the end of the war, and most of the general staff officers in the various war zones and group armies above the rank of colonel were graduates of formal military schools or the War College, many local units lacked a sound staff system. All too often these units adhered to the old notion, "If someone is literate, then he can be a staff officer; if someone is illiterate, then he can be an aide-de-camp." Literacy, while essential to staff work, is hardly in itself an adequate substitute for a solid foundation in administration, logistics, operational planning, or even the elementary military skill of map reading. By way of comparison, during the war 35 percent of the Japanese general staff were graduates of Japan's Army War College.[2] The Japanese staff system had been created along German lines, and had been in place for far longer than its Chinese equivalent, so it is not surprising that the Japanese staff corps was superior to that of the Nationalist army throughout the war.

As one might expect, the dramatic increase in the demand for lower-level officers during the war led to a corresponding increase in the number of men commissioned from the ranks. While this had been a common practice in the prewar army, with the statistics from 1930 showing that 29.1 percent of the total number of officers in the Central Army had been commissioned from the ranks, this number was bound to increase in response to the huge losses suffered in the opening stages of the Anti-Japanese War.[3] Officers from the ranks were not necessarily inferior to their academy-trained counterparts; while acting as the vice chairman of the Central Military Affairs Commission, the wily former foot soldier and warlord Feng Yuxiang went so far as to claim that 85 percent of the bravest and most talented fighting officers came from the ranks.[4] As the number of officers commissioned from the ranks increased, the percentage of military school graduates correspondingly decreased. In 1930, 70.9 percent of the officers in the Central Army were graduates of military schools. By 1944, the percentage of lower-level officers who had passed through some sort of formal military school had dropped to 27 percent.

The factor that most affected the quality of middle- and lower-echelon officers was the kind of education they received. Following the founding of the army, the official tactical doctrines and training standards were changed frequently, which naturally resulted in some confusion in the schools. For example, while still in Guangdong prior to the start of the

Northern Expedition, the army used verbal commands derived from Japanese along with Soviet-style training and organization. During the Nanjing period, the Central Military Academy adopted German tactical doctrine, while the Infantry School continued to follow the Japanese model as laid out in the manuals published by the Inspectorate General for Training. The War College simultaneously used both German and Japanese doctrine. Following the start of the war, Japanese doctrine remained influential, but it was increasingly mixed in with Soviet, German, and American doctrine. Wartime military journals reveal that army officers studied doctrine from many countries, with no one system predominating, but these imported ideas had only a superficial impact on the Nationalist army. Although in the later stages of the war troops trained in India, Yunnan, and Guilin all embraced American doctrine, other units continued to do as they pleased. This lack of standardization, which extended even to the terms the army used in its day-to-day operations, naturally had a deleterious effect on troop training.

The lack of standardized doctrine was but one of the many organizational problems that plagued the Nationalist army. Throughout the 1930s and 1940s, organization and equipment varied widely, and the steady stream of provisional reorganization plans flowing out of Nanjing did not help this situation. Far more important, while the skills emphasized in the schools were usually taught using the most current equipment, it was nearly always the case that when the students graduated and were posted to their units, they would discover that their troops possessed neither modern nor standard equipment. As one horrified observer noted, many supplies and materials were stored like junk in an old warehouse, with no two pieces of equipment identical. As a result, the new officers often felt that the skills they had learned at the various schools were irrelevant to the actual problems they faced once posted to their units. The lack of equipment and logistical support, the high level of illiteracy among the troops, poor morale, and a high desertion rate all combined to thwart even the most motivated of junior officers. In addition, like the higher-echelon officers, mid- and low-level officers of the Nationalist army had to spend much of their time on duties beyond the scope of their normal military responsibilities.

As the army found itself moving into areas either previously beyond the reach of Nanjing or simply overlooked by the resource-starved government, officers found themselves forced to take on the civil duties of an army of occupation in their own country. Only rarely could officers devote themselves exclusively to their military duties, and the need to assume civil administrative functions impaired their ability to fight. Most units considered themselves lucky if they could devote three days a week to training. Even if they were free to focus on their military duties, officers were burdened with an administrative system that was a nightmarish web of overlapping jurisdictions, infested with petty tyrants who wielded power out of all proportion to their actual rank. When it came to dealing with the various organizations that controlled money and supplies, all but the most powerful officers were forced to grovel. In order to get the resources needed to survive on a day-to-day basis, let alone fight, officers had to be willing to appear subservient before even the lowliest of clerks. As the power and position of those they were dealing with increased, so too did the time and effort officers had to expend to obtain what would have been considered normal administrative and logistical support in any other army. Even the relationships with their own immediate superiors could be burdensome in terms of time and money. Reflecting the influence of traditional Chinese bureaucratic practices, officers were expected to socialize with, or perhaps more accurately, court, their superiors or anyone else who could expedite their career progression.

If the officers in the Nationalist army had to concern themselves with so many things tangential to their main duties, how could they be expected to realize their full potential as military commanders? Even if an officer was talented, the conditions that prevailed in the Nationalist army made it unlikely that he would get a chance to prove himself. An American military officer who was in China for many years during the war pointed out that if an officer in the Nationalist army could perform well in China, he would surely also perform well abroad. The historian Ray Huang, himself a graduate of the Central Military Academy, claimed that if Chinese officers were given a chance to go abroad and command English or French troops, they would surely prove to be first-class officers.[5] This was in fact the case when Chinese troops were dispatched to Burma to participate in the Allied campaigns there. Once freed from the political, economic, and administrative constraints that existed in China, the Nationalist officers proved to be every bit as competent as their Allied counterparts.

Aside from suffering from a scarcity of resources and an undertrained, undersized officer corps that was handicapped by a Byzantine bureaucratic culture, the Nationalist army also suffered from a chronic shortage of suitable recruits. Prior to the war, the Nanjing regime relied on a volunteer recruitment system that was essentially identical to that of the earlier Beiyang Army. Individual units were required to send out teams to their favorite hunting grounds to seek recruits, which accounts for the distinctly regional flavor of many regiments. In 1933, as part of a German-inspired plan to modernize China's defense preparedness, the government promulgated a conscription law; however, the law was only put into effect following the outbreak of the war with Japan. According to available statistics, China conscripted a total of 14,049,024 men between 1937 and 1945. This seems like a rather impressive number, but given China's large population it does not represent a high degree of mobilization. F. F. Liu compared the mobilization figures for all of the major powers during World War II, and he calculated that China's mobilization index (average number of men mobilized per year as a percentage of the total population) was only 0.4 percent. That figure falls far short of Japan's 1.3 percent, England's 1.4 percent, the United States's 2.4 percent, Russia's 3.0 percent, and Germany's 3.8 percent.[6]

China's failure to achieve a degree of mobilization comparable to the other combatants was in large part due to the fact that Chinese society failed to meet many of the basic preconditions for the successful implementation of compulsory service. First, China lacked a sound household register system, and without detailed population records it was very difficult to track down all the draft-eligible men. The Nanjing regime had been trying, but following the Japanese attack and the government's retreat into the interior, they found themselves cut off from precisely those areas in which they had made the most progress. Second, the successful implementation of the conscription law depended on the cooperation of cadres at the lowest levels, and many of them were simply not interested in actively enforcing an unpopular law. Sometimes cadres were understandably reluctant to draft their friends and relatives. On other occasions they were threatened by local bullies, and chose discretion over valor in the absence of any concrete help from the central government. Often the cadres simply accepted bribes from local notables, agreeing in exchange to pass over their relatives or accept illegal substitutions. Third, household incomes were generally low throughout the country. The wartime pay of conscripts was appallingly low, even by contemporary Chinese standards, and if the draftee happened to be a key breadwinner or vital source of farm labor, his household could quickly find itself in trouble. The serious economic consequences for families of draftees led many to view military service as the first step on the road to ruin. Finally, the low level of literacy in China and the parochialism it fostered meant that many Chinese simply did not understand the need for conscription during the war, especially if they lived outside the war zones. Military service still suffered from image problems associated with the wanton looting and destruction of the warlord period, and the notion that "good men do not become soldiers" was pervasive in Chinese society. This in turn encouraged the practice of draft avoidance. Because the literate (who presumably knew what was coming), the wealthy, and the powerful could avoid conscription by flight or corruption, most of those ensnared were illiterate peasants from poor households who were often in poor physical condition.

Most military authorities are of the opinion that peasants are possessed of many military virtues, such as simplicity, sincerity, bravery, obedience, tenacity, and the ability to stoically endure great hardship. According to one prewar American military observer, the Chinese peasant was excellent soldier material, having infinite patience, a natural deference to authority, and a robust physique. If provided with suitable training and equipment, enough to eat, and clothes to wear, the Chinese would make good soldiers even by American standards. It was also noted that although most Chinese soldiers were illiterate, their learning ability was quite impressive. An Allied observer noted that whereas it took American GIs four or five days to master the intricacies of the flamethrower, Chinese troops required only two or at most four days to master the same weapon. As was the case with their officers, it seemed that when Chinese troops were freed from the limits imposed on them by their own straitened circumstances, they were capable of performing as well as their Allied counterparts.[7]

Sadly, for the majority of the Nationalist troops who were not part of American training programs after 1941, conditions continued to deteriorate. As China's financial situation worsened, the resources available to the army began to shrink, and this had a negative impact on its fighting strength. The soldiers, who had never really enjoyed an abundance of food, began to manifest signs of malnutrition. In 1944 an American expert undertook a medical inspection of some 1,200 Chinese soldiers from throughout the army. His findings revealed that fully 57 percent of those he examined were undernourished.[8] Prolonged malnutrition, coupled with poor sanitation and a shortage of medical services, resulted in a large number of cases of preventable diseases, such as night blindness, trachoma, scabies, anemia, and parasitic infections. The Nationalist army had only one doctor for every 1,700 to 3,400 men, as compared to one for every 210 men in Britain and one for every 150 men in the United States. This critical shortage of doctors and the primitive state of medical facilities made it impossible for the army to gain the upper hand in its fight against these preventable illnesses.

The real income of the soldiers also experienced a rapid decline, which exacerbated already poor morale. Up until the outbreak of the war, the army's pay and benefits had continued to improve. Relatively high rates of pay and good benefits, coupled with the flowering of Chinese nationalism during the 1930s, meant that the army enjoyed an unprecedented popularity. Even many students indicated their desire to pursue a military career, and one survey showed that military officer ranked higher than both doctor and lawyer on a list of desirable professions.[9] This popularity was fleeting, however, and by the time the war had entered its middle stage after a long succession of embarrassing defeats, an army career had lost its appeal for most Chinese youths. Military pay and benefits declined drastically, and by the midpoint of the war they could not even compare with the earnings of coolies and rickshaw drivers (in 1943 a second-class private earned a monthly salary equivalent to only 7.5 American cents). By the end of the war, the military's position in society had declined so far that common soldiers were seen as little better than beggars.

As serious as the Nationalist army's financial and personnel problems were, its supply difficulties were even greater. Following the establishment of the Nationalist army, its organization and training models changed with bewildering rapidity, leaving weapons-procurement policies in a state of continuous flux. As had been the case with all previous Chinese regimes, the Nanjing government found itself unable to produce domestically the type and quantity of weapons required by its ambitious rearmament program. It was also unable to purchase all that it needed from overseas, and as a result the army was saddled with a collection of unstandardized weapons drawn from every conceivable source. They ranged from centuries-old spears and lances to the very latest automatic rifles and antiaircraft guns. It seemed that no weapon was too old or too exotic for the Chinese, and they had in service at any given time weapons from countries such as Japan, Germany, France, Austria, Czechoslovakia, and Switzerland, along with the products of their own diverse arsenals. As the army planners were well aware, such a hodgepodge of weapons made for a logistical nightmare.

When war broke out, the army found itself dependent on large-scale imports of munitions from Germany, the Soviet Union, the United States, Britain, France, and Czechoslovakia. This diversity of weapons meant that ammunition and parts were not interchangeable, and that in turn greatly increased the burden on the already overstrained supply system. For example, those units that were lucky enough to receive American weapons during the latter stages of the war enjoyed a marked increase in their firepower and mobility. However, when the American government imposed a weapons embargo on Nanjing following the end of the Pacific War (the

American intention being to force a reluctant Nationalist government to abandon a military solution to the CCP problem in favor of a negotiated solution), the combat effectiveness of those same units deteriorated rapidly. In 1947 a reporter visiting Nationalist units at Shenyang discovered that the cargo trucks, armored vehicles, and other transport belonging to some mechanized units had been abandoned at various barracks due to a lack of spare parts. Exposed to the elements, these hard-to-come-by assets were quickly being reduced to piles of rust. In another case, an artillery regiment that was equipped with powerful American 155mm howitzers had been crippled by ammunition shortages and could no longer scrounge sufficient gasoline for the trucks needed to move the guns. Despite their superior equipment, they were less effective than another regiment armed with older, mule-drawn Japanese 150mm guns, which could be supplied from the ample ammunition stockpiles left behind after the war.

Aside from their dependence on external sources of supply, the Nationalist army confronted yet another major logistical problem. China's poor interior infrastructure and the widely scattered battle lines meant that the army had to rely on human labor for many transport and construction tasks. As with its attempts to conscript soldiers, the Nationalist army encountered many problems in trying to raise the necessary civilian levies. The pay offered to the civilian laborers was excessively low, insufficient even to support the workers, let alone compensate them for the cost of whatever tools they may have contributed. Civilians generally recoiled in apprehension at the prospect of serving, and few stepped forward of their own volition. Many simply fled, while others went so far as to destroy their own tools. This stands in stark contrast to the success the Communists enjoyed in mobilizing civilians. According to the memoirs of one Communist commander, one of the key factors in their success at the Civil War battle of Huai Hai (November 1948–January 1949) was the huge number of large and small carts provided by the peasants. During the course of this long battle, the Communists claim to have mobilized more than 5 million civilian workers in five different provinces. Utilizing 230,000 stretchers, 800,000 carts of various types, and their own backs, they moved 110,000 casualties, 342 million kilograms of food, and 3.3 million tons of ammunition.[10] There is still an ongoing debate as to whether their success in mobilizing this type of civilian support was due to their organizational expertise or the allure of their land reform program, but it is an indisputable fact that their ability to evacuate their wounded and maintain a constant flow of supplies to the front contributed in no small measure to their victory.

The actual conduct of the war with Japan and the campaigns against the Communists are discussed elsewhere in this volume. The important thing to remember is that the army that lost to the Communists in 1949 was not the same one that Sun Yat-sen and Chiang Kai-shek set out to build in 1924. When the Nationalist army first emerged on the scene in 1924, its ideological drive—the much vaunted "Whampoa Spirit"—more than compensated for its relative material weakness. Its warlord enemies lacked any sense of higher purpose, and that often proved to be their downfall when they squared off with the Guomindang's party army. Although the success of the Northern Expedition was largely due to the KMT's regional allies, their time was also running out, as Chiang was determined to recentralize power. That goal ruled out the simultaneous existence of warlord and central government armies, so the bulk of Chiang's army-building effort was aimed first at imposing central control, and then on absorbing regional forces. Absorbing such diverse forces made standardization difficult, and given the financial difficulties of the Nanjing government and the ongoing campaigns against the Communists and recalcitrant warlords, it is surprising that Chiang accomplished so much. The Whampoa graduates played a crucial role in this drive for centralization, as did the German advisory group, and collective training courses such as the ones at Lushan and Emei in the 1930s helped to facilitate the assimilation process. However, all of Chiang's drive and determination could not overcome China's objective circumstances.

Poor, with a largely illiterate population, China simply did not have the human or financial resources necessary to undertake a comprehensive rearmament program. The same weakness that hindered Chiang's efforts also made China a prime target for Japanese imperialism, and from the late 1920s on, Japanese pressure on China threatened to thwart the government's plans. Chiang's policy of "pacifying the interior while yielding to those outside" (*an nei rang wai*) simply reflected his desire to consolidate his domestic control and rebuild his army before facing off against the might of imperial Japan. Unfortunately for China, the Japanese army was not prepared to wait for Chiang and his German advisors to finish building a modern army. The outbreak of war in 1937 caught the Nationalist army only partly prepared, and Chiang was forced to make do with whatever he had on hand. Under the straitened circumstances of the war, problems that had not been fully addressed in the 1930s became increasingly serious, and not even American assistance could repair the ravages of eight years of fighting. When the war finally ended in 1945, Chiang had a large army that seemed to be well equipped on paper. The reality, however, was quite different. When the American embargo was put in place, even those units with the latest American equipment found themselves crippled by logistical problems. Others often fared even worse, and in many cases Chiang's units were simply unfit for combat.

Objectively speaking, there were many competent generals within the Nationalist central army, such as Chen Cheng, Tang Enbo, Luo Zhuoyang, Sun Liren, Guan Linzheng, Du Yuming, and Qiu Qingquan. The Japanese grudgingly acknowledged these generals as dangerous foes, and remained wary of them throughout the war. Among the remaining regional power-brokers, Li Zongren, Bai Chongxi, and Huang Shaohong of Guangxi all threw their lot in with Chiang once the war started. In particular, Li and Bai—Chiang's on-again-off-again allies from the Northern Expedition—went on to hold key positions in the Nationalist army. They were responsible for what was arguably one of China's greatest victories over the Japanese at Taierzhuang in 1938. Long before the Allies finally started to stem the Japanese tide in the later stages of the Pacific War, Chinese troops had proved that the Imperial Army was far from invincible. Unfortunately, these talented generals were often unable to exert a decisive influence on the course of the war because they were barred from holding positions of power. As one would expect from a politicized army that had its origins in the warlord period, the Chinese Nationalist forces suffered from factionalism and personal rivalries, and this played a critical role in hindering the development of a sound command stratum.

After being driven from the mainland by the Communist forces in 1949, Chiang and what remained of his army withdrew to Taiwan. Chiang was determined not to repeat the same mistakes, and after reflecting on the causes of his defeat, he initiated sweeping economic reforms and set out to rebuild a proper army out of the remnants from the mainland and an apprehensive Taiwanese population. Chiang believed that the basic reason for his defeat lay with the Guomindang's failure to maintain party bureaus and political officers in all units of the army. He felt that the success of his own army in the 1920s and 1930s, and the Communist success in 1949, were all due to the presence of a sound party structure within the army. Determined to reassert party control over the army and to breathe some new life into political work among the troops, Chiang ordered his son Chiang Ching-kuo, himself a graduate of the Soviet Red Army's Central Political Academy, to spearhead the effort. In effect, Chiang tried to pick up where he had left off in 1937, and with the help of American advisors and material support that flowed in after the outbreak of the Korean War in 1950, he was able to build up a formidable military force that still stands in the way of

Communist China's plan to reclaim Taiwan. Even today, as Chiang's legacy fades away before the economic prosperity and democracy of modern-day Taiwan, the shadow of Whampoa still hangs over the army that he built.

SUGGESTIONS FOR FURTHER READING

For a general history of the Nationalist army, see F. F. Liu, *A Military History of Modern China* (Princeton: Princeton University Press, 1956). In Chinese, the standard work is *Guomin geming jianjun shi* [A History of the Founding of the National Revolutionary Army] (Taipei: Ministry of Defense History Bureau, 1992). For an account of the early days at Whampoa in Chinese, see Wang Zhaohong, *Beifa qian de Huangbu junxiao* [The Whampoa Military School before the Northern Expedition] (Taipei: Dong Da tushu gongsi, 1987). The best English account of the Northern Expedition is Donald A. Jordan, *The Northern Expedition: China's National Revolution of 1926–1928* (Honolulu: University Press of Hawaii, 1976). For a study of party–army relations, see Hsiao-shih Cheng, *Party–Military Relations in the PRC and Taiwan: Paradoxes of Control* (Boulder, CO: Westview Press, 1990). The best social history of the Republican-era armies is Diana Lary, *Warlord Soldiers: Chinese Common Soldiers, 1911–1937* (Cambridge: Cambridge University Press, 1985). The best studies of Chiang's forces during the Anti-Japanese War are Hsi-sheng Ch'i, *Nationalist China at War: Military Defeats and Political Collapse, 1937–45* (Ann Arbor: University of Michigan Press, 1982); Evans Fordyce Carlson, *The Chinese Army: Its Organization and Military Efficiency* (New York: I.P.R. Inquiry Series, 1940); and, in Chinese, Chang Jui-te, *Kangzhan shiqi de guojun renshi* [Anatomy of the Nationalist army, 1937–1945] (Taipei: Institute of Modern History, Academia Sinica, 1993). For a study of Chiang's army-building efforts after withdrawing to Taiwan, see Monte R. Bullard, *The Soldier and the Citizen: The Role of the Military in Taiwan's Development* (Armonk, NY: M. E. Sharpe, 1997).

SUGGESTIONS FOR FURTHER RESEARCH

No comprehensive analysis has yet been made of changes in the Nationalist army's fighting ability over time in terms of administration, intelligence, operations, logistics, and training. There also remains a need for a comparison of the military's role in the wartime state-building efforts of the KMT and the CCP. And most of the major figures in the Nationalist military have yet to receive biographical treatment in English.

NOTES

1. Chiang Kai-shek, "Kangzhan jiantao yu bisheng yaojue" [An examination of the War of Resistance and the key to victory], in *Jiang zongtong sixiang yanlunji*, vol. 14 (Taipei: Zhongyang wenwu gongying she, 1966), 72–73.

2. Alvin Coox, "The Effectiveness of the Japanese Military Establishment in the Second World War," in *Military Effectiveness*, vol. 3, *The Second World War*, ed. Allan R. Millett and Williamson Murray (Boston: Unwin Hyman, 1988), 10.

3. Chang Jui-te, "Nationalist Army Officers during the Sino–Japanese War, 1937–1945," *Modern Asian Studies* 30 (1996): 1048.

4. Feng Yuxiang, *Feng Yuxiang huiyilu* [Memoirs of Feng Yuxiang] (Shanghai: Wenhua chubanshe, 1949), 152.

5. Huang Renyu, *Hexunhepan tan Zhongguo lishi* [Talking about Chinese history by the banks of the Hudson] (Taipei: Shibao wenhua chuban qiye youxian gongsi, 1989), 320.

6. F. F. Liu, *A Military History of Modern China* (Princeton: Princeton University Press, 1956), 136.

7. Yang Anming, "Dui bubing jiaoyu yingyou zhi renshi" [The understanding we should have regarding the education of troops], *Junshi zazhi*, no. 166 (June 1945): 2.

8. Lloyd E. Eastman, Jerome Ch'en, Suzanne Pepper, and Lyman P. Van Slyke, *The Nationalist Era in China, 1927–1949* (Cambridge: Cambridge University Press, 1991), 141.

9. Zhuang Zexuan and Hou Houpei, "Qinghua xuesheng duiyu ge xueke ji ge zhiye xingqu de tongji" [Statistics on the interest of Qinghua students in the various majors and professions], *Qinghua xuebao* 1, no. 2 (December 1924): 297.

10. Chen Yongfa, *Zhongguo gongchan geming qishinian* [Seventy years of the Chinese Communist Revolution] (Taipei: Lianjing chuban shiye gongsi, 1998), 413–414.

TWELVE

The Sino-Japanese Conflict, 1931–1945

Stephen R. MacKinnon

The origins of China's National War of Resistance (or the Sino-Japanese War of 1937–1945) go back at least as far as the late nineteenth century, when tensions over control of the Korean peninsula exploded into the Sino-Japanese War of 1894–1895. Japan decisively defeated China on land and sea, took control of Korea, and colonized Taiwan. For China's elites it was a devastating, traumatic loss, to be humiliated by another—and heretofore minor—Asian power. For Japan, of course, the meaning was the reverse. Japan had come of age as a great power and had begun to build an empire in East Asia. The Meiji leadership of Japan went to war again nine years later against Czarist Russia. The war was fought on Chinese soil, and Japan won decisively at the expense of Chinese sovereignty in Manchuria by taking control of Port Arthur (Lüshun) and the South Manchurian Railway. There followed a ten-year hiatus before Japan took advantage of World War I to demand territorial concessions from the new Chinese Republican government that had replaced the Qing dynasty in 1912.

In the "Twenty-One Demands" presented in 1915, Japan threatened Chinese president Yuan Shikai with war if he did not accede to further concessions of sovereignty in Manchuria and Shandong. The popular response to the demands surprised the Japanese. Mass demonstrations and boycotts of Japanese goods in Chinese cities both helped to bring down the government of Yuan Shikai and provided the background for the politically and culturally important student protests that began on May 4, 1919. The immediate spark for those events was the perception that the Chinese government's representatives at the Paris Peace Conference had yielded to Japanese demands for recognition of their control over the former German concessions in Shandong province.

In other words, by the 1920s Chinese nationalist feeling was running full bore, provoked by Japan's repeated infringements of Chinese sovereignty. Tensions were further heightened by the rise to power in 1928 of the Guomindang, the Chinese Nationalist Party, which had pledged to restore China's territory and full sovereign rights. China and Japan were well on the way to a major conflict, with Chinese nationalist fury now directed more against Japan than against the West. At the same time, Japan was beginning to distance itself from the Western powers and to militarize its economy and polity in preparation for further colonial expansion in Asia. By the end of the decade, the target of many influential Japanese military officers was complete control of Manchuria. The stage was set for a second Sino-Japanese War.

In 1931 the Japanese army seized Manchuria, soon declaring the region to be the independent state of Manchukuo with the last Qing emperor, Puyi, as puppet ruler. In the spring of 1932 the Japanese navy bombed and assaulted the Chinese-controlled part of Shanghai (outside of the International Settlement and the French Concession) in order to teach the Guomindang government of Chiang Kai-shek a lesson. The Chinese organized a spirited defense, and the Japanese forces eventually withdrew from Shanghai, but not before destroying much of the Chinese city and sending the Nanjing government the strong message that central China was vulnerable to Japanese attack.

There had been no formal declaration of war by either side. What followed was an uneasy truce and a series of "incidents" in north China, which the Japanese military used to nibble away at Chinese sovereignty and move troops south from Manchuria toward Beijing (then known as Peiping). This put Chiang Kai-shek's Nanjing-based government on the horns of a dilemma. Needing first to consolidate power by neutralizing rival warlords and wiping out the Communist threat by means of encirclement campaigns, Chiang decided for the time being to resort to diplomacy and appease the Japanese. This would buy the necessary time to build up political and military strength domestically and to better exploit the growing international outrage over Japanese expansion and the possibility of a wider world war.

From the Japanese point of view, expansion into China was another step in the empire-building process that had begun in the late nineteenth century. Japanese diplomats were fond of telling their American counterparts that they were simply hammering out a "Monroe Doctrine" for Asia, implying that what was happening was none of Washington's business. Especially after the Crash of 1929 and the world depression that followed,

Japanese leaders tied national security to the control of natural resources in East and Southeast Asia and saw it as Japan's responsibility to develop the rest of the region through occupation and/or colonization. Overemphasizing the regional divisions of warlord politics, the Japanese did not take Chinese nationalism seriously. They saw China as the "sick man" of Asia, hopelessly divided and backward, needing to be raised up by Japan and brought into the twentieth century. At the same time, orderly constitutional government and democratic politics in Japan were crumbling. After a series of assassinations and attempted coups, the military leadership came to dominate Japanese politics. No parliamentary elections would be held in Japan between 1937 and 1942.

By the end of 1936, popular outrage in China's large coastal cities over Japanese aggression and the subjugation of Chinese populations to the north of Peiping was threatening Chiang Kai-shek's government. Loss of patience with Chiang was demonstrated in no uncertain terms in December when the Generalissimo, visiting the city of Xi'an in northwest China to expedite the campaign against the Communists, was kidnapped by two of his own generals. Their demands were simple. As a condition of release, Chiang would have to agree to call off the military campaign against the Chinese Communists and declare war on Japan. Chiang never publicly acquiesced, but during the spring of 1937, after his return to Nanjing, his government dropped the anti-Communist campaign and abandoned compromise and diplomacy with the Japanese. At the same time there was a stiffening of the Chinese military posture in the north, making an armed confrontation all but inevitable. On July 7, 1937, an "incident" involving clashes between Chinese and Japanese troops at Marco Polo Bridge in the suburbs of Peiping provided the provocation both sides were looking for (though to this day each side claims the other fired the first shot).

Fighting soon spread to other areas around Peiping, and China formally declared war. (Japan never did the same, preferring to label the conflict with China an "incident.") Peiping fell before the end of July, after a large body of Japanese troops arrived by rail from Manchuria. They first surrounded the port of Tianjin (Tientsin), then moved west to lay siege to Peiping. There was significant resistance at Tongzhou, halfway to Peiping, but the Chinese defenders were overwhelmed by Japanese firepower; survivors were massacred and the walled city burned to the ground. The defenders of Peiping got the message and surrendered after relatively little organized resistance. By the end of August, Japanese tanks and airpower had moved south down the Peiping–Hankou railway, laying waste by blitzkrieg and killing large numbers of civilians in Baoding before veering east in a trek across Hebei province toward Shandong, the home of Confucius. In panic, refugees flooded into the Shandong ports of Qingdao and Yantai. Other Japanese units moved west, capturing the strategically important Nankou Pass and then the key railroad and coal mining town of Datong in Shanxi province. This put the Japanese in a position to threaten Taiyuan, the capital of Shanxi, and Xi'an in the heart of northwestern China.

The Japanese demonstration of mobility and firepower confirmed Chiang Kai-shek's worst nightmares. The well-coordinated attacks were devastating. Their morale broken, Chinese troops scattered in panic with the Japanese in hot pursuit. The Japanese practiced selective terror and took revenge on Chinese civilians—in Baoding and Tongzhou, for example—in reprisal for the killing of Japanese civilians. The intention was to terrorize the civilian population and cow Chiang Kai-shek's government into submission. The only bright spot was a minor, morale-boosting victory at Pingxingguan, northeast of Taiyuan, by Communist units of the Eighth Route Army, who captured a cache of weapons and annihilated a Japanese brigade.

In August 1937, further south in central China, a second front was opened as Chiang Kai-shek baited the Japanese into attacking Shanghai. First, Chiang massed hundreds of thousands of troops on the outskirts of Shanghai in violation of the agreement that had concluded the 1932 hostilities. Then, on August 14, his air force attacked a Japanese cruiser moored at the Bund. The Japanese responded by sending strong reinforcements and laying siege to the Chinese-controlled portion of Shanghai. The battle raged for three months. Combining blitzkrieg from the air with amphibious landings, the exercise of Japanese firepower was devastating and prevented coordinated defense or orderly retreat. The Japanese methodically surrounded the Chinese city (with the foreign community watching from the safety of the concession zones), taking advantage of total air and sea superiority to apply tremendous firepower and fully exploit every misstep in the ill-coordinated defense. Many of the Chinese units nevertheless fought heroically. Chiang sacrificed his best divisions and over half of his officer corps in the defense of Shanghai. In the end the Japanese took the city after prolonged and bloody house-to-house combat. The Chinese city was completely in Japanese hands by mid-November. The crush of refugees trying to enter the foreign concessions was unprecedented:

> Refugees poured into the ten square miles of the French Concession and International Settlement, swelling the population from 1.5 to 4 million within a few weeks and increasing the size of the average household to 31

people. Many left the 175 refugee camps to return to their native villages, but tens of thousands of homeless clogged the streets and hundreds of thousands more slept in office corridors, stockrooms, temples, guild halls, amusement parks, and warehouses. With winter came disease, starvation, and exposure; and by the end of the year 101,000 corpses had been picked up in the streets or ruins.[1]

What followed was a chaotic Chinese retreat that was extremely costly in terms of men and material. Much of Shanghai's industrial capacity was left intact to the Japanese. What remained of the defending force fled west, hopelessly disorganized and demoralized. Suzhou was abandoned without a fight on November 19, leaving the route to Chiang Kai-shek's capital of Nanjing wide open and basically undefended. As the Japanese armored units moved west, they laid waste to the Jiading area without encountering much resistance. In such an atmosphere of confusion and fear, the old walled city of Nanjing was gripped by panic. Chiang himself took charge of the city's defense in an attempt to restore order.

By early December 1937, Nanjing was under full land and air assault as Japanese units closed in from three sides. Chiang and General Tang Shengzhi attempted a coordinated defense using concentric circles, but this was quickly breached, trapping tens of thousands of Chinese troops in the city by December 13. The execution of captured troops (many of them buried alive) began the infamous Nanjing Massacre. Once again Japanese troops ran amok, taking revenge on the civilian population, but this time it was on a much larger scale. From the reports of foreign observers and the diaries of the Japanese soldiers themselves, the Japanese army seemed to be trying to butcher every man, woman, and child left in the city. The body count may have been as high as 300,000. There is some controversy today over questions such as the number of civilians killed and whether or not the troops were following orders, but what occurred at Nanjing was certainly one of the major atrocities of World War II.

Meanwhile, Chiang's forces were regrouping and reorganizing at Wuhan, the great commercial capital of the Chinese heartland, three hundred miles inland from Shanghai. In January 1938, Wuhan became the de facto capital of wartime China. All elements of China's anti-Japanese "united front" were represented there, not only the Chinese Communist Party and the Nationalists of the Guomindang, but also third-party movements. Wuhan became a cultural center as well, with refugee intellectuals and military units from all over China mixing as equals on the streets. The defense of the city was likened by the Chinese press to the defense of Madrid by the Spanish Republican forces that was occuring at the same time.

In order to finish Chiang off and break the back of united-front patriotism, the Japanese high command ordered troops from the north and east to carry out a coordinated pincer movement in preparation for an attack on Wuhan that would be launched in the late spring. However, what happened next did not fit the Imperial Japanese Army's game plan. The city did not fall until October 1938, after ten months and a series of costly battles. Both sides lost more men in 1938 than in any other year of the war. Moreover, from the Chinese standpoint it is clear in retrospect that these battles were critically important—win or lose—because they had the effect of prolonging the war. The fall of Wuhan brought mutual exhaustion and depletion of resources and set the scene for the next stage of the war, which was much slower in pace, consisting of smaller-scale engagements punctuated by Japanese bombing raids of varying intensity.

Why did it take the Japanese ten months to capture Wuhan? In other words, what happened militarily and how did the Chinese side prepare its defense? To answer these questions, we need to step back and take stock of Chinese military power at the outset of the war, with special attention to organization and preparedness.

China began the war with an estimated regular force of 1.7 to 2.2 million men. These troops can be divided into six categories based on their political loyalty to their commander-in-chief, Chiang Kai-shek. First, there were the troops controlled directly by Chiang. Second came troops who had been loyal to Chiang in the past but were less directly controlled by him. The third category were provincial troops over whom Chiang could exercise command in ordinary times. These were followed by provincial troops over which Chiang had little direct influence. The fifth category was the Communist forces: the Eighth Route Army headquartered in the caves of the northwest and the New Fourth Army taking shape in the hill country of the central Yangzi region. Finally, there were the Northeastern or Manchurian units that had been defeated and displaced by the Japanese in 1931. These were loyal to the "Young Marshal" Zhang Xueliang (one of Chiang's kidnappers at Xi'an in 1936). The first two categories included roughly 900,000 men, with a million more in the independent provincial armies. About 300,000 men were split between the Communist and Manchurian forces.

As commander-in-chief, Chiang Kai-shek exercised effective command over only about half of the units that could be mobilized against the Japanese when war broke out in July 1937. This meant that military decisions were inevitably slow, procedurally complex, and almost always subject to negotiation. Coordination and communication at the division level proved especially difficult. All of this contrasted starkly with the clean, disciplined command structure on the Japanese side.

Geographically, most of the troops loyal to Chiang Kai-shek were located in the area between the Yangzi and Yellow rivers at the beginning of 1938. They had been heavily involved in the defense of Shanghai and Nanjing and had suffered tremendous losses, retreating to Wuhan at half strength under a decimated officer corps. They now numbered about 400,000 men, with command split between generals Chen Cheng and Hu Zongnan. The independent regional armies of the north—especially the divisions under General Han Fuju in Shandong province—had taken heavy casualties, with some units going over to the Japanese and later serving them as puppet troops. This meant that after the six-month Japanese onslaught, during which the coastal areas from Peiping–Tianjin to Shanghai and inland to Nanjing were lost, the relatively autonomous, sizable armies that remained were either from the southwest or the northwest. They were commanded by leading militarists such as Li Zongren and Bai Chongxi (Guangxi), Long Yun (Yunnan), and Yan Xishan (Shanxi and Suiyuan). About 700,000 of these troops, the bulk of whom came from Guangxi under generals Li and Bai, were committed to the defense of Wuhan. Of less importance were the Communist forces of the Eighth Route Army, who numbered about 100,000 and remained relatively unscathed and isolated in bases north and east of Xi'an. Altogether, there were probably about 1.3 million men under arms for the defense of Wuhan.

Early in 1938, as retreating troops regrouped around Wuhan and were joined by fresh divisions from Guangxi, war zones were reorganized and plans were laid for the defense of the central Yangzi valley. The Fifth War Zone (the area north of the Yangzi in Anhui, Hubei, and Henan provinces) was under the Guangxi general Li Zongren. Li commanded a mixture of his own Guangxi units under his longtime associate, the brilliant strategist Bai Chongxi, and troops more loyal to Chiang Kai-shek who were commanded by generals Zhang Zhizhong and Hu Zongnan. All together, about 280,000 men fought on the Chinese side in the Fifth War Zone.

A new Ninth War Zone to the south of the Yangzi (in Hunan, Jiangxi, and the southern part of Hubei, with Wuhan as its command center) was put under the most able of the Chiang loyalists, General Chen Cheng. He commanded some 380,000 men in seventy-eight divisions. Many of these troops, such as those under the Cantonese general Zhang Fakui, had strong provincial loyalties. They were expected to work closely with units that were more directly tied to Chiang Kai-shek and commanded by graduates of the Whampoa Military Academy (where Chiang had been the commandant). Added to these were displaced provincial troops of questionable loyalty who had formerly been under the militarists Feng Yuxiang and Zhang Xueliang, and the New Fourth Army of Communist-dominated guerrilla units being assembled under General Ye Ting.

At the beginning of the war, the Chinese had a four-to-one superiority over the Japanese in terms of men on the ground. But the advantage of numbers dissolved in the face of the massive superiority of the Japanese in equipment, mobility, and firepower. During the first six months of the war the Japanese swept south employing the latest in mobile warfare, including the free use of tanks, supporting air strikes, and sophisticated logistical support. The Chinese who faced them in north China and later in the defense of Wuhan and the central Yangzi were for the most part equipped more primitively with small arms, machine guns, and hand grenades. A Chinese air force existed, but it was defensive and not employable in a tactical sense. Chinese forces were most effective fighting at night, when their generals could take better advantage of their numerical superiority. Night fighting was a key factor in the biggest Chinese victory of the war: the outmaneuvering and defeat of several Japanese divisions by Li Zongren and Bai Chongxi at Taierzhuang (fifty miles northeast of Xuzhou) in March–April 1938.

With the exception of the Guangxi divisions, Chinese units were seriously handicapped by an unnecessarily complex command structure. Orders from Chiang Kai-shek had to pass down through six tiers of commanders before action was possible. Moreover, in the distribution of equipment Chiang favored the central army units over which he had direct control and which had loyal commanders belonging to the Whampoa clique. Needless to say, Chiang's favoritism bred discord and insubordination at all levels of the Chinese field forces.

There were other problems as well. One was the mixture of approaches to the organization and positioning of forces. The Chinese forces had been reorganized using German models, with large armies grouped together as field armies (called war zones). At the same time, Russian influence was evident in the strategic positioning that Chinese units adopted, with division into "front" and "route" armies as well as rear area service units. Thus, there was a lack of coherence in the forces facing the Japanese. Troop placement and support procedures were not rational. On the one hand, Chiang and his generals consistently tried to avoid decisive confrontation with the Japanese so as to reduce the possibility of meeting with irreversible defeat (as had occurred at Shanghai). On the other hand, Chiang also eschewed a commitment to guerrilla warfare as a widespread tactic. The large, multilayered Nationalist-led units overemphasized holding onto communication lines such as railways, presumably for transport and logistical purposes. This had the effect of immobilizing or tying down their main fighting forces, around which the Japanese could easily maneuver.

During the battle of Wuhan in the summer and fall of 1938, the Chinese enjoyed a six-to-one numerical advantage, throwing 1.1 million men (or 120 divisions) against a Japanese force of 200,000 (10 divisions). But in fact the Japanese still had an enormous military advantage. According to one calculation by an American military observer, the fighting capacity (defined as numbers times firepower) of a Guomindang division ranged from one-third to one-twelfth that of its Japanese counterpart.[2] Not only was Chinese weaponry inferior, but little replenishment of men and arms took place or was even possible. Leaving aside bravery and fighting spirit, this meant that at the front one hundred Chinese divisions were often no better than twelve Japanese divisions in terms of fighting effectiveness. The Chinese units with the least firepower were often exposed to the heaviest Japanese shelling. This was the situation at Shanghai in the fall of 1937, when the Twenty-Ninth Army commanded by Zhang Zhizhong fought valiantly before buckling under the Japanese bombardment.

The conduct of the war in and around Wuhan in 1938 also illustrated the major strengths and weaknesses of the Chinese forces. What made the victory at Taierzhuang possible during the spring of 1938 was the exploitation by General Bai Chongxi of a temporary balance between Chinese firepower and that of overextended Japanese units. The result was a short-lived Chinese victory. Casualties on both sides were heavy but also roughly equivalent. The Chinese failure to follow up this victory by pursuing the fleeing Japanese units as part of a larger strategy of counterattack reflected problems of command structure, especially Chiang Kai-shek's jealousy and distrust of generals Bai and Li. The Japanese were thus given time to regroup and launch a full-scale attack on the strategically important city of Xuzhou in Jiangsu province, headquarters of the Fifth War Zone. Generals Li Zongren and Tang Enbo organized a spirited defense, producing one of the bloodiest and most destructive battles of the war. But the Japanese were now able to bring their full firepower to bear. They soon broke the Chinese defenses and closed in on Xuzhou from three sides. Losing two of their own men for every one Japanese soldier killed, the defenders were forced to retreat, abandoning the smoldering ruin of a city on May 18. It was just after the loss of Xuzhou, at the end of May, that Chiang Kai-shek made the famous decision to blow the Yellow River dikes at Huayuankou, just north of Zhengzhou in Henan, in a desperate surprise move designed to slow down the southward advance of Japanese mechanized units. With the Yellow River now flowing freely south through the Huai River bed to join the Yangzi just west of Shanghai, eleven cities and four thousand villages were inundated by flood waters, which left more than 2 million homeless.[3] But the military objective was accomplished. For a few weeks the floods blocked the main route south to Wuhan and permitted Chinese troops to regroup in the Dabieshan area on the Anhui–Henan border. In the long run, however, the political cost of the move to Chiang's government after the war far outweighed the short-term military benefit from the blowing of the dikes.

The Yellow River flood did not prevent major Japanese army and navy units from moving west from Nanjing into the central Yangzi valley, where they took Anqing with ease on June 12, 1938. Hoping to block the Japanese at Madang, halfway between Anqing and Jiujiang, the Chinese prepared an elaborate defensive position. But once again the Japanese outflanked Chinese forces by taking advantage of their failure to coordinate land and naval units in an effective way. The resulting rout and the fall of Madang by the end of June led to a brutal attack on defenseless Jiujiang shortly thereafter and the slaughter of its remaining civilian population. At this point, the lack of coordination between the war zones had become a major problem for which the Chinese were paying dearly. The defense of Madang had been under the Ninth War Zone commander Zhang Fakui. Throughout the battle, crack Guangxi units remained one hundred miles to the north in the Dabieshan area of the Fifth War Zone, the bailiwick of Guangxi general Bai Chongxi. As a result of the fall of Madang and Jiujiang, Bai's forces became increasingly isolated and vulnerable in the mountains to the north along the Anhui–Henan border. Bai held out until the end of July, when he was finally outflanked by the Japanese and forced to retreat. By August 1938, Wuhan was nearly surrounded and the battle for its survival well underway. Bombing of the city intensified. Recognizing the superiority of Japanese firepower and the convergence on the city of Japanese armored divisions from the north and east, the Guomindang government began planning an orderly evacuation of skilled industrial workers and the shipping of whole factories upstream and into the interior. Wuhan held out longer than expected, but finally fell on October 25, 1938.

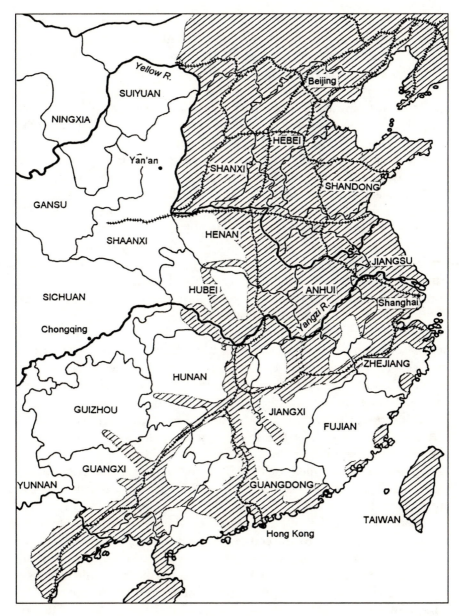

Map 12.1   China during the Sino-Japanese War, 1937–1945, showing major railway lines and maximum extent of Japanese occupation. Adapted by Don Graff based upon *Cambridge History of China,* vol. 13: *Republican China, 1912–1949, Part 2* (Cambridge: Cambridge University Press, 1986), map 8.

After the fall of Wuhan and Canton (or Guangzhou, on October 21, 1938), the war moved to a decidedly different stage, much lower and slower. The Chinese were now practicing a "protracted war" strategy, engaging in a long war of attrition in which head-on confrontations with Japanese field armies were to be avoided. Chiang Kai-shek's military headquarters moved to Sichuan, where the city of Chongqing (Chungking) became the new capital. Provincial armies scattered. The Guangxi army, for example, had taken heavy losses in the battle for Wuhan; Li Zongren led some of the survivors into the Dabie Mountains north of the Yangzi, while other units returned to Guangxi to confront the Japanese moving inland from Canton. The Communists, for their part, turned to guerrilla harassment tactics against the Japanese in north China. The Japanese held the railway lines and cities, but were not able to assert effective control over the vast spaces in between these points and lines.

One reason for the lull in the action was the fact that in 1939 the Japanese turned their attention to an indecisive and costly war against Soviet forces at Khalkin-Gol on the Mongolian–Manchurian border. Over the next four years the Chinese commitment to the protracted war strategy seemed to preclude consideration of serious counterattacks against Japanese positions. Moreover, during the winter of 1940–1941, serious clashes—better known as the "New Fourth Army Incident"—broke out between Nationalist and Communist units in southern Anhui. The latent civil war between Communists and Nationalists had reemerged as a divisive factor on the Chinese side and crippled the united-front posture.

Thus, the military initiative in the Sino-Japanese War would remain with the Japanese. Bombing raids against Chongqing became much heavier in 1940 and continued for the rest of the war. There were important clashes in the hill country of western Hunan and Hubei. Three times (once in 1939 and twice in 1941) Chinese and Japanese units battled for control of Changsha, the capital of Hunan province. But such events had little effect on the big picture. By the end of 1941, the Sino-Japanese War had become part of a much larger conflict as Japan expanded the war to the Pacific and gave Chiang Kai-shek a powerful new partner, the United States.

The merciless Japanese bombing of Chinese cities had already turned American public opinion against Japan, and in 1940 a retired officer of the U.S. Army Air Corps, Claire L. Chennault, brought 100 volunteer pilots from the United States to form the Flying Tigers and contest Japanese control of the skies over parts of China. The outbreak of World War II in Europe in 1939 had seen the virtual removal of French and British influence from East Asia. The Burma Road, China's supply route from the port of Rangoon, was closed by the British in response to Japanese pressure on July 18, 1940. During that same month the Japanese took advantage of the German defeat of France to occupy the northern part of French Indochina, cutting off another channel by which foreign supplies had reached Chiang's forces. The British reopened the Burma Road in October 1940 after Japan adhered to the Tripartite Pact with Germany and Italy, and the United States imposed an oil embargo on Japan in the summer of 1941. This American move provoked a new burst of Japanese aggression. Japan's attack on Pearl Harbor on December 7, 1941, brought the United States into the war on China's side, but the immediate result was the Japanese conquest of the British colonies in Southeast Asia, including Burma, in the first half of 1942. This left the tenuous India–China air route over "the Hump" of the Himalayas as the only link between Nationalist China and the Western Allies.

With the exception of the Japanese Ichi-Go offensive in 1944, the field positions of the opposing armies remained roughly stationary for the rest of the war. There were several reasons for the lack of significant military action from 1942 to 1945. Japanese control of much of the rail network in the populous eastern third of the country hampered Chinese movement of men and supplies, while the invaders had to expend much energy securing the railways and supplying garrisons. For their part, the Chinese depended upon the airlift over the Hump until the long, tenuous Ledo road was opened in 1944. Even then there were serious disputes over strategy in Chongqing, with the China Theatre commander, U.S. Army general Joseph Stilwell, pitted against Claire Chennault and Chiang himself. Without a significant Chinese counterattack, the Japanese were increasingly able to channel their energies into the Pacific War.

Though the land war stabilized, air operations did not. Chennault's U.S. Fourteenth Air Force, supplied over the Hump, became increasingly aggressive, raiding along the southeast coast and even striking Japanese bases in Taiwan. Industrial centers in north China and Japanese shipping on the Yangzi came under attack, as did Shanghai and even the Japanese homeland itself. The last major campaign launched by the Japanese in China, the Ichi-Go offensive of 1944, was designed in part to capture Chennault's air bases and cut U.S. supply lines to western China. It was only partially successful. After a rugged, six-month campaign the Japanese captured Guilin, capital of Guangxi province. From then until the end of the war, the Japanese became more defensive, losing skirmishes in western Hunan. But it was the atomic bombing of Hiroshima and Nagasaki that brought the war to an abrupt end in August 1945. The surrender of the 1.2 million Japanese troops who were still in place in China at the end of the war was seen by the Chinese—both Communist and Nationalist—as a vindication of their strategy of relative inactivity or "protracted war."

IMPACT AND HISTORICAL IMPORTANCE

The importance to modern Chinese history of these eight years of total war is difficult to overestimate, be it in social, cultural, economic, or political terms. Between 1937 and 1945 the country changed dramatically. The cost in lives lost and property destroyed made the Sino-Japanese War even more devastating than the war in Europe, a fact not widely acknowledged in the West. Throughout the coastal provinces, from north to south, the atrocities committed by Japanese troops were of monstrous proportions; the best known, of course, is the Nanjing Massacre of December 1937. In due course, over 100 million homeless refugees (almost a quarter of the population) fled to the interior. Over 20 million civilians lost their lives. Families were torn apart. Countless widows were left to fend for themselves, some alone and others destitute with children. Their husbands and brothers were forcibly pressed into service. Many died on the battlefield, others succumbed to wounds left untreated, and yet others to starvation and disease.

These tens of millions of lives lost will never be accurately calculated. A youthful reporter named Theodore White, fresh from Harvard and the comforts of Boston, tried to grasp what was happening:

> Through the long months of 1938, as the Chinese armies were pressed slowly back toward the interior, they found their way clogged by moving people. The breathing space of winter had given hundreds of thousands time to make their decision, and China was on the move in one of the greatest mass migrations in human history. It is curious that such a spectacle has not been adequately recorded by a Chinese writer or novelist. Certainly the long files of gaunt people who moved west across the roads and mountains must have presented a sight unmatched since the days of nomad hordes; yet no record tells how many made the trek, where they came from, where they settled anew.[4]

With such losses came a brutalization processs that touched the entire population and left a social and cultural scar that went in a variety of directions. One was survivor guilt. Another was the fear of chaos, or *luan*. The Chinese developed a deep-seated fear of social disorder that has no clear counterpart in Western historical experience. This fear survives to this day and has been exploited to the hilt by every major Chinese political figure since the war's end. It has been the crucial factor in justifiying and mobilizing support for the intrusions of the modern Chinese state, first under Chiang Kai-shek and more recently in the post-Mao China of the 1980s and 1990s. Fear of chaos is one part of the survivor mentality that was rooted in the Sino-Japanese War of 1937–1945 and reinforced by the Cultural Revolution of 1966–1976.

By the mid-twentieth century, at least half the Chinese population had been through a refugee experience, either as a result of the Sino-Japanese War or the civil wars that bracket the period from 1931 to 1949. The agonies and uncertainties of being a refugee or living in occupied China created the long-term traumatization of a generation. It reached the point that survival by whatever means became the principal goal of life. With it went guilt: the haunting questions about what compromises may have been made to explain the survival of one family member over another.

Yet out of the ashes of war a drastically new cultural and political landscape emerged, shaping the generation that has led China through the second half of the twentieth century. In this sense the social impact of the Sino-Japanese War was not unlike the sweeping changes that shook European society after World War I. To begin with, the war turned China into what became the most politicized large society of the latter half of the twentieth century. The war forced the population—regardless of class or station—to choose sides. At first the choice was a relatively simple one between living and very likely dying. By the end of the war the choice was not just between Japanese occupation and "free" China; after 1941, Chinese were forced to choose between the competing demands for loyalty from the Communists and Nationalists in their struggle to shape the new, patriotic China that would emerge from the war. Put another way, the war generated the first in a series of mass movements or mobilization efforts. These would only intensify after the war, and become inescapable after "liberation" in 1949, shaking Chinese society to its roots with wave after wave of campaigns that lasted through the 1950s, 1960s, and 1970s.

There was also a positive side to the social changes the Sino-Japanese War produced. Chinese nationalism came of age during the war, with an equalizing effect on the structure of social classes in China and on the status of men and women. War propaganda promising democracy and social and economic justice bound culture and society together into a single package in unprecedented ways. The Chinese upper classes, and intellectuals in particular, voluntarily embraced mass culture and politics in the arts and intellectual life generally, while the commitment to social justice brought investment in a national health care system and social services for the dispossessed.

SUGGESTIONS FOR FURTHER READING

Important recent works on the war and its impact include Frederic Wakeman Jr., *The Shanghai Badlands: Wartime Terrorism and Urban Crime, 1937–41* (Cambridge: Cambridge University Press, 1996); James C. Hsiung and Steven I. Levine, eds., *China's Bitter Victory: The War with Japan, 1937–45* (Armonk, NY: M. E. Sharpe, 1992); and Chang-tai Hung, *War and Popular Culture: Resistance in Modern China, 1937–45* (Berkeley and Los Angeles: University of California Press, 1994). Earlier but still useful accounts which focus on the military and political story are Hsi-sheng Ch'i, *Nationalist China at War: Military Defeats and Political Collapse, 1937–45* (Ann Arbor: University of Michigan Press, 1982); John Boyle, *China and Japan at War, 1937–45: The Politics of Collaboration* (Stanford: Stanford University Press, 1972); Lloyd Eastman, *Seeds of Destruction: Nationalist China in War and Revolution* (Stanford: Stanford University Press, 1984); Paul Sih, ed., *Nationalist China during the Sino-Japanese War, 1937–45* (Hicksville, NY: Exposition, 1977); Dick Wilson, *When Tigers Fight: The Story of the Sino-Japanese War, 1937–45* (New York: Viking, 1982); and Frank Dorn, *The Sino-Japanese War, 1937–41: From Marco Polo Bridge to Pearl Harbor* (New York: Macmillan, 1974). The works by Wilson and Dorn are concerned exclusively with the military story. Dorn's in particular is a classic, well written and based on scholarship as well as the author's own eyewitness observations as the senior U.S. naval attaché in Hankou and Chongqing during the war. The most influential study of the war's impact on Chinese politics is Chalmers Johnson, *Peasant Nationalism and Communist Power: The Emergence of Revolutionary China, 1937–45* (Stanford: Stanford University Press, 1962), a pathbreaking work when it was first published and still very much worth reading.

SUGGESTIONS FOR FURTHER RESEARCH

Given the importance of the Sino-Japanese War to the making of contemporary China, it is surprising how little is known about the military history of the war and how understudied the subject is. Admittedly, a major problem has been point of view—that is, the difficulty of escaping the choice between the distortions of the record that go with either a pro-Nationalist or pro-Communist perspective. Western historiography, although not so committed to one side over another, has still focused less on the war itself than on the political struggle for supremacy between Communists and Nationalists that emerged from the war and the question of why the Communists came to power so soon after the end of the war in 1945. A second problem is that the primary sources are fragmentary and often too politically tainted to be reliable. Statistics about how many were killed and wounded over the course of the war are either nonexistent or invented to prove a point. Private memoir accounts by major players such as Chiang Kai-shek and Mao Zedong either do not exist or are much too self-serving. And finally, the Japanese side is also poorly understood. Much of the detailed Japanese military record, carefully preserved in archives, is only just now becoming available to scholars, who heretofore have had to work almost exclusively with memoir literature, reports from a controlled wartime press, and records captured by the United States.

In other words, only recently has the historical picture of the Sino-Japanese War become more complete in the sense that greater objectivity of analysis has become possible. Moreover, serious multilingual and archival work on the history of the war is now underway. The time is approaching when a comprehensive, detailed, and definitive study of the war can be written.

NOTES

1. Frederic Wakeman Jr., *The Shanghai Badlands: Wartime Terrorism and Urban Crime, 1937–41* (Cambridge: Cambridge University Press, 1996), 7.
2. Frank Dorn, *The Sino-Japanese War, 1937–41: From Marco Polo Bridge to Pearl Harbor* (New York: Macmillan, 1974), 6–10.
3. Diana Lary, "Drowned Earth: The Strategic Breaching of the Yellow River Dyke, 1938," *War in History* 8 (2001): 205–207.
4. Theodore White and Annalee Jacoby, *Thunder Out of China* (New York: William Sloane Associates, 1946), 55.

THIRTEEN

"Political Power Grows Out of the Barrel of a Gun": Mao and the Red Army

William Wei

That Mao Zedong was a military genius is a myth, although a powerful one. It is one that has been embraced by many people, from those seeking to explain how the Chinese Communists came to power in 1949 to those seeking to emulate them. Intimately associated with this Maoist myth is the image of a Red Army invincible once it had subscribed to Mao's military ideas. Accordingly, Mao's military writings have come to serve as the blueprint for many liberation movements in the so-called Third World. For example, Vo Nguyen Giap, the Vietnamese general responsible for defeating the French at Dien Bien Phu, acknowledged Mao's contribution to his army's victories: "We educated ourselves according to the military thought of Mao Zedong. That was the important factor that allowed our army to mature and that led to our successive victories."[1]

In fact, Mao was principally a political leader rather than a military commander, even though he served in that capacity on several occasions, and the Red Army was far from invincible, having suffered many reverses before its ultimate triumph during the Chinese Civil War (1946–1949). In the beginning, Mao was the political commissar of the Central Soviet base area in the Jiangxi–Fujian border region; only later did he become one of the major leaders of the Chinese Communist Party. Paradoxically, Mao owed his rise to political prominence in part to Red Army defeats rather than victories, and to the support of Red Army commanders who were actually ambivalent about his military capabilities.

THE MAKING OF A MAOIST MYTH

Mao's reputation as a brilliant strategist and tactician is mainly a retrospective view resulting from the triumph of the Chinese Communists in 1949 and the cult of personality that developed around him (with an assist from his own talent for self-promotion). His image as a military leader evolved from that of a gallant guerrilla chieftain who started an insurgency in the countryside in 1927 to that of the head of the Red Army during the famous Long March. It was based in small part on the romantic appeal of his underdog status (and his poetry) and in large part on the incompetence of his Nationalist opponents and the competence of his partner Zhu De, an experienced military commander and former warlord. Later, as the leader of the Chinese Communist Party, Mao was given credit for the victory against the Nationalist Party, a triumph that was achieved largely on the battlefield. And as the ruler of China, he was traditionally accorded both civil and martial virtues.

Given the popular "great man" approach to history, it was a matter of convention as well as convenience to attribute martial sagacity to Mao. Journalists, scholars, and others who have delved into his early years point out that while other children were studying the Confucian canon to prepare themselves to be mandarins in the Chinese establishment, Mao was reading picaresque novels about righteous rebels who sought to overthrow the establishment. Among his favorites was *The Water Margin* (*Shui hu zhuan*), whose heroes fought corrupt and greedy officials in the timeless tradition of social bandits around the world. Harrison Salisbury, an American journalist, would refer to the novels as Mao's manuals for conducting guerrilla warfare, pointing specifically to *The Romance of the Three Kingdoms* (*San guo yanyi*) as his "military text" for the Long March.[2]

But Mao's reading of historical romances is hardly unique; many of his contemporaries, including Communist military leaders such as Zhu De, read them as well. In any case, the historical references and literary allusions in Mao's essays testify that he was equally familiar with the traditional Confucian literature. Whatever else Mao was, he was unquestionably a Chinese intellectual. And like intellectuals the world over, Mao felt that he knew what was best in any area he chose to take an interest in, including military matters. Indeed, he was fond of "philosophizing" about war: War was the supreme test of the human spirit, and the human spirit was the decisive factor in the outcome of a war.

Supporting the image of Mao as a military wizard is the cult of his personality, which began in response to the perceived need for a symbol of unity around which to rally the Chinese people. In China's authoritarian political culture, the people needed to be able to identify with someone representing the power of the state. Mao himself advanced this idea in an "anonymous article urging his compatriots to follow Mao's way."[3] "Mao's way" was codified in April 1945, when the Seventh Congress of the CCP adopted a new constitution containing a preamble in which the "Thought of Mao Zedong" was deemed an essential guide to the work of the party. With that, Mao became the party's ideological spokesperson, setting its goals and values. His "words of wisdom" would be encapsulated in the *Quotations from Chairman Mao* (popularly known as "the Little Red Book"), which was widely disseminated throughout the military and then society in general beginning in 1964.

As the object of veneration, Mao subsumed the accomplishments of other leaders so that he became a composite figure incorporating the achievements of Zhu De, Peng Dehuai, Lin Biao, and other Communist military leaders. After 1949, when Zhu sought to commission a biography, Mao prevented it from being published because "it might have suggested that not every single victory on the Long March and at other moments of the Communist struggle was due to the genius of the Chairman."[4]

Those of Mao's writings that analyze the CCP's military situation and present his theories on the role of the military in the Communist revolution are referred to collectively by hagiographers as "The Glorious Military Thought of Comrade Mao Zedong." Lin Biao even elevated Mao's military thought to the level of revolutionary dogma. In "Long Live the Victory of the People's War" (September 1965), Lin advanced the thesis that just as the Chinese Communist revolutionaries in the countryside had encircled and captured the cities, so would the underdeveloped Third World countries surround the advanced capitalist countries.[5]

Ironically, Mao's knowledge of military strategy and tactics was initially slight. It was only in 1936–1938, when preparing to write essays on military tactics, that he finally read Sunzi's *Art of War*, the Chinese classic on warfare. Furthermore, questions have been raised about the authorship of some of the writings published in his name. His work *Basic Tactics*, for instance, may have been plagiarized from a treatise on guerrilla warfare written earlier by Zhu De and other military commanders. Unlike his political essays, which can be "amateurish, verbose, tendentious, repetitious," this book on the operational principles of the Red Army is "thoroughly professional, usually laconic, objective, and to the point."[6] In other words, it is suspiciously unlike his usual work.

Mao the Soldier

In any case, it is evident that Mao had limited experience in military affairs before his arrival at Jinggangshan, Jiangxi, in the autumn of 1927. According to Mao himself, during the 1911 Revolution he decided to join the army of the Republican leader Li Yuanhong after listening to him speak, and while in Changsha, Hunan, Mao enlisted in the Hunan Revolutionary Army. Considering the Chinese armies of the period, he probably received very little if any "training"; he also did very little "soldiering," performing garrison duty for six months before resigning. Mao had hardly anything to say about this experience. Except for learning about and developing an enthusiasm for Socialism (that is, social reform) from reading newspapers and other publications, and writing letters for his fellow soldiers, Mao accomplished hardly anything at all.

Mao's lack of education and training in this area showed in his poor military management style. On more than one occasion, military commanders criticized him for his ineptitude. During the Jinggangshan period, Zhu expressed dissatisfaction with Mao's approach to guerrilla warfare; during the Long March, Lin Biao proposed that Mao confine himself to overall policy and planning, and leave military matters to Peng Dehuai. Liu Bocheng castigated "Mao's rhetorical style of combat instructions, which were often delivered with passion but were couched in such general language as to either confuse subordinate commanders or suggest that Mao was not clear about phasing, objectives, coordination, and other matters of modern military management."[7]

By temperament and experience, Mao preferred political to military battles. His *métier* was maneuvers in the periodic intraparty conflicts that plagued the CCP: He paid particular attention to the ideological disputes that were the staples of such struggles, and assiduously built coalitions with other Communist leaders, including the military commanders. His political style was to criticize the ideas and policies of others while promoting his own in party forums. He was quite adept at capitalizing on the misfortunes of others. In the wake of the disintegration of the "first united front" in 1927, he would challenge Marxist–Leninist orthodoxy by advocating the establishment of a Red Army that would lead a protracted, peasant-based revolutionary movement to victory. In effect, the Red Army would become the revolutionary movement. To Mao, the military would always be a means to political ends.

In 1923, out of a common commitment to anti-imperialism and anti-warlordism, the Communists joined the Nationalist Party. Together, the

Nationalists and Communists undertook the Northern Expedition (1926–1928), a military campaign to overcome the warlords and unify the country. The "united front" alliance collapsed when Chiang Kai-shek, commander-in-chief of the Northern Expedition, launched the "White terror" on April 12, 1927. With the assistance of Shanghai gangsters, Chiang used his army to purge the Communists from the Nationalist Party. As a result of this disaster, Mao realized that the CCP needed its own army, a disciplined and politicized military force that would not only defend it against counterrevolutionaries but would also be in the vanguard of the revolutionary struggle.

In an effort to salvage something from the Nationalist–Communist split, the CCP initiated urban and rural insurrections in the spring and summer of 1927. Assuming that they were in the midst of a so-called revolutionary high tide that would sweep them to power, Communist leaders adhered to the Marxist–Leninist political strategy of seizing urban centers through primarily proletarian uprisings, with the peasantry and military serving in an auxiliary capacity. However, after conducting an investigation (January 4 to February 5, 1927) of a peasant uprising occurring in his native Hunan province, Mao conceived the "heretical" idea that it was the peasantry rather than the proletariat that would lead the revolution. At the August 7, 1927, emergency conference of the CCP's Central Committee, using his now famous aphorism, "Political power grows out of the barrel of a gun," Mao argued that the proposed Autumn Harvest Uprising (September 12, 1927) required an armed peasantry. Presumably, this is why he was designated a special commissioner and sent to eastern Hunan, where the provincial committee appointed him a division commander of the Worker and Peasant Army then being organized. Meanwhile, the agrarian revolution he envisioned started without him.

The Origins of the Red Army

Mao never had a chance to participate actively in the Autumn Harvest Uprising. However, he did arrive in time to organize its survivors into the 1st Division of the Worker and Peasant Revolutionary Army. In October 1927 he led them to Jinggangshan, a remote, mountainous region along the Jiangxi–Hunan border that would serve as a secure rural base from which to renew the Communist movement. It was there that he employed hit-and-run guerrilla tactics against his enemies and became known as a veritable Chinese Robin Hood who robbed from the rich to give to the poor. This behavior is an essential component of his myth, but it did not make him unique. While he did expropriate and redistribute the property of the rich, so did Peng Pai and other Communist leaders waging an armed struggle in the countryside. During this period, Mao's reputation as a daring guerrilla chief was further embellished by his poetry. When he was not outwitting his enemies in the field, Mao was composing poems commemorating the exploits of his troops. His most famous work, however, is "The Immortals," a paean to his beloved wife, Yang Kaihui, who was executed by the Guomindang in 1930. In recent memory, the only person who has ever rivaled Mao's reputation as a romantic revolutionary was Che Guevara, the Argentine-born theoretician and tactician of Marxist guerrilla warfare in Latin America. In reality, Mao was more like Che's comrade Fidel Castro, the political leader of Cuba.

In the following spring, Mao was joined by Zhu De and the remnants of the Nanchang Uprising, a failed urban insurrection by pro-Communist military forces that had taken place on August 1, 1927 (now celebrated as the founding day of the Chinese People's Liberation Army). In Zhu De, a former warlord who became an ardent Communist, Mao found a brilliant military tactician who was known as the Chinese Napoleon. Perhaps even more important from his perspective, Mao had found a military commander who truly believed in subordinating the army to political direction. Zhu De's willingness to defer to political authority would allow Mao eventually to take credit for the Red Army's victories.

Until 1931, when the CCP's Central Committee moved from Shanghai to Jiangxi, Mao Zedong and Zhu De had considerable local autonomy in the supervision of Communist revolution. They had time to regroup and to rethink the CCP's revolutionary strategy, with the immediate aim of taking control of Jiangxi province. They began to develop what might be called a "Communist revolution with Chinese characteristics," to paraphrase Deng Xiaoping's approach to economic reform in the 1980s. At Jinggangshan, they established a rural base area, mobilized the peasantry, and organized a Red Army that fought a guerrilla war. From 1927 to 1929, under the leadership of Zhu and Mao, the Red Army defended the Jinggangshan base area against Nationalist army attacks. After being driven out, Zhu and Mao reestablished themselves along the Jiangxi–Fujian border, which became the Central Soviet, the most important of the several Communist base areas to emerge in various parts of China. Only the Eyuwan Soviet base area (located in the Hubei–Henan–Anhui border region) rivaled it in scope and influence. In April 1931 the Eyuwan base would be placed under the direction of Zhang Guotao, who would become Mao's arch rival.

Together, Zhu De and Mao Zedong made a formidable team. Because of the close working relationship between them, they were often mistaken for a single individual named "Zhu Mao." However, despite their close collaboration, the two men maintained a clear division of responsibility: Zhu De served as the military commander and Mao Zedong as the political commissar of the newly organized Red Army.

As commander, Zhu De was in charge of organizing and training an effective military force and conducting military operations. It was during the Jiangxi Soviet period that Zhu developed several innovations for which the Red Army is known. First of all, out of his experience in fighting the Nationalist army's first three encirclement and suppression campaigns, he evolved the operational principles of mobile warfare summed up in the famous quatrain:

> When the enemy advances, we retreat.
> When the enemy halts and encamps, we harass them.
> When the enemy seeks to avoid battle, we attack.
> When the enemy retreats, we pursue.

Zhu also instituted the after-action debriefings in which Red Army officers and troops had an opportunity to critique the battle they had just fought. Finally, to instill personal discipline in his soldiers, he instituted the "The Main Rules of Discipline and Eight Points of Attention":

Three Rules
   1. Obedience to orders.
   2. Take not even a needle or thread from the people.
   3. Turn in all confiscated goods.

Eight Points
   1. Replace all doors and return all straw on which you sleep before leaving a house. [The doors were used as improvised beds.]
   2. Speak courteously to the people and help them whenever possible.
   3. Return all borrowed articles.
   4. Pay for everything damaged.
   5. Be honest in business transactions.
   6. Be sanitary—dig latrines a safe distance from homes and fill them up with earth before leaving.
   7. Never molest women.
   8. Do not mistreat prisoners.

Adherence to these commandments would make the Red Army markedly different from the existing Chinese armies, particularly the predatory warlord armies that mercilessly victimized the populace. The comparatively good behavior of the Red Army in part explains how Communist soldiers won the "hearts and minds" of the Chinese people.

As the commissar, Mao had an equally important role to play and a significant contribution to make. He was responsible for raising the political consciousness of the troops through indoctrination in CCP principles, ensuring loyalty to the Communist cause, and instilling in them an esprit de corps. Besides fighting their enemies, the troops were expected to work with the peasant masses in order to develop the popular support that was necessary for their survival. The Red Army's relationship to the people was summed up in the saying "the soldiers are fish and the people water." Popular support was generated through such techniques as the "mass line," which involved consulting the people and drawing them into the political process. When done effectively, the mass line motivated and transformed people, and made them amenable to the party's aims. Even more important, Mao also sought to mobilize the masses through social and economic reforms, particularly redistribution of land. It was through the sympathy and support of the peasantry that he was able to set up an intelligence and logistical system that proved indispensable in defeating Chiang Kai-shek's encirclement and suppression campaigns.

THE ENCIRCLEMENT AND SUPPRESSION CAMPAIGNS

Chiang Kai-shek sought to destroy the resurgent Communist movement in Jiangxi once and for all with a major campaign to envelop and eliminate the main Red Army units. But to Chiang's chagrin, the Red Army defeated not only his first but also his second, third, and fourth encirclement and suppression campaigns. There were several contributing factors. During the first three campaigns (December 1930–September 1931) Zhu De and Mao Zedong effectively used a defensive–offensive strategy of "luring the enemy deep." They allowed the enemy forces to enter the base area, even at the expense of the people that the CCP was obligated to defend, trading space for time and forcing the Nationalist army to overextend its communication lines and supply routes. At the appropriate time and place, the Red Army then initiated a counterattack, concentrating its main forces against selected enemy units and annihilating them. Politically, the Communists involved the people in the base area in their own defense. By exposing them to the depredations of enemy troops, they alienated them from the Nationalist government and drew them closer to the Communist cause.

In the first two campaigns, Chiang Kai-shek unwittingly contributed to his own defeat by sending expeditionary forces consisting mainly of assorted former warlord troops that had defected to the National Revolutionary Army during the Northern Expedition. Conflicting interests made them incapable of cooperating in the implementation of the plan to envelop and destroy the numerically inferior Red Army. Instead, the Red Army, taking advantage of its superior military intelligence and employing greater mobility, was able to concentrate its forces on isolated Nationalist units and destroy them.

For the third campaign, Chiang Kai-shek mobilized men and units that were personally loyal to him. Once again, his forces were defeated. However, this defeat was due less to the lack of cooperation among the warlord troops in his army (though that continued to be a factor) than to external distractions: the Canton Secessionist Movement (May 1931) and the Mukden Incident (September 1931), which resulted in the loss of Manchuria to the Japanese.

After the third campaign (July–September 1931), the Chinese Communist Party experienced significant leadership changes. In the CCP's intraparty power struggles, Zhu De was able to retain his power and was even elevated to the position of chairman of the Central Soviet's Revolutionary Military Council because of his military expertise. Mao, however, lost power, presumably because of his unorthodox ideas and political ambitions. At the Ningdu Conference in August 1932, Mao was replaced by Zhou Enlai as the general political commissar and lost his influence in the Red Army.

Under the leadership of the "28 Bolsheviks," a group of young Chinese Communists who had been trained in the Soviet Union, and of Otto Braun, the Comintern military adviser, the Red Army's organization, strategy, and tactics were changed to deal with Chiang's fourth campaign (July 1932–April 1933). The Red Army was transformed into a conventional fighting force capable of engaging in positional warfare. Under the slogan, "Lose no inch of soviet territory to the enemy," the CCP abandoned the previously successful Zhu-Mao strategy of "luring the enemy deep" into the base area in favor of an offensive strategy of attacking the enemy outside the base area. The Red Army launched successful preemptive strikes against Nationalist army units, thus ending Chiang Kai-shek's fourth campaign.

But the fifth campaign (October 1933–October 1934) proved markedly different. Reacting to their repeated failures, the Nationalists changed to a "strategically offensive but tactically defensive" strategy. Synthesizing some of the methods that they had used against the Communists previously, the Nationalists imposed a stringent economic and communications blockade, destroying the self-sufficiency of the Central Soviet base area. The blockade consisted chiefly of a network of mutually supporting blockhouses and trenches built at key points on the periphery of Communist territory. Nationalist forces methodically moved into the base area, building blockhouses and interdicting the flow of goods as they advanced, eventually strangling the Central Soviet base.

Understandably, given their success against the fourth campaign, the Communists at first responded by continuing with their positional warfare strategy, thus playing into the hands of the Nationalists. But the Communists quickly realized that they had insufficient manpower and firepower to prevent the Nationalists from penetrating the base area. They tried Otto Braun's plan of building their own blockhouses in the most vital sectors, only to discover that enemy artillery and air bombardment readily destroyed them. Red Army efforts to lure the enemy out of the blockhouses and ambush them proved fruitless: The Nationalist army declined to engage directly and continued its gradual, inexorable advance, constricting the base area with a wall of steel and concrete. After losing the Battle of Guangchang (April 11–28, 1934), the Communists realized that their situation was becoming increasingly untenable. By the fall, the Red Army had suffered a loss of about 60,000 men, and the base area had been reduced by more than half, now encompassing only six counties. For the CCP leadership, the time had come to abandon the Central Soviet.

Mao later claimed that if the Red Army had continued using mobile warfare and had breached enemy lines to attack from the rear, it could have defeated the Nationalist army once again, but this is questionable. Frankly, it is improbable that the Red Army could have accomplished this feat because the blockade–blockhouse line allowed the Nationalists to apply their superior material strength without exposing themselves to yet another demoralizing defeat. In other words, as long as the Nationalists refused to be lured into Communist territory and fight a battle under unfavorable circumstances, they could not be defeated. For the Nationalists, in the final analysis, not losing was the equivalent of winning.

From a historical perspective, the Jiangxi Soviet period was a watershed in the Chinese Communist revolutionary movement. First, the Communists moved the theater of operations from the urban to the rural areas;

second, they founded base areas from which to engage in a protracted armed struggle against their enemies; and third and most important, they had organized, trained, and indoctrinated a formidable military force: the Red Army. Nevertheless, during the "strategic withdrawal" from Jiangxi, the Communists almost lost that army.

THE LEGENDARY LONG MARCH

On October 16, 1934, under the cover of darkness, approximately 86,000 Communist army, party, and government personnel began what was to be known as the Long March, a year-long organized retreat that at times degenerated into an outright flight. They marched in three columns, two main ones and a heavily burdened headquarters column in the center (which was later dropped). Because of the ponderous nature of the fifth campaign and the secrecy shrouding the departure of the Communists, it took the Nationalists a month to realize that their foes had literally stolen a march on them.

By the time the Long March was completed, the Communists had covered about 6,000 miles, from Jiangxi province in the south to Shaanxi province in the north, over some of the most rugged, least explored territory in the country. The worst came toward the end, when they began to cross the Grasslands, a vast marsh that swallowed many a Red Army soldier during the week-long traverse. Altogether, the Red Army soldiers had to go across eighteen mountain ranges and twenty-four rivers, all the while fending off hostile forces. Often marching twenty to forty miles a day, sometimes for several days straight, the underequipped and undersupplied soldiers fought warlord troops who sought to drive them from their territory; minority peoples, such as the Yi and Tibetans, who ambushed them; and, of course, the Nationalist army, which tried to intercept and destroy them, nearly succeeding on more than one occasion.

In Chinese Communist history, the Long March has attained legendary status. Paradoxically, it represented both the lowest and highest points of the Chinese Communist movement. Even though they left Jiangxi in defeat, the Communists arrived in Shaanxi a year later ready for victory, for the Long March served as the crucible that forged an indestructible Red Army, or so the story goes. The Long March has been idealized as a triumph of revolutionary will over extreme hardship, the Chinese equivalent of Valley Forge.

Unquestionably, the Long March was an unprecedented epic in human survival, and the veterans of the Long March provided living proof that determined people willing to engage in unending struggle and self-sacrifice could prevail even under the most desperate conditions. The Chinese Communists like to claim that the men and women of the Long March were able to survive because they were imbued with a political conciousness that made it possible for them to overcome every natural and man-made obstacle they encountered. That is the essential lesson they passed down to later generations of Chinese. During the Cultural Revolution (1966–1976), Red Guards, young Chinese students, sought to test their own revolutionary resolve by going on their own version of a Long March.

The Long March began with the Red Army heading westward, aiming to cross the Xiang River and join other Communist forces in Hunan province. After arranging a "neutrality pact" with Chen Jitang, the Guang-dong warlord, the Red Army successfully penetrated the southwest zone of the Nationalist blockade–blockhouse line. There they met only token opposition from Guangxi and Guangdong provincial troops manning the defense networks. Facilitating their escape was a Communist rear-guard force whose mission was to distract and delay the Nationalists. Most of this "death legion" would later be captured or killed, though enough of them survived to form the nucleus of the New Fourth Army during the War of Resistance against Japan.

The Nationalists nearly destroyed the Communists at the Battle of the Xiang River (November 25–December 3, 1934), when they caught the Red Army divided, with one half on each side of the river. Though the Red Army escaped, it lost more than half of its troops. By the time it finally arrived at Zunyi, Guizhou, a month later, the Red Army was down to about 30,000 soldiers.

On January 15–18, 1935, at Zunyi, the Communist leaders held a conference to evaluate their defeat during the fifth campaign and their retreat from the Central Soviet base area. This proved to be a historic event resulting in a change in the leadership as well as the direction of the Long March. Since Mao was out of favor politically, no one could blame him for the recent debacles that they had sufffered. However, he was in a position to criticize severely CCP leaders for losing the Central Soviet base area by following the erroneous policy of "pure defense" rather than "mobile warfare," and for failing to exploit the rebellion by Chiang Kai-shek's Nineteenth Route Army that had erupted in Fujian during the fifth campaign. And, of course, he reproached them for the recent disaster at the Xiang River. In this Mao was supported by others, most notably the senior military commanders, whose voices were particularly influential since the problems during the Long March were mainly military ones.

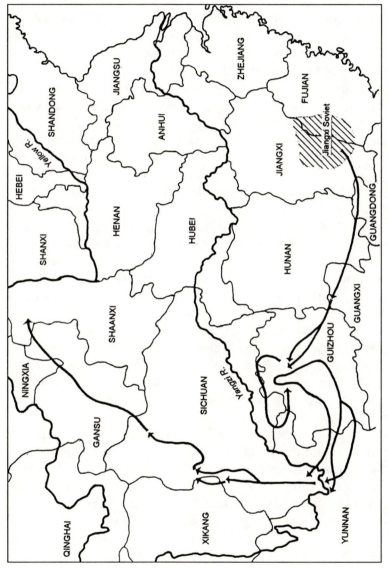

Map 13.1 The Long March, 1934–1935, showing route of the Communist First Front Army. Adapted by Don Graff based upon *Cambridge History of China*, vol. 13: *Republican China, 1912–1949, Part 2* (Cambridge: Cambridge University Press, 1986), p. 210.

As a result of the Zunyi Conference, Mao's political stock went up. As Benjamin Yang observes, he developed a "reputation as the only man who had represented a correct Party line in the past and who had the potential to lead the Revolution to victory in the future."[8] Mao became a member of the Standing Committee of the Politburo and strategic adviser to Zhou Enlai, who along with Zhu De was now in charge of the Long March. Taking advantage of Zhou's illness and Zhu's deference to political authority, Mao became the de facto leader of the Long March within weeks following the Zunyi Conference. By March 1935, Mao became political commissar and Zhu De commander-in-chief of the Long March. Mao had come full circle, returning to where he started at Jinggangshan, with considerable authority to make decisions. As a result of his leadership during the Long March, Mao would eventually rise to become the preeminent leader of the CCP.

Under Mao's general direction, the Red Army sought to cross the Yangzi River and head north, with the objective of joining Zhang Guotao's forces from the Eyuwan Soviet and establishing a new base area in the Yunnan–Guizhou–Sichuan border area. But the marchers were ignorant of Zhang's exact whereabouts; all they knew was that he was somewhere in the northern part of Sichuan province. Depending on how one interprets Mao's leadership during this period, either he engaged in some ingenious maneuvers, using feints to confuse the enemy, or himself was confused, leading the Red Army aimlessly across southwest China. In either case, Mao had the initiative, forcing the Nationalists to guess his next move. In what was later regarded as a stroke of genius, he ordered the Red Army to go south toward Yunnan province as a prelude to heading north. Finally, the Red Army crossed the River of Golden Sands, a western extension of the Yangzi, into Sichuan.

It was in Sichuan that Red Army soldiers performed their most famous act of courage, the capture of Luding Bridge. In order to escape the pursuing Nationalist army and avoid the fate of the Taiping army that had been destroyed there a century earlier, the Red Army had to take the bridge spanning the raging Dadu River below. Enemy troops held the opposite end of the chain suspension bridge and had removed most of the wooden planks that formed a catwalk across it. Twenty-two Red Army soldiers volunteered to be members of an assault team to take the bridge. Under enemy machine-gun fire, they crawled 100 yards hand over hand across the swaying bridge chains to reach the remaining planks and attack enemy positions. Capturing the bridge enabled the Red Army to cross the river safely and continue the march to northern Sichuan.

After crossing the Great Snowy Mountains, the Red Army finally found Zhang Guotao and his troops. Instead of the expected happy reunion, it proved to be a problem-riddled meeting, marred by policy disputes, personality conflicts, and power rivalries. The major problem was Zhang's rivalry with Mao and his desire to take control of the entire Communist force. It is alleged that at one point Zhang even threatened to attack Mao's forces unless he complied. The Mao camp wanted to continue north and then east to join Communist forces in the Shaanxi–Gansu border region, ostensibly for the purpose of fighting the Japanese, who continued to encroach on Chinese territory. But the Zhang camp had other ideas. They wanted to head south to establish a soviet base in the Sichuan–Xikang border region. In a compromise brokered by Zhu De, Mao and Zhang agreed to reorganize their combined forces and go their separate ways. As part of the deal, Zhu accompanied Zhang as his hostage.

After crossing the deadly Grasslands of the Qinghai–Gansu border region, Mao's ragtag force of about 4,000 finally met up with Communist forces in north Shaanxi on October 20, 1935, ending the Long March. A year later, after suffering defeats in western China, Zhang Guotao and his forces rejoined Mao.

While the Long March was a victory of the human will, it was also a defeat for the Chinese Communist movement. After all, it began as a military retreat and ended up as a military disaster, with over nine-tenths of the Red Army lost along the way. To the veterans of the Long March, the future must have appeared rather bleak indeed. The Nationalists had defeated the Communists repeatedly, decimating the early revolutionary movement, devastating the Central Soviet base area, and nearly destroying the Red Army during the Long March. After unparalleled hardship, the remnants of the Red Army had reestablished themselves in a new base area at Yan'an, Shaanxi, only to be blockaded once again by the Nationalist army.

RED ARMY REDUX

The Nationalists were poised to defeat the Communists and probably would have done so if not for a significant external factor: Japanese aggression. In 1937 the Japanese launched a full-scale invasion of China as the first step in their effort to establish a so-called new order in Asia under their domination. In the face of a common enemy, Chinese closed ranks. Chiang Kai-shek reluctantly forged a "second united front" with the Communists to oppose the invading Japanese. Under the nominal command of its erstwhile enemies, the Red Army was designated the Eighth Route Army, with Zhu De as commander-in-chief and Peng Dehuai as deputy commander. Until the New Fourth Army Incident (1941)—when the Nationalist army attacked Communist troops in southern Anhui, killing 3,000 of them—both sides cooperated, more or less, in the war against the Japanese.

During the War of Resistance against the Japanese (1937–1945), Nationalist forces shouldered the heaviest burden and suffered the severest losses. In the summer and fall of 1937, for example, the Nationalist army sustained as many as 250,000 casualties, almost 60 percent of its finest forces, in the heroic defense of Shanghai. Eventually, Chiang Kai-shek and his army were forced to retreat to Chongqing (Chungking), Sichuan, where he set up his wartime capital. With American assistance, Chiang's armies fought the Japanese in the western and southern parts of China. In fleeing west, Chiang left behind a political vacuum that would be filled by the Communists. Led by the survivors of the Long March, the Communists entered the northern and eastern areas abandoned by the Nationalists to wage a guerrilla war against the Japanese. Their greatest offensive was the "Hundred Regiments Campaign" (1940) in north China. Under the command of Peng Dehuai, Communist forces attacked enemy strong points and lines of communication, losing about 100,000 men. Together, the Nationalist and Communist armies succeeded in inflicting severe losses on the Japanese army and tying down at least two-fifths of its available troops during World War II. In fighting a land war in Asia, the Japanese army foolishly found itself in a quagmire from which it could not extract itself.

At Mao's direction, Communist cadres went behind enemy lines to organize the people against the Japanese. Under their political leadership, the Chinese populace learned to survive the chaotic wartime conditions and to defend themselves against marauding Japanese troops who treated the areas they controlled as a vast "free fire zone." Employing such cruel measures as the "Three-Alls" policy—"kill all, burn all, destroy all"—Japanese soldiers committed countless atrocities, with the worst being the infamous Rape of Nanjing (1937). By implementing select socioeconomic reforms that had been developed earlier in the Jiangxi Soviet base area and mobilizing the peasants to resist the Japanese, the Communists were able to build political legitimacy in the countryside. By the tens of thousands, peasants joined the CCP, enrolled in the mass organizations, and, most important, enlisted in the Red Army. By the end of the War of Resistance (August 1945), the Communists had about 2 million in militia units and over 900,000 regular troops under their command, placing them in a postion to defeat the Nationalists in the civil war that ensued.

At the beginning of the Civil War (1946–1949), the Nationalists were quite successful. In the first year, they seized key cities and towns; in the second year, they were even able to capture the Communist capital of Yan'an. It was all for naught. Using mainly guerrilla warfare, the Communist forces gained control of the countryside and began surrounding the cities occupied by the Nationalists. By 1948, Communist forces were strong enough to shift to conventional warfare against the Nationalists. At the Battle of Huai Hai (November 7, 1948–January 10, 1949), Communist forces decisively defeated the Nationalists, forcing Chiang Kai-shek to resign the presidency of the country and flee to Taiwan, where he established a government in exile.

CONCLUSION

Mao's personality cult portrays him as the all-knowing, all-wise leader who led the party through "storm and stress," overcoming every sort of difficulty to achieve final victory in 1949. This is far from the truth, certainly when it comes to his military role. Mao's military role in CCP history has been much exaggerated by the party as well as by others. The Communist preference for making political theory paramount ensured that Mao as the party leader would be given credit for the party's military triumph. Without much regard for historical truth, the party promoted his cult by rewriting its history in such a manner as to establish the supremacy of Mao and his thought. It has placed him at the center of the revolutionary movement while relegating other Communist leaders to subsidiary roles as either supporters or opponents of his "correct" policies. For the sake of group solidarity and to present a unified front to the outside world, none of the other leaders opposed Mao's personality cult, at least in the beginning. This facade would eventually fall apart and the military commanders would be among those to challenge him publicly. In July 1959, Peng Dehuai reproved Mao for undertaking the Great Leap Forward (1958–1960), which led to a famine resulting in an estimated 30 million deaths, and implicitly questioned his concept of "people's war." For his temerity, Peng suffered demotion and imprisonment.

In reality, Mao was essentially a political leader. He was, however, an exceptionally effective politician, persistent in his pursuit of power and magisterial in his manipulation of others. He first attained prominence in Jinggangshan, but was later forced to share the limelight with others, such as the 28 Bolsheviks, who eventually eclipsed him politically toward the end of the Jiangxi Soviet period. On the Long March, he regained political power and attained a high position in the CCP largely because his rivals were held responsible for the loss of the Jiangxi Soviet base area. He was able to carry out this coup only because he had the support of the senior Red Army military commanders, who had reservations about Mao's military ability but thought he had a better grasp of China's political situation than his rivals did. Besides, Mao gave the Red Army a place of prominence in the revolutionary movement, and they returned the compliment. Mao's symbiotic relationship with the Red Army's military commanders would serve as the foundation of his political power for years to come. For Mao, the aphorism "Political power grows out of the barrel of a gun" would have a dual meaning: The Red Army would prove to be indispensable in his own quest for political power as well as the party's.

SUGGESTIONS FOR FURTHER READING

Cold War politics has produced quite a number of works on or about Maoist military strategy, especially as it pertains to insurgency or counterinsurgency in the Third World. None of them, however, is a substitute for Mao's original essays. His most important works are conveniently compiled in Mao Zedong, *Selected Military Writings of Mao Tse-tung* (Beijing: Foreign Languages Press, 1963). Two books provide informative commentaries in addition to translations of some of Mao's essays: Mao Tse-tung, *Basic Tactics*, trans. and with an introduction by Stuart R. Schram (New York: Praeger, 1966), and *Mao Tse-tung on Guerrilla Warfare*, trans. and with an introduction by Brigadier General Samuel B. Griffith (New York: Praeger, 1961).

Since Mao was more a politician than a warrior, perhaps it should not be surprising that there is so little on him as a soldier. Jacques Guillermaz, "The Soldier," in *Mao Tse-tung in the Scales of History*, ed. Dick Wilson (Cambridge: Cambridge University Press, 1977) remains the only evaluation of Mao as a military man. But as Guillermaz cautions, it is only a preliminary assessment. What is remarkable is that except for Agnes Smedley, *The Great Road: The Life and Times of Chu Teh* (New York: Monthly Review Press, 1956) there is no study of Zhu De, the father of the Chinese Red Army. For the other military commanders, the situation is equally bleak; except for Lanxin Xiang, *Mao's Generals: Chen Yi and the New Fourth Army* (Lanham, MD: University Press of America, 1998), existing works focus on their political lives.

As a real or potential adversary during the Cold War, the Chinese Red Army has been much written about. But as Edward J. M. Rhoads, *The Chinese Red Army, 1927–1963: An Annotated Bibliography* (Cambridge: Harvard University Press, 1964) shows, not many of these works pertain to the Jiangxi Soviet period and the Long March. Since the publication of Rhoads's bibliography, there have been few additions. For the Jiangxi Soviet period, the only monograph-length study available is Peter W. Donovan, *The Red Army in Kiangsi, 1931–1934* (Ithaca, NY: China–Japan Program, Cornell University, 1976). Most other works tend to treat the Jiangxi period as part of a larger study on Chinese Communist military forces or military doctrine. Among them, one of the most analytical is William W. Whitson with Chen-hsia Huang, *The Chinese High Command: A History of Communist Military Politics, 1927–71* (New York: Praeger, 1973). Focusing on Chinese Communist military politics, it discusses three competing models of military "ethics" and "style" in the history of the Red Army, beginning with the Jiangxi Soviet period.

There are related works that offer important insights into Chinese Communist policy issues and power disputes that affected the Red Army during the Jiangxi Soviet period, such as Ilpyong J. Kim, *The Politics of Chinese Communism: Kiangsi under the Soviets* (Berkeley and Los Angeles: University of California Press, 1973), which recounts the development of Chinese Communist mass-mobilization policies and techniques. No discussion of the Red Army would be complete without a consideration of its opponents, for which see William Wei, *Counterrevolution in China: The Nationalists in Jiangxi during the Soviet Period* (Ann Arbor: University of Michigan Press, 1985), which provides a comprehensive analysis of Chiang Kai-shek's political, socioeconomic, and military policies and programs to eliminate the Red Army from Jiangxi.

The Long March has attracted more studies. For readability and drama, the journalistic accounts by Dick Wilson, *The Long March 1935: The Epic of Chinese Communism's Survival* (New York: Avon Books, 1971) and Harrison E. Salisbury, *The Long March: The Untold Story* (New York: Harper and Row, 1985) are still the best. Benjamin Yang, *From Revolution to Politics: Chinese Communists on the Long March* (Boulder, CO: Westview Press, 1990) is a much-needed scholarly treatment of this legendary episode in modern Chinese history. On the basis of new documents, Yang corrects previous explanations of Mao's rise to power during the Long March. Lest it be forgotten, the Communist forces left behind had a hard time of it. Gregor Benton, *Mountain Fires: The Red Army's Three-Year War in South China, 1934–1938* (Berkeley and Los Angeles: University of California Press, 1992) is an encyclopedic treatment of the fate of those left behind in Jiangxi as well as other Communist base areas in south China.

SUGGESTIONS FOR FURTHER RESEARCH

Since so little scholarly work has been done on Mao and the Red Army during the Jiangxi Soviet period and the Long March, the field is more or less wide open. Certainly, a comprehensive assessment of Mao as a military man and military thinker is long overdue. Such an evaluation, of course, would have to get beyond his cult of personality and the a priori assumption of his "military genius." A natural corollary would be studies on Zhu De, Peng Dehuai, Lin Biao, and the other Chinese military commanders who conducted the Red Army operations. For these studies to be complete, it would be necessary to consider the challenge their enemies posed, so a parallel set of studies on the Nationalist generals and their armies is in order.

The Chen Cheng Collection, a large body of primary sources on the Jiangxi Soviet Republic, enables scholars to reconstruct the history of the Red Army.[9] In addition to studying the usual military topics, such as the strategy and tactics that the Red Army employed against its enemies, it is essential to examine its interaction with the local population. After all, it has been an article of faith that the success of the Red Army depended heavily on the people's willingness to provide military intelligence and logistical support. An analysis of the socioeconomic and other effects that the Red Army had on the people living in Jiangxi would prove immensely valuable in understanding the significance of "People's War."

The Long March warrants a similar analysis, and also deserves to be studied as a major military event rather than as a vehicle for the playing out of intraparty struggles or a test of the participants' commitment to the Communist cause. A study of the effect that the Red Army had on the people it encountered on the Long March would help explain the Chinese Communist Party's subsequent relationship with the minority peoples whose territories the Red Army crossed.

NOTES

1. Stéphane Coutois, Nicolas Werth, Jean-Louis Panné, Andrzej Paczkowski, Karel Bartošek, and Jean-Louis Margolin, *The Black Book of Communism: Crimes, Terror, Repression*, trans. Jonathan Murphy and Mark Kramer (Cambridge: Harvard University Press, 1999), 465.

2. Harrison E. Salisbury, *The Long March: The Untold Story* (New York: Harper and Row, 1985), 172.

3. Dick Wilson, *The Long March 1935: The Epic of Chinese Communism's Survival* (New York: Avon Books, 1971), 55.

4. Ibid., 63.

5. Lin Piao, "Long Live the Victory of People's War!" *Peking Review* (September 3, 1965): 9–30.

6. Brigadier General Samuel B. Griffith, "Foreword," in Mao Tse-tung, *Basic Tactics*, trans. and with an introduction by Stuart R. Schram (New York: Praeger, 1966), 7.

7. William W. Whitson with Chen-hsia Huang, *The Chinese High Command: A History of Communist Military Politics, 1927–71* (New York: Praeger, 1973), 64.

8. Benjamin Yang, "The Zunyi Conference as One Step in Mao's Rise to Power: A Survey of Historical Studies of the Chinese Communist Party," *China Quarterly*, no. 106 (1986): 258.

9. The Chen Cheng Collection is held by the Hoover Insititution at Stanford University; microfilm copies of many of these materials can be found in other major research libraries. See Tien-wei Wu, *The Kiangsi Soviet Republic, 1931–1934: A Selected and Annotated Bibliography of the Ch'en Ch'eng Collection* (Cambridge: Harvard-Yenching Library, Harvard University, 1981).

FOURTEEN

Always Faithful:
The PLA from 1949 to 1989

Dennis J. Blasko

At the founding of the People's Republic of China on October 1, 1949, the People's Liberation Army was 5.5 million strong. Its twenty years of experience in guerrilla fighting against both the Nationalists and Japanese had culminated in large-scale conventional operations during the Civil War. China's senior military leaders were also its senior political leaders and the army pledged its loyalty to the Chinese Communist Party above all. For the next forty years, China's enemies would change; the PLA's size, force structure, doctrine, equipment, and role in society would vary; and the balance between "red" (politics) and "expert" (professionalism) would be a constant source of tension within the PLA. However, in every test the Chinese military remained faithful to the Communist Party.

In the months prior to the establishment of the PRC, the PLA was basically an infantry-heavy ground force organized into five field armies:

The First Field Army led by Peng Dehuai operated in the northwest provinces of Shanxi, Shaanxi, and Ningxia.

The Second Field Army under the command of Liu Bocheng, with Deng Xiaoping as political commissar, operated in Henan, Hubei, and Anhui.

The Third Field Army commanded by Chen Yi operated in Shandong, Jiangsu, and parts of Anhui.

The Fourth Field Army under the command of Lin Biao first operated in Manchuria and then moved south into Hunan and Guangdong.

The Fifth Field Army commanded by Nie Rongzhen, with Xu Xiangqian as political commissar, fought in Hebei, Inner Mongolia, and parts of Shanxi.

The field armies were composed of numbered armies, each composed of several numbered corps. Over the next four years, the field army structure would dissolve, but the personal relationships among the leaders would remain influential for decades.

Mao Zedong was the chairman of the Military Affairs Committee (known later as the Central Military Commission, CMC) of the Chinese Communist Party's Central Committee, with Ye Jianying as vice chairman. Zhu De was named commander-in-chief, Peng Dehuai his deputy, Xu Xiangqian the first chief of the general staff, and Nie Rongzhen deputy chief of the general staff. Except for Mao, these leaders were professional, technically oriented officers.

Most senior military leaders also held high positions in the central government in Beijing, and many lower-level military leaders continued to perform the duties of civilian governance in China's six administrative regions as they did in the "liberated areas" during the Anti-Japanese War and the Civil War. From 1952 to 1954 most military officers were gradually relieved of their civil administration duties.

The earliest elements of the PLA Navy were formed in the spring of 1949, and were composed mainly of ex-Nationalist ships and sailors; the leaders were former ground-force commanders. One of the navy's earliest leaders, Liu Huaqing, came to epitomize professionalism in the PLA. In the early 1950s, Liu served as the vice commandant of the First Naval Academy and then studied at the Voroshilov Naval Academy in the USSR. In the late 1960s he was deputy director of the Defense Science and Technology Commission under Nie Rongzhen, rose to command the PLA Navy in 1982, and ended his career as the most senior uniformed officer in the PLA.

The PLA Air Force was established in November 1949 and also was equipped with captured Nationalist and Japanese aircraft. Its first commander, Liu Yalou, had no aviation experience. He was assisted by Xiao Hua, considered one of the PLA's most effective political commissars.

"People's War" was China's basic military doctrine. As conceived by Mao Zedong, People's War was primarily a defensive strategy that relied on the mobilization of the Chinese people to make up for China's inferiority in weapons. It emphasized stealth, deception, and initiative. "Active defense," which calls for taking the tactical offensive within a defensive strategy, was (and remains) a principal concept of People's War.

Until the outbreak of the Korean War in June 1950, the PLA's main mission was to complete its military victory over the Nationalists. However, China's final campaign against Chiang Kai-shek's forces was prevented by the presence of the U.S. Seventh Fleet in the Taiwan Strait immediately after the outbreak of hostilities on the Korean peninsula. Despite the fighting in Korea, the PLA was reduced in size to 3 million in early 1952.

ALLIANCE WITH THE USSR, CONFRONTATION WITH THE UNITED STATES

In February 1950, China and the Soviet Union signed a Treaty of Friendship, Alliance, and Mutual Assistance. After about a year of fighting in Korea, the PLA began to receive massive infusions of military equipment from the USSR. When faced with superior firepower in the positional warfare that developed on the peninsula, the Chinese "volunteers" were forced to adopt much more conventional tactics than they had used in the first months of the war. After the cease-fire in 1953, the PLA reorganized using Soviet military organizational structures, doctrine, and tactics, and welcomed Soviet advisers and equipment. The USSR also provided plans and assistance for military factories so China could produce its own conventional weapons. The PLA instituted a Soviet-style system of military ranks in 1955, which Mao and many others in the party opposed because it shattered the PLA's tradition of equality among soldiers and leaders.

The Ministry of National Defense was formed in 1954 with Peng Dehuai as the first minister of defense. The experience of fighting U.N. forces in Korea led by the technologically advanced United States convinced the PLA leadership of the necessity of modernization and the importance of military professionalism. Long a proponent of professionalism within the PLA, Peng was just the man to lead the PLA down this road. However, many in the party preferred for the army to retain Mao's emphasis on revolutionary zeal and the supremacy of man over weapons. In particular, Peng made many enemies among the political commissars with his preference for "one-man command," by which commanders held final authority in decision making over the commissars.

By 1956 thirteen Military Regions had been formed, placing the forces of one or more provinces under a single commander. PLA ground forces were organized into main force units that could be transferred from one part of the country to another, local or regional forces responsible for security only in their own limited locales, and militia forces that would provide manpower and logistics support to the main and local force units. Main force units were primarily the thirty-five infantry corps that had been part of the field army structure, as well as air and naval forces.

General military modernization was not paramount on Mao's national priority list in the mid–1950s. Mao believed that a protracted-war strategy, relying on China's size and manpower resources, was the proper response to the threat posed by the United States, which had signed a mutual defense treaty with Taiwan in 1954. The PLA was to be used for non-military, economic functions, and to serve as a model for the rest of Chinese society. The best way to modernize the military was first to build a strong civilian industrial base. In a major policy speech in 1956, Mao stated that if the army wanted to build atomic bombs, then it should reallocate resources within its own military budget. In 1957, the PLA was reduced to about 2.4 million in a decision that would help limit the size of the defense budget.

Though he publicly denounced atomic weapons, Mao had actually decided that for both prestige purposes and military necessity China must have its own nuclear arsenal. At a meeting of the Politburo in January 1955, Mao declared that China would immediately begin a major effort to develop atomic energy for military purposes. Moscow also announced it would provide aid to China and several East European countries to "promote research into the peaceful uses of atomic energy." Over the next three years, the USSR and China signed six accords related to the development of nuclear science, industry, and weapons. In the New Defense Technical Accord of 1957, the Soviet Union agreed to supply China with a prototype atomic bomb and missiles, as well as technical data.

In part, Mao was reacting to a threat from the United States, which at the time was developing the doctrine of massive nuclear retaliation to deal with an international Communist movement that increasingly challenged the "Free World" through military and revolutionary actions. In early 1953, the new Eisenhower administration had warned that it might use nuclear weapons to break the deadlock in negotiations at Panmunjom. Over the next five years, the United States also threatened China with nuclear strikes to gain leverage in the two Taiwan Strait crises over the Nationalist-held offshore islands of Quemoy and Matsu in 1954 and 1958; another such threat was the U.S. deployment of nuclear-capable Matador surface-to-surface missiles on Taiwan. Up until the 1958 crisis, Mao appeared to believe that the Soviet Union would provide China with a nuclear umbrella in the event of a confrontation with the United States. Moreover, he believed that the PRC could triumph in a nuclear war, even with the loss of millions of lives.

Nie Rongzhen was placed in charge of developing China's conventional military industry as well as its nuclear and missile programs. Zhang Aiping was given responsibility for research and development of conventional weapons and assigned to command the First Atomic Bomb Test

Commission. Returned U.S.-trained scientist Qian Xuesen led China's missile program. Development of both nuclear weapons and surface-to-surface missiles was given high priority by both central and local governments through the assignment of highly trained personnel, allotment of funds, and access to resources such as land and material. A large assortment of commissions and ministries, including the Fifth Academy in charge of missiles and the Second Ministry of Machine Building for the nuclear program, were established to conduct research and build the equipment necessary for the bomb and missile programs. Though they encountered problems during the Great Leap Forward (1958–1960), when Mao attempted to mobilize the masses for economic development, these strategic programs received high-level attention and survived the political and economic turmoil China suffered in the late 1950s and early 1960s.

Moscow did provide nuclear weapons expertise and a few surface-to-surface missiles to China, but it did not transfer a complete atomic bomb as it had pledged in 1957. Following the death of Stalin, the rise of Khrushchev, differences over grand strategies, and Russian perceptions of Chinese ingratitude led to a political rift between Moscow and Beijing. By early 1959, Khrushchev had decided China was an unreliable partner, a conclusion that paralleled the one Beijing had reached the previous year during the second Taiwan Strait crisis. As a result, over the next year all Soviet advisors returned to the USSR, many defense projects were left uncompleted, and much of the material originally promised to China was never delivered. At the same time, an important leadership change was taking place in Beijing.

Peng Dehuai was removed from his position as defense minister in 1959, mainly for his criticism of Mao's economic policies in the Great Leap Forward. His emphasis on military professionalism also contributed to his fall. Lin Biao, a well-respected commander who had been ill and relatively inactive in the mid–1950s, replaced Peng as defense minister. Lin's task was to reestablish the PLA's political and ideological foundation, as well as modernize the forces. Luo Ruiqing, a former political commissar, was named chief of the general staff.

Lin restored the balance between commander and political commissar. He reemphasized military training, yet allotted 30 to 40 percent of the PLA's time for political work. Lin also modified Mao's concept that "men are superior to material" by stating that "men and material form a unity with man as the leading factor." This formulation opened the door for a strengthening of the PLA's more technical arms—the air force, the navy,

and the soon-to-be-formed strategic missile force—while remaining ide-
ologically safe.

On October 16, 1964, China exploded its first atomic bomb, developed
on its own after the Soviet advisers had departed. Four months earlier
China had tested its first indigenously designed missile, the Dong Feng 2
(DF–2). (Previously China had produced and deployed a few shorter-
range missiles based on the Soviet SS–2.) The crash strategic program begun less than a decade before was a success. Immediately after its first nuclear test, Beijing announced that it would never be the first to use nuclear
weapons and called for a conference to discuss their complete prohibition
and destruction.

In the years that followed, a plan was implemented to develop an assortment of missiles with ranges that could reach U.S. bases in Japan, the
Philippines, Guam, and the continental United States, as well as China's
other regional neighbors. The Second Artillery Corps, China's strategic
missile force, was established on July 1, 1966. A PLA Air Force bomber
dropped China's first hydrogen bomb on June 17, 1967.

Over the next two decades, China produced and deployed approximately 150 strategic missiles of all types, though none with multiple independently targetable reentry vehicles (MIRVs), and an unknown number
of atomic bombs to be delivered by aircraft. China first achieved the capability to strike the United States in August 1981 with the deployment of
the DF–5 in hardened silos. China first successfully tested a submarine-
launched ballistic missile in 1982 and later deployed one submarine with
twelve missiles. The relatively small number of single-warhead missiles
with large circular error probable (i.e., low accuracy) indicated that
China's nuclear missile force was a minimum deterrent force, capable of
second strike, retaliatory, and countervalue strategic missions consistent
with its declared "No First Use" policy.

REDEFINITION OF THE THREAT AND DOMESTIC INVOLVMENT

In the mid–1960s, Mao attempted to prepare China for an "early war, big
war, and all-out nuclear war." To protect China's strategic and conventional weapons industries from nuclear attack, he ordered a massive construction program in the interior provinces of Sichuan, Shaanxi,
Guizhou, Hubei, and Yunnan. Industries in these areas were called the
"Third Line." Though they were relatively less vulnerable to attack, these
factories were also far from markets and sources of raw materials; transportation and communications in these regions were poor, and educated,

skilled workers were in short supply. Construction of Third Line industries continued through the end of the 1970s, but the problems of the Third Line plagued the defense industries well into the period of reform that followed.

During the 1960s, the PLA once again became an ideological model for Chinese society. Lei Feng, a selfless truck driver who died trying to help a comrade in trouble, was perhaps the most widely known model soldier. Mao wrote an inscription on Lei's "diary" (though the diary was actually a fraud created by PLA propagandists) and exhorted the country to "learn from the PLA."

By the mid–1960s, Defense Minister Lin had also taken the lead in promoting radical Maoism to the point that the "red" versus "expert" argument was extrapolated into a struggle between the proletariat and the bourgeoisie for control of the armed forces. According to the radical Maoists, politics was a prerequisite for technical expertise; technical training itself was of secondary importance. Disobedience of military orders could be condoned if subordinates believed that the orders given them did not conform to Mao's thought. Professionalism in the army was equated with "the bourgeois military line" and "Soviet revisionism." In June 1965, military ranks were abolished to minimize the distinction between the military and society. Peng Dehuai and Luo Ruiqing, who was removed from his post as chief of the general staff in late 1965, were accused of promoting the "bourgeois military line" under the pretext of modernization.

Differences in strategic outlook had created a split between Lin Biao, who was soon to be designated as Mao's political heir, and his chief of the general staff, Luo Ruiqing. Their disagreements were based upon differing interpretations of the threat to China from the U.S. war in Vietnam and the proper response by the PLA. Luo advocated finding a way to bring China back under the Soviet Union's nuclear umbrella and, if necessary, conducting a defense of the mainland much closer to its borders by moving more quickly into an offensive, counterattack mode. Lin, on the other hand, stressed the necessity for China's self-sufficiency and adhered to Mao's classical strategy of "luring the enemy deep." These differences led to Luo's greater emphasis on main force units, while the Maoists focused more attention on the local forces and militia in a People's War. Luo's challenge to Lin's military leadership and Mao's national policies resulted in his removal from office. Nevertheless, many of Luo's recommendations were later implemented by the PLA.

Lin's political rectification of the army prepared it for its role during the Cultural Revolution. The PLA initially was tasked to provide logistics and transportation support to the Red Guards as they held mass rallies in Beijing and traveled throughout China. But by the fall of 1966, the students' activities had begun to get out of hand and undermine the authority of party and government organizations. In the summer of 1967, radical Red Guard "rebels" attacked military headquarters in the city of Wuhan and other parts of China. As the chaos spread, the PLA was called upon to restore order; however, in the fighting that followed main force units and their local force brethren often backed rival Red Guard factions. Violence continued through the spring of 1968 until Beijing finally committed itself to ending the chaos. Military "Mao Zedong Thought and Propaganda Teams" and "Three Supports and Two Militaries Teams" were dispatched to exercise control in much of the country. In areas where the PLA could not form an alliance with remaining revolutionary cadres and the revolutionary masses, Military Control Committees were established to maintain order.

As a result of the need for the PLA to reestablish domestic tranquility, military leaders were reintroduced into both local and central government functions in numbers that had not been seen since the end of the Civil War. By 1971, military officers occupied approximately 50 percent of civilian central leadership positions and 60 to 70 percent of most provincial leadership jobs. The PLA also grew in size to over 4 million to cope with its domestic responsibilities during the Cultural Revolution. However, professional military training suffered immensely.

Not long after Lin and Luo were debating the degree of danger from the United States in Vietnam, a new threat began to emerge on China's northern border. In the mid–1960s, the Soviet Union increased its forces and logistics capabilities in the Far East. In 1967, the Soviet Union and the Mongolian People's Republic signed a mutual defense treaty and Soviet forces were stationed in Mongolia. In 1968, the USSR held large-scale military exercises in Mongolia and tensions between Moscow and Beijing rose. The decade-long ideological dispute between China and the USSR turned into a series of armed clashes along China's northeast and northwest borders in the spring and summer of 1969. Mao began to assess the Soviet Union as a greater threat to China at about the same time that U.S. president Richard Nixon began looking for a way out of Vietnam and a strategic partner to balance the Soviet threat to America.

Concurrently with Mao's strategic reevaluation, Defense Minster Lin began to voice contrary opinions. While Mao sought to withdraw the PLA from its civil governance responsibilities assumed during the Cultural Revolution, Lin advocated that it remain involved in local politics. He also

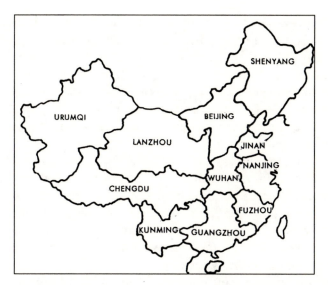

Map 14.1   China's military regions, 1970s. Adapted by Don Graff based upon *From Muskets to Missiles,* Harlan Jencks (Boulder, CO: Westview Press, 1982), p. 301, map G-1.

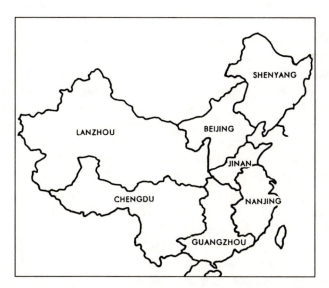

Map 14.2   China's military regions, 1990s. Adapted by Don Graff based upon *The Armed Forces of China,* You Ji (London and New York: I. B. Tauris, 1999), p. 48, figure 2.2.

opposed Mao's rapprochement with the United States as a balance against the Soviet Union. Rather, he believed that China's traditional "luring in deep" strategy would be sufficient to counter the Soviet mechanized forces growing on China's borders. By 1971, instead of being Mao's successor, Lin had become a challenger to Mao. Lin, his wife, and his son died in a plane crash in Mongolia in September 1971. Allegedly, he was attempting to escape to the Soviet Union after a coup he was plotting against Mao was uncovered.

In the aftermath of Lin's death, the general staff was purged of his supporters and the number of military officers in the party's Central Committee was cut in half. PLA units "returned to their barracks" and military officers in large part were removed from their duties in local governments. The reassignment of eight of the commanders of the eleven military regions (two of the original thirteen military regions having been reduced to provincial military districts in the late 1960s) in late 1973 and early 1974 was an important symbol of the PLA's exit from local politics.

Toward the Rebirth of Professionalism

Deng Xiaoping returned to the central leadership as a vice premier and member of the Politburo after having been "deprived of all posts" in 1966. In 1975, he became a vice chairman of the Central Military Commission and chief of the general staff. Premier Zhou Enlai proposed the "Four Modernizations" of agriculture, industry, defense, and science and technology. At an enlarged meeting of the CMC, Deng made a scathing criticism of "overstaffing, laxity, arrogance, extravagance, and indolence" within the PLA. The stage was set for a new era of military professionalism, but death and politics intervened once more.

Following Zhou's death in January 1976, Deng came under political attack from radical Maoists and was removed from all posts in April. Zhu De's death in July gave the new premier, Hua Guofeng, the opportunity to deliver Zhu's eulogy. In late July, the PLA redeemed the image that had been blemished in the Cultural Revolution during its rescue efforts following the Tangshan earthquake, which to many Chinese presaged the death of the emperor. Approximately six weeks later, Mao Zedong died.

Hua was able to consolidate his position with the help of Ye Jianying and Nie Rongzhen. Less than a month after Mao's death, Hua ordered Wang Dongxing, Mao's former bodyguard and commander of the PLA's 8341 Unit, an elite force responsible for protection of the central leadership, to arrest the radical "Gang of Four": Zhang Chunqiao, Wang Hongwen, Yao Wenyuan, and Mao's wife Jiang Qing. Hua then became chairman of both the Party Central Committee and the CMC. In July 1977, Deng was rehabilitated again and reinstated to his government and military posts, including his membership in the CMC and his post as chief of the general staff.

Deng gradually became the most powerful leader in China, even though Hua officially held important titles for a few more years. The Third Plenum of the Communist Party's Eleventh Central Committee in December 1978 was the watershed event that redirected China's national focus to economic modernization. The Four Modernizations were adopted as national policy, and as this was done the ranking of defense modernization was slipped to last. This minor change basically meant that the PLA was tasked to modernize and professionalize, but it would be low on the list for government resources. Thus, military modernization became a long-term goal, dependent upon first strengthening the overall Chinese economy.

The United States's formal normalization of relations with China on January 1, 1979, strengthened Beijing's position in the U.S.–USSR–PRC triangle. The break in diplomatic relations between Washington and Taipei and the abrogation of the U.S.–Taiwan defense treaty, which were part of the normalization deal with the United States, also strengthened China's position vis-à-vis Taiwan. Beijing stopped the shelling of Quemoy and Matsu that had begun in 1958, proposed talks with Taiwan, and removed some PLA units from Fujian province directly across from Taiwan. However, increased Soviet aid to Vietnam, the Vietnamese occupation of Cambodia, and the Soviet invasion of Afghanistan all contributed to Beijing's perception of Moscow's efforts to encircle China.

Ostensibly in reaction to Vietnamese border incursions, the PLA launched a "counterattack" into northern Vietnam in February–March 1979. The PLA's tactical performance during this brief but bloody campaign revealed serious shortcomings in its doctrine, training, logistics, and equipment, and added further impetus for military modernization.

Thus, at the beginning of China's period of reform, a bloated PLA of over four million personnel was structured to defend the Chinese mainland using the doctrine of People's War. At the same time, the Soviet Union was increasing both its conventional and nuclear capabilities in the Far East opposite China.

The PLA was dominated by ground forces and had a definite continental orientation. Its main force units were organized around infantry corps, generally composed of three infantry divisions and smaller armor, artillery, engineer, and other combat support and combat service support units. Most equipment was of 1950s vintage. In theory, a large militia would provide logistical and some combat support to main and local force units as they "lured the enemy in deep" and drowned him in the vastness of continental China. Air and naval forces primarily had a defensive mission and, for the most part, operated independent of the ground forces. China's nuclear forces were small (compared to U.S. or Soviet strategic forces), structured for deterrence and, should deterrence fail, to conduct retaliatory strikes against population centers in the USSR.

The PLA had completed the process of "returning to the barracks" (i.e., removing itself from involvement in all aspects of civil society), and had subordinated its modernization to the larger task of national economic development. Except for a spike that resulted from the campaign against Vietnam, the low priority for military modernization translated directly into low defense budgets for the 1980s. The PLA was required to grow much of its own food, and produce in its factories many of the light industrial goods necessary for basic survival and mission accomplishment. The fact that the senior PLA leadership accepted its low priority in China's national modernization strategy is a reflection of its discipline and loyalty to the Communist Party and China's civilian leaders.

In June 1981, Deng Xiaoping replaced Hua Guofeng as chairman of the CMC. Hu Yaobang took Hua's position as party chairman. Deng began to fill senior positions in the military with officers loyal to him: Zhang Aiping was named defense minister, Yang Dezhi became chief of the general staff, Liu Huaqing assumed command of the PLA Navy, and Yang Shangkun was made secretary-general of the CMC. In 1982, the National Defense Industrial Office under the State Council was merged with the Defense Science and Technology Commission and the Science and Technology Equipment Committee of the CMC to form the Commission on Science, Technology and Industry for National Defense (COSTIND). COSTIND reported to both the CMC and State Council and was responsible for overseeing production in the defense industries and planning military research and development.

In another government reform, in accordance with the State Constitution of 1982, a State Central Military Commission, responsible to the National People's Congress, was established. This body was, in theory, different from its counterpart in the Communist Party structure, but in reality consisted of the same set of leaders. It is possible that this development will eventually lead to the creation of an army loyal first to the government of China rather than the leadership of the Chinese Communist Party.

Changes in Force Structure and Doctrine

In the first few years of the 1980s, the PLA underwent another reduction in its forces. Faced with limited funding from the central government, a cut in the PLA's size permitted the money that was available to be spread among fewer units. More important, this streamlining also removed organizations with largely nonmilitary missions from the force structure. The Railroad Construction Corps was turned over to the Ministry of Railways, and the Capital Construction Corps (founded in 1966) and Xinjiang Production and Construction Corps (created in the early 1950s) were removed from the PLA's control.

Security and border defense units were transferred to the newly created paramilitary People's Armed Police (PAP). The PAP's main mission was (and is) domestic security, which, in theory, allowed the PLA to concentrate more on its external defense role. Still, the PLA retained a secondary mission of internal security, and the PAP forces assigned to each province retained an external defense role to act as local forces during an invasion of the mainland. In 1984, a reserve force was established that began to assume some of the tasks that traditionally were assigned to the militia. Demobilized soldiers would man the new reserve units, which could be maintained for much less cost than active-duty forces.

In the late 1970s and early 1980s, PLA strategists began considering a doctrinal modification that envisioned defending China closer to its borders and fighting the Soviets in a more mobile style of war with a combined arms and joint force. Nuclear weapons were considered likely to be used. This new doctrine was named "People's War under Modern Conditions," and called for a more flexible PLA that incorporated increased numbers of modern weapons into its inventory. Ironically, the PLA was adopting many of the concepts advocated by Luo Ruiqing fifteen years earlier.

Emphasis in the ground forces shifted from light infantry to mechanized, combined arms operations with tanks, self-propelled artillery, and armored personnel carriers. This type of equipment added more mobility to portions of the force and, if properly outfitted, could provide a degree of protection from the nuclear, biological, and chemical weapons the Soviets were expected to employ. However, because of the size and backwardness of the force, the cost of equipping enough of it with sufficient modern weapons to fight the Soviets was prohibitive.

The Chinese defense industries were not up to the task of producing state-of-the-art weapons, so the PLA basically had to make do with the weapons in its inventory, upgraded with a few modifications. Because of its improved relations with many Western countries, for the first time China had the opportunity to shop for weapons from foreign suppliers, including the United States, France, Italy, the United Kingdom, and Israel. The Chinese defense industries used this access to foreign technology to improve their capabilities by obtaining licenses for production or reverse engineering some of these systems. However, only a few small purchases of more modern equipment and subsystems could be afforded, and these went only to selected units and were used primarily for experimental purposes. Out of necessity, a large portion of the PLA remained best structured for the old-style People's War.

Nevertheless, improvements in general force readiness were made. Something as simple as equipping PLA infantry units with enough trucks to make them road mobile was a relatively inexpensive improvement that greatly increased the speed and distance forces could maneuver. Military training received renewed emphasis. In 1981, the PLA held a large multi-service training exercise near Zhangjiakou northwest of Beijing that began the process of incorporating more complex tasks into Chinese military operations. The Zhangjiakou exercise featured extensive PLA Air Force involvement, including the use of airborne troops. (China's first parachute unit was formed in 1950 and subordinated to the PLA Air Force. In 1961, that division-size unit was incorporated into the Fifteenth Airborne Army, which had been formed out of the army's Fifteenth Army that had fought in Korea.) Officer training was enhanced and many older cadres were forced to retire. Age limits were established for the various levels of command, allowing younger officers with a more modern approach to war the opportunity to advance.

In a major strategic reassessment, Deng declared in 1985 that the threat of a major war was remote. Instead, Deng forecast the more likely scenario would be limited, "Local War" fought on China's periphery. A reduction of another million personnel was also announced. Military planners began to think about how such a Local War would be fought and how the PLA should be structured to meet its new challenges. While the doctrine to fight Local War was being developed, People's War under Modern Conditions remained the PLA's primary doctrine for planning and training purposes. Because both doctrines were modernizations over the People's War concept, many of the changes applicable to People's War under Modern Conditions also were appropriate for Local War. At the same time, a small number of theoreticians in a few academic institutions began playing with concepts that later would become known as "Information Warfare," but these ideas did not receive much attention with all the other changes underway in the PLA.

By 1988 the personnel reduction was complete, and the force numbered slightly over three million. Perhaps the changes that most symbolized the professionalization of the PLA were the reintroduction of ranks and the issuing of new uniforms. (The soft caps with their big red stars and the "Mao" jackets were replaced by larger "saucer" caps with hard bills and Western-style jackets with insignia of rank on the shoulders; neckties were introduced for both men and women.) Among other changes, the eleven military regions were reduced to seven, the thirty-five infantry corps were reduced to twenty-four group armies (corps-size combined arms units), and hundreds of units at the regimental level and above were disbanded.

A major organizational development peculiar to the doctrine of Local War was the formation of small, mobile "Fist" or "Rapid Reaction Units" (RRU). RRUs were found in all military regions and could be deployed locally or wherever needed in the country. Among the group armies and within the PLA Air Force and Navy, a few units were at least partially equipped with new weapons and placed on call to be deployed within hours of alert. RRUs received priority in training and would take part in the experiments that tested tactical concepts necessary for implementing the Local War doctrine. The air force's airborne army of three divisions was designated the primary strategic RRU. The navy's 5,000-man marine brigade, formed in 1980, could also perform rapid reaction missions.

In 1986, an Army Aviation Corps, composed mainly of helicopters, was established. This organization would be the backbone for the new helicopter units that would be added over the next decade. Still, in absolute terms, the number of helicopters available to the ground forces was extremely limited. With only a few helicopter units spread out all over the country, the percentage of infantry units that could be trained to proficiency in air mobile operations was very small.

A New PLA Leadership and New Problems for the 1990s

By the late 1980s, China's military leadership had undergone further changes. In 1988, Yang Shangkun became president of the PRC and retained his position as vice chairman of the CMC; Qin Jiwei was named minister of national defense. A year earlier, Chi Haotian had succeeded Yang Dezhi as chief of the general staff and Yang Baibing, the half-brother of Yang Shangkun, was appointed director of the General Political Department and later became a member of the CMC.

Defense budgets remained tight through the end of the 1980s. Even as the civilian economy expanded, the PLA was encouraged to support itself through commercial activities in addition to its traditional sideline agricultural and light industrial production. The Chinese defense industries sought foreign markets for their weapons and to develop new systems for export. The PLA created import–export companies to sell excess weapons from its own inventory. At first, most of the actual commercial activity was conducted by elements at higher headquarters, but gradually combat units also got into the act of running hotels and restaurants and performing other services. Transportation and construction engineer units hired themselves out to work on projects with no direct military application. Within a few years, up to 20,000 PLA enterprises were in operation, but the actual number of companies and how much they were earning, or losing, was not known. In the rush to reap profits, economic competition developed among PLA units and local governments and businesses. Some units became involved in smuggling operations. Graft and corruption spread. Profits were problematic. The PLA's participation in this sector of Chinese society was not turning out as expected.

Following the death of Hu Yaobang in April 1989, the PLA's loyalty to the party was put to its greatest test. Over a six-week period, as demonstrators calling for democracy, government reform, and an end to corruption grew in numbers in Beijing, normal daily life around Tiananmen Square and throughout much of the city (and country) was increasingly disrupted. Party and government leaders were particularly embarrassed during the long-scheduled summit with Soviet leader Mikhail Gorbachev in May. Beijing was placed under martial law and PLA units from all over the country were ordered to the city to assist in maintaining order. Efforts to talk with the demonstrators or intimidate them with the use of nonlethal force failed.

Though some military leaders, both active and retired, opposed the use of force against the peaceful demonstrators, Deng Xiaoping exerted his personal influence with the military high command. When the domestic police and PAP forces were unable to disperse the crowds from Tiananmen, the PLA was called in. In the chaos that followed, hundreds and possibly thousands of civilians (as well as some soldiers) were killed as tanks, armored vehicles, and truckloads of soldiers moved to retake the center of the city. The PLA obediently but reluctantly followed the orders of its civilian leadership and restored order. In doing so, it tarnished the reputation it had rebuilt with the Chinese people in the years since the Cultural Revolution.

A few weeks after the bloodshed, many of the soldiers who were involved in the military action in Beijing received silver wristwatches for their participation. At the top of the watch's pale yellow face was a red outline of the Tiananmen rostrum; on the bottom, a profile of a PLA soldier wearing a green helmet. Under the soldier were the figures "89.6" (for June 1989) and the characters "In Commemoration of Quelling the Rebellion." Inscribed on the back were the characters "Presented by the Beijing Committee of the Chinese Communist Party and the People's Government of Beijing." In the following years, these watches were often found in flea markets in Beijing, broken, their hands no longer working, discarded by the soldiers to whom they had been presented.

SUGGESTIONS FOR FURTHER READING

This chapter relies heavily on the two-decades worth of books and articles by three scholars who lead the field in the study of Chinese military professionalism. For further information about the development of the PLA's military doctrine and strategy, force structure, and "red" versus "expert" debate, see Harlan Jencks, *From Muskets to Missiles: Politics and Professionalism in the Chinese Army, 1945–1981* (Boulder, CO: Westview Press, 1982); Paul H. B. Godwin, *The Chinese Communist Armed Forces* (Maxwell Air Force Base, AL: Air University Press, 1988); Ellis Joffe, *The Chinese Army after Mao* (Cambridge: Harvard University Press, 1987); or any of their other shorter works.

Michael Swaine, *The Military & Political Succession in China* (Santa Monica, CA: RAND Corporation, 1992) updated William Whitson's classic *The Chinese High Command* and outlines the PLA's personal relationship networks into the early 1990s. Monte Bullard, *China's Political–Military Evolution: The Party and the Military in the PRC, 1960–1984* (Boulder, CO: Westview Press, 1985) covers the entry and exit of the PLA in domestic politics, as well as its efforts toward professionalization in the early 1980s.

Kenneth W. Allen, Jonathan Pollack, and Glenn Krumel, *China's Air Force Enters the 21st Century* (Santa Monica, CA: RAND Corporation, 1995) provides a level of detail about the PLA Air Force's history and current status unmatched in any other work.

John Wilson Lewis and Xue Litai, *China Builds the Bomb* (Stanford: Stanford University Press, 1988) and John Wilson Lewis and Hua Di, "China's Ballistic Missile Programs: Technologies, Strategies, Goals," *International Security* 17 (1992): 5–40 describe the strategic setting and research and development efforts that resulted in the creation of China's nuclear arsenal.

SUGGESTIONS FOR FURTHER RESEARCH

When the political situation in China permits it and the PLA opens its records for research, a military analysis of the events of April through June 1989 would be illuminating. Timothy Brook, *Quelling the People* (New York: Oxford University Press, 1992) has already attempted a military analysis based on non-Chinese sources for this sensitive time in PLA history.

FIFTEEN

China's Foreign Conflicts since 1949

Larry M. Wortzel

China has tended to use force as an instrument of foreign policy when its leaders believe it to be important to take a strong stand on matters affecting sovereignty, including reinforcing territorial claims, to maintain safe buffer zones free from what Beijing perceives as foreign intervention, and to back up strong diplomatic threats with the coercive power to make other countries take China seriously. This approach is deeply rooted in Chinese history, where strong states established relations of suzerainty over weaker ones, regarding them as "vassal states" (*shuguo*) and punishing them with military expeditions when they failed to do the bidding of the stronger kingdom.

From the time of the establishment of the People's Republic of China in 1949 to 1988, Beijing used force to resolve international disputes in numerous cases: the Korean War in 1950, two artillery bombardments and crises over Taiwan's offshore islands in 1954 and 1958, incursions into Burma in 1960 and 1961, constructing roads in Laos and providing air defense protection there in the 1960s, the war with India in 1962, a mobilization on the Indian border in 1965 to relieve pressure on Pakistan by Indian forces, border skirmishes with the Soviet Union in 1969, large military deployments to Vietnam in the 1960s and 1970s, the seizure of the Paracel Islands in 1974, a standoff with Japan over the Senkaku Islands in 1978, the Chinese attack into Vietnam in 1979, and the seizure of islands in the Spratly Archipelago in 1988.[1] China has also exercised its military might by firing missiles off Taiwan in 1995 and 1996, by seizing Mischief Reef, claimed by the Philippines, in 1995, and by threatening the use of nuclear weapons against the United States in the event America comes to the aid of Taiwan should Beijing use force to reunite the island with the mainland. In every instance that China has used force, its leaders have claimed that their actions were based solely on the need for self-defense. And because of its expansive territorial claims, China's diplomatic and military establishments maintain that it is only in rare cases that China's forces enter foreign territory: Korea in 1950 and Vietnam in 1979. In some cases, of course, Beijing doesn't acknowledge that its forces were deployed in combat, as in Vietnam and Laos during the war with the United States in the 1960s and 1970s.

It is useful to clarify what the use of force may mean in general military terminology, for what is true in general is also applicable to China. The simplistic understanding of the term would be the conduct of overt military action by the People's Liberation Army in an actual attack on another country or sovereign state. But the use of force can be subtler than that, and may not amount to actual combat. Military demonstrations are also a use of force, as are well-timed military exercises, weapons tests, and troop, naval, or air deployments. In November 2000, for instance, Beijing tested its newest-generation road-mobile missile, the DF–31, while the chairman of the Joint Chiefs of Staff of the United States, General Hugh Shelton, was visiting China. This was a not-so-subtle demonstration of force meant to underscore just how seriously Beijing takes American military sales to Taiwan. China's aggressive intercepts of American reconnaissance flights—as on April 1, 2001, when a fighter aircraft of the People's Liberation Army Naval Air Forces collided with a U.S. EP–3 reconnaissance aircraft seventy miles off Hainan Island—represent demonstrations of force. In late May and early June 2001, the PLA conducted an extensive series of amphibious exercises in the area of Dongshan Island in south China, exercises timed to show Beijing's displeasure over the transit of Taiwan's president Chen Shui-bian through New York on May 21–23 and his meetings with American citizens. Thus, a military training evolution involving an overflight of the Spratly Islands by Chinese bombers is just as much a use of military force as was the seizure of the Paracel Islands from the Republic of Vietnam (South Vietnam) in 1974. Indeed, some uses of force are mutually reinforcing. For instance, China's entry into the Korean War in 1950 and its willingness to fight India in 1962 made China's warnings to the United States about the scope of combat in the Vietnam War all the more credible.[2]

Two researchers from the RAND Corporation in Santa Monica, California, Michael D. Swaine and Ashley J. Tellis, have identified "five core features" of Chinese security behavior over the past one thousand years in which the use of force is a significant feature. In their book *Interpreting China's Grand*

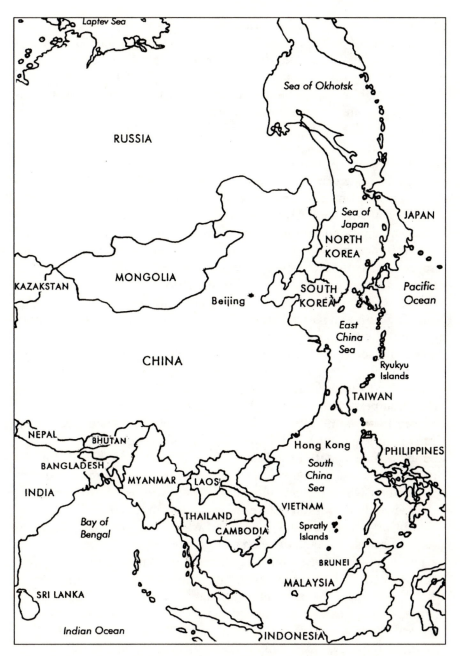

Map 15.1 China and its neighbors at the end of the twentieth century. Adapted by Don Graff based upon "Eurasia," in *Fire in the East*, Paul Bracken (New York: HarperCollins, 1999).

Strategy: Past, Present, and Future, Swaine and Tellis argue that the broad historical pattern of the use of force by China has five key features: (1) An effort to protect a central heartland while maintaining control over China's "strategic periphery," (2) expansion or contraction of peripheral control dependent on the strength of the regime and its capacity, (3) "the frequent yet limited use of force against external entities, primarily for heartland defense and peripheral control, and often on the basis of pragmatic calculations of relative power and effect," (4) a reliance on less than coercive strategies when the state is weak, and (5) a strong relationship between the power and influence of domestic leadership and the use of force.[3] Imperial China, like the PRC, used force frequently. In the Ming dynasty (1368–1644), China engaged in an average of one external conflict a year.[4]

It is equally important for students of history to note not only when Chinese leaders have tended to resort to force in international affairs, but also to pay attention to how they tended to exert it. In times of crisis or threat, Chinese leaders have tended to resort to force to create a political shock that reinforces an important principle, such as sovereignty. Despite Beijing's claims that its actions are defensive, China has often used force in a preemptive manner after what the Chinese Communist Party's leaders perceived to be clear threats or signals that a certain action by a foreign country would trigger a reaction by the PLA seemed to have been ignored. Part of the justification for Beijing's resort to force is often based on the perception perpetuated by the Chinese Communist Party that the period between 1840 and 1949 consisted of a "century of national humiliation" of China by foreign imperial powers. This period between the Opium War and the establishment of the People's Republic of China is treated in the history books as a period when foreign countries used force of arms to impose their will on China, including the acquisition of extraterritorial privileges and the creation of foreign concession areas.

John Garver has set out a typology of when Chinese leaders decide to use force based on the underlying goals of the action: "(1) deterring superpower attack against China; (2) defending Chinese territory against encroachment; (3) bringing 'lost' Chinese territory under Chinese control; (4) enhancing regional influence; and (5) enhancing China's global stature."[5] These goals are not mutually exclusive, but may well be complementary. For instance, when China entered the Korean War in 1950, Mao Zedong and the CCP leadership believed that they were not only defending Chinese territory against encroachment, but also strengthening China's regional influence and global stature. The DF–31 missile test cited earlier was also designed to deter a superpower from intervening and attacking Chinese forces engaged in any future attempt to bring the "lost" territory of Taiwan back under Beijing's control. With this typology in mind, this chapter will examine a few of the major cases in which China resorted to force in external affairs and will discuss which of the five underlying goals of action seemed to be in play. Tibet and Xinjiang are not discussed here because they involve areas that were ruled from China during the Yuan (1279–1368) and Qing (1644–1912) dynasties, and there is no challenge to China's sovereignty over these areas by the United States or the United Nations. The case of the offshore islands held by the Republic of China (ROC) on Taiwan is included because the 1958 Taiwan Strait Crisis involved the United States.

THE KOREAN WAR

The Korean War began on June 25, 1950, when Communist North Korea (the Democratic People's Republic of Korea; DPRK) invaded the Republic of Korea (South Korea; ROK). On the same day, the U.N. Security Council condemned the aggression. The North Korean People's Army (NKPA) rapidly overcame the ROK forces. Seoul fell to the NKPA on June 27, 1950, and the South Korean army was defeated. On the same day, the United Nations asked its members to assist South Korea.

Responding to the crisis, President Truman ordered U.S. ground forces into Korea on June 30, 1950. The newly formed unit sent into action, Task Force Smith, was created out of units from U.S. occupation forces in Japan. It confronted NKPA forces in the vicinity of Osan on July 5, 1950. The U.S. force was easily overrun. Its troops were not trained to fight as an organized team, they were out of shape for combat, and their outdated weapons were no match for the NKPA's Soviet-made tanks and artillery. U.S. forces fell back and established the Pusan Perimeter on August 4. The U.S. commander, Lieutenant General Walton H. (Johnny) Walker, and his Eighth Army held the perimeter stubbornly against determined attacks from the NKPA forces through August and into September 1950.

At the outbreak of the Korean War, China and the United States had no diplomatic relations because the United States still recognized the Republic of China as the legitimate government of China. Thus, there was no direct means by which American and Communist Chinese diplomats could engage in a dialogue. On September 1, 1950, referring to North Korea, Mao Zedong publicly stated that China could not tolerate the invasion of a neighbor, a public signal in the press intended to deter the U.S. and U.N. forces from going into the DPRK. Two days later, Zhou Enlai formally passed a warning to the U.S. and the U.N. through the Indian ambassador Sardar K. M. Panikkar that the Chinese would intervene if U.S. forces entered North Korea. These warnings, however, were dismissed by the United States as unreliable or mere bluff.

The momentum of the war dramatically shifted against the NKPA after the successful amphibious landing by U.S. forces at Inchon, south of Seoul, on September 15, 1950. On September 18, U.N. forces broke out from the Pusan perimeter and attacked north and west. The NKPA, caught between MacArthur's "anvil" at Inchon and Walker's Eighth Army "hammer" in pursuit, rapidly collapsed. Seoul was liberated on September 26.

Four days later, Zhou Enlai publicly reiterated the warning that China would not tolerate the invasion of one of its neighbors. This was an important way of declaring that China viewed an attack on its neighbors as an encroachment on its sphere of influence that undermined its stature in the region and the world. Continuing to discount these warnings, however, the U.N. forces pushed north. On October 1, ROK forces crossed the 38th parallel, and General MacArthur called for the surrender of the North Korean capital, Pyongyang. On October 7, U.N. forces crossed the 38th parallel. Pyongyang was captured on October 19.

China began to react to the U.S. move into the north. The first campaign of the Chinese People's Volunteers (CPV) was launched in secret, surprising American and ROK forces. Chinese forces, primarily consisting of light infantry, had begun crossing the Yalu River border between China and North Korea on October 18–19, under the command of Peng Dehuai. The CPV moved at night and hid during the day to conceal its movements.

On November 1, the CPV ambushed the U.S. 1st Cavalry Division at Unsan on the western side of the peninsula. Although intelligence reports had indicated the presense of Chinese forces, they were believed to be no more than about 70,000 strong. In reality, there were over 200,000 Chinese soldiers already in Korea. The U.S. X Corps, which had landed on the east coast of North Korea at Wonsan on October 26, moved toward the Yalu River between November 10 and 26, while the U.S. Eighth Army advanced in the west. General MacArthur launched his final, "Home by Christmas" offensive on November 24, 1950.

The second CPV campaign, from November 25 to December 24, 1950, not only succeeded in stopping the U.N. drive to the Yalu River, but also succeeded in driving the U.N. forces completely out of North Korea. On November 25, the CPV attacked the Eighth Army at Ch'ongch'on River in the west. Two days later, CPV forces in the east assaulted the U.S. 1st Marine Division and the Army's 7th Infantry Division at Chosin Reservoir.

Between November 26 and December 1, the U.S. 2nd and 25th Infantry Divisions were defeated along the Ch'ongch'on River and forced to retreat. In the east, between November 27 and December 10, the X Corps fought through CPV forces to the port of Hungnam, while the 1st Marine Division was forced to retreat from Kot'o-ri. By December 24, when the X Corps sailed from Hungnam, U.N. forces had been completely expelled from North Korea.

The third CPV campaign was launched on December 31, 1950, against Peng Dehuai's advice. Peng attempted to convince Mao that the U.N. forces had consolidated into an in-depth defensive position and the CPV forces lacked experience fighting against fortified positions. The CPV logistics lines were also overextended, Peng argued, and Chinese troops lacked sufficient food, winter clothing, and other essential supplies. Further, after pushing from northeast China through the length of North Korea, CPV soldiers were exhausted and in need of rest and reorganization. A desire to end the war quickly, combined with the sweeping victories over the U.N. forces, however, encouraged Mao to order the CPV to continue to push southward despite Peng's concerns. On January 4, 1951, Seoul fell, and by January 14 the U.N. line was pushed back to the 37th parallel.

On January 25, 1951, U.N. and U.S. forces resumed the offensive. Within two days, the CPV bagan its Fourth Campaign, which lasted until April 21. On February 14, the U.S. 23rd Infantry Regiment, with help from the French Infantry Battalion, turned back a CPV counteroffensive at Chipyong-ni. The United Nations seized the initiative between February 17 and March 17, 1951, and moved north. Seoul was liberated for a second time on March 18. During this fighting, on April 11, General MacArthur was relieved of command and General Matthew B. Ridgeway assumed command of U.N. and U.S. forces.

The fifth CPV campaign was launched between April 22 and May 21, 1951. On April 22, the CPV attacked the British Brigade northwest of Seoul near the Imjin River with a force of 50,000 men. U.N. lines held and the CPV broke contact on April 30. U.S. forces halted the CPV Soyan Offensive between May 16 and 22, 1951. U.N. forces began to push north on May 23, and reached the 38th parallel on June 13. The Soviet delegate at the United Nations, Jacob Malik, proposed a truce on June 23. Talks began at Kaesong on July 10, but an armistice was not signed until July 23, 1953. The bloodiest fighting of the war (and an intensive Communist propaganda campaign) occurred during the intervening two years.

From August 1 to October 23, 1951, in an effort to straighten its lines, the United Nations launched a series of limited battles, known as Bloody

Ridge and Heartbreak Ridge. In late October, peace talks resumed at Panmunjom, and a cease-fire was agreed to at the line of contact. Between November 1951 and April 1952 there was a stalemate along the battlefront while the Panmunjom talks continued.

On January 28, 1952, the CPV headquarters reported that U.S. and U.N. planes had spread smallpox in areas southeast of Inchon. On February 18, Radio Moscow accused the United States of using bacteriological warfare against North Korea. By March, a campaign against germ warfare had been launched in China. Although the Chinese have never retracted their charge that the Americans used germ warfare in Korea, their claim has never been supported by scientific evidence.

Between June and October 1952, truce talks were deadlocked over how to handle the repatriation of prisoners of war (POWs). A number of hill battles were fought, including Baldy and Whitehorse. On October 8, 1952, truce talks recessed and fighting resumed. The ROK army was faced with particularly heavy fighting in the Kumwha sector until November 1952, during which the South Koreans distinguished themselves as tough and courageous soldiers.

India offered a proposal on the POW issue to the U.N. in November 1952, and on March 30, 1953, Zhou Enlai indicated the Chinese would accept the Indian proposal. The talks at Panmunjom resumed. As the negotiations continued, one of the bloodiest battles of the war, the Battle of Pork Chop Hill, occurred on April 16–18, 1953. From April 20 though 26, both sides exchanged sick and wounded POWs at Panmunjom.

On June 4, 1953, the Chinese and North Koreans agreed to accept U.N. truce proposals and the fighting ceased. On September 4, screening and repatriation of POWs began at Freedom Village, Panmunjom. CPV forces remained in North Korea until 1958.

The Korean War stands out as China's only sustained foreign conflict in the second half of the twentieth century. The war took place at a time when the new Communist regime had the determination, confidence, and trained manpower to confront the might of the United States and its allies in battle. The indecisive outcome was considered a moral victory by the Chinese and made the point that the PRC was not to be trifled with.

TAIWAN STRAIT CRISIS OF 1958

Sino–U.S. talks in Geneva over bilateral recognition and the return of U.S. prisoners of war from the Korean War broke down by 1957. When the U.S. ambassador in Geneva, U. Alexis Johnson, left for another diplomatic assignment in December 1957, no replacement was assigned. By June 1958, after requesting the continuation of talks and the assignment of a new U.S. ambassador, Beijing decided to use military force to demonstrate to the Americans why they had no choice but to deal with China. The CCP Central Military Commission met over a period of two months, during May–July 1958, to decide on a means to bring military force to bear on the situation.

Beijing first initiated a strong propaganda campaign in its internal and external media calling for the "liberation of Taiwan." This lasted through June and July. Following a July 1958 visit to Beijing by Soviet premier Nikita Khrushchev, during which plans for Chinese military action reportedly were withheld from Khrushchev by Mao Zedong, the PLA Air Force began to deploy to forward airfields. On August 23, the PLA began shelling the Nationalist-held offshore island of Quemoy (Jinmen), firing more than 30,000 rounds on the first day of the campaign. The United States, meanwhile, rushed six aircraft carrier battle groups to the area and sent in combat aircraft and transports. U.S. ships even escorted Nationalist vessels up to the three-mile territorial limit while they resupplied the offshore islands. Other U.S. support arrived, including atomic-capable 8-inch howitzers (which were deployed on the offshore islands) and air-to-air missiles. Taiwan and the mainland fought seven air battles between August 23 and the end of October. China, meanwhile, began to receive surface-to-air missiles (the SA–2) from Moscow. In the end, no invasion of Quemoy or the other major Nationalist-held offshore island of Matsu was mounted. China and the Soviet Union split over assessments of whether the United States was willing to risk war with the socialist camp, and U.S. support continued to flow into Taiwan.

THE SINO–INDIAN WAR

After driving Indian forces out of the area around the hamlet of Longju in August 1959, China continued to observe the McMahon Line, drawn in 1914, as the de facto border between Tibet and India's northeastern region of Assam.[6] Chinese forces pulled back from disputed territory that same month to avoid further incidents. In the western sector of the border, where China and India had clashed in October 1959, Indian forces, under New Delhi's orders, began a "forward policy" designed to push the disputed boundaries out to geographical features favorable to, and claimed by, India.

In the east, on the McMahon Line, Indian forces had avoided patrolling within two miles of the border after 1959. But in December 1961 they were ordered to move forward and begin patrolling again along the disputed line. During the first six months of 1962, the Indian army was to establish twenty-four new border outposts. In June 1962, a platoon of the Indian Assam Rifles moved about four miles north of the McMahon Line to the Thagla Ridge, which they treated as the border. Indian troops established a position there on June 4, even though India's own maps showed the ridge to be in Chinese territory. On September 8, a Chinese force advanced on the Thagla post, attempting to press the Indians to withdraw. Beijing also issued a diplomatic protest on September 16, complaining about the presence of the Indian troops.

The Indian government took the position that when Sir Henry McMahon drew the line in 1914 he intended that it run along the line of the highest ridges. They argued that the Thagla Ridge was the dominant terrain feature and, therefore, should be the border. The Chinese reaction, according to India, was the implementation by Beijing of a central policy to advance the border into Indian territory. India began a buildup of forces that was logistically insupportable and militarily dangerous, while Chinese forces increased their strength and weaponry along the border using a road system that would support five- and even seven-ton vehicles. Through September, there were skirmishes around the Thagla area, in the course of which both sides took casualties. By October, faced with bad weather and unfavorable terrain, the Indians attemped a buildup of forces.

The Indian army was ordered to carry out Operation Leghorn, designed to push the Chinese back, on October 10, 1962. But Chinese intelligence was aware of the operation, and Beijing issued a warning to India in the form of a diplomatic note on October 6. Meanwhile, the PLA concentrated superior forces and artillery in the area. On the night of October 19, Chinese troops assembled in assault positions, and on the morning of October 29 they attacked the Thagla Ridge, wiping out the Indian 7th Brigade and capturing its commander.

In the western sector of the border, along the Galwan River, the PLA launched a simultaneous attack against Indian forces in the Chip Chap River valley. The Chinese government declared these to be self-defensive counterattacks to clear Indian troops out of Chinese territory. American supplies, meanwhile, began to flow into India, with about twenty tons of military equipment arriving each day. Great Britain also provided assistance.

An Indian counterattack along the McMahon Line was beaten back by Chinese forces in November, while Indian troops in the west were also trounced by the Chinese. By November 21, China had announced a unilateral ceasefire. The Chinese simultaneously announced a December 1, 1962, withdrawal to positions twenty kilometers behind the "line of actual control" that had existed between China and India on November 7, 1959, reviving a formula that had been used to defuse the crisis in that year. Indian figures indicate that 1,383 troops were killed, 1,696 were missing in the operation, and 3,968 were captured by Chinese forces. The Chinese, having incurred far fewer losses, were left in control of the Aksai Chin plateau.

The Zhenbao Island Clash

After about a year of confrontation between the PLA and the Soviet army over demarcation on the eastern border, on March 2, 1969, a major clash broke out at Zhenbao Island (called Damansky by the Russians), located on the Ussuri River between the cities of Khabarovsk and Vladivostok. The Chinese maintained that the border between the two countries followed the "Thalweg Principle," or the central line of the main channel, putting the island on the Chinese side. Moscow claimed that the Chinese banks of the Amur and Ussuri rivers were the border, putting some 600 disputed islands on the Russian side.

As each side patrolled, physical clashes became more common, until on March 2, 1969, a Chinese patrol crossing the frozen river to the island was challenged by Russian forces. Automatic weapons fire from the Chinese bank hit the Russian forces, killing seven Russians and wounding twenty-three. The Chinese, who said the Russians fired on their patrol first, also claimed to have had several casualties. It is not clear from accounts by either side, however, whether the PLA instigated the incident or the Soviets initiated fire. On March 4 and 12, the Russians reinforced the island and flew reconnaissance aircraft along the border. Then, on March 15, 200 Russian infantrymen supported by thirty armored vehicles again tried to seize the island. Clashes continued through March 17, when both sides deescalated the conflict. Tensions continued, however, for several years.

Paracel Islands

A neomaritime spirit arose in China in 1973 with the reappearance of Deng Xiaoping as vice chairman of the CCP Central Military Commission.

Soon after that, the PRC initiated its campaign to seize the Paracel (Xisha) Islands from South Vietnam. Deng had close contacts with the head of the navy, Su Zhenhua, and was a leading voice supporting a more maritime-oriented approach for the PLA Navy, which had been principally a coastal, or "brown water," force. Thus, Deng appears to be closely linked with events in the Paracel Islands, just as he would be with the 1979 attack into Vietnam described later. The seizure of the Paracels, therefore, must be viewed as a means of developing a more active maritime role for China as well as a statement of sovereignty and control over claimed territory in the South China Sea.

On January 11, 1974, the PRC Ministry of Foreign Affairs released a public warning that the PRC had indisputable sovereignty over the Paracels, adding that the "sea areas around them also belong to China." Four days later, the PLA Navy began moving forces into position. According to South Vietnamese survivors, China first began to move fishing vessels into the area, a tactic that seems to be common when China is seeking to reinforce its maritime claims. The fishermen not only serve as a visible representation of what China sees as its rights to the area, but also as advanced reconnaissance for the Chinese navy.

On January 15, South Vietnamese ships allegedly attempted to displace the fishermen, and two Chinese patrol boats in their vicinity, from the waters surrounding the islands. By that time, the PLA had assembled a naval force consisting of about eleven warships, some of which carried more than 600 assault troops. Fighter aircraft based on Hainan Island, about 130 miles northeast of the Paracels, were available for air cover. On January 17, several Chinese patrol vessels arrived, followed by ten other warships. The South Vietnamese had a former U.S. Coast Guard cutter with a 5-inch gun and four destroyer escorts, each armed with two 3-inch guns. They had no air support. In the ensuing naval engagement, a missile from a Chinese patrol craft reportedly hit one of South Vietnam's destroyer escorts. Within two days, Vietnam's naval forces were overwhelmed and forced to withdraw. The 600 PLA assault troops, trained for amphibious operations, had landed and taken control of the Paracels. Chinese press releases on the incident emphasized the participation of "people's-militia fishermen" in the seizure of the islands, a common theme in Chinese military actions involving what Beijing considers its sovereign territory. The Chinese claim that South Vietnamese forces suffered 300 casualties in the engagement and that the PRC captured 49 Vietnamese military personnel who were later returned to Vietnam.

This action marked the first time China had used military force after the United States had improved relations with China in January 1972. Washington took no action, and Hanoi was not in a position to react either. The Paracel Islands operation of 1974 is notable because it marked the only Chinese amphibious operation involving the projection of troops across any distance, even if it only involved eleven ships and some 600 ground troops.

The "Self-Defensive Counterattack" against Vietnam

Between 1978 and early 1979, Vietnamese military forces began operations in Cambodia designed to drive the Chinese-supported leader, Pol Pot, and his Maoist-oriented regime from power. By January 1979, Vietnamese forces had seized Phnom Penh and were soon poised on the Cambodian–Thai border, where they threatened Thailand. Beijing, a major supporter of Pol Pot, had good relations with the Thai government. In response to Vietnam's military moves, the Chinese government complained about a series of violations along the Sino–Vietnamese border, threatening punitive action over alleged incursions into China. During January and into mid-February the PLA moved main field-force armies and divisions from around China to staging areas north of the Vietnamese border. Between thirty and forty divisions were eventually assembled, often moving by rail under cover of night. At the same time, fearing a Soviet response in the north because Moscow and Hanoi had signed a treaty of Friendship and Cooperation in November 1978, China made preparations to defend the north against any potential Soviet counterattack.

Chinese forces aligned on the Vietnamese border in one front, while another front was formed in the north. The Northern Front comprised the Shenyang, Beijing, Jinan, Lanzhou, and Xinjiang military regions (MR). Li Desheng, commander of the Shenyang MR, was appointed front commander along the Sino–Soviet border. Preparations in the north were mainly defensive, including the evacuation of civilians along the border and raising the readiness levels of Chinese forces.

The Southern Front along the Sino–Vietnamese border was divided into two theaters of war or zones of operation (*zhanqu*): the Eastern in Guangxi province opposite Lang Son, and the Western in Yunnan province opposite Lao Cai. Xu Shiyou, who as Guangzhou MR commander was also commander of the Eastern Theater of Operations, commanded the Southern Front. Yang Dezhi, the Kunming MR commander,

was in control of the Western Theater of Operations. In Beijing, Deng Xiaoping controlled forces on both fronts for the Central Military Commission, with marshals Xu Xiangqian and Nie Rongzhen as deputies. Geng
Biao, chief of the general staff of the PLA, was responsible for coordinating the operation.

On February 17, 1979, Chinese forces attacked across the Vietnamese
border, advancing along five main axes: in the Eastern Theater of Operations against Lang Son and Cao Bang, and in the west against Ha Giang,
Lao Cai, and Lai Chao. Logistics and service support for Chinese forces
came from local-force and militia units in the two military regions.

The Vietnamese had responded to the preattack Chinese buildup by
moving forces north from around Hanoi and by withdrawing some main
force units from Cambodia. Vietnam also relied heavily on local-force
and militia units. China had announced its attention only to "punish
Vietnam" for border incursions and said that the attack would be limited
to an advance of no more than fifty kilometers into Vietnam. After initial
progress against very heavy resistance, Chinese forces halted, concentrating on consolidation around major cities, and began an orderly withdrawal that was completed by March 17, 1979. In the process of the campaign the Vietnamese claimed to have killed or wounded 42,000 Chinese,
while Beijing said it had inflicted 50,000 casualties on Vietnam with a
loss of only 20,000. The Vietnamese estimates are probably closer to the
actual outcome.

In the conflict, the PLA units suffered from poor command and control, poor logistics, and an inability to coordinate large formations on the
battlefield. After the attack on Vietnam, the PLA began to discuss restruc-
turing its group armies and restoring a rank structure to facilitate battlefield command and control. In combat training, the PLA began to focus
on combined arms operations so that its infantry, armor, artillery, and engineers worked in coordination. The PLA also sought to develop rapid reaction forces, and to reorganize its military logistics structure.

NANSHA (SPRATLY) ISLANDS INCIDENTS

Since the Nansha, or Spratly, archipelogic chain in the South China Sea
may be the site of a major oil source as confirmed by recent Chinese and
international seismic surveys, the question of sovereignty has become a
matter of serious concern among the claimants to the islands: China,
Vietnam, Malaysia, and the Philippines. Taiwan also occupies one of the
islands, Itu Aba.

A January 30, 1980, white paper published by the PRC claimed "indisputable sovereignty over the Xisha (Paracel) and Nansha (Spratly) Islands." Since both Beijing and Taipei regard Taiwan as a province of China, the Taiwan garrison on Itu Aba reinforces the Chinese claim to sovereignty. China's claims to the islands are based on historic usage by Chinese fishermen as early as 200 B.C.E., and on the 1887 Chinese–Vietnamese Boundary Convention, while Vietnam claims historic links with the islands primarily on the basis of having inherited modern French territory. The Nationalist Chinese abandoned Spratly Island in 1950. At the time that South Vietnam fell in 1975, the Saigon regime occupied four islands. The successor Hanoi government built up the total number of occupied islands to about twenty.

Vietnam remains China's principal antagonist, as exemplifed by the March 1988 incident in which the PLA Navy sank three Vietnamese supply vessels. For the PLA Navy, the key to control of the Spratly Islands is not so much continuing the development of a growing "blue water" naval capability, but rather establishing control over the associated airspace. This problem will not be solved until the PLA Navy either is able to deploy an aircraft carrier or develops an operational air-to-air refueling capability for its naval air arm, thereby ensuring dominance over Vietnam and all other claimants to the Nanshas.

With the perceptions of the Association of Southeast Asian Nations (ASEAN) member countries in mind, China continues to proceed slowly in exercising its claims over the Nanshas. In a statement issued in Manila in 1994, the Chinese embassy stressed Beijing's "indisputable sovereignty" over the Nansha Islands and adjacent waters. China has contracted a U.S. oil company to drill exploratory wells near the Nanshas and has said it will defend its claimed sites if necessary. In February 1995, China continued to expand its presence in the Nanshas and took over Mischief Reef, a fifteen-square-mile set of shoals 150 miles west of the Philippine island of Palawan. China acknowledged building several structures on the barely submerged coral reef, ostensibly as "shelters for Chinese fishermen." China also deployed several ships, believed to be naval vessels, to the area. Philippine president Ramos said the Chinese actions were "inconsistent with international law" and with the 1992 declaration on the Nanshas that was endorsed by China and other claimants to the islands. As recently as the July 1995 ASEAN Regional Forum conference in Brunei, China agreed to abide by the Law of the Sea in negotiating claims to the islands. In spite of that agreement, from time to time Beijing has continued to pressure the ASEAN states by sending naval units or fishing fleets into contested areas.

CONCLUSION

In its own National Defense White Paper of October 2000, China claims to be a country that seeks to resolve disputes in the international arena through negotiations. However, Beijing has clearly stated its right to use force inside whatever area it defines as its own territory, even if that territory is in dispute. The 1988 naval engagements against Vietnam in the Spratly Islands come to mind, as do the 1974 seizure of the Paracel Islands and the 1979 attack on Vietnam. Of course, Beijing has always been careful to couch its actions in terms of a "defensive counterattack" or an action to regain territory it claims. More recently, China seized and occupied Mischief Reef, claimed by the Philippines, and demonstrated massive force against Taiwan as a way to express its dissatisfaction with what CCP leaders believed was a trend toward independence. Thus, it is clear that China continues to rely primarily on threats of force and coercion in its relations with neighbors, and has shown that it will not hesitate to use force to achieve foreign policy goals.

SUGGESTIONS FOR FURTHER READING

To understand how China views the use of force and characteristically warns countries before using force, one of the seminal books is Allen S. Whiting, *The Chinese Calculus of Deterrence: India and Indochina* (Ann Arbor: University of Michigan Press, 1975). Whiting provides an excellent set of case studies of how China uses strategic warning and diplomacy in combination before using force. As a case study of the same subject, the reader would do well to obtain a copy of Neville Maxwell, *India's China War* (Bombay: JAICO Press, 1971). Maxwell had access to the Indian classified diplomatic archives, giving his conclusions great credibility.

From the standpoint of strategic culture—when China might resort to force and why—two authors have done an excellent job of putting classical and modern Chinese military thought into perspective. Thomas J. Christensen, *Useful Adversaries: Grand Strategy, Domestic Mobilization, and the Sino–American Conflict, 1947–1958* (Princeton: Princeton University Press, 1996) has used the early Cold War confrontations between China and the United States to illustrate China's strategic culture. Alastair Iain Johnston, *Cultural Realism: Strategic Culture and Grand Strategy in Chinese History* (Princeton: Princeton University Press, 1995) provides a more historical perspective on the same questions.

Three of the best texts dealing with China's military actions in the Korean War are T. R. Fehrenbach, *This Kind of War* (New York: Macmillan, 1963); Alexander L. George, *The Chinese Communist Army in Action: The Korean War and Its Aftermath* (New York: Columbia University Press, 1967); and Shu Guang

Zhang, *Mao's Military Romanticism: China and the Korean War, 1950–1953* (Lawrence: University Press of Kansas, 1995). Fehrenbach deals with the conduct of the war from the perspective of the United States, including strategy, foreign policy issues, and military actions. George provides an assessment of how the Chinese military functioned as an instrument of national policy. Shu Guang Zhang's book is an excellent complement to the other two because he has exploited internal Chinese documents that provide a view of why the PRC entered the war. Zhang has also interviewed a number of Chinese officers who took part in the Korean War.

Accurate materials on China's seizure of the Paracel Islands and its actions in the Spratly Islands are not available yet, so one must rely on more general works about China's military activities. Greg Austin, *China's Ocean Frontier: International Law, Military Force and National Development* (Canberra: Australian National University, 1998) is one book that covers the matter well. Ken Allen, a former U.S. Air Force attaché in China, has studied some of the instances of the use of force by China; see Kenneth W. Allen, Jonathan Pollack, and Glenn Krumel, *China's Air Force Enters the 21st Century* (Santa Monica, CA: RAND Corporation, 1995).

The very best work on the Chinese attack into Vietnam in 1979 is Harlan Jencks, "China's Punitive War on Vietnam: A Military Assessment," *Asian Survey* 19 (1979): 801–815. This quick and accurate assessment written only months after the conflict remains mandatory reading.

SUGGESTIONS FOR FURTHER RESEARCH

China is increasingly dependent on foreign trade and exports and on imports of energy and food. As China expands its strategic reach through military improvements, it is bound to develop the capabilities to act in its own interest when it perceives its interest as threatened. Military strategic writings from China have made it clear that the PRC does not intend to challenge the United States or other great powers directly in a military sense. There is a need for new research that examines how China can obtain the energy resources it requires, and what military and diplomatic measures it will employ to secure them. It is increasingly evident that China's shipping companies are gaining footholds at ports near strategic waterways such as the Panama Canal, the Bosporus, and the Malacca Strait. Will China use arms sales or military deployments to back up its state-owned corporations if access to resources is threatened? What can one learn from an examination of the history of the Yuan dynasty and the early Ming (including the voyages of Zheng He), when China pursued maritime expansion that used both force and commerce to advance national interest? Are these actions reflected in modern strategic writings? Will the introduction of effective ballistic missile submarines capable of extended voyages change China's military strategy and how it uses force?

NOTES

1. John W. Garver, *Foreign Relations of the People's Republic of China* (Englewood Cliffs, NJ: Prentice Hall, 1993), 250–265.

2. This point is the thesis of a seminal book on the subject; see Allen S. Whiting, *The Chinese Calculus of Deterrence: India and Indochina* (Ann Arbor: University of Michigan Press, 1975).

3. Michael D. Swaine and Ashley J. Tellis, *Interpreting China's Grand Strategy: Past, Present, and Future* (Santa Monica, CA: RAND Corporation, 2000), 21.

4. Alastair Iain Johnston, *Cultural Realism: Strategic Culture and Grand Strategy in Chinese History* (Princeton: Princeton University Press, 1995), 184.

5. Garver, *Foreign Relations of the People's Republic of China*, 253–254.

6. Brigadier J. P. Dalvi, *Himalayan Blunder: The Curtain-Raiser to the Sino–Indian War of 1962* (Bombay: Thacker, 1969), 43–45.

SIXTEEN

Recent Developments
in the Chinese Military

June Teufel Dreyer

There have been three major formative influences on the People's Liberation Army in the past decade: the demonstrations at Tiananmen Square and elsewhere in China in 1989, the collapse of the Soviet Union that began later the same year, and the Gulf War of 1990–1991. Taken together, these three events resulted in marked changes in strategy, budgets, civil–military relationships, recruitment, training, and weapons acquisition.

With regard to the demonstrations, the leadership's use of the PLA to forcibly suppress unarmed civilian protestors resulted in significant numbers of dead and injured. The exact figures are in dispute, but range from a low of 200 deaths given by official sources to a high of several thousand given by dissident groups. A number of military commanders are known to have been opposed to using the army in this way. They argued that the people's army should not be used against the people, lest the people look upon it as their oppressor rather than their protector. These commanders' reluctance notwithstanding, the military obeyed Deng Xiaoping's orders. As predicted, the army's image among the Chinese people did suffer. This was more noticeable among better-informed urban dwellers than peasants, particularly those who lived in rural areas, where news of the demonstrations had little salience.

The central government launched a massive propaganda effort to discredit the demonstrators and portray the military as the protectors of the people against the "black hands" of counterrevolution who sought to undermine the party and government and plunge China into chaos. At the same time, the leadership sought to ensure that the military would not again hesitate to carry out orders: Units held repeated discussion meetings designed to instill the message that the army belongs to the party, whose directives it must carry out immediately and unquestioningly. Individuals and groups pledged their loyalty to the party leadership with Jiang Zemin, Deng's newly anointed successor, as its core. The leadership itself was none too popular with the Chinese people. Jiang Zemin did not have the revolutionary credentials possessed by Mao Zedong and Deng Xiaoping. There were conscious efforts to promote a sense of Chinese nationalism, most of them seemingly directed against external powers, particularly the United States.

The Chinese leadership was also stung by negative international reaction to its actions at Tiananmen Square. Several countries, most notably the United States, imposed sanctions on the PRC that fell particularly heavily on the military. President Bush announced the suspension of high-ranking visits, including military visits, and banned military sales to China of all items controlled by the State Department and cited in the department's Munitions Control List until such time as China could amend its human rights behavior. Congress went further, introducing legislation suspending military sales, nuclear cooperation, and the export of American-made satellites for launching by Chinese rockets. It also halted further liberalization of export controls for U.S. products with potential military application going to China. Despite opposition from the Bush adminstration, a movement to revoke the PRC's most-favored-nation trade status with the United States gained momentum.

While the American actions were undertaken to induce the Chinese government to modify its behavior, they had the effect of provoking additional belligerence. The Chinese media accused the U.S. leadership of plotting to peacefully undermine socialism and the leadership of the socialist state, substituting capitalist values that were inappropriate to the Chinese context. The PLA was reminded that it was the protector of the cherished socialist system and its leadership. And although the American military sanctions actually had relatively minor effects—President Bush waived certain of these soon after imposing them, and alternate channels existed—the Beijing leadership began to look for new sources of weapons procurement.

The second major factor influencing the development of the PLA, the disintegration of the Soviet Union, reinforced the Chinese leadership's anti-American and antiliberal feelings deriving from the aftermath of the Tiananmen demonstrations. A few months after the demonstrations were suppressed, the Berlin Wall was dismantled, the Romanian army refused to support the country's president when he ordered it to move against demonstrators (he was then executed) and the USSR began to shatter into what would become fifteen successor states. The Chinese leadership had always been skeptical of the wisdom of *perestroika*, or liberalizing the political system. It interpreted the collapse of the USSR as vindication of its arguments that economic reform under the firm guidance of authoritarian rule was far preferable as well as less risky than political liberalization. The demise of the Soviet Union carried substantial defense risks for the PRC. Beijing had been adept at playing off Moscow against Washington to advance China's interests. Chinese leaders saw their maneuverability in the new geopolitical configuration sharply reduced. While the Russian Federation had but a fraction of the power of its predecessor, it was *faute de mieux* an ally worth cultivating. Russia, with its shattered economy and oversupply of reliable weapons, could also serve as an alternate supplier of arms.

The final event shaping the development of the PLA in the last decade of the twentieth century was the Gulf War of 1990–1991. In August 1990, when Iraq invaded Kuwait, the United States spearheaded a U.N. resolution ordering Iraqi leader Saddam Hussein to withdraw his forces. Saddam refused, whereupon President Bush, working through the U.N. Security Council, organized a multilateral coalition to forcibly expel the Iraqis from Kuwait. The PRC declined to participate and hinted that, as a permanent member of the Security Council, it might veto the resolution to establish the U.N. force. Chinese diplomats took the view that sovereignty alone was absolute. While it was wrong for one country to invade another, it was also wrong for third parties to interfere to undo the situation: Two wrongs did not make a right. The concept of sovereignty meant that a nation was supreme within its borders. Hence, no other state had the right to interfere in its internal affairs, much less invade it. President Bush eventually persuaded the PRC not to exercise its veto, perhaps by promising that he would veto congressional attempts to revoke China's most-favored-nation status. Beijing abstained in the Security Council vote.

Beijing's attitude may in part be explained by the leverage its Security Council vote gave it in influencing a continuation of its trade relations with Washington, but there was a more important reason for China's opposition to the U.N. coalition. In arguing that human rights—in this case, the fate of the conquered Kuwaiti people—outweighed sovereign rights, the United States was setting a precedent that the Beijing leadership feared could be applied to its own plans to "return" Taiwan to its control. In addition to its repeated insistence that the Taiwan question be settled peacefully, the United States had also expressed support for human rights in Tibet and Xinjiang, where ethnic minorities resisted Beijing's control and argued for independence. This was further confirmation that the sole remaining superpower was trying to impose its value system on China, undermine the country's integrity, and perhaps cause its disintegration.

In addition to convincing the Beijing leadership that the United States was bent on proselytizing its ideology, the Gulf War showed that the United States would be a formidable adversary militarily. The military modernization program that Deng Xiaoping had instituted in 1979 had achieved significant advances, albeit from a low starting point. China's official media regularly reported on military developments, describing the design of the latest simulator or the test of a new model of rocket as evidence that the PLA had now reached "advanced world standards." When PLA generals saw videos of the performance of American weapons in the Gulf War, they were said to have been despondent, wondering how China could ever catch up. Yet they were convinced that it must if the PRC were to take its proper place in the New World Order. The United States as sole remaining superpower was behaving not just as a bully, but as a bully who was exceedingly dangerous militarily.

STRATEGY

An immediate response to these three events was a change in strategy. The PLA was ordered to prepare for limited high-technology war with emphasis on information warfare. There was also interest in the "revolution in military affairs" (RMA). As defined by the American military analysts who developed it, the RMA is a dramatically new concept of war. Often described as a "system of systems," a synergy of developments that includes significant progress and change in the related areas of technology, systems, operations, organization, and strategy. Through linked computers, satellites, and weapons delivery systems, a commander can be aware of all aspects of the battlefield and able to deliver crippling blows to the enemy's most vulnerable points. This synergy fundamentally alters the nature of warfare.

Chinese strategists were aware that the creation of a revolution in military affairs is both technologically difficult and financially expensive. Effecting an RMA would require a fundamental change in the party–bureaucratic managerial system that discouraged scientific and technological innovation. Those in charge were understandably reluctant to relinquish control of this system. While those who felt the existing system would have to be reformed were hesitant to attack it openly, frequent references to the need to emancipate thought and throw off the fetters of outdated strategic concepts indicate their misgivings.

Aided in part by the American military's own effort to learn from its mistakes in the Gulf War, Chinese analysts scrutinized the U.S. performance and decided that the superpower had a number of vulnerabilities that the PLA could exploit. High technology was both an advantage and a disadvantage: In a confrontation, the Chinese military would seek to maximize the vulnerabilities of American technological superiority.

The efforts of the North Atlantic Treaty Organization (NATO), led by the United States, to reverse Serbian efforts at ethnic cleansing in Kosovo reopened the strategy debate in China. For seventy-eight days, from March through June 1999, the air forces of thirteen NATO states bombed the territory of the Federal Republic of Yugoslavia (FRY) in an impressively coordinated fashion. No allied combatants were killed. However, there was also general agreement that the Serbs had endured this terrible pressure impressively. In the end, NATO compromised its original demands sufficiently that Russia, the FRY's only meaningful ally, sided with NATO and the FRY capitulated.

Chinese analysts contrasted the Gulf War with the Kosovo action, describing the former as having some characteristics of modern high-technology war whereas the latter was a truly modern high-technology war with "hyperconventional" features. America had proved that it was capable of learning from its own mistakes. These new features would have to be analyzed and digested if the PRC were to be able to defend itself properly. Three different schools of thought contended.

One group argued that the Kosovo conflict had shown the continuing relevance of Mao Zedong's strategy of People's War. The FRY's population, they noted, had stood fast in the face of repeated attacks, thus dealing a devastating psychological blow to their technologically superior attackers. Citizens had formed human chains to protect bridges and held mass sports events in defiance of the bombing raids. The military had set up false targets that deceived the enemy into expending his firepower uselessly while missing the real targets. Troops and planes had been hidden underground or camouflaged against attack. This showed the continuing relevance of the tried and true strategy that had enabled the Communists to defeat the American-aided Chiang Kai-shek in 1949.

A second group stressed the need to fight high technology with high technology. China is not Yugoslavia, they pointed out, and should not expect to employ the same strategy. As a nuclear power and emerging superpower, the PRC needed whatever weapons the advanced capitalist countries had. Only a strategy that was thoroughly grounded in the most advanced scientific and technological weapons could hope to win. A system of systems must be constructed that would link all PLA computers on ground, air, and sea through satellite communications. Network-centered warfare would increase the command speed of the component parts and permit continuous monitoring of the battlefield. Not to possess such capabilities could doom China to losing a war before a single shot was fired.

A third group advocated a strategy of doing more with existing weapons while selectively developing high-technology weapons in order to take advantage of the enemy's vulnerabilities. They argued that the use of "asymmetric warfare," such as inserting viruses into the enemy's computers and blinding his satellites with laser rays, would enable the PLA to defeat a technologically superior adversary at relatively low cost. While the development of technologically state-of-the-art weapons across the entire military spectrum might be desirable in the abstract, it was unnecessary for the attainment of victory. Moreover, it would have extremely negative consequences for the PRC's economic development. Some suspected that the United States had a conscious plan to lure China into an arms race that would destroy its economy. This strategy had, they pointed out, worked with regard to the Soviet Union. If the PRC succumbed to a similar temptation and invested in its military to the detriment of industrial growth, China would be the next power to collapse.

A variation on the asymmetric warfare school advanced a strategy of "unrestricted warfare." In a book by the same name published in 1999, two PLA senior colonels argued that the PRC must be prepared to act without regard for the "rules of war," since these rules had been devised by the West in order to advantage itself in any confrontation. Hence, in formulating strategy, military planners should be prepared to act outside those rules. The authors stressed the need to exploit (1) the tendency of the West to worship technology and (2) its obsession with avoiding casualties. Their preferred strategy would employ terrorism, biological and chemical warfare, and the manipulation of environmental conditions; for example, producing harmful climate changes in the enemy's territory.[1]

There has been no clear resolution of these differences of opinion, which continue to coexist within the broad rubric of "Local War under High Technology Conditions." All would have advantages and disadvantages in time of confrontation; projects are being funded that fit with the arguments of each of the schools. For the immediate future, the leadership hopes to avoid armed conflict until the country's economy has strengthened and it is better capable of sustaining a confrontation with a technologically superior adversary.

BUDGETS

The official defense budget began a steady rise in 1989. The initial increment, from 22 billion yuan to 25 billion, or a 13-percent rise, had been announced shortly before the demonstrations at Tiananmen Square began, but subsequent increases, all in comparable double-digit figures, caused some foreign analysts to conclude that the military was being rewarded for moving against the dissidents. Others saw the rising defense budget as evidence that China was intent on an expansionist policy internationally. In February 1992, the National People's Congress unilaterally passed a law that reinforced these views. It declared that the territorial sovereignty of the PRC included not only the mainland but Taiwan, the offshore islands administered by Taiwan, the Diaoyu Islands (administered by Japan and known to the Japanese as the Senkaku Islands), and the Xisha (Paracel) and Spratly Islands in the South China Sea. In 1974 the PRC seized the Xisha from Vietnam, which still claims jurisdiction. The Spratlys are claimed by Vietnam, Malaysia, Taiwan, the Philippines, and Brunei as well as the PRC. The same law asserted Beijing's right to "adopt all necessary measures to prevent and stop the harmful passage of vessels through its territorial waters and empowers the Chinese military to expel violators out to open sea."

The 1999 defense budget was 104.7 billion yuan, or more than four times as large as a decade before. Official spokespersons reacted sharply to foreign accusations of a growing China threat, pointing out that the PRC's military expenditures were far lower than those of other large countries. In 1997, to take a typical example, they were a mere 3.67 percent of those of the United States, 61.25 percent of Russia's, 27.53 percent of Britain's, 26.7 percent of France's, 22.79 percent of Japan's, and 56.98 percent of South Korea's. In addition, the increases in China's defense budget had barely kept pace with inflation. Most expenditures had in fact gone to improve the extremely spartan living conditions of officers and recruits. Personnel costs accounted for just under 35 percent of total defense costs.

Skeptics observed that the defense budget continued to rise in 1998 and 1999, when the economy had slipped into deflation. Moreover, given frequent complaints from local areas about the burden of supporting the PLA units stationed there, a significant amount of personnel costs did not appear in the official defense budget. The costs of research and development for nuclear weapons, believed to be quite large, were likewise not included in the defense budget. Neither were the costs of acquiring weapons systems from abroad, nor the profits from the PLA's large and diversified business empire. Also, since wages in China are far lower than those in the industrialized countries, more weapons can be produced and more troops paid in the PRC than for a comparable amount of money spent in the industrialized states.

In July 1998, the PLA was ordered to divest itself of its business empire, which party and government leaders believed to be a major factor in the worrisome degree of corruption within the armed forces. Divestiture, they felt, would also be helpful in focusing the military on its functional role of defending the country, as opposed to the pursuit of profits. The large budget increases of the late 1990s despite the absence of inflation could be explained by the need to compensate the PLA for the loss of its businesses. While some units did sever ties with factories, guest houses, and entertainment establishments, others found ways to avoid doing so or maintained "back door" relationships. Still others reportedly looted the enterprises of their assets before turning them over. It is not yet clear how successful the move to sever the PLA from its commercial activities has been.

The debate over the actual size of the defense budget continues. Estimates range from a low of 30 percent over the official figures to a high of ten times. Most analyses fall into the range of three to four times.

CIVIL–MILITARY RELATIONS

For a time after the Tiananmen incident there were intensive efforts to instill in officers and recruits the necessity for absolute and unswerving loyalty to the party and its orders. PLA members were reminded that theirs was a party army, not a state army. Strict adherence to the directives of the party center with the newly appointed Jiang Zemin as its core was the sine qua non of political orthodoxy. Those deemed to have been insufficiently responsive to this message, as well as those who had evinced hesitation when ordered to move against the demonstrators, were purged.

The immediate effect was to advantage the dominant faction in the PLA. Even before the Tiananmen demonstrations began, Chinese critics described the military as "the Yang family village," after the surname of its leading figures. Yang Shangkun was both secretary-general of the Central Military Commission and president of China. In the former position, he supervised the day-to-day functioning of the military, since CMC chair Deng Xiaoping was concerned with the myriad other details of running China. Yang Shangkun's younger half-brother, Yang Baibing, served as a vice chair of the CMC. Good relationships with the Yangs were believed crucial to the enhancement of one's military career. When the post-Tiananmen purges took place, many of the vacant slots were filled with members of the Yang faction.

Jiang Zemin, Deng's hand-picked successor, had no military experience, and the high command was reportedly suspicious of him. When new military appointments were announced, Yang Baibing would frequently award them, even to the extent of visiting far-flung military districts to do so. Foreign analysts pointed out that a military that was brought out of its barracks to deal with the Tiananmen incident would not easily return to the barracks afterward, and predicted that the PLA was likely to play the role of kingmaker after Deng died.

While a logical prediction, this is not what happened. In 1992, just before the Fourteenth Party Congress was to meet, rumors began to circulate about the Yangs' disloyalty. Among other allegations, it was charged that Baibing and some of his officers had gathered in a Beijing hotel to make plans to ensure social stability at the time of Deng's death. While there is nothing inherently disloyal about this act, it was said that Deng had not been informed beforehand, and was furious. Yang Shangkun also allegedly declared that the PLA would be the "escort" of Deng's reforms. Again, there is nothing overtly subversive about the statement, but it was interpreted as showing an improperly activist attitude. Whether the details were accurate or not, the Party Congress accepted the Yangs' resignations. The stated reason for Yang Shangkun's retirement was his advanced age of eighty. Yang Baibing relinquished his military posts while receiving an appointment to the Party Politburo that appeared to be mainly ceremonial. The result was to detach the Yangs from their military power base, thus removing a potential obstacle in Jiang Zemin's path. Deng Xiaoping formally retired as chair of the Central Military Commission, with Jiang assuming the position.

His way thus cleared, Jiang moved with alacrity. Laws were passed on mandatory retirement ages: For miltary district commanders and commissars, this was sixty-five. These age limits were scrupulously enforced, the existence of a two-year-extension "escape clause" notwithstanding. Regional commanders and commissars were transferred from one region to another with some regularity in order to prevent their becoming too enmeshed with the local power structure. New appointees were believed to be chosen for their loyalty to Jiang. Jiang also provided positive incentives for loyalty. Regional commanders and commissars were promoted to the rank of full general—three stars under the Chinese system—and both officers and recruits received pay raises. Jiang began a regular practice of visiting units throughout the country. These tours were heavily publicized. Jiang was extravagantly praised for braving bitterly cold weather in the north and hot sun in the south to share meals with troops, inspect their barracks, and show his concern for the smallest details of their daily life. By the mid–1990s it seemed clear that the party, in the form of Jiang, did indeed control the gun. However, some foreign analysts observed that since the army was now commanded by people without military experience and had also embarked on a more specialized professionalization program, it might develop a more separate corporate existence that could bring it into conflict with the civilian leadership.

RECRUITMENT

The military had suffered from a shortage of willing volunteers ever since Deng Xiaoping's economic reforms had made it more lucrative to stay in civilian life. Given the huge number of young people available for military service relative to the PRC's needs, there had heretofore been no shortage of eager volunteers. After the reforms, however, party and government had to exercise considerable pressure to get able-bodied youth to present themselves during annual recruitment periods. Hence, although still technically volunteers, many were in reality conscripts. Popular indignation against the army's role in Tiananmen Square notwithstanding, its recruitment did not suffer in the period immediately thereafter. Party and government leaders were aware that dissatisfaction with rising inflation rates had motivated many of the demonstrators, and hence introduced deflationary policies. This succeeded in bringing down inflation, though at the cost of reducing economic growth. Fewer jobs were created, and a sufficient number of draft-age males found military service preferable to unemployment.

When economic growth picked up again a few years later, memories of Tiananmen had faded somewhat, but recruitment again had to contend with reluctant enlistees. In early 1996, a long-rumored announcement was made that the size of the PLA was to be cut by 500,000 over the next few years, to an eventual end strength of 2.5 million. Stated reasons for the cut were, first, so that the money saved on personnel costs could be devoted to the development and acquisition of more modern weapons, and second, to lessen problems of "instability" caused by some soldiers' dissatisfaction with the low pay and difficult living conditions in comparison to civilians.

In keeping with its goal of being able to fight high-technology wars, the PLA also sought to recruit soldiers with better educational backgrounds. The goal was to have ordinary soldiers with at least a middle school education and officers who had graduated from military academies or other institutions of tertiary education. In the interests of recruitment from all areas of society, these standards could be relaxed as appropriate in remote areas and among certain ethnic minorities where standards of education were low. In practice, few university graduates were interested in joining the military. However, when the economy again contracted in 1998–1999, some recent graduates were inducted into the officer corps.

TRAINING

Training exercises seem to have been curtailed in favor of political indoctrination for the first few months after the Tiananmen incident, but soon resumed. The Gulf War showed Chinese planners that the PLA was not agile enough to cope with a fast-moving modern opponent. As is Western military practice, a "Red Team" (the color of communism) and a "Blue Team" (its adversary) were formed to conduct mock battles. Exercises were set up such that the Blue Team could triumph if it could show superior performance. This would have been unthinkable only a few years before. The air force practiced night flights in difficult weather conditions, low-altitude and high-altitude flying, and emergency mobility maneuvers. Ground forces instituted live-ammunition target practice. Units also participated in a wider variety of exercises in diverse geographic areas: the arid Gobi Desert, the high-altitude Kunlun Plateau, the mountainous Greater Xing'an Range, the steamy Yunnan jungles, and areas in and around the contested Taiwan Strait and Spratly Islands. The air force set up a tactical training base with air and ground training ranges, simulated runways built to scale, and a surface-to-air missile range. An exact copy of the Chinchuankang Air Base in central Taiwan was constructed in Gansu to train units to attack it.

Military academies were ordered to enhance the science and technology portions of their curricula, and a wider variety of courses was added to enhance the professional specialization of the officer corps. The National Defense University offered a special course on high-technology warfare and its implications for those senior officers whose school years were far in the past. A PLA engineering university was set up in the central China city of Wuhan in 1999, the same year that the PLA's missile arm, the Second Artillery, instituted a scholarship program at Northwest Engineering

University in Xi'an to train future missile officers. Articles stressed the need for "scholar generals."

Recognizing that even well-trained troops' ability to perform in battle depends on having the proper resources available to them, modifications were made to the military logistics system. To cope with a fast-moving opponent, the PLA must be able to quickly transfer its elite units to the site of conflict. Given the expectation that these troops will become more dependent on high-tech weapons, a way must be found to quickly repair or resupply their equipment. This entails a revamp of the former logistics system that relied on replenishment from a fixed-site depot. Military regions have experimented with various organizational structures to provide mobile support. The navy has instituted emergency support detachments to repair warships at sea rather than send them to dockyards for repair, and the air force has tried assembling elements from several different organizations to accompany fighter units deploying forward to airfields. There are also plans to civilianize logistics. Some inventory-control processes have been automated.

These advances notwithstanding, there were contraindications as well. The existence of a number of different solutions to logistics problems would seem to portend an adverse effect on standardization, to the detriment of the PLA's ability to deploy units from different parts of the country. There are already complaints that training lags behind weapons acquisition: New equipment languishes in storage because troops are not able to use it. However, in January 1999, in deference to the unpopularity of military service, the PLA reduced the period of compulsory service from three years to two. This will mean less time to train and to become familiar with increasingly more complex weapons.

WEAPONS ACQUISITIONS

The PLA appears to be focusing on "credible intimidation," acquiring weapons that will make it expensive enough in terms of lives and money that potential adversaries will be inclined to accept the PRC's terms without actually going to war. Some of these weapons are indigenously developed, either wholly so or with assistance from Israel and/or Russia. Others have been bought, mostly from Russia. Still other designs and technology may have been stolen from the United States, a charge the Chinese government has vehemently denied. According to a controversial U.S. congressional committee report, classified information on seven thermonuclear warheads, including every currently deployed thermonuclear warhead in the American ballistic missile arsenal, was stolen. The report also charged that the PRC illegally obtained classified information on a number of associated reentry vehicles, as well as the design for an enhanced radiation weapon or neutron bomb that neither the United States nor any other nation has yet deployed.[2]

Missiles

The military has devoted particular attention to missile research and development. New land-attack cruise missiles are enhancing the PLA's ability to strike targets within the Asian region accurately with conventional warheads. By 2005, China is expected to have deployed a first-generation land-attack cruise missile (LACM), as well as two types of short-range ballistic missiles (SRBMs). The SRBM force is growing rapidly. The CSS–6, also known as the DF–15 or M–9, is a solid-propellant, road-mobile missile that can deliver a 500-kilogram payload to a maximum range of 600 kilometers. The PLA already has one regimental-size CSS–6 unit deployed in southeast China. The CSS-X–7 or M–11 is also a solid-propellant, road-mobile SRBM with a shorter, 300-km range. An improved, longer-range version is being developed. It is anticipated that both will incorporate satellite-assisted navigation technology to improve their accuracy. Chinese sources have already boasted that they could hit the desk in the presidential office of Taiwan. LACMs have a high development priority, which is being facilitated by help from Russia. Antiship cruise missile (ASCM) capabilities will be improved by the acquisition of SS-N–22/Sunburn ASCMs from Russia. American maritime experts consider that the Sunburns would be a threat even to the U.S. Navy.

Air Force (PLAAF)

While the bulk of the air fleet is composed of second- and third-generation planes, fourth-generation platforms are gradually entering the inventory. The F–10, the PRC's first domestically produced (with Russian and Israeli assistance) fourth-generation fighter is currently being tested. It is expected to be armed with advanced beyond-visual-range active radar and air-to-air missiles, and may be air refuelable. Slow progress is being made in mastering air refueling techniques. Sixty Su–27 fighters were purchased from Russia with a license to produce more such planes in China. The Su–27 is the only fighter currently in the PLAAF's inventory with a large enough combat radius for extended operations beyond China's borders.

Su–27s are equipped with Russian-built antiair AA–11/Archer infrared missiles that are superior to those of most of the PRC's neighbors. Forty Su–30s, a more advanced multipurpose warplane that was designed to compete with the U.S. Air Force's F–15, are being acquired as well. These have ground attack capabilities and can be refueled in flight.

Bombers are mostly obsolescent and vulnerable. The newer BADGER models, which incorporate cruise-missile technology, could expect some success in combat. Troop transport has been aided by the purchase of a dozen IL–76MD/CANDID planes from Russia; additional IL–76s or other similiar planes are expected to be purchased. The PRC's civilian aircraft fleet is expanding rapidly, and some of these planes could be diverted to troop-transport duties if hostilies should occur. With regard to air defense, China is expending great efforts to establish an integrated air defense system, though it is not expected to be operational for at least five years.

Navy (PLAN)

During the past decade, the PLA Navy has eliminated large numbers of older ships and replaced them with fewer, more modern units, including the Luhu-class guided-missile destroyers, Jiangwei-class guided-missile frigates, and fast-attack missile boats. Sovremenny-class destroyers have also been purchased from Russia. These are collectively enhancing the PLAN's readiness and capability for extended operations. With regard to subsurface operations, China has acquired Kilo-class submarines equipped with advanced sonar systems from Russia, and a new Type 094 ballistic-missile submarine is being developed. If successful, the 094 could give the PRC a true maritime strategic-strike capability. The issue of whether to acquire aircraft carriers, and if so whether through reverse engineering or purchase, has been debated for more than a decade with minimal results. PLAN's amphibious fleet is capable of transporting approximately one infantry division; this could be augmented with barges, small landing craft, fishing boats, and civilian merchant ships if hostilities should occur.

Ground Forces

The ground forces have received lowest priority in the PLA's modernization. The leadership considers it more likely that a confrontation would involve Taiwan or the Spratly Islands, where the need for air and sea assets is of greater importance. Only about 20 percent of ground force units are considered elite or rapid reaction units. The 500,000-man cut in the PLA already discussed will mainly affect ground units. It is anticipated that streamlining the force will enable the creation of a larger number of RRUs. Newer Type 80 tanks are entering the inventory, and infrastructure improvements are being made.

Information Warfare

The major focus of China's information warfare (IW) efforts is defensive, consonant with the leadership's belief that the PRC's information systems are vulnerable. Efforts are being made to provide computer antivirus solutions, network security, and advanced data communications. Chinese media have said that the PLA has incorporated IW-related scenarios into recent training exercises. As the military becomes more proficient in defending its own networks against attack, it is apt to increase its efforts to penetrate the enemy's information systems. This is consonant with the asymmetric warfare strategy already discussed.

Antisatellite (ASAT) Programs

The PRC is now able to detect and track most satellites with enough accuracy to target them. However, its only means of destroying or disabling a satellite is to launch a ballistic missile or space launch vehicle equipped with a nuclear weapon. Programs are underway to develop an antisatellite laser to remedy this situation.

Telecommunication Infrastructure

Modernization of the PRC's command, control, communications, computer, and information (C^4I) is receiving high priority. Multiple transmissions systems exist, creating a military communications system that is survivable, secure, flexible, mobile, and less vulnerable to exploitation, destruction, or electronic attack. The country's C^4I system could be degraded, but it is unlikely to be completely denied.

Deception

Efforts are being made to enhance capabilities for military denial and deception to counter American precision weapons, advanced reconnaissance sensors, and command and control warfare doctrine. The PLA hopes to force its enemy to reach erroneous conclusions about the activities, deployment, and combat objectives of its forces. Camouflage and deception, features of the People's War strategy, can disperse the enemy's troops, waste its firepower, and disrupt its high-technology weapons.

SUMMATION

Plans do not automatically translate into capabilities. While it cannot be doubted that the PLA has made impressive progress over the past decade and would be a formidable opponent for most of its Asian neighbors, much remains to be done. For example, while the military now conducts interservice exercises at the tactical level, the services are not fully integrated into a cohesive combat force. The component parts train simultaneously and near each other, but are not controlled at operational level by a joint commander. The PLA has not yet found a way to relate joint warfighting to strategic doctrine. And despite progress in logistics, the system would have difficulties in sustaining a large-scale, long-term, high-intensity conflict.

The PLAN has already fallen behind on plans for it to be able to control the area delineated by a "first island chain"—north to south from the Aleutians through the Kuriles, Japan, the Ryukyus, Taiwan, the Philippines, and Indonesia—by 2000. This may set back plans to control the area to the "second island chain," which includes the Bonins, the Marianas, and the Carolines, by 2020, and to become a global maritime force by 2050. The navy's ability to transport and land troops under combat conditions is not good, and progress in improving it has been slow. The marines' most conspicuous role thus far has been standing guard on a select number of islands in the South China Sea. The nuclear submarine development program has been unimpressive, with a wide gap between rhetoric and reality. An aircraft carrier, if built, may represent more of a target for China's enemies than a power-projection platform for its airplanes.

PLAAF pilots remain hesitant to push their planes to the limits of their capabilities, thus degrading their performance in combat. The issue of spare parts for Russian planes is apt to be difficult to solve; despite an agreement to produce Su–27s in the PRC, many parts will be manufactured in Russia for some years to come. This problem could be even more troublesome for the Su–30s. Morale is poor, particularly among enlisted personnel and in the ground forces. Officer corruption has been held responsible for sporadic reports of food shortages among the rank and file. Finally, the PLA as a whole lacks combat experience.

SUGGESTIONS FOR FURTHER READING

Several publications in Chinese are basic for keeping up with the rapidly changing People's Liberation Army. These include *Jiefangjun Bao* (*Liberation Army News*), published by the PLA's General Political Department, and monthly or quarterly journals such as *Xiandai Bingqi* (*Modern Weaponry*), *Zhongguo Junshi Kexue* (*China Military Science*), *Xiandai Junshi* (*Conmilit*), *Xiandai Jianchuan* (*Modern Ships*), and *Guofang* (*National Defense*). Translations from these occasionally appear in the Foreign Broadcast Information Service (FBIS), available in internet or e-mail form for a monthly fee from National Technical Information Service, Springfield, Virginia (*http://www.ntis.gov*).

Western defense periodicals such as *Defense Week* and *Aviation Week and Space Technology*, both published in Washington, DC, and *Jane's Defence Weekly* (London) regularly report on developments in China's weapons technology. The International Institute for Strategic Studies, also of London, publishes research on the Chinese military in its Adelphi Papers series, as well as assessments of Chinese capabilities in its annual reviews *Strategic Survey* and *The Military Balance*.

The American Enterprise Institute of Washington, DC, sponsors an annual invitation-only conference on the People's Liberation Army. The papers presented to the conference are published in book form. Recent titles include James R. Lilley and David Shambaugh,eds., *China's Military Faces the Future* (Armonk, NY: M. E. Sharpe, 1999) and Larry M. Wortzel, ed., *The Chinese Armed Forces in the 21st Century* (Carlisle, PA: Army War College Strategic Studies Institute, 1999). The respective service arms of the U.S. military sponsor research on the PLA, which has appeared in the publications series of the Counterproliferation Center of the Air War College at Maxwell Air Force Base, in the Air Force's Maxwell Papers, and in the publications of the Army War College's Strategic Studies Institute and the Navy's Center for Naval Analyses.

The RAND Corporation of Santa Monica, California, and the Stockholm International Peace Research Institute of Sweden regularly report on Chinese military developments. Scholarly journals including *The China Quarterly*, published by the School of Oriental and African Studies in London, and *Issues and Studies*, published bimonthly by the Institute of International Relations in the Republic of China on Taiwan, devote significant attention to Chinese military issues. There are several Web sites devoted to the Chinese military, including *http://216.87.213.144/plaboard*.

SUGGESTIONS FOR FURTHER RESEARCH

While states are in general reluctant to divulge information regarding their defense, the People's Republic of China is unusually secretive. Although sources are far more diversified and available than they were twenty years ago, research on the military continues to be limited by lack of transparency in the data released. The more sensitive the area, the scarcer the information and the greater the foreign interest in it. Examples of such topics are research and development on missile programs, the process by which high-level promotions and transfers are decided, and the precise process by which the PLA makes its corporate voice known to civilian policy makers.

Research topics that can be addressed from open sources, however imperfectly, include recruitment and demobilization, strategy, training, comparisons of published defense budgets over time, weapons acquisition, and the PLA's exchange programs with foreign militaries.

Notes

1. Qiao Liang and Wang Xiangsui, *Chao xian zhan* [Unrestricted warfare] (Beijing: PLA Literature and Arts Publishing House, 1999). English translation is avaible online at *http://www.terrorism.com/documents/unrestricted.pdf.*

2. *Report of the Select Committee on U.S. National Security and Military/Commercial Concerns with the People's Republic of China, submitted by Mr. Cox of California, Chairman* (Washington, DC: U.S. Government Printing Office, 1999); also available online at *http://www.house.gov/coxreport.*

CHINESE PLACE NAMES

The "Post Office" system has been used in English-language writing about China since the nineteenth century. The Pinyin system, official in the People's Republic of China, has been prevalent since about 1980.

Post Office	Pinyin	Post Office	Pinyin
Anhwei	Anhui	Mukden	Shenyang
Canton	Guangzhou	Nanking	Nanjing
Chekiang	Zhejiang	Ninglsia	Ningxia
Chungking	Chongqing	Peking	Beijing
Fukien	Fujian	Quemoy	Jinmen
Heilungkiang	Heilongjiang	Shanghai	Shanghai
Honan	Henan	Shansi	Shanxi
Hopei	Hebei	Shantung	Shandong
Hunan	Hunan	Shensi	Shaanxi
Hupei	Hubei	Sian	Xi'an
Jehol	Rehe	Sinkiang	Xinjiang
Kiangsi	Jiangxi	Szechwan	Sichuan
Kansu	Gansu	Taipei	Taibei
Kiangsu	Jiangsu	Tientsin	Tianjin
Kirin	Jilin	Tsinghai	Qinghai
Kwangsi	Guangxi	Tsingtao	Qingdao
Kwangtung	Guangdong	Yenan	Yan'an
Kweichow	Guizhou	Yunnan	Yunnan
Liaoning	Liaoning		

About the Contributors

Dennis J. Blasko served as army attaché in Beijing and Hong Kong from 1992 to 1996 and has written extensively on developments in the Chinese ground forces over the past decade.

Chang Juit-te is research fellow and deputy director at the Institute of Modern History, Academia Sinica. He is the author of *Anatomy of the Nationalist Army, 1937–1945* (1993, in Chinese) and is currently working on *Chiang Kai-shek's Personal Staff in Wartime China, 1936–1945*.

Edward L. Dreyer received his Ph.D. from Harvard University, and has taught Chinese history and military history at the University of Miami since 1970. His publications include *Early Ming China: A Political History, 1352–1435* (1982) and *China at War, 1901–1949* (1995).

June Teufel Dreyer is professor of political science at the University of Miami and analyst of the contemporary Chinese military. She is a member of the congressionally-established U.S.–China Security Review Commission.

David A. Graff, assistant professor of history at Kansas State University, is the author of *Medieval Chinese Warfare, 300–900* (2002).

Robin Higham is professor emeritus of history at Kansas State University and author or editor of many books in military history and other subjects, including the *Dictionary of Contemporary Chinese Military History* (1999), *A Guide to the Sources of United States Military History* (1975–1998), and *The American Civil War*.

Richard S. Horowitz, assistant professor of history at California State University, Northridge, is currently completing a book manuscript entitled *Imperial Power and State Transformation in Late Qing China: The Zongli Yamen, 1861–1880*.

Paul Lococo Jr. is assistant professor of history at the University of Hawaii, Leeward. He is co-author of *War in World History* (forthcoming).

Peter Lorge teaches Chinese history and film at Vanderbilt University. He is currently finishing a book on the political and military history of the early Song dynasty.

Edward A. McCord is associate professor of history and international affairs at The George Washington University. He is the author of *The Power of the Gun: The Emergence of Modern Chinese Warlordism* (1993).

Stephen R. MacKinnon, is a professor of history at Arizona State University. He co-edited *Scars of War: Impact of Warfare on Modern China* (2001) and is completing a book-length study of the battle for Wuhan and central Yangzi, 1938.

Ralph D. Sawyer, an independent scholar, has spent some three decades in the study of Chinese military history and translation of key military writings.

William Wei is professor of history at the University of Colorado, Boulder, specializing in modern China and Asian America. His major works are *Counterrevolution in China: The Nationalists in Jiangxi during the Soviet Period* (1985) and *The Asian American Movement* (1993).

Larry M. Wortzel is director of the Asian Studies Center of the Heritage Foundation in Washington, DC. He is a retired U.S. Army colonel who served at the American embassy in China from 1988 to 1990 as assistant army attaché, and from 1995 to 1997 as army attaché. He is a graduate of the U.S. Army War College and earned his Ph.D. in political science at the University of Hawaii. His other books include *China's Military Modernization* (1988) and *The Chinese Armed Forces in the 21st Century* (1999).

David C. Wright is assistant professor of history at the University of Calgary in Alberta, Canada. His book on Song–Liao diplomacy is forthcoming.

Maochun Yu, associate professor of history at the U.S. Naval Academy, is the author of *OSS in China—Prelude to the Cold War* (1997). He is currently writing a history of the People's Liberation Army.

INDEX